Outdoor Recreation

An Introduction

Ryan Plummer

Routledge
Taylor & Francis Group

NEW YORK AND LONDON

First published 2009
by Routledge
270 Madison Ave, New York, NY 10016

Simultaneously published in the UK
by Routledge
2 Park Square, Milton Park, Abingdon, Oxon OX14 4RN

Routledge is an imprint of the Taylor and Francis Group, an informa business

Typeset in Perpetua and Bell Gothic by Wearset Ltd, Boldon, Tyne and Wear
Printed and bound in Great Britain by CPI Antony Rowe, Chippenham, Wiltshire

British Library Cataloguing in Publication Data
A catalogue record for this book is available from the British Library

Library of Congress Cataloging in Publication Data
Plummer, Ryan.
Outdoor recreation : an introduction / Ryan Plummer.
p. cm.
1. Outdoor recreation. I. Title.
GV191.6.P59 2008
796.5–dc22   2007051731

ISBN10: 0-415-43040-2 (hbk)
ISBN10: 0-415-43041-0 (pbk)
ISBN10: 0-203-09075-6 (ebk)

ISBN13: 978-0-415-43040-1 (hbk)
ISBN13: 978-0-415-43041-8 (pbk)
ISBN13: 978-0-203-09075-6 (ebk)

Outdoor Recreation

Outdoor Recreation: An Introduction provides students following courses in outdoor recreation, leisure, and environmental studies with a comprehensive and informative overview of this broad and fascinating field.

Covering both theory and practice, and including case studies and examples from around the world, this is the first student text in outdoor recreation to draw on such a diverse range of interdisciplinary approaches and methods. The book introduces students to every key theme in the study of contemporary outdoor recreation, including:

- key concepts and definitions;
- history and development of outdoor leisure;
- management of outdoor recreation;
- development and management of parks, protected areas, and wilderness;
- psychology of the outdoor experience;
- ecology and the natural environment;
- outdoor education and interpretation;
- economics of outdoor recreation;
- outdoor education, leadership, and personal development;
- contemporary issues in, and the future of, outdoor recreation.

Student learning is supported throughout the book with helpful features such as learning objectives, case studies, weblinks, chapter summaries, study questions, and definitions of key terms. Representing a definitive guide to an important and rapidly growing field, this book is essential reading for all students of outdoor recreation, leisure management, tourism, and environmental studies, and will be an important resource for all professionals working in outdoor recreation and leisure.

Ryan Plummer is Associate Professor in the Department of Tourism and Environment at Brock University, Canada.

To Patty—for encouraging my neuroplasticity

Contents

Boxes

Plates

Figures

Tables

Acknowledgments

Many people have generously supported, and contributed to, the development of writing this book. I am fortunate to work in an environment that encourages creativity and embraces initiative. Gratitude is extended to the Department of Tourism and Environment as well as Dean David Siegel at Brock University for their support. Appreciation is also extended to my network of colleagues who enriched ideas contained in these pages through our conversations. More specifically, I would like to thank David Fennell and Cynthia Stacey for frequently discussing many aspects of the manuscript and Reid Kreutzwiser for his written comments on an earlier draft. For their contributions, I also wish to thank: Colleen Beard, Jennifer Fresque, Ann Grimwood, Bryan Grimwood, Emily McIntyre, Mark Montgomery, Karen Natho, Cheryl Plummer, Andrew Spiers, and Nick Pujic.

In terms of making this book a reality, I would like to thank the team at Routledge (Ygraine Cadlock, Samantha Grant, Brian Guerin, and Simon Whitmore) for their masterful command of the publishing process. Guidance from Simon Whitmore is specifically recognized for nurturing the development process.

The publishers would like to thank the following for permission to reprint their material:

Chapter 1:
Marcus Brunmeier for permission to reprint his photograph as Plate 1.1

Chapter 3:
Michigan Technological University for permission to reprint Peterson, R. O. (figure) "Prey relationship between moose and wolves" in Nebel, B. J. & Wright, R. T. *Environmental Science: The Way the World Works*, (5th ed.), Prentice-Hall, Inc., 1996, p. 87

Springer and *Population and the Environment Journal*, Vol. *21*(1) 5–26, 1999, p. 8, Price, D. (figure) "Carrying Capacity Reconsidered" with kind permission from Springer Science and Business Media

Reprinted from *Technological Forecasting and Social Change*, Vol. 52, Marchetti, C., Meyer, P. S. & Ausubel, J. H. (figure) "Human population dynamics revisited with the logistical model: How much can be modeled and predicted?," p. 30, 1996, with permission from Elsevier

Bryan Grimwood for permission to reprint his photograph as Plate 3.1

Emily McIntyre for permission to reprint her photograph as Plate 3.2

Chapter 4:
The McGraw Hill Companies for permission to reprint Edgington, C. J., Hanson, C. R., Edginton, S. R. & Hudson, S. D. (figure) "Maslow's Hierarchy of Needs" *Leisure Programming*, (3rd ed.), 1998, p. 138

Nick Pujic for permission to reprint his photographs as Plate 4.1 and Plate 4.2

Chapter 5:
The McGraw Hill Companies for permission to reprint Howard, D. R. & Crompton, J. L. Financing, (figure) "The Main Arguments Against User Fees" *Managing and Marketing Recreation and Park Resources*, 1980, p. 415

Resources For The Future for permission to reprint Clawson, M. & Knetsch, J. L. (figure) "Schedule of Visits, Costs per Visit and Total Expenditure, Hypothetical Recreation Area" *Economics of Outdoor Recreation* The John Hopkins Press Table, 1966, p. 51

Sagamore Publishing for permission to reprint Cordell, H. K. et al., (table) "Percent and Number of People 16 Years and Older in the U.S. Participating in Land-Resource-Based Outdoor Activities" *Outdoor recreation in American Literature: A national assessment of demand and supply trends*, 1999. p. 223

Sagamore Publishing for permission to reprint Cordell, H. K. et al. (table) "Percent and Number of People 16 Years and Older in the U.S. Participating in Snow- and Ice-Based Outdoor Activities, 1994–95" *Outdoor Recreation in American Literature: A National Assessment of Demand and Supply Trends*, 1999, p. 228

Routledge for permission to reprint Hall, C. M. & Page, S. J. (table) "Positive and Negative Dimensions of the Impacts of Tourism on Host-Communities" *The Geography of Tourism and Recreation: Environment, Place and Space*, 1999, p. 122

Sagamore Publishing for permission to reprint Cordell, H. K. et al. (table) "Land and Water Area Administered by Federal Land-Managing Agencies by Agency and Region" *Outdoor Recreation in American Literature: A National Assessment of Demand and Supply Trends*, 1999, p. 41

Chapter 6:
Fulcrum Publishing Inc for permission to reprint Hendee, J. C., Stankey, G. H. & Lucas, R. C. (figure) "The LAC process provides a framework for prescribing and maintaining acceptable wilderness conditions" *Wilderness Management*, (2nd ed. rev.), 1990, p. 222

Mark Montgomery for permission to reprint his photograph as Plate 6.1

Emily McIntyre for permission to reprint her photograph as Plate 6.2

Recreation Heritage and Wilderness Resources for permission to reprint USDA Forest Service (table) "Appropriate Setting Description for Each of the Six Classes in the Recreational Opportunity Spectrum" *ROS Users Guide*, 1982, in Hammit, W. E. & Cole, D.N. *Wildland Recreation: Ecology and Management*, (2nd ed.), John Wiley and Sons, Inc., 1998, pp. 211–212

Sagamore Publishing for permission to reprint Manning, R. E. (table) "Visitor Experience and resource protection: A framework for managing the carrying capacity for national parks" *Journal of Park and Recreation Administration*, Vol. *19*(1) 93–108, 2001, p. 169

Chapter 7:
Ann Grimwood for permission to reprint her photograph as Plate 7.1

"Yellowstone to Yukon" by Jeff Gailus was reprinted with permission from *Alternatives*, Vol. 27:4, 2001, www.alternativesjournal.ca, pp. 36–39

Canadian Press for permission to reprint Harrington C., "Elk Out of Bounds on Golf Course" *Victoria Times Colonist*, 11 December, 2000, in Eagles, P. F. J. "Environmental Management" from Dearden, P. & Rollins, R. (Eds.) *Parks and Protected Areas in Canada: Planning and Management*, (2nd ed.), Oxford University Press, 2002, pp. 283–284

Chapter 8:
Mark Montgomery for permission to reprint his photograph as Plate 8.1

Sagamore Publishing for permission to reprint Beck, L. & Cable, T.T. (table) "Principles of Interpretation" *Interpretation for the 21st Century: Fifteen Guiding Principles for Interpreting Nature and Culture*, 2002, p. 31

From "Interpretation and Environmental Education" by Jim Butler and Glen Hvenegaard, in *Parks and protected areas in Canada: Planning and management*, 2nd edition, edited by Philip Dearden and Rick Rollins. Copyright Oxford University Press Canada 2002. Reprinted by permission of the publisher.

Chapter 9:
Dave McCarthy for permission to reprint his photograph as Plate 9.1

Ann Grimwood for permission to reprint her photograph as Plate 9.2

Stephen Finucane for permission to reprint his article "Death on the Water; The Masters knew not what they were doing" as it appeared in *Toronto Star*, 30 June, 2002, p. D15

Chapter 10:
The Easter Seal Society, Ontario and Karen Natho for permission to reprint "Easter Seals Camp Merrywood"

Colleen Beard for permission to reprint "Geocaching"

Allyn & Bacon for permission to reprint Kelly, J. R. & Freysinger, V. J. "Debate: Outdoor Recreation is Antienvironmental" *21st Century Leisure: Current Issues*, 2000, pp. 244–246

Leave No Trace Center for Outdoor Ethics for permission to reprint "The Leave No Trace Principles of Outdoor Ethics," 2004, retrieved June 21 2004 from http://www.lnt.org/teachingLNT/LNTEnglish.php

Introduction

OBJECTIVES

This chapter will:

- introduce the importance of outdoor recreation;
- explain why outdoor recreation is at a critical juncture;
- articulate the rationale of this book;
- develop an interdisciplinary framework for outdoor recreation;
- present the structure of this book.

INTRODUCTION

The subject of outdoor recreation is immensely important. Outdoor recreation has shaped the human–environment relationship throughout history and is an engrained part of many cultures. The popularity of outdoor recreation activities is undeniable as participation rates continue to increase and new forms of activities are developed. Popular media has heightened awareness and hyped outdoor related activities through television programs such as *Survivor* and *The Amazing Race*. As a form of human behavior, outdoor recreation is free time activity that occurs in the outdoors and embraces the interaction of people with the natural environment. A diverse array of benefits is realized from outdoor recreation. Individuals may derive personal meaning from these experiences and achieve a state of "flow" or oneness. Relationships among friends and family may be strengthened and enriched. Society and community may benefit as activities contribute towards the process of socialization and as individuals transfer lessons learn to their "everyday" lives and enhance their functioning in society. The economic implications from this "industry" are substantive and accompanied by a complex network of service providers.

At the same time, outdoor recreation is at a particularly critical juncture. All outdoor recreation activities have an impact on the natural environment. These impacts are often magnified by the fact that participants travel to the activity site and that some of these areas are ecologically sensitive. The Intergovernmental Panel on Climate Change (IPCC) recently released their fourth assessment on climate change. Scientists from around the world concur that system warming is now unequivocal and very likely (more than a 90% chance) due to anthropogenic activities (IPCC, 2007). Implications of environmental change on outdoor recreation demonstrate the complexity of the issue as opportunities may disappear, shift, or emerge. The possibility of outdoor recreation being anti-environmental has become a point of debate (Kelly & Freysinger, 2000). Ethical concerns have prompted considerable attention as to how we should behave in the out-of-doors. Serious questions are also being asked about the morality of consumptive outdoor recreation activities such as fishing and hunting. The very essence or meaning of outdoor recreation appears to be at stake as technology pervades wilderness and the demarcation between foundational categories (e.g., indoors vs. outdoors; real vs. reality; humans vs. machines) blurs (Ryan, 2002).

The future value of outdoor recreation is contingent upon successfully negotiating the contemporary situation. Meeting these dynamic challenges requires an appreciation of our rich outdoor recreation heritage, understanding of fundamental concepts, and willingness to pursue innovative research. It necessitates taking an interdisciplinary perspective to highlight interconnections, realize complexities, and capture holistic qualities. Most importantly, the prospects for outdoor recreation hinge on the engagement of people in the process of transformative change.

RATIONALE FOR THE BOOK

This book aims to introduce students to the subject of outdoor recreation. In endeavoring to reveal the considerable breadth of information associated with the subject matter a conscientious effort was made to revisit many of the classic and timeless works that have shaped our field. Attention was also directed to a diverse array of contemporary information such as peer-reviewed articles, synthesis monographs, technical reports and websites. Notwithstanding the difficulties of communicating "experiential" elements via print medium, frequent examples are utilized throughout the book to enhance understanding of both theoretical and practical considerations.

College and university students are primarily the intended audience of this book. Therefore, it also conveys the potential depth of knowledge associated with outdoor recreation. Scholarly inquires across a number of research traditions are therefore presented throughout the book. Evidence from inquiries is used to support central concepts, raise methodological considerations, and enhance understanding of the phenomenon. In this regard, the book is a precursor to avenues of future study.

As a textbook, this work strives to synthesize existing material and effectively communicate it to learners. Innovation comes from the interdisciplinary perspective employed as a means of integrating information and structuring this volume. More importantly, it offers a novel and logical way to systematically think about outdoor recreation. The approach also gives further evidence that the study of outdoor recreation has indeed "come of age."

Achieving the intent outlined above will be accomplished by:

- introducing concepts fundamental to the study of outdoor recreation;
- exploring the context which has shaped both practice and study;
- examining influences from various disciplines which contribute to understanding the phenomena of outdoor recreation;
- describing the breadth of outdoor recreation research and practice; and,
- critically examining emerging issues facing people interested in outdoor recreation.

AN INTERDISCIPLINARY PERSPECTIVE ON OUTDOOR RECREATION

As an area of study outdoor recreation has come of age (Manning, 1999). Maturation is evidenced by increasing theoretical contributions as well as the identified need to employ an interdisciplinary approach (Manning, 1999; Wall, 1989). When considering undertaking interdisciplinary inquiry individuals require comprehension and appreciation of what inter-disciplinary research entails as well as an understanding of core concepts, research themes, and basic questions associated with the area of study (Mitchell, 1989). Therefore, this prologue to interdisciplinary inquiry is an appropriate starting point for readers as the remainder of the book addresses the core concepts and research themes associated with outdoor recreation.

Brewer explains that:

> interdisciplinarity generally refers to the appropriate combination of knowledge from many different specialties—especially as a means to shed new light on actual problems. In notably effective efforts, the combination of disciplines adds value: the total is more interesting than the sum of the individual contributions or parts.
>
> (1999, p. 328)

The concept of interdisciplinary inquiry is distinguished from other forms of research in Figure I.1. Jantsch stresses that:

> Only with inter- and trans-disciplinarity the science/innovation system becomes alive; in the sense that disciplinary contents, structures, and interfaces change continuously through co-ordination geared to the pursuit of a common system purpose. *Inter- and trans-disciplinarity thus become the key notion for a systems approach to science, education and innovation.*
>
> (1972, p. 224)

Many potential benefits may be realized through interdisciplinary research. This approach is particularly well suited to outdoor recreation because it focuses on solving problems that fail to adhere or "fit" into a discipline (Brewer, 1999; Manning, 1999; Savory, 1988). Jantsch (1972) recognizes the merits of such an approach in light of complexity, dynamic systems and uncertainty. These characteristics are commonly found in the realm of environmental studies with which outdoor recreation is often concerned.

3

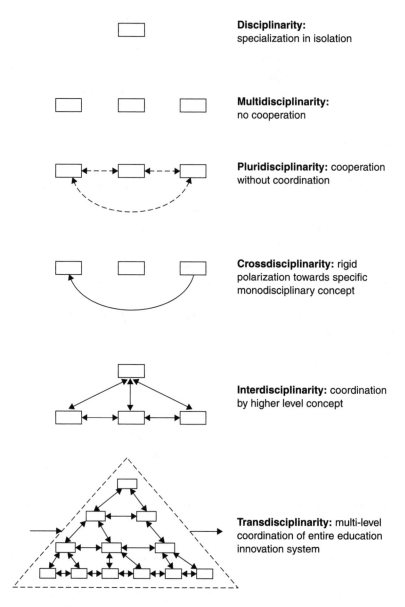

Disciplinarity:
specialization in isolation

Multidisciplinarity:
no cooperation

Pluridisciplinarity: cooperation
without coordination

Crossdisciplinarity: rigid
polarization towards specific
monodisciplinary concept

Interdisciplinarity: coordination
by higher level concept

Transdisciplinarity: multi-level
coordination of entire education
innovation system

Figure I.1 Different Forms of Research.
Source: Jantsch, 1972.

This problem orientation requires information from multiple knowledge areas and therefore potential synergies between discipline-based approaches may be realized (Mitchell, 1989). Similar to other areas of study that have followed a comparable progression, outdoor recreation is well poised to take advantage of such opportunities. In 1959 Snow observed that "the clashing point of two subjects, two disciplines, two cultures—of two galaxies, as far as that goes—ought to produce creative chances. In the history of mental activity that has been where some of the break-through came" (p. 16). Some 50 years later the association between interdisciplinarity and innovation is well established. Atkins writes "there seems to be general recognition that many of the most interesting and challenging intellectual debates lie at interfaces between disciplines, and opportunities are increasingly opening up that allow these debates to be progressed in a practical sense" (2004, p. 2).

Interdisciplinary inquiry illuminates holistic qualities of systems which are not always immediately identifiable by looking at individual components. Savory (1998) views this as the most valuable contribution of an interdisciplinary approach and is a strong proponent of holistic resource management. It is important to recognize when undertaking interdisciplinary work that "since greater wholes have qualities and character not present in any of their constituent wholes (parts) *one must seek to understand the greater whole in order to understand its parts, not vice versa*" (Savory, 1988, p. 30).

Interdisciplinary inquiry is also conducive to developing and organizing knowledge at a large scale. Many contemporary challenges, especially involving the natural environment, require an approach which is both holistic and large scale. Brewer explains:

> Much high-quality science illuminates environmental problems, but it is often poorly organized and incomplete. It often does not have an interdisciplinary integration and synthesis that permit problems to be seen in a larger context, especially in an ecologically sensitive and sensible one. It is often not geared to the scale needed to shed light on environmental problems of long-term importance to human well-being. In short, much essential knowledge is not capable of guiding the development of policy, heightening public awareness, or even informing and enlightening political debate.
>
> (1995, p. 4)

There are also many challenges to undertaking interdisciplinary inquiry. Issues often stem from the organization of academic institutions which structure disciplines in isolation (Jantsch, 1972). Well-entrenched disciplines also tend to emphasize the value of specialization and isolation (Jantsch, 1972; Savory, 1988). These challenges can be linked to the underlying mechanical or scientific method of knowledge creation (Savory, 1988). Even in cases where multiple individuals work together on a project and/or have experience in multiple disciplines, challenges arise as they often speak different languages (jargon), negotiate according to disciplinary criteria, and lack a holistic perspective (Savory, 1988). Brewer presents an excellent synthesis of common obstacles faced by those undertaking interdisciplinary inquiry to include:

- different cultures and frames of reference;
- different methods and operational objectives within and between the disciplines;
- different "languages" within the disciplines and between the disciplines and the world at large;
- personal challenges related to gaining the trust and respect and others working in different disciplines and fields;
- institutional impediments related to incentives, funding, and priorities given disciplinary versus interdisciplinary work.

5

- professional impediments related to hiring, promotion, status, and recognition (1999, p. 335).

Conceptual frameworks are "organizational devices, used to structure a problem and to identify its various parts" (Mitchell, 1989, p. 28). An interdisciplinary perspective provides a way to conceptualize the phenomenon of outdoor recreation, as illustrated in Figure I.2. Coordination of the framework is given by the problem domain or higher order concept. Jantsch explains that "in a purposeful science/innovation system, inter-disciplinarity has to be understood as a *teleological* and *normative* concept. Above all, we must ask? Inter-disciplinarity to what end?" (1972, p. 220). A system of inquiry must be coordinated by a common purpose and those involved committed to that end for the system to be meaning-ful. In this way, the concept of outdoor recreation serves as a problem domain and/or higher level concept. As established earlier, outdoor recreation is a form of human behav-ior. It involves voluntary participation in free-time activities that occur outdoors and stresses interactions between people and the natural environment.

The second level of the framework consists of disciplinary-based approaches or know-ledge areas which have concerted considerable attention to the study of outdoor recreation. These terms are purposefully employed to clearly differentiate them from fundamental branches of knowledge discussed. A "critical mass" of knowledge is particularly evident in environmental studies, social-psychology and economics. Environmental studies is a some-what ubiquitous title and it must be acknowledged that aspects of the human–environment relationship are pursed in both disciplines (e.g., biology, sociology, geography) and applied areas of study (e.g., forestry, ecology, environmental planning, natural resources manage-ment). Put simply, the natural world distinguishes outdoor from other forms of recreation. Social-psychology combines the distinct disciplines of psychology and sociology to focus on the experience of the phenomenon. The social-psychology approach has been utilized to examine leisure behaviors in terms of individual cognitions, social context, temporal occur-rences and physical environment (Iso-Ahola, 1980). Economics is a knowledge area with a long-running history regarding outdoor recreation. Human choices and values are central to economics and therefore the importance of such discourse is immediately apparent due to demands for scarce resources, efficiency of allocation and competing/alternative interests (Krutilla & Knetsch, 1974).

The second level of the framework has thus far been presented using disciplinary-based boundaries for the point of illustration. In reality, those studying and/or conducting research regarding outdoor recreation frequently assimilate information from one or more of these knowledge areas. Arrows among the three discipline-based approaches reflect this potential flow of information. Given the interdisciplinary nature of the framework, the discipline-based approaches are coordinated by the higher order concept of outdoor recre-ation, as shown by the downward pointing arrow. Such an approach acknowledges that outdoor recreation does not occur in a vacuum. Regardless of what aspect of the phenome-non may be of particular interest, it is necessary to understand, at some level, other import-ant facets of outdoor recreation.

Management of outdoor recreation is purposefully positioned between the second and third levels of the framework because in many ways outdoor recreation management constitutes both

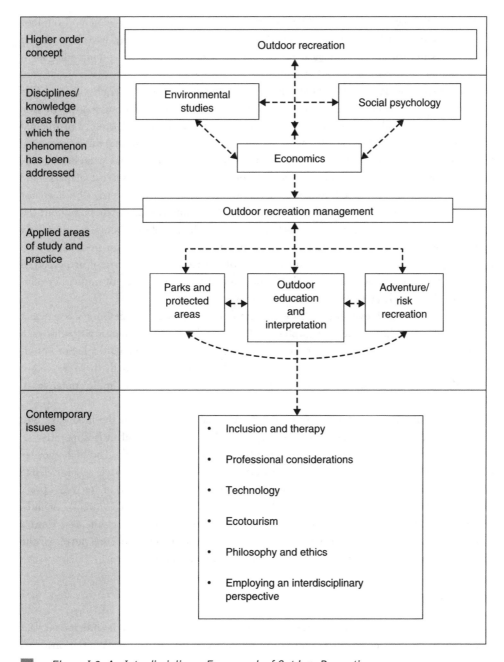

Higher order concept	Outdoor recreation
Disciplines/ knowledge areas from which the phenomenon has been addressed	Environmental studies — Social psychology / Economics
Applied areas of study and practice	Outdoor recreation management / Parks and protected areas — Outdoor education and interpretation — Adventure/ risk recreation
Contemporary issues	• Inclusion and therapy • Professional considerations • Technology • Ecotourism • Philosophy and ethics • Employing an interdisciplinary perspective

Figure I.2 An Interdisciplinary Framework of Outdoor Recreation.

a knowledge area as well as an applied topic of study and practice. As a knowledge area, it now constitutes a mass of information as well as considerable conceptual developments. These are largely the outcome of the increasing attention and ability to discern impacts, the incorporation of more general administrative knowledge and the advancement of organizational structures to foster innovation. This is largely the result of integrating information from the disciplinary approaches, as indicated in Figure I.2 by the arrow from their center. Management of outdoor recreation also maintains an applied focus. Applied aspects of this element have been chiefly concerned with ensuring the ecological integrity of the natural environment and providing high-quality outdoor experiences desired by humans.

Considerable breadth is also evident in management as it is directly applicable to other applied areas of study and practice that constitute the third level of the framework. The title "applied areas of study and practice" is used here to specifically refer to topics of focused investigation that provide a basis for practice and which represent potential career domains. The three topics constituting this level of the framework are parks and protected areas, outdoor education and interpretation and adventure recreation. The subject of parks and protected areas has developed alongside outdoor recreation and emphasizes the need for conservation and preservation of natural areas. Outdoor education is instruction about the natural world and the manner in which it functions. Interpretation aims to ultimately develop appreciation of the natural world as it fosters revelations from people's innate curiosity. Adventure recreation encompasses activities that involve either real or perceived risk. Similar to the previous levels of the framework, these subjects are not mutually exclusive and in both study and practice considerable overlap exists.

The fourth and final level of the conceptual framework involves contemporary issues that require dialogue. These issues are located at the fourth level because familiarity with each and every part of the framework is necessary for such discourse. Although the list of potential issues from which these have been selected is long and distinguished, these issues are selected as they represent critical decision points and have important implications to all aspects of the framework.

Arrows connecting parts of the framework are equally important as the individual elements. In addition to the relationships among variables at any one level, it is imperative to recognize the reciprocal exchange between all levels of the framework. The higher order concept of outdoor recreation acts to coordinate discipline-based approaches. Knowledge gained from one or more of these areas may be employed in applied areas of study and practice. Information gained from any of the above levels may also be applied (directly or indirectly) to the contemporary issues. The arrows that make these connections also form a feedback loop. In this way information gained at one level may inform other levels of the framework and ultimately enhance the understanding of outdoor recreation.

USING THIS BOOK

This book introduces students to the study of outdoor recreation. It is anticipated that increased awareness and understanding of outdoor recreation will foster realization of its importance as both a course of academic study and personal pursuit.

Communicating the subject matter to readers in a meaningful way is paramount to this enterprise. To engage readers and facilitate the learning process numerous features are employed in this book. These include:

- images and captions that underscore the topic of each chapter;
- objectives which identify the main ideas contained in each chapter;

- graphics and tables that complement information conveyed in the text;
- boxes which highlight important issues and/or get across novel examples from practice;
- summaries which succinctly appraise the essence of each chapter;
- key concepts that make accessible the major ideas that learners should be familiar with;
- suggested sources for more information that learners may consult to gain an in-depth understanding on specific topics; and,
- review questions that learners may use to evaluate their progress and to initiate critical thinking.

STRUCTURE OF THIS BOOK

The interdisciplinary framework employed to conceptualize outdoor recreation also serves as a useful device to organize the ten chapters constituting this volume.

Context to the higher level concept of outdoor recreation is given in the initial chapters. Chapter 1 begins with a "simple" question—what is outdoor recreation? In the process of responding to this question, fundamental concepts in leisure studies are probed, characteristics of outdoor recreation are defined, and a general model of the outdoor recreation experience is introduced. Reviewing the evolution of outdoor recreation research acknowledges important approaches to inquiry and supports the need to employ an interdisciplinary perspective. The historical and cultural context of outdoor recreation is documented in Chapter 2. Chronicling experiences with outdoor recreation in the past makes clear its longstanding and extensive roots. Recognizing individuals and organizations instrumental in advancing discourse and practice is fundamentally important as their work provides the foundation upon which the contemporary situation has been built.

Chapters 3 through 5 reflect the second level of the framework. The natural environment is recognized as being the defining characteristic of outdoor recreation and knowledge pertaining to it is essential for those studying outdoor recreation. Chapter 3 discusses the human–environment relationship, components of the natural world, and landscape features available for outdoor recreation. Chapter 4 examines outdoor recreation through the lens of social-psychology. Attention is focused on understanding it as a particular form of human behavior with an emphasis on both individual and societal aspects. Chapter 5 delves into economic analysis and applies the concepts of demand and economic impacts to outdoor recreation. The provision of outdoor recreation opportunities by the public, volunteer and private sectors is also described.

Chapter 6 addresses outdoor recreation management. Managers have the dual mandate of insuring the integrity of the natural environment while concomitantly providing high-quality opportunities for outdoor recreation. Therefore, the chapter is concerned with impacts from outdoor recreation as well as their management. The process of outdoor recreation management and more specific techniques are covered.

The third level of the framework encompasses applied study areas. Chapter 7 explores parks and protected areas that both offer protection to natural ecosystems and opportunities for outdoor recreation. Ecological values associated with wilderness areas are emphasized and international initiatives are examined as competing uses of resources intensifies.

Outdoor education and interpretation are pursued in Chapter 8. These topics share a common theoretical basis in learning theories and communication as well as a shared goal of fostering awareness, developing understanding, and ultimately, instilling a sense of steward-ship towards the natural environment. Chapter 9 details the human fascination with adven-ture recreation. Associated conceptualizations are examined to explain the allure of risk and applications of adventure to education and therapy are presented. Challenge emerges as a powerful mechanism to achieve optimal experiences, facilitate self-development, foster team-building and promote leadership.

The final part of the book takes an integrative and summative orientation. Chapter 10 identifies emerging issues confronting outdoor recreation that are not profiled elsewhere in the text. Constructive dialogue is required by participants, students, practitioners and researchers to appreciate the multi-faceted nature of these issues. The interdisciplinary framework is specifically applied to a case study to illustrate the interconnected, complex and holistic reality of outdoor recreation. The book closes with a succinct reflection on the journey undertaken and musings about future expeditions.

SUMMARY

This opening discussion established the importance of outdoor recreation and reflected upon current tensions confronting it, such as climate change, ethical concerns and technology. Outdoor recreation is at a critical juncture. In an effort to foster learning, this text intro-duces readers to the breath and depth of topics within the subject of outdoor recreation. Interdisciplinary inquiry provides an appropriate perspective to consider outdoor recreation and the rewards and challenges of it were discussed. An interdisciplinary conceptual frame-work for outdoor recreation was developed which provides a way to think about the phe-nomenon as well as a structure to organize material covered in this book.

KEY CONCEPTS

Conceptual framework
Disciplinarity
Interdisciplinarity
Outdoor recreation

SUGGESTED KEY SOURCES FOR MORE INFORMATION

Brewer, G. D. (1999). The challenges of interdisciplinarity. *Policy Sciences, 32*, 327–337.
Jantsch, E. (1972). *Technological planning and social futures*. New York: Halsted Press.
Kelly, J. R. & Freysinger, V. J. (2000). *21st century leisure current issues*. Needham Heights, MA: Allyn & Bacon.
Ryan, S. (2002). Cyborgs in the woods. *Leisure Sciences, 21*, 265–284.
Savory, A. (1988). *Holistic resource management*. Washington, DC: Island Press.

REVIEW QUESTIONS

1. Why is outdoor recreation at a critical juncture?
2. What is the future value of outdoor recreation contingent upon?
3. Describe the potential benefits and pitfalls of an interdisciplinary approach.
4. Why is an interdisciplinary approach important to those studying outdoor recreation?
5. Identify and describe the four levels which constitute the interdisciplinary framework of outdoor recreation.

Chapter 1

The Concept and Study of Outdoor Recreation

OBJECTIVES

This chapter will:

- introduce key concepts within leisure studies;
- define outdoor recreation and describe associated characteristics and objectives;
- present a model of the outdoor recreation experience;
- probe the relationship between other forms of leisure and outdoor recreation;
- outline how outdoor recreation has evolved as an area of academic study.

INTRODUCTION

What is outdoor recreation? Your answer may be quick and intuitive—activities such as camping, fishing and skiing are examples of outdoor recreation. Why do you consider these activities to be outdoor recreation? What attributes do they display? Can outdoor recreation be distinguished from other pastimes such as leisure, recreation, sport and tourism? How can outdoor recreation be studied?

Chapter 1 introduces the concept of outdoor recreation. Key ideas in leisure studies (leisure, recreation, sport, tourism) are presented to set the contextual background for defining and understanding outdoor recreation. The concept of outdoor recreation is developed through a discussion of its characteristics, objectives and experiences. In probing the connections between outdoor recreation and other key concepts in leisure a relational understanding is established. The second half of this chapter directs attention to outdoor recreation as an area of academic study. Innovations and challenges are identified in tracing the development of outdoor recreation research. Emerging evidence of maturity supports the appropriateness of pursuing an interdisciplinary perspective.

KEY CONCEPTS IN LEISURE STUDIES
Leisure

Leisure is the good life. It is being able to do what you want. Leisure experiences are often accompanied by a special feeling of transcendence, in which an individual experiences "oneness" with an activity or environment. For individuals with a keen interest in the outdoors, leisure experiences often occur while interacting with the natural environment. In seeking to understand this phenomenon, scholars have discussed leisure as free time, activity, state of mind and state of existence (Edginton, Jordan, DeGraaf & Edginton, 1995; Godbey, 1999; Searle & Brayley, 2000).

Leisure is typically associated with free time or situations in which individuals have the luxury of choice (Godbey, 1999). This association between leisure and free time is so strong that the terms are often used synonymously (Edginton et al., 1995). Think about your daily routine and the amount of time you spend on each activity. The typical American spends ten hours on fulfilling biological requirements (existence), nine hours on garnering economic necessities (subsistence), and five hours on free-time activities each day (Jensen, 1995). This amount of free time when considered over the course of life is staggering. When a person reaches the age of 75 he/she has had at least 156,000 hours of non-obligated time (Godbey, 1999). Does this mean that a person experiences leisure during all of this time?

Leisure has also been defined by the activities undertaken during free time. From this perspective leisure is characterized as activities which are pleasurable, purposeful, and undertaken voluntarily (Edginton et al., 1995; Godbey, 1999; Searle & Brayley, 2000). Dumazedier's understanding of leisure is frequently associated with this view, he states that "leisure is activity—apart from obligations of work, family and society—to which the individual turns at will, for either relaxation, diversion or broadening his knowledge and his spontaneous social participation" (1967, pp. 16–17).

A third way of thinking about leisure is as a state of mind. Writing in this tradition, Kelly explains that "leisure is a mental condition that is located in the consciousness of the individual" (1990, p. 21). Leisure here is both subjective and personal. What is leisure to you may be very different than what it is to someone else. Particular attention has been directed at how attitudes and values shape the experience of leisure. Godbey (1999) observes that for an individual to experience leisure he/she must perceive free choice. Edginton et al. (1995) go further and emphasize that individuals must be both positive and open to the experience.

Leisure was historically associated with status and considered a state of being (Sylvester, 1999). Godbey (1999) traces leisure back to the Athenian political system which privileged a small minority to experience the "absence of necessity." Although not to the same extent, the association between social status and leisure has persisted. At the turn of the twentieth century Veblen (1934) observed the emergence of a "leisure class" who derived status from displaying extravagance and using time unproductively. Today leisure remains an important avenue for people to convey an image of themselves as goods and services associated with leisure are often used to claim status (Edginton et al., 1995).

Although each of the above perspectives describes a view of the term leisure, they have all been subject to criticism. Godbey (1999) provides one of the most comprehensive critical assessments, asserting that:

1   the concept of freedom is not absolute;
2   defining leisure as external activities excludes consideration of important internal or subjective factors;
3   regarding leisure solely as a state of mind negates consequences of reality; and,
4   an "absence of necessity" contradicts purposeful and willful undertaking required to experience leisure. In addition to these arguments, he urges for consideration of more broad questions regarding the applicability of the leisure concept to all persons regardless of gender, race and/or class.

Shortcomings identified with each of the above perspectives have prompted the proposal of more holistic definitions. Writing in the early 1980s, Kelly defined leisure as "the quality of activity defined by relative freedom and intrinsic satisfaction" (1982, p. 82). This definition signaled a shift towards a multi-dimensional definition of leisure. As illustrated in Figure 1.1., the multi-dimensional definition of leisure involves time, activity and experience. These three dimensions appear enduring as they are also reflected in Godbey's most recent definition of leisure. He writes that "leisure is living in relative freedom from the external compulsive forces of one's culture and physical environment so as to be able to act from internally compelling love in ways that are personally pleasing, intuitively worthwhile, and provide a basis for faith" (1999, p. 12).

Recreation

The term recreation is often interchangeably used with the term leisure, even though the two terms are not the same. Recreation is derived from the Latin words *recreatio* and *recreare* which respectfully mean "to refresh" and "to restore" (Edginton et al., 1995). It was traditionally understood in opposition to work and gained currency during the Industrial Revolution as both employers and employees searched for ways to become rejuvenated from long hours of toil (Searle & Brayley, 2000).

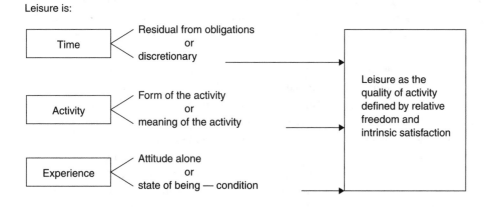

Leisure is:

Time — Residual from obligations or discretionary

Activity — Form of the activity or meaning of the activity

Experience — Attitude alone or state of being — condition

Leisure as the quality of activity defined by relative freedom and intrinsic satisfaction

Figure 1.1 Multidimensional Definition of Leisure.

It was also during the Industrial Revolution that concern arose regarding popular activities such as gambling, drinking and related violence. Capitalists worried about production and citizens alarmed by "such ills" viewed recreation as an instrument to prepare citizens for employment and to better society (Edginton et al., 1995; Godbey, 1999). These views prompted recreation to become an entrenched part of institutions and organizations throughout the twentieth century (Edginton et al., 1995). Although a wider range of recreational activities are embraced today in a society of cultural pluralism (pleasurable activities selected by individuals), socially positive values associated with recreation endure.

Considerable disagreement exists regarding the definition of recreation. These differences are contingent upon:

> whether or not recreation is a means to an end (such as achievement) or an end in itself, whether or not it should be limited to "moral" activity, whether or not it must refresh the individual for work, and whether or not it is determined primarily by the nature of the activity, the attitude of the respondent toward the activity, or the respondent's psychological state during the activity.
>
> (Godbey, 1999, p. 14)

For the purposes of this book recreation is defined as "voluntary non-work activity that is organized for the attainment of personal and social benefit including restoration and social cohesion" (Kelly, 1996, p. 27). The term recreation is further illuminated by eight key characteristics. According to Sessoms (1984) recreation involves activity, has multiple forms, occurs during leisure, is motivated by satisfaction, resembles play, and has by-products. These characteristics reflect the scope of potential definitions and are helpful to detail subtle nuances that distinguish an activity as recreation (Searle & Brayley, 2000).

Sport

The term sport is also widely used with many meanings. Application of the term has become so diverse that even popular sources have identified the challenge of defining it. The Internet Encyclopedia, as an example of a popular source, states that "despite the fact that everybody thinks that they know what sport means, defining sport is a very complex matter; the term constantly evolves to cover new ranges of human behaviour" (2007, online).

Given this complexity, the term sport is recognizable by key characteristics. These characteristics are consistently identified across popular sources (e.g., Internet Encyclopedia, 2007) and academic sources (Hinch & Higham, 2001; Searle & Brayley, 2000). Sport is characterized by physical activity (strength, agility, speed), structure or rules concerning space and time, competitiveness or goal orientation either among contestants or with oneself, and uncertainty of outcomes. A definition of sport incorporates many of these key characteristics. Kelly defines sport as "organized activity in which physical effort is related to that of others in some relative measurement of outcomes with accepted regularities and forms" (1990, p. 196).

Compared to recreation, which encompasses various forms of activities, sport focuses on activities that exhibit a narrower set of characteristics. The International Olympic Committee (IOC), for example, promotes the Olympic Movement by recognizing International Federations that administer sport(s) at a world level and are constituted by national level organizations in many countries (IOC, 2007, online). Even with a more restrictive definition of sport, a diverse range of activities and events are still encompassed (IOC, 2007).

Many activities classified as sport also fit into categories of leisure and recreation. An individual may be intrinsically motivated to participate in such activities during free time and therefore consider his/her involvement as leisure. The same activity may be undertaken for the purpose of physical rejuvenation. This connection between recreation and sport is particularly strong because a majority of sport occurs at the local level and is considered as recreation (Hinch & Higham, 2001).

Tourism

The notion of travel has changed considerably in a relatively short period of time. More than 150 years ago travel was an experience reserved for the affluent and adventurous (Fridgen, 1991). The Grand Tour (1500–1820), for example, took sons of English aristocracy to France, Rome, Germany, and the Netherlands for as long as 40 months for studying, aesthetic appreciation, and experiencing culture (Fridgen, 1991). Today, travel is integrated both into everyday life and undertaken for specific purposes. This centrality and popularity are reflected by the recognition that tourism is the largest industry in the world (Hall & Page, 1999).

Tourism has also been defined in a number of ways. In a general sense, tourism is understood as "voluntary travel to a destination which is more novel than the place from which one traveled" (Godbey, 1999, p. 217). Hall and Page (1999) suggest that most definitions of tourism either conceptually or technically narrow this general idea. Conceptual definitions specifically understand tourism as "the temporary movement to destinations outside the normal home and workplace, the activities undertaken during the stay and the facilities created to cater for the needs of tourists" (Mathieson & Wall, 1982, p. 1). In this regard tourism is characterized by:

1. the movement of people;
2. the journey and the stay;
3. the distinction between normal residence and work (both of the traveler and of citizens at the destination);
4. its temporary nature; and,
5. purposes other than residency or employment (Burkart & Medlik, 1981 as cited by Hall & Page, 1999, p. 58).

Technical definitions are frequently employed by organizations in an attempt to capture information or measure specific populations (Hall & Page, 1999). Numerous organizations and government agencies have adopted technical definitions of tourism. One such example is the World Tourism Organization (WTO). The WTO was formed in 1975 and is the only organization with a global scope focusing on international tourism (Fridgen, 1991). According to the WTO "tourism comprises the activities of persons travelling to and staying in places outside their usual environment for not more than one consecutive year for leisure, business and other purposes" (2007, online). Other government agencies have advanced definitions that are even more prescriptive or technical. For example, the National Tourism Resources Review Commission based out of the United States in 1973 recognized a tourist as being, "one who travels away from home for a distance of at least 50 miles (one way) for business, pleasure, personal affairs, or any other purposes except to commute to work, whether he stays overnight or returns the same day" (as cited in McIntosh, Goeldner & Ritchie, 1995, p. 11). In Canada, the Canadian Travel Survey similarly recognizes a person who travels the one-way distance of 50 miles (80 kilometers) as a tourist.

Outdoor Recreation

The term outdoor recreation has been part of the leisure studies lexicon for over 50 years. Over this period of time many definitions of outdoor recreation have emerged. Unlike many of the other contested concepts in leisure studies, the term outdoor recreation has been employed with remarkable consistency. Characteristics associated with numerous definitions of outdoor recreation are summarized in Table 1.1. From this summary, outdoor recreation can be defined as voluntary participation in free-time activity that occurs in the outdoors and embraces the interaction of people with the natural environment.

While characteristics provide a way to recognize outdoor recreation, they fail to entirely capture the intent of such experiences. Therefore, Jensen (1995) asserts that the aims of outdoor recreation need to be clear and purposeful. The very essence of outdoor recreation is reflected in the realization of specific opportunities. In this regard Jensen (1995) proposes the following five objectives of outdoor recreation:

1. Appreciation of nature—outdoor recreation should build knowledge and enhance understanding of ecological processes as well as develop an awareness of sensitivity of natural environments to human impacts.

Plate 1.1 Why is Kayaking Considered an Outdoor Recreaction Activity?

2. Personal satisfaction and enjoyment—outdoor recreation provides a vehicle by which people may positively experience nature, derive personal pleasure and/or intuitive enrichment.
3. Physiological fitness—outdoor recreation frequently provides opportunities for active physical engagement.
4. Positive behavior patterns—outdoor recreation should instill an attitude of respect, consideration, and sincerity toward fellow participants and resource managers.
5. Stewardship—outdoor recreation provides opportunity for the exercise of moral and ethical values towards the environment, stewardship should be a chief aim and spirit fostered by outdoor recreation.

The nature of the outdoor recreation experience itself also requires elaboration. Outdoor experiences are frequently (either explicitly or implicitly) limited to the occurrence of an activity at a particular site for a period of time (Clawson & Knetsch, 1966; Jensen, 1995). Considering outdoor recreation in this way omits many important aspects. Clawson and Knetsch (1966) have approached outdoor recreation in a holistic way and developed a model of the total outdoor recreation experience. The impact of their work is noted by Fennell who states that "one of the most oft quoted models of tourism and outdoor recreation research is one proposed by Clawson and Knetsch's (1966)" (2002, p. 7). As illustrated in Figure 1.2, the total outdoor recreation experience consists of five distinct phases. The experience begins with anticipation and planning. During this time an individual eagerly thinks about the forthcoming activity, may read extensively about what to expect and consults with others regarding proper equipment. The second phase involves some amount of travel to the site at which the activity is to occur. It is important to highlight "some amount of travel" to recognize that the site where an activity occurs may vary considerably from a short walk to a local greenway to the most remote reaches of the earth, such as the Arctic. The third phase involves actual participation in the intended activity. This is the phase of the experience that is typically solely associated with outdoor recreation. Return travel is the fourth phase. It is distinguished from travel to the site (phase two) because the participants are changed from the experience. Recollection, recalling aspects of the experience, is the fifth and final phase of the total outdoor recreation experience.

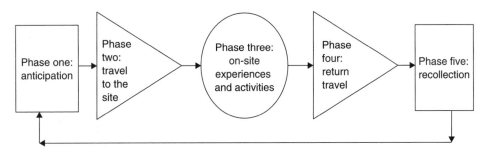

Figure 1.2 Phases of the Outdoor Recreation Experience.
Source: adapted from Clawson & Knetsch, 1966.

19

Table 1.1 A Synthesis of Outdoor Recreation Definitions

Definition	Source	Enjoyable	Occurring outdoors	Appreciation of natural environment	Involving activity	Knowledge	Use of natural environment	Occurs during leisure	Occurring in man-modified environments	Interaction with the natural environment
"Outdoor recreation is an enjoyable leisure-time activity pursued outdoors or indoors involving knowledge, use, or appreciation of natural resources."	Carlson, 1960, as cited in Ford & Blanchard, 1993, p. 5.	•	•	•		•	•	•		
"those activities that occur outdoors in an urban and man-modified environment as well as those activities traditionally associated with the natural environment. With the advent of indoor–outdoor facilities, such as convertible skating rinks and swimming pools, an additional dimension has been added to the complex of areas and facilities encompassed in the term outdoor recreation."	ORRRC, 1962, as cited in Ford & Blanchard, 1993, p. 4.		•		•				•	
"Outdoor recreation is simply recreation that is typically carried on outdoors."	Clawson & Knetsch 1966, p. 7.		•							

"The term "outdoor recreation" includes that sector of the recreation profession relating to large open spaces, mountains, lakes, forests, plains, and all the features and phenomena thought of as "wild, primitive, and natural." To some environmentalists, outdoor recreation identifies solely with hiking shoes, backpacks, and human beings pitted against the elements. On the other hand, outdoor recreation today can range from the wilderness camper atop a 6,000-foot mountain, to a busy administrator struggling with garbage disposal in the crowded campgrounds of a national park. The spectrum of outdoor recreation is broad."

Curtis, 1979, p. 32.

"Outdoor recreation has a complexity of meanings and includes a variety of disciplines such as landscape architecture, forestry, ecology, physical education, conservation, and civil engineering ... and ... is the wholesome recreation that is done without the confines of a building. It covers a broad field of topics from a backyard barbecue to a Boy Scout Jamboree. It can mean recess on the paved playground of a downtown grade school or a two-week pack trip into the Bob Marshall Wilderness area in Montana."

Douglass, 1982, p. 6.

"Outdoor recreational experiences can be gained through participating in a wide variety of activities. In undertaking these activities, man interacts with his environment. Outdoor recreation is also a land use. It competes with agriculture, forestry, mining, housing, industry and a variety of other activities for the same scarce resources of land and water."

Marsh & Wall, 1982, p. 1.

"[Outdoor recreation] refers to leisure activities that take place in open green spaces away from one's home and backyard and that generally refer to the hinterland rather than to outdoor settings in urban areas. Also included are problems related to the recreational use of areas that make up the nation's wilderness-preservation system."

Driver & Brown, 1983, p. 309.

21

Table 1.1 continued

Definition	Source	Enjoyable	Occurring outdoors	Appreciation of natural environment	Involving activity	Knowledge	Use of natural environment	Occurs during leisure	Occurring in man-modified environments	Interaction with the natural environment
Outdoor recreation includes, "virtually all those constructive leisure activities that occur in parks and other open space areas. They include everything from playground and playfield activities to wilderness trips and camping."	Knudson, 1984, p. 11.		•		•			•	•	
"The term "outdoor recreation" has been used to describe those activities of a recreational nature that normally take place in a natural environment and depend primarily upon that environment for satisfaction."	Sessoms, 1984, p. 237.	•	•		•					
"Outdoor recreation is defined as the interaction between an activity and an outdoor natural environment that recreates an individual physically, psychologically, emotionally, and socially."	Leitner, Leitner & Associates, 1996, p. 338.		•		•			•		•

Principles exhibited

22

"Outdoor recreation is defined as the organized free-time activities that are participated in for their own sake and where there is an interaction between the participant and an element of nature."	Ibrahim & Cordes, 1993, p. 13.
"Outdoor recreation is just what the category "outdoor recreation" portrays—recreation that occurs outdoors in urban and rural environments."	Pigram & Jenkins, 1999, p. 6.
Outdoor recreation is understood to involve those activities that "are undertaken outside the confines of buildings (i.e. in the outdoors); and do not involve organized competition or formal rules; and can be undertaken without the existence of any built facility or infrastructure; and may require large areas of land, water and/or air; and may require outdoor areas of predominantly unmodified natural landscape."	Queensland Outdoor Recreation Federation, 2001, online. http://www.qorf.org.au/app/index.asp•page=qorfandyou

Recounting events and showing pictures of the activity to family and friends are common examples. This final phase also acts as a feedback loop which influences both anticipation of and planning for future outdoor recreation experiences.

Connecting Key Concepts

Leisure, recreation, sport, tourism, and outdoor recreation have thus far been treated as mutually exclusive or discrete concepts. Although it is initially helpful to introduce these key concepts in this way, it is important to recognize that many commonalties exist. Overlap between these concepts may be illustrated through the example of playing golf (see Box 1.1). Golf may be considered leisure if it is voluntarily undertaken due to a passion for the activity. Golf is also considered to be an activity which has inherently "recreational" qualities and offers external rewards to participants such as physical fitness and social belonging. Golf certainly mirrors the characteristics of sport (physical participation, rules, skills, competition), which is a more specific type of recreational activity. It may also qualify as tourism if travel of greater than 50 miles or 80 kilometers is involved. Golf is also usually played outdoors and thereby provides an amount of interaction between humans and the natural environment. Yet the degree of interaction between the participant and nature in golf is not as extensive as in other outdoor pursuits.

BOX 1.1 IS GOLF OUTDOOR RECREATION?

Golf is an increasingly popular activity, but is it outdoor recreation? This is a difficult issue and the definitions provided at the start of this chapter are useful in attempting to classify this particular activity. According to these definitions, golf may be considered leisure, recreation, tourism and sport. Many individuals undertake golf out of an internal love or passion for the activity during their free time from which they derive immense personal satisfaction. The Golf Nut Association illustrates the way in which individuals are drawn towards golf in an almost compulsive fashion. Other individuals may participate in golf as a recreational activity; deriving satisfaction from the experience and viewing it as a means of social obligation, exercise and/or relaxation. Travel is involved both to and from the golf course. Travel may also be initiated with the sole purpose of playing golf. Golf also certainly qualifies as a sport as it has well-defined rules, involves physical skills and has many levels of competition.

Golf certainly meets two of the criteria to be considered outdoor recreation. It may be both a free-time activity and may occur outdoors. But, does it emphasize interaction with the natural environment? This is a point of debate. Some argue that elements of nature (ponds, trees, wind) are important aspects of golf with which the golfer must interact. Others argue that interaction with the natural environment is not a primary focus, that golf courses are largely constructed or built environments which are, for the most part, meticulously maintained and that interaction between golfers and natural elements (water hazards, forests, gusts of wind) often result in great frustration.

Like many other activities, the classification of golf is largely subjective and strongly influenced by the manner in which it is undertaken. On the same golf course individuals may be experiencing leisure, participating in recreation, or taking part in tourism. The very nature of golf most closely aligns it with the concept of sport as it involves rules, physical skills and competition. Although many golfers may enjoy being outside, it is argued here that golf ought not be viewed at the resource end of the recreation continuum because it does not emphasize interaction with "natural environments."

As the above example illustrates, an activity may qualify as more than one concept. It is therefore necessary to probe, at a more refined level, the relationship between outdoor recreation and other key concepts. Mieczkowski's (1981) work in *Canadian Geographer* is acknowledged as being important in clarifying the inter-relationships among leisure, recreation and tourism (see Fennell, 2002; Searle & Brayley, 2000). As illustrated in Figure 1.3, leisure serves as a foundation for each of the other concepts. Mieczkowski (1981) views recreation, consisting of local and non-local forms, to occur entirely within the domain of leisure. Tourism extends beyond the reach of non-local recreation and incorporates the host of other reasons for which people travel including business and visiting family and friends.

Probing the relationships among these concepts continues to be of interest to scholars. Hall and Page observe that "there is increasing convergence between the two concepts [recreation and tourism] in terms of theory, activities and impacts, particularly as recreation becomes increasingly commercialised and the boundaries between public and private responsibilities in recreation change substantially" (Hall & Page, 1999, p. 5). They consequently assert that boundaries between these concepts should be considered "soft."

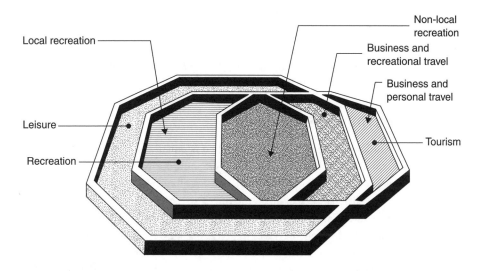

Figure 1.3 Inter-Relationships Among Leisure, Recreation, and Tourism.
Source: Mieczkowski, 1981, cited in Murphy, 1985.

Fennell (2002) observes that such convergence is the subject of perceptual debate. While tourism and recreation are sometimes similar, technical distinctions remain in most definitions. Reflecting upon definitions of tourism leads Fennell to observe that "space—the movement of travelers beyond a predetermined spatial limit—seems to be the key criterion in distinguishing tourism from other forms of recreation" (2002, p. 4).

Consideration of outdoor recreation more specifically reveals that, as a form of recreation, it fits within the purview of leisure when it is an activity that is both freely chosen and intrinsically undertaken. Differentiation is also warranted among the various potential forms of recreation. Jensen (1995) has developed a classification scheme that is helpful to make such a distinction. He suggests that recreation activities may be classified along a continuum. At one end of the continuum are forms which are resource-oriented (occur in natural settings and rely on natural resources). Activities that are user-oriented (occur in built or modified environments and depend on performance) are on the other end of the continuum. By following this classification scheme, outdoor recreation can be regarded as a category of activities that are located at one end of Jensen's (1995) continuum of recreational pursuits.

The model by Clawson and Knetsch (1966) provided an excellent starting point for understanding the total outdoor recreation experience but confounds the relationship between tourism and outdoor recreation. Travel is clearly embedded in their model as part of the outdoor recreation experience. Hall and Page come to the same conclusion from the opposite perspective in stating that "natural settings and outdoor recreation opportunities are clearly a major component of tourism, perhaps especially so since the development of interest in nature-based and ecotourism activities" (1999, p. 5). Their statement confirms the convergence between recreation and tourism at a broad level and recognizes that the relationship between outdoor recreation and particular forms of tourism is even closer. Despite this relative proximity, outdoor recreation is distinct from tourism. Hall and Page (1999) identify that how individuals define the activity themselves is important. Differences are also contingent upon the perspective taken in understanding and analyzing these activities. Outdoor recreation tends to focus on "recreational" and ecological elements whereas tourism tends to focus on spatial and "ecological" elements. Despite taking the former perspective in this book, which does not highlight spatial elements, the closely related topics such as ecotourism are discussed in the final chapter.

THE STUDY OF OUTDOOR RECREATION

Understanding how outdoor recreation has been studied is equally as important as defining it. Essentially, this section establishes the epistemology of outdoor recreation. Epistemology is a Greek word that means the theory of knowledge (Welbourne, 2001). Campbell and Hunter explain that "a traditional task of epistemology is to establish and defend systematic standards, norms, or criteria that must be satisfied in order for us to have knowledge or simply have beliefs that are justified or warranted" (2000, p. 1). This task is relevant to developing an understanding of knowledge acquisition regarding outdoor recreation.

Manning (1999) provides a historical account of outdoor recreation research and development in his book *Studies in Outdoor Recreation*. In this work he traces early studies of outdoor recreation back at least 50 years and recognizes that they tended to be ecologically focused due to the biological training associated with resource management. A shift in focus occurred after World War II when outdoor recreation emerged as an area of study for social scientists, largely through the presidential-commissioned Outdoor Recreation Resources Review Commission (ORRRC) in the United States. The association of social issues with outdoor recreation (e.g., crowding, conflict, access) and recognition of social variables of interest (e.g., economics, preferences, attitudes) in the 1960s and 1970s increased the breadth of early research to include social science disciplines such as sociology, economics, and psychology. Based on these historical observations, Manning describes that:

> research in outdoor recreation has, then, evolved in the classic manner of most emerging fields of study. Most early studies were descriptive and exploratory, substituting data for theory, and were disciplinary-based. An expanding database allowed more conceptual and analytical developments, and ultimately a more multidisciplinary and interdisciplinary approach.
>
> (1999, p. 8)

The above account of outdoor recreation research makes clear three important approaches to acquiring outdoor recreation knowledge. Initially, inquiry was undertaken from a disciplinary approach. A discipline, in the traditional academic sense, is considered a basic branch of knowledge. Conventional academic disciplines, often associated with foundational methods, have been used to structure academic institutions, construct basic knowledge, and pursue specialization with increasing refinement and isolation (Brewer, 1999; Savory, 1988). Yet outdoor recreation does not exactly fit within the traditional disciplinary approach and is more accurately described as disciplinary-based. Manning makes clear this distinction as he writes that:

> outdoor recreation is not a discipline in the conventional academic sense. That is, it is not a basic branch of knowledge like biology, mathematics, or sociology. It is an applied field of study focused on an issue or problem that has attracted the attention of a broad segment of society.
>
> (1999, p. 4)

As a repository of outdoor recreation information developed, a second tactic emerged in which research began to shift away from initial disciplinary-based approaches. Wall views this as a significant issue in that "recreation is a phenomenon which does not respect traditional disciplinary boundaries and is best understood by those willing to transgress the artificial barriers constructed by those who wish to segment knowledge into academic departments" (1989, p. 4). Consequently, it is not a surprise that a decade later Manning observes:

> contributions from the traditional social science disciplines of sociology, psychology, and economics have declined relative to the contributions from researchers in the broader park, recreation, and related departments, whose studies are broader in nature and more appropriate to problem solving in an inherently interdisciplinary field.
>
> (1999, p. 7)

While outdoor recreation remains a subject of interest to some researchers working from disciplinary perspectives, it emerged during this second approach as a substantive area of study in and of itself. This is the process of knowledge specialization. As a result, the subject of outdoor recreation constitutes a significant area of focus in professional schools or applied areas of study including natural resource management, forestry, ecology, tourism, environmental studies, planning, community health and leisure studies.

The relationship between a discipline-based and an applied approach has, at times, confounded advancement and recognition of outdoor recreation research. This tension primarily arises from systemic differences between basic and pragmatic approaches to research (Manning, 1999). Following in the positivistic tradition associated with the disciplinary approach, scholarly research focused on testing hypotheses to generate new knowledge. On the other hand, applied research tends to be pragmatic and aimed at addressing manageable variables of concern.

Partly due to the classical development of outdoor recreation as a field of study and to some extent a consequence of the basic versus applied schism, outdoor recreation research has been frequently criticized for lacking a theoretical basis (Crandall & Lewko, 1976; Hendricks & Burdge, 1972; Manning, 2000; Moncrief, 1970; Napier, 1981; Riddick, DeSchriver & Weissinger, 1984; Smith, 1975; Witt, 1984). In commenting on the state of recreation and leisure research, Hendricks and Burdge explained:

> It is difficult to convince colleagues not steeped in leisure that we are engaged in meaningful research—not because we lack statistical and methodological expertise but because we lack a theoretical framework, a conceptualization scheme and a cumulative focus.
>
> (1972, p. 217)

Smith (1975) also recognized that recreation research often specifies intractable, vague non-problems that resultantly do not hold up in practice. Others (e.g., Hultsman, Cottrell & Hultsman, 1998) have reinforced the need to be broadly applicable.

These once pervasive criticisms appear to be waning with time (Manning, 1999, 2000). Henderson (1994) explored the presence of conceptual and theoretical frameworks in four recreation journals during the 1980s and found that most articles included a theoretical basis. Research from disciplinary-based and applied approaches are becoming recognized as being complementary and together have advanced the state of outdoor recreation research. Important trends in the development of outdoor recreation research are the transition to theoretically-based investigations and understanding and synthesis of literature into conceptual/organizational frameworks (Vaske & Manning, 2008). Although sometimes these terms are employed interchangeably (e.g., Wall, 1989) they are distinct. Berkes and Folke offer further refinement by linking these concepts. They observe that "models describe how things work, whereas theories explain phenomena. Conceptual frameworks do neither; rather they help to think about phenomena, to order material, revealing patterns—and pattern recognition typically leads to models and theories" (1998, p. 15).

Conceptual frameworks are organizational devices which structure how we think about a particular phenomenon. Geoffrey Wall (1989), in his book *Outdoor Recreation in Canada*, proposed a framework which details variables influencing leisure generally and outdoor recreation specifically. To Wall:

> Outdoor recreation may be considered to have two basic aspects: the supply of recreational facilities and the demand for participation. Supply and demand interact through intervening decision-making processes to give rise to patterns of outdoor recreation. These patterns of outdoor recreation have associated economic, environmental, and social impacts.
>
> (1989, p. 9)

The various linkages that connect the main elements are equally important. Supply (available resources) and demand (persons requiring the resource) relate through the decision-making process and ultimately shape participation. Wall (1989) refers to this as patterns of recreation consisting of quantitative measures, spatial elements, duration of activities, temporal distributions, nature of accommodations and group composition. The result of pursuing outdoor recreation is manifest in economic, environmental and socio-cultural consequences. Wall encourages others to pursue organizational devices as he writes that "the theoretical [conceptual] framework which has been presented is by no means the only possible one . . . nor is it exhaustive in its content" (1989, p. 16).

A third approach to outdoor recreation inquiry emerges with the accumulation of a critical mass of outdoor recreation research and ongoing conceptual refinements. Outdoor recreation in this third approach is identified as being multidisciplinary (Manning, 1999) and/or interdisciplinary (Manning, 1999; Wall, 1989). An interdisciplinary perspective of outdoor recreation is pursued in this book because it facilitates exploration of topics that transcend boundaries, permits incorporation of both pragmatic and conceptual considerations and reflects the continued logical progression of outdoor recreation inquiry.

SUMMARY

This chapter developed the contextual background in which outdoor recreation may be understood. Key concepts within leisure studies were discussed (leisure, recreation, sport and tourism) prior to concentrating on defining the term outdoor recreation. Unlike some of the other key concepts that have been widely interpreted, the term outdoor recreation has been employed with remarkable consistency and is considered a behavior that:

1. involves voluntary participation in free time activity;
2. occurs in the outdoors; and,
3. embraces the interaction of people with the natural environment. Probing differences among these key concepts highlights the importance of employing the terms with precision.

The second half of the chapter was dedicated to documenting how outdoor recreation has been, and may be, studied. Outdoor recreation has followed a "classical" progression from a primarily descriptive discipline-based approach to a conceptual and interdisciplinary scheme. In putting an interdisciplinary framework front and center in this volume, readers may gain an appreciation for its importance as well as the major elements that constitute the study of outdoor recreation.

KEY CONCEPTS

Applied approach

Disciplinary approach

Epistemology

Leisure (multi-dimensional definition)

Objectives of outdoor recreation

Outdoor recreation

Phases of the outdoor recreation experience

Recreation

Sport

Tourism

SUGGESTED KEY SOURCES FOR MORE INFORMATION

Clawson, M. & Knetsch, J. L. (1966). *Economics of outdoor recreation*. Baltimore: Hopkins Press.

Godbey, G. (1999). *Leisure in your life: an exploration* (5th ed.). State College, PA: Venture Publishing.

Great Outdoors Recreation Page (GORP): GORP.com

Hall, C. M. & Page, S. J. (1999). *The geography of tourism and recreation: Environment, place and space*. New York: Routledge.

Manning, R. E. (2000). Coming of age: History and trends in outdoor recreation research. In W. C. Gartner & D. W. Lime (Eds.), *Trends in outdoor recreation, leisure and tourism* (pp. 121–131). New York: CABI Publishing.

Mieczkowski, Z. T. (1981). Some notes on the geography of tourism: A comment. *Canadian Geographer, 25*, 186–191.

Natural Resources Research Information Pages: Outdoor Recreation http://www4.ncsu.edu/~leung/recres.html

Virtual Library of Sport http://sportsvl.com

REVIEW QUESTIONS

1. Define the terms leisure, recreation, sport and tourism.
2. What is outdoor recreation?
3. Explain the similarities and differences among leisure, recreation and sport.
4. Is golf outdoor recreation?
5. Describe the total outdoor recreation experience?
6. How has the study of outdoor recreation evolved during the past 50 years?

Chapter 2

Perspectives on the Past

OBJECTIVES

This chapter will:

- explain the contribution of historical analysis;
- document the heritage of outdoor recreation;
- consider the presence of outdoor recreation activities before European contact;
- trace the evolution of outdoor recreation in North America;
- explore the major social and political forces that have influenced the development of outdoor recreation;
- recognize the contributions of prominent individuals and organizations.

INTRODUCTION

This chapter takes a historical look at the development of outdoor recreation. Roots are traced back to early civilizations, significant developments in Europe that prompted general advances in leisure are documented, and the presence of outdoor activities preceding the European settlement are acknowledged. Considerable attention is given to chronicling the development of outdoor recreation in North America. Special consideration is given to recognize changing perceptions regarding leisure and wilderness as well as precipitous social and political forces. Accounts of inspirational works and pragmatic efforts by individuals and organizations are presented as they changed early views towards nature, positively altered human actions, and shaped the development of outdoor recreation.

SETTING THE CONTEXT

The task of historians is to study the past and offer their interpretation of events and the forces which influenced them (Conrad, Finkel & Jaenen, 1993). History goes beyond simply reporting what happened. It provides insights as to why an event happened and retrospective commentary on the consequences. The context for outdoor recreation is indicative of the historical approach as it involves interpretation of important events, key people and organizations, and the forces that shaped them.

The Roots of Outdoor Recreation

The earliest records of civilization include the creation of parks and gardens for aesthetics and hunting, elements that we now consider as outdoor recreation. Gothein (1928) traces the creation of parks to the Sumerian people and specifically King Gudea (approximately 2340 BC) who had both vineyards and fish ponds. The Egyptians are also recognized as an important early influence in park development. Sessoms writes that "the hunting preserves of the Egyptians and the hanging gardens of Babylon might be considered early signs of interest in setting aside outdoor areas for personal enjoyment—exactly the purpose of the modern park" (1984, p. 34). Often these areas were intended for use by royalty and public officials (including priests) while slaves and serfs were responsible for planting and the upkeep of these early gardens (Wright, 1934).

Although ancient India is identified as an early provider of public parks and baths (Gothein, 1928), it was Greek and Roman cultures which formally established the idea of leisure and recreation through an emphasis on sports and art. According to Murphy:

> the term leisure is derived from the Latin word *licere* or "to be permitted to abstain from occupation or service," with direct reference to the Athenian ideal of absolving select citizens from daily physical (*ponos*) and freeing them to engage in intellectual, cultural, civic, and artistic endeavors.
>
> (1981, p. 24)

Roman culture maintained a parallel concept of *otium* in reference to similar endeavors (Murphy, 1981). Both arts and sports were important components of Greek civilization and were emphasized through their belief in balanced education (physical activity, art and philosophy). Sessoms writes that "to encourage and facilitate athletic performances, public parks, hunting preserves, gymnasiums, and related athletic facilities were constructed" (1984, p. 35).

Although some of these early conceptions of leisure came from Greek society, it was the Roman civilization which emphasized free time. Recreation and leisure are enduring influences of Roman society, although it is important to recognize that these activities did not include everyone. Slaves and those living a subsistence lifestyle were commonplace and these individuals did not enjoy large amounts of relative freedom. Citizens of Rome, in the fourth century for example, were given as many as 175 holidays per year and provided with diverse recreational opportunities (Boren, 1977; Godbey, 1999). Many of these opportunities were not provided out of stately benevolence, but rather "emperors and kings have always found it prudent, especially when they rule from large capital cities, to try to keep the lower classes in their capitals quiescent and reasonably happy" (Boren, 1977, p. 205). Entertainment in Roman society included theatrical performances, horse and chariot races, staged naval combat, circus events and gladiator competitions (Boren, 1977). Roman society also maintained a keen interest in outdoor recreation as game preserves, private and public gardens, and baths were all popular; "by the fourth century, there were over 800 public baths available which could accommodate crowds of 60,000 persons on any given day" (Sessoms, 1984, p. 36).

Following the demise of the Roman Empire were the Dark Ages. Scholars studying leisure during this period note relatively little if any recreation opportunities, with the exception of feudal lords who had sufficient power and land to maintain hunting preserves (e.g., the New Forest preserve established by William the Conqueror in 1087) and limited gardens (Godbey, 1999; Jensen, 1995; Sessoms, 1984). Interest and opportunity for recreation, and particularly outdoor recreation, re-emerged during the Renaissance. The Renaissance "can usefully denote a particular complex of ideas and a definable civilization. In the realms of thoughts, literature, art, and scholarships the three centuries after 1300 have a reasonably coherent character of their own" (Elton, 1968, p. 39). The almost exclusively private ownership of gardens and hunting preserves began to shift towards public garden parks (e.g., Kensington Gardens in London) and the provision of public hunting opportunities (Sessoms, 1984).

One of the most auspicious events to change the pattern of daily life, including recreation, was the Industrial Revolution. Spielvogel, in his discourse on western civilization, remarks that "although it took decades for the Industrial Revolution to spread, it was truly revolutionary in the way it fundamentally changed Europeans, their society, their relationship to other peoples, and the world itself" (1991, p. 703). The Industrial Revolution started in Britain in the 1780s and was precipitated by the agricultural revolution, increasing markets for manufactured goods, surplus labor, ready capital investments, infrastructure improvements, energy sources, and trade relations (Spielvogel, 1991). The combination of these factors lead to a tremendous shift from an agricultural-based rural economy that was labour intensive, highly interactive, and non-regimented to a capital-based economy involving machinery, factories, and high levels of regimentation (Spielvogel, 1991). Some of the immediate consequences of such a transformation were realized a relatively short time later (around 1850) as large numbers of people migrated from the countryside into cities searching for jobs. Rapid urbanization, particularly by those seeking employment in factories, resulted in living conditions with poor-quality food, few shelters, and a general lack of sanitary disposal. Indignant living conditions were accompanied by equally poor working conditions in both factories and mines. These places of employment hired large numbers of children and women and mandated long hours of labour (12–16 hours daily). Working conditions were often unsafe and meager wages were offered with no guarantee of employment. Spielvogel observes that at a societal level "the creation of a wealthy industrial middle class and a huge industrial middle class (or proletariat) substantially transformed traditional social relationships" (1991, p. 703). Recognition by the middle class of the squalor conditions resulted in social investigations. These investigations had multiple motivations including moral consequences of such conditions, fear of violence by these masses, and desire to maintain their position which required a motivated labor force (Spielvogel, 1991).

Leisure was central to the critique of capitalism and the class structure resulting from the Industrial Revolution. In 1899, Thorstein Veblen provided a social commentary that argued the existence of a leisure class which displays extravagance through the consumption of leisure (defined as the non-productive use of time). According to Veblen:

The conditions apparently necessary to its emergence in a consistent form are (1) the community must be of a predatory habit of life (war or the hunting of large game or both); that is to say, the men who constitute the inchoate leisure class in these cases, must be habituated to the infliction of injury by force of stratagem; (2) subsistence must be obtainable on sufficiently easy terms to admit of the exemption of a considerable portion of the community from steady application to a routine of labour. The insitituion of a leisure class is the outgrowth of an early discrimination between employments, according to which some employments are worthy and others unworthy.

(1975, pp. 7–8)

Many variations are possible within Veblen's leisure class, some of which represent the roots of early social movements and voluntary associations concerned about other well-being such as the Chartist Movement (Godbey, 1999; Spielvogel, 1991). As slight improvements were made through legislative efforts and reform, attention was directed to reforming leisure activities popular during the Industrial Revolution (e.g., gambling, drinking, blood-sports) with planned and "respectable" activities such as reading, structured sports and education (Godbey, 1999). Although these changes did not replace or eliminate previous leisure pursuits, the move towards industrialization (increasing value of time, possibility of travel and increased pace of life) continued to influence the awareness of potential opportunities (Godbey, 1999).

Outdoor recreation in the post-industrialized era has uniquely developed in nation states and specific regional areas, shaped largely by social context and geography. Although a comprehensive review of how outdoor recreation has developed in various locations is beyond the scope of this book, a few examples illustrate the range of experiences. In the United Kingdom, for example, the above changes in leisure did not translate into pursuit of outdoor activities but rather quiet enjoyment of landscapes (Curry, 2004; Ibrahim & Cordes, 2002). Open-air schools were introduced in England in the early portion of the 1900s to resist the influence of industry (Hughes, 2004). A demand for increased access to the countryside in the United Kingdom, which was largely privately owned, met considerable opposition and it was not until 1949 that legislation (the National Parks and Access to the Countryside Act) acknowledged safeguarding some of the English countryside, although parks largely remained in private ownership (Curry, 1994, 2004; Seabrooke & Miles, 1993). Redressing this situation occurred relatively recently with the Countryside and Right of Way Act in 2000 which permits public access to open land after 2005 and requires the conservation of habitat by governments (see Curry, 2004; Torkildsen, 2005). Initial values pertaining to outdoor recreation in New Zealand were quite different, with an emphasis on social elements and universal access (Curry, 2004). With increasing globalization, however, there has been an increasing coalesce between the United Kingdom and New Zealand in terms of leisure lifestyles and market orientation (Curry, 2004). A country such as Norway illustrates a very different course of development. In Norway legislation (Outdoor Recreation Act) specifically aimed at outdoor recreation was enacted in 1957 and outdoor activities are nationally promoted (Riese & Vorkinn, 2002). Riese and Vorkinn explain that "outdoor recreation is one of the most important leisure activities in Norway, and is practiced by a large part of the population. It also has special cultural meaning as a national symbol, and is a prominent issue in both political life and administration" (2002, p. 199).

34

Outdoor Recreation before European Settlement

Leisure and recreation were also present in many societies prior to European contact. These societies have been the subject of interest to scholars because leisure played an important role in their functioning (Godbey, 1999; Ibrahim, 1991). Contemporary societies with similar characteristics act as reliable sample, and may also provide valuable insights (Ibrahim, 1991).

Both Ibrahim (1991) and Godbey (1999) investigate the case of Australian Aborigines or Australoids. Although one of the technically least complex societies known, this group was found to have both considerable leisure time and activities. Godbey (1999) notes that this group only required between three and four hours per day for work. Ibrahim (1991) described many types of rituals observed by this group to include dances and movements, spear-throwing and wrestling. In his review and synthesis of anthropological literature, Godbey (1999) recognizes a similar pattern among many other primitive groups. The Maori, Machiguenga and Australian Aborigines all take an integrative approach to daily activities with play-like characteristics, thus blurring the dichotomy between work and leisure.

The manner by which the Americas became inhabited and the number of inhabitants at the time Europeans reached the continent (40 million to over 100 million people) are topics of great debate (Conrad et al., 1993). It is clear from studies of history that the First Nations people of North America had vibrant cultures which included leisure and recreation long before European settlement. The following examples illustrate the presence of such activities in a diverse number of groups or tribes who occupied the continent at the time when the Europeans arrived.

The northernmost First Nations group was the Eskimo or Inuit. Ibrahim (1991) and Horna (1994) characterize their daily existence as playful. Dancing and wrestling in this society were observed as forms of ritual entertainment or celebration (Burch, 2004; Price, 1971). Dancing partnerships between men were often created as a ceremonial way of creating bonds between families and communities (Burch, 2004). Festivals were also a part of Inuit culture, often lasting for weeks at a time (Price, 1971).

Navajo people, located in the southwestern United States, had many forms of recreation. Stories were conveyed through the telling of folk tales and "sings" were popular (Ibrahim, 1991). Rituals observed contained many elements of "recreation" including running races, painting and wrestling (Ibrahim, 1991; Kluckhohn, Hill & Kluckhohn, 1971). Conversely, aspects of religion and ritual were inherent in traditional Navajo games (Kluckhohn et al., 1971).

The First Nations people of what is presently Canada also exhibited rich traditions of recreation and leisure. Ibrahim (1991) asserts that the geographical landscape of Canada and the First Nations populations contribute to recreation activities which are uniquely Canadian. One of the recreation activities popular with many tribes was Baggataway or a ball game. Kah-Ge-Gah-Bowh in 1850 offered the following description of the Ojibwa version of this game. He observed:

Each man and each woman (women sometimes engage in the sport) is armed with a stick, one end of which bends somewhat like a small hoop, about four inches in

35

circumference, to which is attached a net work of raw-hide, two inches deep, just large enough to admit the ball which is used on the occasion. Two poles are driven in the ground at a distance of four hundred paces from each other, which serves as goals for the two parties. It is the endeavor of each to take the ball to this pole. The party which carries the ball and strikes its pole wins the game.

(1972; as cited in Conrad et al., 1993, pp. 27–28)

This particular game was adopted by the French who renamed it *lacrosse*; it remains popular today and is Canada's national sport.

Many of the activities engaged in for subsistence (e.g., fishing, gathering, canoeing) are considered to be outdoor recreation today. The canoe, an important mode of transportation for First Nations peoples and vital to the development of Canada, is fundamental to the recreational activity of canoeing today. Archery and hunting are additional examples that were central for defense and subsistence which have become primarily recreational activities.

Outdoor Recreation in North America

The settlement of North America was the product of many influences. European motives for expansion were multi-faceted as they wanted to discover new lands, deliver religious messages, and expand economically by acquiring new materials (Spielvogel, 1991). Coincidental "discovery" of North America occurred while explorers searched for trade routes. It was the presence of resources that provided economic incentives for more permanent settlement as individuals were searching for new opportunities and/or to escape existing conditions (Conrad et al., 1993).

In the Colonial period, early settlers of North America brought with them their attitudes about both leisure and wilderness. In his discussion of the influence of religion on leisure, Godbey (1999) focuses on the Puritan settlers of North America who emphasized the ideas of original sin and predestination in their religious practices. These beliefs combined with class conflict (indignation towards the leisure class) to result in a value system which renounced pleasure and idleness and by extension leisure and recreation. These settlers were also confronted with the reality of arriving in previously unexplored territories. Nash, in *Wilderness and the American Mind*, traces early attitudes towards wilderness in America back to "when William Bradford stepped off the *Mayflower* into a 'hideous and desolate wilderness' he started a tradition of repugnance" (1982, pp. 23–24).

Elements of outdoor recreation were present in early colonial settlements. Areas of common land (used for grazing, harvesting and recreation) can be traced to 1634 in Boston (Jensen, 1995). In Canada, Halifax Common was established in 1763 and was used for a number of recreational activities including skating, tennis and archery (Wright, 1984). Conservation legislation also has its roots in early colonial development. Jensen (1995) cites an ordinance passed in 1626 by the Plymouth colony which prohibits the unauthorized harvesting of timber. Despite these few early examples, the pioneers' attitude towards the environment remained largely adversarial. Two reasons account for this attitude: the acute need for survival by pioneers (food, shelter, and safety) faced with the harsh reality of wild and unknown environments and the dark symbolism associated with the wilderness (Nash, 1982). In this regard Chubb and Chubb write that wilderness was "regarded as something that had to be conquered. Protestant theology tended to represent it as an earthly hell that Christians had a duty to subdue by clearing and farming" (1981, p. 21).

At the dawn of the Victorian period attitudes about leisure in general and outdoor recreation specifically began to shift in North America. Chubb and Chubb (1981) refer to this period as the recreation renaissance; changing attitudes by some religious leaders resulted in the "Muscular Christianity" movement that encouraged participation in physical activity. Other societal changes were equally important and also played an important role on the influence of recreation. Chubb and Chubb (1981) as well as Searle and Brayley (2000) recognize three important developments:

1. urbanization and increased rights for workers raised the amount of individuals looking for leisure and recreation;
2. the widely held idea that women should find recreation in the domestic domain started to change as public recreation became increasingly acceptable for women; and,
3. the development of transportation systems which opened difficult to access geographical areas and increased the speed and comfort of travel.

Outdoor recreation during this time period was also confronted with the stark reality that conservation was necessary. Jensen (1995) notes that 12 of 13 colonies enacted seasonal closures for various types of game. Ideas of the romantic period appeared to sway attitudes about natural landscapes as the residents of cities and towns became concerned about rapid urbanization. In this regard, the city of Toronto established the Public Walks and Gardens in 1851 (McFarland, 1970). The most recognized manifestation of the concern about public spaces is Central Park in New York. According to Chubb and Chubb (1981) civic leaders concerned about urban development purchased an 840-acre parcel of swamp north of the city and held a design competition to award the contract. Frederick Law Olmsted and Calvert Vaux were successful with their design which emphasized rural and functional elements of natural landscapes.

In addition the establishment of public spaces within cities containing natural elements, interest developed in the preservation of wilderness. John Muir prompted legislation in 1864 for the protection of the Yosemite Valley (Chubb & Chubb, 1981). This legislation pertaining to a relatively small area provided the foundation for larger scale enterprises. Nash writes "the world's first instance of large-scale wilderness preservation in the public interest occurred on March 1, 1872, when President Ulysses S. Grant signed an act designating over two million acres of northwestern Wyoming as Yellowstone National Park" (1982, p. 108). Of equal importance to the preservation is the wording contained in the following passage from the associated legislation:

[The Yellowstone region] is hereby reserved and withdrawn from settlement, occupancy, or sale ... and set apart as a public park or pleasuring ground for the benefit and enjoyment of the people.... [The Secretary of the Interior] shall provide for the preservation ... of all timber, mineral deposits, natural curiosities, or wonders within said park ... in their natural condition.

(United States Statues at Large, 1872; as cited in Nash, 1982, p. 108)

Formulation of the first Canadian national park was precipitated by the discovery of hot springs by employees of the Canadian Pacific Railway. Rather than accepting the employees' claim, the Federal Government formed a 26 sq. km reservation in 1885 (McNamee, 1993). According to McNamee "wilderness preservation had little to do with the establishment of the Banff hot springs reserve and other national parks around the turn of the century" (1993, p. 18). Parks are integral to the history of recreation and in recognition of this enduring influence are described in detail in Chapter 7.

The early part of the twentieth century was characterized by increasing government involvement in the provision of recreation services (Chubb & Chubb, 1981). Momentum for the continued formation of parks in cities continued to grow rapidly at this time with the number increasing tenfold in the United States from 1880 to 1900 (Chubb & Chubb, 1981). Two major events had profound influence on outdoor recreation in the twentieth century— the closing of the American frontier and the production of the automobile.

The American frontier officially closed in 1890 (Nash, 1982). Although those living on the frontier retained an antagonistic attitude, this seminal event had a profound impact on future generations. Nash observes:

although there were a few exceptions, American frontiersmen rarely judged wilderness with criteria other than a military metaphor. It was their children and grandchildren, removed from a wilderness condition, who began to sense its ethical and aesthetic values. Yet even city dwellers found it difficult to ignore the older attitudes completely.

(1982, p. 43)

Exceptions to the dominant attitudes toward the natural environment at the time the frontier closed are noteworthy because of their unprecedented nature and considerable scope. The closing of the frontier, to some, signaled the need to conserve resources in an effort to avoid resource scarcity. The commitment by the federal government in the United States, under the leadership of Theodore Roosevelt, himself an outdoor enthusiast, was striking. From 1880 to 1920 the federal government in the United States created the United States Forest Service, established the first wildlife refuge, initiated the National Park Service, and launched a national conservation commission (Chubb & Chubb, 1981; Jensen, 1995). The National Parks Conservation Association was formed in 1919 as a non-partisan voice to advocate for national parks (National Parks Conservation Association, 2007). Others also reached out to embrace the values and qualities associated with wilderness as the frontier closed. Sir Robert S. S. Baden-Powell began the scouting movement in 1907 which quickly caught on in the United States (Nash, 1982). Nash asserts that the magnitude and vigor of such success was far more than just a growing organization; he writes "the Boy Scouts' striking success (it quickly became the largest youth organization in the country) is a significant commentary on American thinking in the early twentieth century" (1982, p. 148).

Accompanying these more philosophical changes were technological advancements and in particular development of the automobile. The invention of the Model T by Henry Ford in 1909 made outdoor environments increasingly easier to access (Chubb & Chubb, 1981). Although the relatively high price of the car and the lack of corresponding infrastructure were restraining factors, automotive use increased as well as foreshadowed future changes.

Although the period of time from the 1920s until the end of World War II is often characterized by hardship, it was a booming period of development for outdoor recreation (Jensen, 1995). In both the United States and Canada much development came from government investment through work projects. In the United States it was Roosevelt's "New Deal" program which developed infrastructure and facilities, frequently in parks (Chubb & Chubb, 1981). Government agencies (e.g., Public Work Administration, Civilian Conservation Corps, National Parks Service) associated with outdoor recreation were particularly influential (Chubb & Chubb, 1981; Jensen, 1995). The emphasis on recreation and provision of public services largely came to a halt with the onset of World War II. Although attention was certainly not focused on outdoor recreation, technological developments and events would influence postwar outdoor recreation. Major influences included improvements in international systems of travel, advancements in equipment for outdoor living and exposure to "camping"—the use of tents although certainly not for pleasure (Searle & Brayley, 2000).

Outdoor recreation boomed in the post-World War II era. Trends in demand, systematic collection of user information and legislative and policy initiatives represent significant developments in both the United States and Canada in the 1950s and 1960s. Chubb and Chubb (1981) identify the most auspicious event of this era as the mechanization of recreation. Although this can largely be attributed to Ford's earlier creation of the automobile, a shorter work week, and the urge to travel combined to result in the dramatic increase for the quest for recreation (Chubb & Chubb, 1981). The influence of mechanized recreation was also not limited to roadways as motorcycles and the snowmobile were also introduced at this time (Searle & Brayley, 2000). Limitations of natural resources were quickly realized as a result of the insatiable appetite for outdoor recreation resources in the postwar era. One of the most important early works that called attention to the void developing between those demanding resources and the potential availability of resources was by Clawson (1959) who called attention to *The Crisis in Outdoor Recreation*. The article clearly articulated the impending consequences of unchecked use of recreational resources in the United States.

Concerns from conservationists, such as the Izaak Walton League of America, prompted Congress to systematically study the phenomena. The terms of reference for this task:

> in order to preserve, develop, and assume accessibility to all American people of present and future generations such quality and quantity of outdoor recreation resources as will be necessary and desirable for individual enjoyment, and to assure the spiritual, cultural, and physical benefits that such outdoor recreation provides; in order to inventory and evaluate the outdoor recreation resources and opportunities of the Nation, to determine the types and location of such resources and opportunities which will be required by present and future generations; and in order to make comprehensive information and recommendations leading to these goals available to the President,

the Congress, and the individual States and Territories, there is hereby authorized and created a bipartisan Outdoor Recreation Review Commission.

(An Act for the establishment of a National Outdoor Recreation Resources Review Commission, Statutes at Large 72, Part 1, 1958, p. 238; as cited in Chubb & Chubb, 1981, p. 36)

Outcomes of the Outdoor Recreation Resources Review Commission (ORRRC) were communicated in a 28-volume report which is regarded by Chubb and Chubb as "probably the most important recreation event of the era" (1981, p. 37). In Canada the National and Provincial Parks Association was formed as a voice to protect parks (McNamee, 1993). Canada also initiated study of outdoor recreation in 1967 with the Canadian Outdoor Recreation Demand Study (CORDS) which aimed at "measuring outdoor recreation demand, developing alternatives from which policy could be determined for the federal government, preparing predictions of the future use, and guiding the management of the outdoor recreation system in Canada" (Searle & Brayley, 2000, p. 25).

The collection of information pertaining to outdoor recreation prompted unprecedented government involvement (Sessoms, 1984). Government agencies, legislation and policy initiated in the 1960s responded to the increasing demand for outdoor recreation and the establishment of conservation measures in the United States. Outdoor recreation officially became the purview of the National Forest Service; the Bureau of Outdoor Recreation was formed two years later within the Department of the Interior; and, under the Land and Water Conservation Act (1965) individual states gained responsibility for the development of outdoor recreation resources (Jensen, 1995). Progress by state governments, acting under the Tenth Amendment of the Constitution, was facilitated by such granting opportunities as the Land and Conservation Fund (Chubb & Chubb, 1981; Kraus, 2001). A myriad of legislation was also introduced for outdoor recreation. The Wilderness Act of 1964 formally acknowledged the importance and values of wildernesses and formed a system for their preservation; the Scenic Rivers Act of 1968 acknowledged the special place of free-flowing rivers; and, the National Trails System Act of 1968 directed attention towards land-based paths of significance (Jensen, 1995).

Momentum developed for recreation in general throughout the 1960s slowed considerably in the 1970s due to the prevailing economic climate, an energy crisis, and environmental concerns (Chubb & Chubb, 1981; Searle & Brayley, 2000). While some forms of recreation development stalled during this time, considerable legislation and planning for outdoor recreation continued in the United States. The first National Recreation Plan was put forward. Although it was not implemented, it provided guidance to the second and more useful 1973 Nationwide Outdoor Recreation Plan (A Legacy for America) (Jensen, 1995). Governmental change in 1977 had a profound effect as the National Parks and Recreation Act provided $1.2 billion for major projects; large tracts of land were added under the Endangered American Wilderness Act; and, the amount of lands in the existing park system roughly doubled under the Alaska National Interests Land Conservation Act (Chubb & Chubb, 1981; Jensen, 1995).

Economic pressures of recessions, unemployment, and public support for reduced government expenditures were enduring features of the late 1970s and characterized the better part of the next two decades in the United States (Jensen, 1995). Canada faced similar pressures, although the specific concern about government spending surfaced later in the 1990s (Searle & Brayley, 2000). As a consequence of these pressures there has been a shift towards conservatism and the corporate economic model in which large corporations influence policy decisions and the roles held by public and private sectors are altered (Jensen, 1995; Kraus, 2001; Reid, 1995).

These socio-political changes which characterize the 1980s and 1990s have had a profound affect on outdoor recreation. Very few new initiatives or programs by governments occurred during these two decades. Jensen (1995) identifies a single act with direct consequences to outdoor recreation formed during this 20-year period. Conservation organizations continued to voice their concerns about conservation. In Canada, for example, the NPPAC merged with the Wildlands League to form the Canadian Parks and Wilderness Society (CPAWS), which directed attention to problems associated with habitat fragmentation (CPAWS, 2005).

The manner in which current programs were maintained and funded was sharply called into question. During the 1980s parks and recreation agencies responded by accepting a marketing orientation in which new opportunities were explored and aggressively promoted in an attempt to create solutions to funding cutbacks (Kraus, 2001). As a result of changing government roles "many recreation, park, and leisure-service agencies resorted to privatization—subcontracting or developing concession arrangements with private organizations—to carry out functions that they could not themselves fulfill as economically or efficiently" (Kraus, 2001, p. 107). Governments are also increasingly relying on other organizations to meet the demand for outdoor recreation as well as natural resource protection. LaPage states that "volunteerism is a form of activism and like other expressions of social and environmental activism, it is triggered by a combination of dissatisfaction with the status quo and a citizenry that is willing to get involved" (2000, p. 366).

While volunteerism and co-production or co-management continue to be pursued for service delivery and resource protection, other concerns confront the contemporary situation. Interest is emerging on ecological justice pertaining to outdoor recreation, and specifically the accessibility of outdoor recreation to minorities and low-income populations (Floyd & Johnson, 2002). Private lands are coming under increasing pressure from urban areas and access to private lands is becoming increasingly restricted, particularly in the eastern United States (Mozumder, Starbuck, Berrens & Alexander, 2007). Growing concern is also mounting for environmental impacts from outdoor recreation and eco-tourism activities on land (e.g., all-terrain vehicles) (Pigram & Jenkins, 2006) as well as in water (e.g., whale-watching) (Cater, 2003). Climatic changes and alterations to the very essence of outdoor recreation discussed in the introductory remarks of this book underscore the need for a meaningful response.

PROMINENT FIGURES IN THE HISTORY OF OUTDOOR RECREATION

The historical account of outdoor recreation provides a broad contextual overview. Although socio-political forces exert considerable influence, many advances can be traced to specific individuals whose extraordinary efforts and insights require acknowledgment. The following synopsis introduces some of the prominent figures in outdoor recreation and summarizes their contributions. Readers are encouraged to both enjoy the works written by these prominent figures and explore the volumes that have been written about each of these individuals.

Ralph Waldo Emerson, 1803–1882

Emerson was born on May 25, 1803. He was raised in Boston, Massachusetts where he experienced a challenging childhood. His father, a Unitarian Minister, as well as his sister, died when he was young and his mother raised him and his four brothers (Rusk, 1949). The family existed on church charity and proceeds from a boarding house run by his mother to send the boys to school. Emerson, like his brothers, attended Harvard where he was appointed the "President's Freshman" and gained free board to undertake his studies (Ibrahim & Cordes, 1993). Assessments of his literary accomplishments during his time at Harvard are less than remarkable (Baym, 1995).

After graduating from Harvard, Emerson attempted teaching at one of his mother's schools. This foray was short lived and accounts of his experience underscore his inability to control students and unhappiness with the vocation (Baym, 1995; Ibrahim & Cordes, 1993). He returned to Harvard's Divinity School in 1825 to study theology and was ordained in 1829, the same year he married Ellen Tucker (Rusk, 1949). The marriage ended 16 months later when she died of tuberculosis. In the two years after her death Emerson, according to observers, had some type of religious experience, which in combination with his earlier readings of various religions, led him to notify his church that "he had become so skeptical of the validity of the Lord's Supper that he could no longer administer it" (Baym, 1995, p. 436). Resigning his ministerial post in 1832, he traveled to Europe where he embarked on an educational journey encompassing both arts and sciences.

Emerson emerged from his trip to Europe renewed and upon receiving his late wife's legacy no longer had to work. He chose to settle into rural life in Concord, Massachusetts (Baym, 1995). In 1835 he married Lydia Jackson with whom he started a family. It was in the small rural community of Concord that Emerson "became involved in local affairs and was a respected and valued member of the community" (Ibrahim & Cordes, 1993, p. 30).

Although Emerson wrote his entire life, as evidenced by his journals, it is the writings undertaken while at Concord for which he is renowned. His first book was published in 1836 with the simple title *Nature* (Sealts & Ferguson, 1969). The book, which was paid for by Emerson and published anonymously, espoused the values of the natural environment and established the roots of Transcendentalism. In the following passage from the first chapter of *Nature* he clearly signaled an aesthetic appreciation:

> The stars awaken a certain reverence, because though always present, they are always inaccessible; but all natural objects make that kind of impression, when the mind is open to their influence. Nature never seems to wear a mean appearance. Neither does the wisest man extort all her secret, and lose his curiosity by finding out all her perfection. Nature never became a toy to a wise spirit. The flowers, the animals, the moun-

tains, reflected all the wisdom of his best hour, as much as they had delighted the simplicity of his childhood.

(1969, p. 7)

Such sentiment starkly contrasts with the dominant view of the time. Vickery explains that "hand-in-hand with the pioneer aversion to nature was the Puritan belief that civilization transmitted *the* sacred lifestyle . . . theirs was a spirit of conquest, of control, fired with religious zeal and self-righteousness" (1986, p. 130).

Emerson went further than just appreciating the natural environment. He offered the intellectual formulation and developed the proposition of Transcendentalism. Transcendentalism was conceived by Emerson as a complex conceptualization among three elements—man, nature and God (Nash, 1982). In an attempt to decipher the complex nuances of this relationship Nash writes:

> the core of transcendentalism was the belief that a correspondence or parallelism existed between the higher realm of spiritual truth and the lower one of material objects. . . . Transcendentalists had a definite conception of man's place in a universe divided between object and essence. His physical existence rooted him to the material portion, like all natural objects, but his soul gave him the potential to transcend this condition. Using tuition or imagination (as distinct from rational understanding), man might penetrate to spiritual truths.

(1982, p. 85)

Transcendentalism was a sharp departure from religious doctrines of the time, arguing that any individual could have this individual relationship with God as well as contesting the inherent evilness contained in wilderness as asserted in Calvinism (Nash, 1982; Vickery, 1986).

As was customary of the period, Emerson delivered a number of lyceum or lectures. His lectures were also highly controversial. As a result of his address to the Divinity School graduates in 1838, where he discussed the state of Christianity, he was barred from speaking at Harvard for three decades (Baym, 1995). Despite such controversy, other like-minded individuals sought him out. Emerson founded a discussion group called the Transcendentalists. He also became editor of their magazine, *The Dial* (Rusk, 1949).

Emerson traveled both in the United States and to Europe where his reputation continued to increase in stature. His subsequent works, two collections of essays, addressed a diverse range of issues and established him as an "intellectual liberator." Of equal importance has been the publication of journals and notes which add even greater depth to his writings (Baym, 1995).

Henry David Thoreau, 1817–1862

Thoreau was born in rural Concord where, as a boy, he enjoyed the outdoors (Sterling, Harmond, Cevasco & Hammond, 1997). His mother, Cynthia, decided that Henry should be the child in the family to attend college. Although barely passing the entrance examinations, he started attending Harvard in 1833 with funding supplied from the family's pencil factory and contributions from other family members (Ibrahim & Cordes, 1993; Vickery, 1986). Thoreau was generally ambivalent while at Harvard (Vickery, 1986). Even though he immersed himself in the library, reading mainly classics and travel books, he longed for interaction with nature and remained somewhat quiet.

Following his time at college Thoreau attempted many different types of employment. He started teaching at the Concord Center School, from which he resigned on principle. A string of jobs followed as he formed a school with his brother John, was employed as a handyman, tutored students, and worked in his father's pencil factory. Thoreau's love of nature grew during this time and was fostered through his many exploratory trips. Unsatisfied by the lack of meaning in his employment endeavors and sensitive of his own mortality after the death of his brother John, Thoreau set out to live purposefully.

Nash (1982) identifies two factors which shaped Thoreau's thinking. The first was Emerson, of whom "biographers Harding and Lebeaux believe Emerson was a surrogate father for Henry, whose own father was not intellectual" (Vickery, 1986, p. 11). Their friendship grew and Emerson encouraged Thoreau to write and engage in discussions with the group of Transcendentalists. The second factor was the influence of an increasingly materialistic and mechanistic civilization. As a consequence of viewing civilization in this way:

> his whole life, after the period of uncertainty about an occupation in his early manhood, became a calculated refusal to live by the materialistic values of the neighbours who provided him with a microcosom of the world. By simplifying his needs—an affront to what was already a consumer society devoted to arousing "artificial wants" he succeeded, with minimal compromises, in living his life rather than wasting it, as he saw it, in earning a living.
>
> (Baym, 1995, p. 769)

To live purposefully, Thoreau set about constructing a cabin on Emerson's property at Walden Pond. In his own words:

> I went to the woods because I wished to live deliberately, to front only the essential facts of life, and see if I could not learn what it had to teach, and not when I came to die, discover that I had not lived. I did not wish to practice resignation, unless it was quite necessary. I wanted to live deep and suck out all the marrow of life, to live so sturdily and Spartan-like as to put rout all that was not life, to cut a broad swath and shave close, to drive life into a corer, and reduce it to its lowest terms.
>
> (1992, p. 61)

The two years spent at Walden Pond gave Thoreau both a chance to observe nature and write. *A Week on the Concord and Merrimack Rivers*, despite Emerson's attempt to influence publishers, was paid for by Thoreau himself, received unfavorable reviews and sold poorly—Thoreau himself retained over 700 of the 1,000 copies printed (Vickery, 1986). As a consequence of much urging from Emerson, Thoreau worked his journal entries into a second book, *Walden or Life in the Woods*, which received largely positive reviews and from which Thoreau received $100 in royalties (Vickery, 1986). Although literary commentators remain divided as to the actual message delivered in *Walden*, Baym observes that:

> throughout Walden that purpose is to force his readers to evaluate the way they have been living and thinking ... he ultimately wants his readers to reevaluate any institution, from the Christian religion to the Constitution of the United States, but first he makes his readers work up their courage by reevaluating on a smaller scale.
>
> (1995, p. 772)

Throughout his lifetime, Thoreau walked daily around the countryside of Concord. He also undertook many trips into the wilderness which became both the subject of future books and influenced his thinking. Thoreau's journeys took him to Maine, Canada, Cape Cod and Minnesota. These adventures were respectively published as *Excursions* (1863), *The Maine Woods* (1864), *Cape Cod* (1865) and *A Yankee in Canada* (1866) (Ibrahim & Cordes, 1993). These sojourns had a profound effect on him:

> the wilderness of Maine shocked Thoreau. He reported it as even more grim and wild than you had anticipated, a deep and intricate wilderness. Climbing Mt. Katahdin, he was struck by its contrast to the kind of scenery he knew around Concord. The wild landscape was "savage and dreary" and instead of his usual exultation in the presence of nature, he felt "more lone than you can imagine." It seemed as if he were robbed of his capacity for thought and transcendence. Speaking of man's situation in wilderness seemed "a place for heathenism and superstitious rites—to be inhabited by men nearer of kin to the rocks and wild animals than we." On the mountain, Transcendental confidence in the symbolic significance of natural object faltered. Wilderness seemed a more fitting environment for pagan idols than for God.
>
> (Nash, 1982, p. 91)

This contradiction, like many confronted by Thoreau, was fodder for further musings (Oates, 1989). In reconciling these two positions, Thoreau asserted that a combination of civilization and wilderness is ideally required (Nash, 1982; Sterling et al., 1997). Throughout his life Thoreau followed this pattern, oscillating between immersion in wilderness and civilized refinements, as well as seeking balancing (proportioning) by advocating benefits of rural equilibrium.

The magnitude of Thoreau's work was largely not realized during his lifetime. Although recognition was slow in coming, he is now exalted for both his contributions as a social philosopher and a lover of nature (Baym, 1995). His stance on abolition, writings on civil liberties (*Civil Disobedience* and *Life Without Principles*), and outright rejection of mechanistic/materialistic ways influenced major figures such as Mahatma Gandhi and Martin Luther King, Jr. as well as other counterculture movements (Baym, 1995). He is perhaps best known as a systematic observer and lover of nature, advocate of wilderness and Transcendentalist philosopher. Vickery recognizes the extensiveness of his influence in stating that "Thoreau has been praised by almost every naturalist of note: John Muir, John Burroughs,

Theodore Roosevelt, Aldo Leopold, Joseph Wood Krutch, Edward Abbey ... the list is endless, so seminal was Thoreau's influence" (1986, p. 3).

John Muir, 1838–1914

John Muir was born in 1838 in Scotland. His family immigrated to the United States when he was 11 and settled near Madison, Wisconsin. Muir's love of wilderness and youthful explorations were brief as he was the eldest son of a father who had "taken his Calvinism to the limit of insanity" (Vickery, 1986, p. 55). By all accounts, Muir's adolescent years were characterized by extremely hard physical labour involving clearing the land and farm chores. Muir slept little, preferring to read and create inventions which failed to impress his strict father (Vickery, 1986).

Encouraged by his friends, Muir left the farm at 22 and headed for the Wisconsin State Fair to show his inventions. His friends were right to encourage Muir as his "mechanical devices won acclaim as the work of a genius" (Nash, 1982, p. 123). After a short stint working, Muir enrolled in the University of Wisconsin which exposed him to the natural sciences (geology and biology), classics and Transcendentalist philosophy of Emerson and Thoreau. He left the University of Wisconsin prior to the completion of his degree to undertake trips in the Great Lakes region of the United States and Canada, frequently taking odd jobs where his creative skills garnered him promotions (Sterling et al., 1997). Tragedy struck while he was working in a carriage shop in Indiana. A file slipped from his hand and punctured the cornea of his eye which left him blind for a month (Vickery, 1986).

After recovering from the accident, Muir set out on a thousand-mile walk to the Gulf of Mexico. Although frequently without food, Muir made his way from Kentucky to Florida where, extremely sick with malaria and typhoid fever, he was forced to stop to recover (Vickery, 1986). He abandoned plans to push further south and instead went to San Francisco where he found the Sierras. Working a variety of odd jobs permitted Muir the opportunity to explore the area, become the first non-native to climb Mt. Whitney's east side, and established himself as an expert on the ecology of the area (Ibrahim & Cordes, 1993). It was also here that he continued to refine his philosophy. The influences of both Emerson and Thoreau were obvious as "for John Muir Transcendentalism was always the essential philosophy for interpreting the value of wilderness" (Nash, 1982, p. 125). Despite the intellectual debt to early Transcendentalist thought, Muir also recognized, with disappointment and displeasure, shortcomings of these early philosophers. Eager anticipation by Muir of Emerson's arrival in Yosemite quickly dissipated as Emerson and his colleagues refused Muir's offers to worship wilderness as they opted for more civilized lodging (Nash, 1982). Unlike Emerson, and in contrast to the balance advocated by Thoreau, Muir embraced pure wilderness and continued undertaking many journeys, including to Alaska.

Throughout his life Muir kept journals in which he detailed observation on the natural world as well as people's interactions and attitudes towards it. At the urging of his friends he submitted his first articles on glaciers to the *New York Tribune* who published them in 1871 (Vickery, 1986). Although Muir lamented about the speed and ease at which he wrote, success continued as he published articles about his glacial studies. Muir's preponderance for writing and the systematic study of wilderness corresponded with "the advent of national concern over conservation" (Nash, 1982, p. 129). Robert Underwood Johnson, of the nation's largest monthly, *Century*, discovered Muir while on a visit to San Francisco (Vickery, 1986). Muir guided Johnson in the Sierras and the two struck a friendship agreeing that Yosemite should be protected and agreed that the best course of action was for Muir to write two articles for *Century* on Yosemite. In these articles, which reached an estimated 200,000 people, Muir clearly outlined that wilderness was something to be protected (Nash, 1982). As a result of these articles, Johnson's lobbying of the House of Representatives Committee on Public Lands, and support from the Southern Pacific Railroad, the Yosemite Act was passed (Nash, 1982). Recognizing that the need for protection extended far beyond legislation, Muir, again at the urging of Johnson, helped to develop the Sierra Club.

Muir also became active in the national protection of forests under the Forest Reserve Act. Although disturbed by the lack of intent conveyed in this legislation, Muir applauded the protection of forests and participated in the advisory commission to determine policies for their management. While the commission could not agree on a single purpose, Muir initially attempted to negotiate between preservation and conservation (or wise use proposed by Gifford Pinchot). Ultimately a schism resulted between the conservation and preservation groups (Nash, 1982; Sterling et al., 1997). In *Our National Parks* Muir writes:

> Any fool can destroy trees. They cannot run away; and if they could, they would still be destroyed—chased and hunted down as long as fun or dollar could be got out of their bark hides, branching horns, or magnificent bole backbones. . . . Through all the wonderful, eventful centuries since Christ's time—and long before that—God has cared for these trees, saved them from drought, disease, avalanches, and a thousand straining, leveling tempests and floods; but he cannot save them from fools—only Uncle Sam can do that.
>
> (1991, p. 272)

Muir subsequently turned his attention to the preservation of national parks and took the opportunity to guide Theodore Roosevelt during his visit to Yosemite. Muir's propositions, that Yosemite Valley be ceded to the federal government and that the Grand Canyon be protected, were received favorably (Nash, 1982). He continued to travel and toured the world with Sargent collecting various botany species (Vickery, 1986). From 1908 to 1913 Muir directed much of his attention to fight the damming of the Hetch Hetchy Valley, a battle which was eventually lost, but greatly increased public awareness and passion for wilderness preservation (Vickery, 1986). The final year of his life he largely devoted to writing about his time in Alaska.

Frederick Law Olmsted, 1822–1903

Frederick Law Olmsted, born April 26, 1822, was raised in New England. Olmsted spent a considerable amount of his childhood exploring the countryside, studying the natural environment and learning about human attitudes toward it (Hall, 1995; Roper, 1973). His passion for scenery and the natural environment was fueled by family excursions which further nurtured his adventurous spirit. According to Olmsted biographer, Laura Roper (1973), the happy memories of such excursions were juxtaposed with his ambivalent to negative experience with educational tutors.

This affinity for nature drew him to an early profession in agriculture and writing. According to Wright he had "been involved in scientific farming and was widely known for works on agriculture and for a series of articles on the social conditions in the southern slave states" (1984, p. 30). Olmsted traveled broadly during this time and as a *New York Times* correspondent reported on the south prior to the civil war (Ibrahim & Cordes, 1993).

Although relatively successful in his initial career endeavors, Olmsted began a second career in environmental planning during his early to mid-thirties. A chance meeting with the commissioner of Central Park prompted Olmsted to make application for the position of superintendent which he was granted in 1857, despite concerns about his literary and non-practical nature (Roper, 1973). In addition to being named superintendent, he was invited by British architect, Calvert Vaux, to enter a public design competition for the park. Their design was successful and Olmsted was appointed Architect-in-Chief the following year (Wright, 1984, p. 31).

Their proposal, Greensward, was significant because it brought innovation to environmental design and sparked the development of parks elsewhere. Ibrahim and Cordes reflect that:

> the two planners felt that a park is a single coordinated work of art that should be framed upon a single, noble motive. The park should allow for some relief from the confinement of urban life. Yet uses of the park are not necessarily compatible, and accordingly different areas of the park should be spatially separated to reduce conflict and confusion.
>
> (1993, p. 40)

The success of their design for Central Park established the reputation of both Olmsted and Vaux as environmental planners and, although they frequently differed as to purpose, fortuitously formed their consulting company in 1863 (Hall, 1995). Innovative design features which make their parks distinguishable included rural-type settings in urban spaces providing multi-use recreation opportunities, forested areas for conservation, formulation of linear greenspaces and integration of greenspaces into urban areas so all citizens had opportunities for recreation (Ibrahim & Cordes, 1993; Wright, 1984).

Acclaim for Central Park sparked a larger movement of attempting to bring recreational opportunities to city dwellers. Organizations, cities and towns consequently enlisted Olmsted's assistance and followed similar design principles. Some of Olmsted's famous parks designs include the University of California at Berkley, Fairmount in Philadelphia and Lincoln Park in Chicago (Ibrahim & Cordes, 1993). His influence also extended beyond the United States. Olmsted was directly responsible for planning Mount Royal Park in Montreal and assisting in the development of the Niagara Falls Park (Wright, 1984).

As Olmsted approached the end of his career he increasingly directed more attention to educating others. Olmsted reflected that:

I know that I shall have helped to educate in a good American school a capable body of young men for my profession. I know that in the minds of a large body of men of influence I have raised my calling from the rank of a trade, even of a handicraft, to that of a liberal profession—an art, and Art of design.

(as cited in Hall, 1995, p. 238)

Olmsted is regarded as having created the profession of landscape architecture and advancing social change (Hall, 1995; Ibrahim & Cordes, 1993; Roper, 1973; Sterling et al., 1997). His early observations of the environment and social sensitivity greatly influenced the philosophy or vision he brought to each design. According to Olmsted:

That other objects than the cultivation of beauty of natural scenery may be associated with it economically, in a park, I am not deposed to deny; but that all other objects should be held strictly subordinate to that, in order to justify, the purchase and holding of these large properties . . . cannot be successfully disputed.

(1881, p. 20; as cited in Wright, 1984, p. 31)

Ernest Thompson Seton, 1860–1946

The Thompson family emigrated from England to Canada in 1866 in search of new opportunities when Ernest was only six (Anderson, 1986; Polk, 1977). The family settled and started farming in the small community of Lindsay, Ontario where Ernest was captivated by the natural environment. A lack of success at farming cut the family's "frontier" venture short; they moved to Toronto a mere four years later where Ernest and his brothers experienced a difficult school and more troubling home life as their father had a short temper and frequently physically punished his boys (Anderson, 1986; Polk, 1977). Despite his overbearing father, Ernest found salvation in nature and was intrigued with indigenous traditions at an early age—these were enduring influences and made possible his contributions to understanding the joys of outdoor life, as a nature artist and writer, and as an educator.

Although his father frowned upon outdoor adventures, Ernest always found ways to explore the natural environment. Plagued with various afflictions, especially as a young person, Ernest found strength in the outdoors and was most healthy when close to nature (Polk, 1977). Reflecting upon his escape from routine beatings and the importance of nature as a boy he wrote:

After one of the worst beatings given by my father I got away from the house as fast as I could. I hoped soon to quit it forever. There was only one place to which I could go for quiet—for absolute aloofness; that was my cabin, far off in the woods. Here I could ponder and plan in peace; without doubt, temporary residence in that cabin would be part of my plan for escape.

As I drew near this happy spot, my aching back grew less and less painful. I felt glad stimulus; a little gleam of hope grew brighter in me—became a glow.

(Seton, 1940, p. 106)

49

This close connection to the outdoors and his particular interest in living creatures heavily influenced his vocation. Concerned about his own well-being, his aging father Joseph repeatedly queried his son as to his career intentions; to which Ernest answered "I've already told you what I want to be. A naturalist" (Polk, 1977, p. 30). While this initially appeared to be a lofty dream, he enrolled in classes at the Ontario School of Art where he was recognized for his outstanding work; subsequently he went to London to study art and was ultimately able to combine his affinity for creatures and art as he began illustrating scientific drawings with incredible accuracy (Anderson, 1986; Polk, 1977). Ernest was able to combine his superior abilities as an illustrator with his gift for story telling as his realistic tales of animals gained immense popularity—*Wild Animals I Have Known* (1898) became an international bestseller (Polk, 1977). Popularity of this and other books aside, Ernest, who had by this time reinstated his family's traditional name of Seton, was told by Theodore Roosevelt that "Burroughs and the people at large don't know how many facts you have back of your stories. You must publish your facts" (Polk, 1977, p. 54). Such encouragement provided fodder for Seton who enthusiastically pursued his work and subsequent publishing.

In addition to actively pursuing outdoor life and being one of the foremost naturalists of his time, Seton was also an astute and passionate educator. His philosophy of outdoor education was heavily influenced by his lifelong fascination with the practices of First Nation people. It was while on vacation in Lindsay that Ernest found a kindred spirit and friend in Sam Blackwell; the two started practicing "Indian" ways, learning from those in the community, activities that eventually Seton turned into his now classic book, *Two Little Savages* (1903) (Polk, 1977). While studying art in London Seton had a profound epiphany, induced by his ill health at the time, he started to hear a voice. Seton recalls that:

> I remember it was in the summer of 1881 that I had the longest message. I had assumed that my life would thenceforth be in London, in the world of art, where already I had won a footing as an illustrator. But my Voice said: "No. A year from now you will be living on the Plains of western Canada. You will regain your health, and have your wish [i.e., to get rid of the rupture]. Your future will be, not in Canada or London, but in New York, where as an illustrator and writer, you will make your fortune. Go to Canada, and rejoice in life on the Plains. But do not stay too long. Go soon to New York, and there you will find your way."
>
> That was the message that came; and here I was supposing that my destiny was London—on and on. But no, I was hearing the Buffalo Wind! That to me was the call of the West.
>
> (1940, p. 147)

This message both charted his course of actions and further reinforced his close connections with "Indian" ways.

Seton's start into outdoor education was unusual as it came about in response to a gang of young boys who had vandalized his Connecticut property. Rather than create conflict, he went to the local school and invited the boys to his property as guests where they would undertake "constructive" outdoor activities (Keller, 1984; Polk, 1977). Unlike his father, and in stark contrast to his Presbyterian upbringing, Seton believed that boys were not inherently bad, but rather such characteristics were due to circumstances experienced during their formative period of youth (Keller, 1984). His guests responded positively to developing outdoor skills and thereby an organization began. Not surprisingly, Seton shaped both the philosophy and structure of this organization from his fascination with First Nations peoples. As Keller observes:

> Seton's choice of the Indian tribe as the unit of organization for his boys' group was inevitable. He had come to believe that "those live longest who live nearest to the ground, that is, who live the simple life of primitive times, divested, however, of the evils that ignorance in those times begot." To Seton, the Indian living in harmony with his environment came the closest to this ideal, and the Indian form of organization was most clearly responsible for promoting that ideal.
>
> (1984, p. 162)

Seton crafted these basic ideas into an organization and presented it in *Ladies Home Journal* (1902) and his subsequent book *The Birch-Bark Roll of the Woodcraft Indians* (1906). The organization grew quickly, expanding throughout Canada and the United States, with Seton, or "Black Wolf" as its leader. In an attempt to bolster the concept in England he wrote and subsequently met with Baden-Powell who informed Seton of his similar intentions. This exchange set in motion questions regarding the precise origin of the Scout movement. Keller (1984) observed that "Robert Baden-Powell had, in fact, been trained to make the most of every opportunity, and when Seton sent him a copy of *The Birch-Bark Roll*, he did what he had been trained to do: he used it as the basis for his own scouting program in Britain and saved himself immeasurable time and energy" (Keller, 1984, p. 169). Although initially given the title of Chief Scout in the Boy Scouts of America, Seton ultimately resigned the post due to political tensions and concentrated on promoting woodcraft and writing (Anderson, 1986; Keller, 1984; Polk, 1977).

Seton exerted considerable influence as a naturalist, writer and educator. He was also instrumental in the advancement of Native American issues as well as the scouting movements (Anderson, 1986; Polk, 1977). His character was summarized best by his wife, Julia, who wrote:

> He stands out above all else not as a writer, artist, or student, but as a man. It is the lovable trivia which comes to mind—the intangible foibles, the frailties, the misbehaviors, the peccadillos—all the insignificant things that constitute the warm quality in him, the wholesome spirit that was the foundation of his charm and his greatness.... He could never have settled into a rut, for the whole world was his to deal with and to make his own.
>
> (as cited in Anderson, 1986, p. 251)

Aldo Leopold, 1887–1948

Aldo Leopold was born in 1887. His family lived in Burlington, Iowa and he was the eldest of four children. The abundance of nature surrounding the Mississippi River provided a haven for Leopold in his youth. His parents were very supportive of his endeavors to identify birds which eventually led him to Yale where he studied ornithology (Nash, 1982). In these early years and throughout his life Leopold kept journals in which he recorded observations of nature (Ibrahim & Cordes, 1993).

After the completion of his initial degree, he remained at Yale to study forestry. Due to the influence and philanthropy of the Pinchot family, Yale had become the foremost forestry school in the United States (Nash, 1982). Graduate work prepared Leopold to be a Forest Assistant, and he quickly undertook his first assignment in Arizona where he was promoted to supervisor of New Mexico's Carson National Forest (Ibrahim & Cordes, 1993). After a year-long battle with Bright's disease, Leopold returned to the service where he increasingly became concerned about the rapid decline of wildlife. As a concerned sportsman, Leopold helped to form game associations and authored both articles and a book on game management. His efforts received national acclaim as he received a medal from the Permanent Wild Life Protection Fund (Nash, 1982).

After a brief departure from the Forest Service due to ideological differences, Leopold returned to a changed climate in which non-utilitarian forest values (e.g., outdoor recreation) were also embraced (Nash, 1982). Leopold became increasingly determined that some areas of the national forests should remain wild and be used primarily for outdoor recreation. In his 1921 article, Leopold wrote that:

> the argument for such wilderness areas is premised wholly on highest recreational use. The recreational desires and needs of the public, whom the forests must serve, vary greatly with the individual. Heretofore we have been inclined to assume that our recreational development policy must be based on the desires and needs of the majority only. The only new thing about the premise in this case is the proposition that inasmuch as we have plenty of room and plenty of time, it is our duty to vary our recreational policy, in some places, to meet the needs and desires of the minority also.
>
> (1921, p. 719)

In 1924 Leopold accepted the position of Assistant Director of the Forest Products Laboratory. It was in this position that Leopold both developed and began to articulate his belief of the importance of wilderness conservation (Nash, 1982). He wrote: "A policy of wildlife conservation ideally should precede the penetration and development of any country new to civilized man" (Leopold & Darling, 1953, p. 11). Although some within his own organization did not share these sentiments, support for such ideas among Americans was evident and eventually led to increased preservation within national forests (Nash, 1982).

Leopold left the Forest Service in 1933 to accept a faculty position at the University of Wisconsin in wildlife management. His lifelong observations of wildlife and interactions with nature coincided with the emergence of ecology and resulted in the publication of one of his two seminal works—*Game Management* (1933). The innovative aspects of this work are captured by Ibrahim and Cordes who wrote that "Leopold's concepts, based on the emerging science of systems ecology, synthesized the most progressive knowledge of population dynamics, food chains, and habitat protection" (1993, p. 44). Underlying the publication was Leopold's fundamental belief toward the environment. Nash (1982) contends that

Leopold's philosophy came from his practical experiences in Mexico, strong understanding and insights into ecology, and broad intellectual foundation.

Leopold brought together his wealth of ecological observations and his knowledge of human attitudes towards the environment in his other seminal work—*A Sand County Almanac* (1949). In this work Leopold (1966) asserted that "conservation is getting nowhere because it is incompatible with our Abrahamic concept of land. We abuse the land because we regard it as a commodity belonging to us" (p. xviii). To provide a way forward, Leopold formulated a land ethic in which humans may consider themselves as part of nature:

> All ethics so far evolved rest upon a single premise: that the individual is a member of a community of interdependent parts. . . . The land ethic simply enlarges the boundaries of the community to include soils, waters, plants, and animals, or collectively: the land. . . . In short, a land ethic changes the role of *Homo sapiens* from conqueror of the land-community to plain member and citizen of it. It implies respect for his fellow-members, and also respect for the community as such.
>
> (1966, pp. 239–240)

In this work the range of skills and depth of insight associated with Leopold are clearly evident. Sterling et al. (1997) best summarize the exceptionality of his contribution in stating that "Leopold was a gifted communicator of the scientific basis of conservation as well as the imperative need for environmental awareness, adept at modifying his style to suit his audience and able to employ these qualities in person as well as in print" (1997, p. 460).

Rachel Carson, 1907–1964

Rachel Carson was born and raised near Springdale, Pennsylvania. Her passion for writing emerged at a young age, as she published in literary periodicals and was an English major upon entering the Pennsylvania College for Women (Budwig, 1997). It was while at the college that her interest in nature was reawakened through a biology class. Upon graduation she passionately pursued a Master's degree in zoology at Johns Hopkins University (Sterling et al., 1997).

Carson taught during her early career at the University of Maryland and summer school at the Johns Hopkins University, while also being published in *Atlantic Monthly* (Budwig, 1997). She subsequently accepted a position with the United States Bureau of Fisheries (she was the first woman to pass the civil-service test) where she initially crafted radio scripts and advanced to the position of editor-in-chief of all publications for the United States Fish and Wildlife Service in 1947 (Ibrahim & Cordes, 1993; Lear, 1998). While working in these positions, Carson continued to write both articles and books—*Under the Sea Wind* (1941), *The Sea Around Us* (1951) and *The Edge of the Sea* (1955). Carson gained broad recognition for advancing the field of marine biology and received the Eugene F. Saxton Memorial Fellowship, the George Westinghouse Foundation, and a Guggenheim Fellowship for her work (Lear, 1998).

Her penchant for writing and inclination as a naturalist prompted her to resign from the Bureau of Fish and Wildlife in 1952 (Lear, 1998). Lear writes that "disturbed by the profligate use of synthetic chemical pesticides after World War II, Carson reluctantly changed her focus in order to warn the public about the long term effects of misusing pesticides" (1998, online). These concerns were delivered in her fourth and seminal work, *Silent Spring*, which effectively combined scientific and eloquent writing styles. In this book Carson writes:

> The current vogue for poisons has failed utterly to take into account these most fundamental considerations. As crude a weapon as the cave man's club, the chemical barrage has been hurled against the fabric of life—a fabric on the one hand delicate and destructible, on the other miraculously tough and resilient and capable of striking back in unexpected ways. These extraordinary capacities of life have been ignored by practitioners of chemical control who have brought to their task no "high minded orientation," no humility before the vast forces with which they tamper.
>
> (1962, p. 297)

The work was immediately controversial as Carson was critical of products and practices of both companies such as Monsanto and government representatives (Ibrahim & Cordes, 1993; Lear, 1998). However, it reached a receptive public audience and consequently led to a presidential advisory committee and ultimately the ban of many harmful chemicals such as DDT (Ibrahim & Cordes, 1993). The book also provided clear articulation of the environmental message which had previously not been done (Sterling et al., 1997).

Carson's contribution to shaping resource management and environmental awareness is twofold. Her efforts enhanced knowledge of marine biology and acted as a catalyst to environmentalism. Ibrahim and Cordes write that:

> Carson would have preferred to be remembered for her sea books, and it is there that the grandeur of her style is visible. She was not by nature a scholar, but her reverence for life called her to bring the message of modern crisis to public attention in *Silent Spring*.
>
> (1993, p. 39)

Due to her conviction to spread this message and the timeliness of her delivery she is commonly regarded as the mother of the modern environmental movement.

PROMINENT ORGANIZATIONS IN THE HISTORY OF OUTDOOR RECREATION

While today many non-governmental organizations are actively promoting conservation, preservation and interest-specific participation in outdoor pursuits, the following organizations did so at a time when this was not the norm. These organizations have endured over long periods of time and are today international in scope. They have significantly influenced the character of outdoor recreation through shaping government policy, fostering innovative ideas, and/or providing unique services.

Sierra Club

As John Muir was contemplating his essays on Yosemite, Robert Underwood Johnson urged him to consider initiating some type of association (Cohen, 1988). In this regard, Muir met with Johnson and other distinguished gentlemen in San Francisco, some of whom had already been contemplating the formation of an alpine organization. The Sierra Club emerged as an outcome of this meeting. Articles of incorporation for the Sierra Club made clear that the members sought:

> To explore, enjoy, and render accessible the mountain regions of the Pacific Coast;
> To publish authentic information concerning them;
> To enlist support and cooperation of the people and the government in preserving the forests and other natural features of the Sierra Nevada Mountains.
>
> (Cohen, 1988, p. 9)

Muir was elected the first president and provided much of the early direction for the organization. Precipitated by the issue of Hetch Hetchy, controversy quickly emerged within the organization. Tensions primarily reflected tensions between preservation and wise use. As a result of this division, the Society for the Preservation of National Parks was formed, bringing national attention to the issue of dams and starting the organization down a political path (Cohen, 1988).

Hjelmar (1996) observes that after this initial controversy the Sierra Club entered a second consolidation phase. During this time less emphasis was placed on politics and more attention was directed to recreational pursuits and opportunities to venture into the very areas that the organization was working to protect. The first of many trips to become an annual tradition was organized in 1901 by Will Colby (Cohen, 1988). Others within the club focused on a variety of outdoor pursuits including mountaineering, skiing and rock climbing (Turner, 1991).

Expansion and interest in the Sierra Club increased sharply after World War II due to the general upswing in popularity of outdoor recreation throughout the United States, the printing of Ansel Adams' stunning photographs of the Sierras, and publication of a biography about John Muir (Cohen, 1988; Hjelmar, 1996; Turner, 1991). The size of the organization expanded from 7,000 members, with chapters only in California in 1951, to 113,000 in 1970, with members in every state (Hjelmar, 1996). David Brower was hired as the first Executive Director in 1952, and immediately reinvigorated the political interests of the organization in conservation with the case of the Dinosaur National Monument (Turner, 1991). Expansion of the Sierra Club continued through their publication program as well as through the development of their political practices.

The outcome of the Dinosaur National Monument, which pitted the Sierra Club against development interests and the Secretary of the Interior, established the ability for the Sierra Club to positively influence change as well as the need for professional staff with the time and resources for such undertakings. This dichotomous structure of those with amateur conservation interests and the professional support staff has remained with the club. The Sierra Club, largely through Brower's initiatives, also established new tactics for environmental challenges

55

including the successful use of litigation (Hjelmar, 1996). Despite establishing such precedents, the Sierra Club was reluctant to embrace the environmentalism of the 1960s and efforts by Brower to do so created tension within the organization and ultimately led to his resignation (Hjelmar, 1996). The importance of his contribution to the Sierra Club was summarized in the meeting minutes in the following "Eulogy":

> David Brower has served the club with dedication and brilliance first as director and then since 1952 as Executive Director. More than any other person he has involved the public in our fight to preserve a liveable world. He has pioneered in the effective use of films, Exhibit Format Books, paperbacks, posters, full page newspaper ads and other parts of the mass media. He has sought to expand the concerns of the club to include all of the environment. David Brower has been a leader. He has tried to bring along those who have lagged behind, not always with success. And now his role in club affairs must diminish. We are saddened by this prospect. We wish him well in his new efforts to save and restore the quality of our environment. We salute David Brower and wish him to know that his unique contribution to the Sierra Club is appreciated.
>
> (Cohen, 1988, p. 433)

The Sierra Club remains an important conservation organization today. Similar to many other environmental organizations, the club has tended to become increasingly professional, enhancing both their expertise and staff (Hjelmar, 1996). The Sierra Club continues to pursue political strategies that includes lobbying, electoral strategies, litigation—the latter is made possible by the tremendous amounts of money they are able to raise (Hjelmar, 1996; Turner, 1991). Turner (1991) described the status of the Sierra Club at their centennial as thriving and continuing to grow. Speaking at the occasion of their centennial, the Executive Director, Michael Fisher, remarked "we have two big challenges ahead in the next ten years. The first is how to maintain the Club's unique structure as it gets larger. The second is how to enhance its ethnic diversity" (Turner, 1991). Ten years after the centennial celebrations of the organization the strength of the membership appears to remain with over 1.3 million friends and members (Sierra Club, 2007).

Scouts

In the early 1900s many different types of scout organizations existed in the United Kingdom—Boys' Brigade, Boys' Life Brigade, and Church Lads' Brigade (The British Boy Scouts, 2007). Concern about militant overtones and disgruntled with the increasing amount of bureaucracy fostered opportunities for a new organization. Robert Baden-Powell, an English hero and scout in the Boer War was returning from South Africa and received word that his book to train scouts, *Aids to Scouting* (1899), was being used to train boys (Reynolds, 1942). Practical experience in the army combined with his observations of the Boys' Brigade led Powell to apply and test his scouting principles. The success inspired him to author the book *Scouting for Boys* (1907) which began a worldwide movement that he eventually quit the army to direct (Reynolds, 1942).

Scouting quickly spread to other countries. In the United States it is popularly traced back to 1909 when William D. Boyce lost his way in London due to fog and was assisted by an unknown scout who would not accept gratuity for his good deed (Boy Scouts of America, 2007). Boyce was so impressed with the organization he incorporated and organized The Boy Scouts of America as a business. Ernest Thompson Seton and James West also played important roles in the founding of the organization. Seton had traveled to England in 1904 to meet Powell and provided him with a copy of his handbook for Woodcraft Indians, a boys' program which he developed. Seton's influence is noted in his introduction to the *Boy Scouts of America Boy Scout Handbook*, as he wrote "in 1904, I went to England to carry on the work [of fostering a "Woodcraft and Scouting movement"] there, and, knowing General R. S. S. Baden-Powell as the chief advocate of scouting in the British Army, invited him to cooperate with me, in making the movement popular" (Snowden, 1984, online). James West, an attorney, played a critical role in the early development as he crafted a national structure for the organization. The first Chief Scout and Chief Scout Executive had differences of opinions of how the organization should develop which resulted in Seton being pushed out in 1916 (Snowden, 1984).

A complementary organization for girls was formed in 1912. It was founded by Juliette Low and was also initially known as scouting. Despite the common name early on, in many countries the organization was referred to as Girl Guides (Ibrahim & Cordes, 1993). The Girl Guide movement emerged from a rally at the Crystal Palace in London, England in 1909 that established girls were also interested in scouting (World Association of Girl Guides and Girl Scouts, 2007). The girls, who were expected to be "lady like," pleaded to Baden-Powell to be involved. A girl-guiding organization was started with Agnes Baden-Powell becoming the first President of the Girl Guides. The Girl Guide movement quickly spread throughout the world where its value was recognized. The Canadian Government, for example, through an Act of Parliament recognized the value of Guiding by approving the Constitution of the Canadian Girl Guides Association in 1917. This was later changed to the Girl Guides of Canada in 1961.

Although the Scout programs have undergone some changes since inception, the basic concept has endured. Boys and young men, organized in troops by age range and rank, learn skills and earn badges. Changes in leadership styles have moved away from earlier models in which Scoutmasters directly ran their troop to a model by which they provide guidance to Senior Patrol Leaders and Patrol Leaders (Boy Scouts of America, 2007). According to the Boy Scouts of America (2007) all adult leadership positions are, as of 1988, open to both men and women. Another recent advancement in scouting is an attempt to retain older Scouts through the creation of Venture Scouts in 1990 and the introduction of Venturing, a co-ed program for individuals in high school or college (Boy Scouts of America, 2007).

The growth and popularity of scouting arguably makes it one of the most successful youth organizations aimed at outdoor recreation. There are currently more than 28 million scouts in over 155 countries throughout the world (World Organization of the Scout Movement, 2007). The 100th anniversary of scouting will be hosted by the Scout Association of the United Kingdom in 2007 (Boy Scouts of America, 2007).

Outward Bound

Outward Bound can be traced back to the 1920s and the ideas of educator Kurt Hahn. Hahn believed that every individual contained inherent goodness which in adolescence becomes eroded by "social diseases," including:

1. the decline in fitness due to the modern methods of locomotion;
2. the decline of initiative and enterprise due to the widespread disease of spectatoritis;
3. the decline of memory and imagination due to the confused restlessness of modern life;
4. the decline of skill and care due to the weakened tradition of craftsmanship;
5. the decline of self-discipline due to the ever-present availability of stimulants and tranquilizers;
6. the decline of compassion due to the unseemly haste with which modern life is conducted (Outward Bound, 2007, online).

It was these rudimentary ideas from which Hahn developed the educational philosophy that was the hallmark of his schools.

Hahn came from a wealthy German industry family and attended Oxford. Following his studies he served as a secretary to Prince Max of Baden (Hogan, 1968). Prince Max's interest in education was instrumental to Hahn, who in the position of Headmaster, successfully directed the Salem School to great success and international acclaim (Hogan, 1968). Hahn was a sharp critic of Hitler and was forced into exile in England where he started the Gordonstoun School. Hahn viewed the connection between education and peace as fundamental and viewed that "it is our duty to equip this growing generation, irrespective of class, with willing bodies. It is our duty also to train them in self-discipline. Freedom and discipline are not enemies, they are friends" (1936, p. 3). At the school, Hahn offered short courses in which students were able to pursue outdoor skills and personal development. Lawrence Holt, a Gordonstoun parent and owner of Blue Funnel Shipping Line, appreciated Hahn's approach and discussed concerns about targeted merchant ships and the susceptibility of young seamen due to a lack of experience, self-reliance and camaraderie (Miner & Boldt, 2001).

Hahn, drawing upon his philosophy, diagnosed the problem as a lack of confidence and with the assistance of Lawrence Holt and Jim Hogan formed the Sea School on the west coast of Wales in 1941 (Outward Bound, 2007). The name "Outward Bound" was coined by Holt which makes reference to the departure of a ship from safe harbour to undertake adventure (Miner & Boldt, 2001). Twenty young men participated in the first 28-day residential experience which gave students a chance to experience success through mastering a progressive series of challenges (Outward Bound, 2007). The program reflected Hahn's philosophy as it combined Greek education ideals of "know thyself" and "nothing to excess" with four pillars of compassion, service, fitness, and skill. The results of the program were encouraging as participants gained valuable memories, strengthened themselves in the above areas, and were introduced to training (Outward Bound, 2007).

The success of Aberdovey School prompted formation of the Outward Bound Trust in

1946 to facilitate expansion (Outward Bound, 2007). In his 1960 address to the Outward Bound Trust Hahn stated:

> Mr. Chairman I consider that Outward Bound is at the crossroads today. Will you be satisfied for your five schools to continue improving their practices as they are doing? Will you be satisfied to increase at a slow and safe rate the number of new schools, or will you hear the cry for help from bewildered and frustrated youths all over the world and accept a missionary assignment? The assignment of giving advice and guidance wherever it is wanted and wherever other institutions want to introduce those health-giving activities which you have helped to develop.
>
> (1960, p. 2)

Outward Bound quickly expanded. In 1950 Josh Miner, who had taught for Hahn at the Gordonstoun School, started to cultivate the idea of Outward Bound in the United States, establishing the first school in the western hemisphere in Colorado in 1962 (Miner & Boldt, 2001; Outward Bound, 2007). Growth in the number of Outward Bound Schools has continued to increase. Today, 40 Outward Bound Schools exist in 32 countries and reach approximately 200,000 people each year (Outward Bound, 2004; Outward Bound International, 2005). The schools have also increased the breadth of program offerings from young men to include women, couples, families and persons with disabilities (Outward Bound, 2007).

National Outdoors Leadership School

The founder and heart of the National Outdoors Leadership School (NOLS) was Paul Petzoldt. Unlike many early mountaineers who had privileged upbringings, Petzoldt endured great hardships as a child. His father died when he was three, creditors seized his family's farm and home when he was 15, and he became independent at this early age as his family disbanded due to financial pressures (Ringholz, 1997). Making his way by taking odd jobs, Petzoldt was an energetic adventurer and mountaineer who made his first ascent of the Grand Teton at age 16 (Ringholz, 1997). This passion for mountaineering endured for his entire life, although he himself had difficulty explaining it to others:

> All my life, people have asked the question, directly or indirectly, "why the hell do you climb mountains?" I can't explain this to other people. I love the physical exertion. I love the wind, I love the storms: I love the fresh air. I love the companionship in the outdoors. I love the reality. I love the change. I love the oneness with nature: I'm hungry; I enjoy clear water. I enjoy being warm at night when it's cold outside. All those simple things are extremely enjoyable because, gosh, you're feeling them, you're living them, senses are really feeling, I can't explain.
>
> (Paul Petzoldt, n.d.; as cited in Neill, 2003, online)

Desiring employment that would permit mountaineering prompted Petzoldt to join the newly established Outward Bound School in Colorado where he served in the position of Chief Instructor (NOLS, 2007). It was while working at Outward Bound that Petzoldt made observations which secured, in his mind, the need for a leadership training center. Petzoldt adamantly states:

> I had a definite reason for starting NOLS ... I wasn't a way out person, I didn't think that we shouldn't cut a tree ... but I was in favour of the wilderness bill. I testified before Congress on the wilderness bill.... At the same time, here we were at Outward Bound taking people out and ... devastating the wilderness. Bad camping, crapping all over ... I was dismayed at the ideas kids were getting about how to treat wilderness.
>
> At Outward Bound we didn't try to teach them, we didn't go into any depth. That wasn't our purpose ... but I thought gosh ... we're passing this wilderness bill and they don't know any more in the Sierra Club than we know here.... We've got to train leaders who can go back and teach people in their community. And I was successful. NOLS has done more than all of the outdoor groups together.
>
> (as cited in Absolon, 1995, online)

Determined to increase both the quality and numbers of outdoor leaders, Petzoldt founded NOLS on March 23, 1965 in Wyoming (NOLS, 2007). Ringholz (1997) observes that Petzoldt viewed NOLS as a logical extension and complementary program to Outward Bound. The first few years of operation for the organization were meager as student clothing came from US Army surplus and Petzoldt designing unavailable equipment (NOLS, 2007). Enrolment in the School increased dramatically in 1970 (from 250 to 750 individuals) upon the release of a *Life* magazine article on Petzoldt and a television program that profiled the organization (NOLS, 2007). NOLS expanded the number of course offerings, the range of clientele, and the types of geographic locations throughout the 1970s. Expansion came at a price as disenchantment grew between Petzoldt and the Board of Directors, which ultimately led to his end as Executive Director (NOLS, 2007).

Throughout the 1980s NOLS looked inward and focused on organizational developed rather than rapid expansion. This was a time which emphasized "staff and instructor training with an increased emphasis on safety, public outreach, involvement with environmental issues, financial security, controlled growth and conscious planning for the future" (NOLS, 2007, online). NOLS reemerged from this internal focus with a new direction of public outreach, more specialized programs and training, and further expansion plans such as an International Base Camp Initiative. From humble beginnings with 100 students, NOLS has now graduated more than 75,000 students from their 11 schools throughout the world (NOLS, 2007).

SUMMARY

This chapter provides the backdrop for outdoor recreation today. This historical perspective is important because it imbues contextual understanding to each of the subsequent chapters. The initial part of this traced the roots of outdoor recreation to Greek and Roman cultures which strongly established the public provision of gardens or common areas. It also considered how events such as the Industrial Revolution effectively separated work and leisure and gave rise to a "leisure class" that had both time and means to pursue such activities. Evidence was also presented that outdoor recreation activities were integrated with societal functioning prior to European contact. In considering the development of outdoor recreation in North America substantial changes were revealed as a negative view of leisure and an adversarial or antagonistic attitude towards wilderness gave way to the need for preservation and/or conservation. Major societal forces (e.g., technological advancements, more discretionary income, etc.) combined with the extraordinary foresight of key individuals to increase the affinity for outdoor activities, demand for parks, and consideration of the environment. Manifest public pressure influenced the formation of government agencies with a mandate for outdoor recreation and environmental protection and prompted formative and ongoing legislation. Organizations also emerged in response to these needs with a mandate related to the natural environment or outdoor activities.

KEY CONCEPTS

A leisure class

Athenian ideal of leisure

Closing of the American frontier

Conservation

Landscape architecture

Leopold's land ethic

Modern environmental movement

Outdoor Recreation Resources Review
   Commission (ORRRC)

Preservation

Puritan belief system

Social-political influences on outdoor
   recreation

The historical approach

The Industrial Revolution

Transcendentalism

SUGGESTED KEY SOURCES FOR MORE INFORMATION

Baym, N. (Ed.) (1995). *The Norton anthology American literature*. New York: W. W. Norton & Company.

Carson, R. (1962). *Silent spring*. Boston: Houghton Mifflin.

Clawson, M. (1959). The crisis in outdoor recreation. *American Forests, 65*(3), 22–31.

Leisure sciences www.tandf.co.uk

Leisure studies www.tandf.co.uk

Nash, R. (1982). *Wilderness and the American mind* (3rd ed.). New Haven, CT: Yale University Press.

National Outdoor Leadership School http://www.nols.edu

Outward Bound http://www.outwardbound.net

Sierra Club http://www.sierraclub.org

World Organization of the Scout Movement http://www.scout.org

REVIEW QUESTIONS

1. Why is historical analysis important?
2. Describe outdoor recreation activities in Greek and Roman times.
3. Identify significant changes brought about by the Industrial Revolution and their effect on leisure.
4. Describe outdoor recreation pursuits in societies prior to European settlement.

5. What is Transcendentalism?
6. What was the predominant view of pioneers toward the environment?
7. Why did participation in outdoor recreation markedly increase after World War II?
8. The 1960s was an important decade in the history of outdoor recreation. Identify and describe three seminal events.
9. Explain the main message in Aldo Leopold's *Land ethic*.
10. Describe the differences between Outward Bound and the National Outdoor Leadership School.

Chapter 3

The Natural Environment and Outdoor Recreation

OBJECTIVES

This chapter will:

- engage readers in the enterprise of environment philosophy;
- examine various approaches to the human–environment relationship;
- introduce the subject of ecology and discuss the workings of the natural environment;
- consider the supply of recreational resources;
- critically assess the influences of climate change.

INTRODUCTION

The natural environment sustains life and is central to outdoor recreation. This chapter begins by examining how humans have approached their relationship with nature. Given the centrality of natural settings to outdoor recreation, familiarity with key environmental concepts and processes is essential. Ecology is used as an entry point to discuss key ecological ideas. Knowledge of natural processes is important to temper the negative impacts from outdoor activities on the natural environment and inform management strategies.

Notwithstanding environmental philosophies that emphasize the inherent value of all living things, the western paradigm or worldview endures. From this perspective "stuff" in the environment is viewed with neutrality until it is useful to humans and accessible through technology at which time it becomes a resource. Discussion of recreational resources occurs in terms of supply, classification schemes, and attributes. Specific landscape features are used to illustrate the breadth of outdoor recreation resources and the influence of climate is explored. The chapter closes by reflecting upon supply trends in outdoor recreation.

ENVIRONMENTAL PHILOSOPHIES

Struggling with environmental issues and questioning the human–environment relationship are not new endeavors and can be found at any point throughout human history (Evernden, 1993). Belshaw explains that:

> we think in the main of there being one environment, rather than many, and that we think of this environment as it exists in outdoor places (so excluding the home and office), whether inhabited by human beings or not (and so including both cities and the few wild places that are left on earth), but inhabited nevertheless (and so excluding, at least until we get there, the distant reaches of outer space).
>
> (2001, pp. 2–3)

This book is specifically concerned with the elements of nature, as opposed to human or built surroundings, and therefore the adjective natural frequently precedes the term environment.

Despite the common conceptions of philosophy, the term itself and particular tasks of philosophers require explanation. Miller (1984) proposes that philosophy is made distinguishable through its meaning, fields, and characteristics. The term philosophy is of Greek origins and means "love of wisdom" (Miller, 1984, p. 3). Halverson interprets the meaning of philosophy in daily life, clarifying that "philosophy is concerned precisely with the fundamental beliefs through which men try to make sense of their lives and by which they try to order their lives" (1972, p. 4). The pursuit of philosophy has taken many different directions. Common fields of study include: metaphysics (theory of reality); epistemology (theory of knowledge); ethics (theory of moral values); aesthetics (theory of beauty); and logic (theory of right reasoning) (Halverson, 1972; Miller, 1984; Wolff, 1976). In each of these areas philosophical inquiry is characterized as being rational (coherent and well-founded), analytical and critical (Miller, 1984).

According to Belshaw (2001), philosophy informs inquires of the natural environment in two ways. First, as the pursuit of knowledge, it offers a means to clarify pressing issues and ascertains the status of specific situations. Second, and of particular concern in this section, are the moral and value questions which it raises pertaining to the environment. While the first branch of philosophy often requires advanced knowledge gained through years of study, the second branch (moral and value questions) pose questions that we all must ultimately address (Belshaw, 2001).

The following sections therefore document ways in which the environment has been approached by humans. Philosophies and actions of indigenous cultures are explored prior to accounting for the pervasive influence of Christianity and European worldviews. Although the latter has had an enduring influence and provides the basis for the dominant western paradigm, glimmers of novelty have emerged in the human–environment relationship. These approaches to morals and values are discussed under the headings of conservation and ecocentric philosophies. Environmental philosophies are important because they are made operational through the political process and thereby substantially influence outdoor recreation. They directly affect resource allocation and land use planning decisions upon which outdoor recreation depends and indirectly shape the way people behave. Readers are encouraged to think critically about the ideas presented and reflect upon their own morals and values.

Indigenous Environmental Philosophies

Considerable diversity is evident when considering the actions and philosophies of indigenous peoples. Historical examples from archeological evidence document instances of disregard for nature and shortsightedness for environmental consequences. During the late Neolithic and Early Bronze Age periods in Greece, grazing and farming led to severe erosion, causing loss of vegetation and extreme flooding (Runnels, 1995). Belshaw (2001) cites extermination of indigenous animals in New Zealand by the Maoris as another example. When Maoris arrived in New Zealand roughly 1,000 years ago a "hunting blitzkrieg" occurred eliminating many indigenous species including the moa, a large flightless bird (Diamond, 2000, p. 2170). On Easter Island, extensive resource use by inhabitants resulted in the loss of the palm forest native to the island (Rainbird, 2002). These trees were mostly utilized to build large stone statues which remain today.

Despite a lack of regard and detrimental actions by some cultures, others exhibited strong ties and connections to the natural environment. Hinduism, one of the oldest documented religions, is one such example of a culture with a strong ethical connection with the earth. Hindus viewed themselves as part of nature, not separate from it (Coward, 1997; Coward, Sidhu & Singer, 2000). They believe that the divine spirit is present in all elements of the natural world, and as such should be treated with respect and care. Similarly, the G'wi tribe, an early hunter-gatherer group native to Zambia, believed that killing or gathering more than what was necessary to sustain their tribe would anger their Supreme Being (Evernden, 1993). This belief led to "direct conservation" practices of the surrounding area (Evernden, 1993, p. 7).

In North America, First Nations people held the environment in similar high regard. In viewing the world as one interconnected entity, they believed that all elements of life and nature had a place and a purpose (Ibrahim & Cordes, 2002). Consequently, ceremonies and rituals were undertaken to "maintain the harmony with the pervasive powers of nature, stressing the relationship of people with the cosmos" (Ibrahim & Cordes, 2002, p. 19).

Christianity and European Philosophy

In *Wilderness and the American mind* Roderick Nash (1982) clearly identifies folklore, Christianity and European philosophy as dominant influences shaping values towards nature. The mysterious and unknown qualities of wilderness made it an important element in both mythology and folklore. Classical mythology contains numerous lesser gods or demons which were frequently portrayed being hideous or gross in appearance, aggressive, uncivilized, and above all else dangerous (Nash, 1982). Such themes endured as hideous beasts that lived in the wilderness became standard fare in European folklore of the Middle Ages (Nash, 1982).

Judeo-Christian beliefs have also been an important influence on attitudes towards

65

wilderness. Analyzing terminology associated with wilderness reveals that "the authors of the Bible gave wilderness a central position in their accounts both as a descriptive aid and as a symbolic concept. The term occurs 245 times in the Old Testament, Revised Standard Version, and thirty-five in the New" (Nash, 1982, p. 13). Negative associations with the natural world continued throughout medieval Christianity where wilderness became both a symbolic force to overcome through missionary work to northern tribes and emblematic of the human condition of sinful temptation that had to be denied to reach heaven (Nash, 1982). Such morals and values towards nature also compounded the perceptions of leisure and recreation.

Although Christianity wielded considerable influence, noteworthy exceptions to this dominant view emerged with Peter Waldo, St Francis of Assisi and eastern religious traditions (Nash, 1982). Peter Waldo advocated Christian asceticism and fled with his followers to the Piedmotese Alps where they obtained religious freedom. St Francis of Assisi held respect for all of nature and alone believed in equality of all creatures. Nash accounts that "the Church stamped St. Francis' beliefs as heretical. Christianity had too much at stake in the notion that God set man apart from and gave him dominance over the rest of nature (Genesis 1:28) to surrender it easily" (1982, p. 19). It is also important to recognize that the Christian attitude of dominance was not evident in other cultures. Many eastern religious traditions embraced nature with compassion (e.g., Jainism, Buddhism and Hinduism) or viewed wilderness as preferential (e.g., Shinto, Taoism) (Nash, 1982).

A third factor influencing western morals and values about the natural environment was that of European philosophy and science. Spielvogel observes that:

> the Scientific Revolution brought Europeans a new way of viewing the universe and their place in it. The shift from an earth-centered to a sun-centered cosmos had an emotional as well as an intellectual effect upon those who understood it. Thus the Scientific Revolution, popularized in the eighteenth-century Enlightenment, stands as the major force in the transition to the largely secular, rational, and materialistic perspective that has defined the modern Western mentality since its full acceptance in the nineteenth and twentieth centuries.
>
> (1991, p. 562)

Sir Isaac Newton's work pertaining to universal laws for gravity established the basis for mechanistic explanations and revelations of nature; René Descartes' formulation of Cartesian dualism (separation of mind and body) asserted that the material world can be known through the mind thereby shifted human identity; and, Francis Bacon's conceptualization of the scientific method which was conceived to empower humans (Spielvogel, 1991). The implications from each of these advances were realized as "scientific" knowledge spread and the principles of mechanization were ultimately realized in the Industrial Revolution.

Culture, religion, and philosophy have combined to fuse a paradigm, or worldview, which clearly places humans in a superior position to the natural environment (Belshaw, 2001; Evernden, 1993; Spielvogel, 1991). The major tenants of this western world view, which has dominated Europe and America, are:

(1) a conviction that man's role on earth is to exploit the rest of nature to his own advantage; (2) an exception of continuing population growth; (3) a belief in progress and history; and, (4) a concern for posterity.

(Tuan, 1971, p. 218)

This worldview is also anthropocentric in orientation. Belshaw explains that anthropomorphism refers to "seeing nature as having certain plans or intentions, possessed of a certain character, and bearing certain relationships, either sympathetic or hostile, to human ends" (2001, p. 196). Although different perspectives have always existed, the dominant and pervasive characteristics of this view, in combination with recent human impacts on the environment, have resulted in increasing attention being focused on alternative ways of looking at the human–environment relationship.

Conservation Philosophies

The western worldview has had both far-ranging and negative consequences on the natural environment. Conservation-oriented philosophies are largely a response to the affects of the dominant western paradigm and can be traced to the closure of the American frontier and the rapid extinction of once plentiful species (Nash, 1982). The most recognized mass loss stemming from human exploitation in America are the bison and the passenger pigeon. During the nineteenth century it was estimated that approximately 60 million bison and approximately 136 million passenger pigeons existed—two wild bison herds are all that remain today due to human misuse (Matthiessen, 1987).

While examples of rapid extinction are shocking, the widespread and more general depletion of resources (e.g., forests, rivers, game animals) evoked reaction from passionate individuals including John Muir, Gifford Pinchot, Stephen Mather and Aldo Leopold. As described in Chapter 2, the concern expressed by these individuals over the rapid use of resources struck a general chord with the public and found a political audience with the United States president Theodore Roosevelt (Victor & Ausubel, 2000). Although initially allied and united in purpose, it quickly became apparent that divergent avenues of thoughts existed among this early movement. Differences centered on the relative merits of conservation and preservation, a debate which continues today (Gray, 1993).

Gifford Pinchot coined or appropriated the term conservation and made it synonymous with wise use pertaining to forestry—forests could be utilized if done so in a planned fashion (DesJardins, 1993; Nash, 1982). The idea was popular because it represented a compromise; a move away from previous destruction, yet it did not prohibit use. Similar notions were employed for other resources including game management by Leopold (Hargrove, 1989). Conservation ideas persist today, prompted by the same basic concern of 100 years ago.

The contemporary conservation argument has been repackaged and popularized under the title of sustainable development. Alarmed at the contemporary situation, the United Nations asked the World Commission on Environment and Development to circumscribe "a global agenda for change" (WCED, 1987, p. ix). The result of the request was straightforward:

> Humanity has the ability to make development sustainable—to ensure that it meets the needs of the present without compromising the ability of future generations to meet their own needs ... sustainable development is not a fixed state of harmony, but rather a process of change in which the exploitation of resources, the direction of investments, the orientation of technological development and institutional change are made consistent with future needs as well as present needs.
>
> (WCED, 1987, pp. 8–9)

Since popularized, the concept of sustainable development has been the focus of much attention. The manner in which a dynamic equilibrium may be struck between humans and other components of the earth's natural system is integral to the continuing debate regarding sustainability.

Although at one time most individuals and organizations with an interest in the natural environment referred to themselves as conservationists, many positions now exist along a conservation continuum (Belshaw, 2001; Nash, 1982). The initial schism between Gifford Pinchot and John Muir is a useful illustration. While Pinchot advocated the use of forests, Muir strongly advocated for their preservation (Hargrove, 1989). According to Belshaw:

> preservation is desired for things that should be saved, not for later use, but just because it is good that they continue to exist, either for essentially aesthetic reasons, or in relation to their scientific interests, or—although perhaps this is in the end deeply mysteriously—simply for their own sake.
>
> (2001, p. 17)

Ecocentric Philosophies

Ecocentric philosophies take a fundamentally different view of the human–environment relationship. Worster (1994) likens this philosophical split to that of a divergence between two roads, one road containing the basis for the imperial tradition and the other containing the basis for harmonious existence. While attention here is focused on ecocentric philosophies advanced since industrialization, it is imperative to acknowledge the resemblance to both indigenous and eastern traditions.

Although once a strong proponent of conservation, Aldo Leopold became disenfranchised with the philosophy, explaining that:

> Conservation is getting nowhere because it is incompatible with our Abrahamic concept of land. We abuse land because we regard it as a commodity belonging to us. When we see land as a community to which we belong, we may begin to use it with love and respect. There is no other way for land to survive the impact of mechanized man, nor for us to reap from it the esthetic harvest it is capable, under science, of contributing to culture.
>
> (1966, pp. xviii–xix)

In formulating his famous land ethic, Leopold provides an eloquent critique of conservation as well as articulating a way forward for humans. In addition to advancing a holistic means of co-existence, the land ethic extends rights to nature. The general popularity of Leopold's writing leads Oelschlaeger to observe that "it is the best known environmental ethic of our time" (1995, p. 335). The idea of extending rights to nature has become the hallmark of other ecocentric philosophies.

In deep ecology Norwegian philosopher Arne Naess developed a non-technical statement of principles from which humans may gain a holistic understanding or perspective (Evernden, 1993; McLaughlin, 1995). Deep ecology embraces all life and clearly rejects anthropomorphism (McLaughlin, 1995). It is distinguished from shallow ecology as it concerns the willingness to question both economic and public policy (Naess, 1995). Deep ecology theory is also unique as it "is not a philosophy in any proper academic sense, nor is it institutionalized as a religion or an ideology. Rather, what happens is that various persons come together in campaigns and direct actions" (Naess, 1995, p. 71). Therefore, much of the deep ecology literature is multi-faceted and directed at politicians, resource managers and individuals (Devall & Sessions, 1985).

THE NATURAL ENVIRONMENT

A recurring theme among both environmental philosophers and proponents is a well-developed understanding of the natural environment. Awareness and knowledge of the natural environment is also essential to the study of outdoor recreation. This section broadly introduces readers to ecology. It specifically covers fundamental ecological concepts and interactions. Learning about environmental processes can both be a rewarding part of participation (Chapter 4) as well as a requirement for outdoor education and interpretation (Chapter 8). An understanding of the natural environment is also necessary for outdoor recreation managers who have a responsibility to ensure the ecological integrity (Chapter 6).

Ecological Concepts

The phrase ecology was first coined by M.I.T. chemist Ellen Swallow and envisioned a discipline which focuses on the interactions among living things and their non-living environments (Miller, 1996). Ecology is "the study of how organisms interact with one another and with their environment, including factors such as sunlight, temperature, moisture, vital nutrients, and all other physical and chemical influences to which organisms are exposed" (Miller, 1996, p. 89). For pragmatic purposes ecologists classify or divide the whole of nature according to distinctive ecosystems. An ecosystem refers to a distinct living community in a particular environment (Enger & Smith, 1995; Miller, 1996; Nebel & Wright, 1996).

Although classification and investigation of specific ecosystems are useful in many situations, ecology also embraces a systems perspective. As a system, each part (distinct ecosystem) connects with and influences other ecosystems. Unlike simple systems that can be easily anticipated, the environment is considered a complex system that is paradoxically characterized by both chaos and stability (Miller, 1996). This complexity is apparent in responses to ecosystem pressures that are frequently delayed and/or protected through

69

negative feedback. Negative feedback occurs when "the systems' response is in the opposite direction from the output" (Botkin & Keller, 1995, p. 36). Botkin and Keller (1995) use the example of an increase in environmental temperature. When it becomes hot, people begin to sweat in order to cool down. Sweating (negative feedback or change to the system) is the body's (system) reaction to the heat (influence from another part of the larger environmental system). Although the above example is relatively simple, it is useful to illustrate negative feedback and makes clear both the magnitude and intricacies of these connections between ecosystems.

Complexity has also been utilized by scientists in the form of the "ecosystem approach" which highlights the need to incorporate social or human effects when considering ecological systems (Marsh & Grossa, 2002). An ecosystem approach involves studying the organization of the environment and all of the influences and interactions that take place (Marsh & Grossa, 2002). As ecosystems regularly interact with one another, it is important to understand that human influences on one ecosystem will also likely impact other ecosystems.

A succinct overview of ecological principles follows to familiarize readers with the structure of ecosystems. With the caveat of their complex and systematic nature, three basic components are examined—living organisms, the non-living environment, and the processes by which the two interact. These components are considered holistically in the final part of this section which discusses the ecosystem boundaries through a nested approach.

Living Organisms

Recollection of outdoor recreation activities often involves other living parts of the environment. Examples include grasses, shrubs, trees, wildlife, fish, insects and other humans. Organisms encompass any manner of life and are considered biotic (biological or living) components of ecosystems (Botkin & Keller, 1995). It is possible to further classify these organisms into three different categories (Miller, 1996, p. 93):

> **Species**: groups of organisms which resemble one another in appearance, behaviour, chemistry, and in the genes they contain. Organisms that reproduce sexually are classified in the same species if under natural conditions they can breed with one another and produce live, fertile offspring.
> **Population**: consists of all members of the same species occupying a given area at the same time.
> **Community or biotic community**: populations of all the different species occupying and interacting in a particular place.

In addition to classifying living organisms, it is also important to recognize their biotic structure or the manner in which they fit together (Nebel & Wright, 1996). At the broadest level, three basic types of organisms (producers, consumers and decomposers) are recognized in all ecosystems (Enger & Smith, 1995; Nebel & Wright, 1996; Raven, Berg & Johnson, 1995). Producers or autotrophs are usually a diverse variety of green plants that convert sun energy and chemicals through photosynthesis to produce oxygen and sugars (Raven et al., 1995). Consumers (heterotrophs) rely on others to meet their food requirements and may be further identified as:

1. herbivores or primary consumers which eat plants;
2. carnivores including secondary consumers which feed on herbivores and tertiary consumers which feed on carnivores; and,
3. omnivores which consume both plants and other animals.

Decomposers, the final type of organism found in all ecosystems feed on detritus or dead organic material and waste (Enger & Smith, 1995; Raven et al., 1995).

The biotic structure of an ecosystem interacts through a complex series of consumptive relationships. Initial pathways pertaining to an organism are recognized as food chains whereas the effects among food chains form a more intricate pattern of food webs. Despite the inherent sophistication of these connections a basic pattern emerges among feeding or trophic levels (Nebel & Wright, 1996). In any ecosystem interactions can be conceptualized as a pyramid with producers occupying the first trophic level, consumers occupying the second, and additional levels being added to represent subsequent feeding relationships.

The Non-living Environment

Miller (1996) provides a useful analogy for the non-living components of the environment. He suggests that these elements may be thought of as the earth's support systems. Theses systems are composed of a series of concentric spheres or layers beginning at the center of the earth with the core and moving outward through the mantle, crust, biosphere and atmosphere (Miller, 1996). Ecology is mainly concerned with the biosphere, a thin layer encompassing the earth in which air, water, soil and organisms interact (Miller, 1996).

Non-living components of ecosystems are termed abiotic and may be further classified according to their physical or chemical properties. Physical properties concern the structural composition of components and may include sunlight, temperature, altitude, soil and water currents, while chemical properties relate to the basic composition of the components and include nutrients, salinity and dissolved oxygen (Miller, 1996). Considerable interplay occurs in most ecosystems between the physical and chemical factors. In rivers, for example, physical characteristics of depth and flow have a strong influence on chemical properties such as dissolved oxygen. Physical and chemical components also combine to exert considerable influence in shaping ecosystems, a reality well illustrated later in the chapter by the profound effects of climate.

Ecosystem Processes

Ecology emphasizes the interactions of organisms with their non-living environment. The importance assigned to understanding these interactions is well founded as without these exchanges an ecosystem would not function. There are three basic processes which connect organisms and their non-living environments. These processes include energy flow, matter or nutrient cycling, and gravity (Miller, 1996; Nebel & Wright, 1996).

Energy flow refers to the process by which solar energy travels through an ecosystem (Botkin & Keller, 1995). Of the energy which reaches the troposphere, only 66% actually penetrates it, and only 0.023% is actually used by green plants in the process of photosynthesis; the rest drives other processes including temperature, wind and water cycles (DeAngelis, 1992; Marsh & Grossa, 2002; Miller, 1996). Energy converted through photosynthesis flows through food webs as living organisms derive nourishment. Other flows are also vital. It is energy retained in the atmosphere by various gasses, commonly known as the greenhouse effect, which permits a sufficiently warm climate for life to exist. Climate and the implications of climate change are explored later in this chapter.

The second of these processes focuses on chemical components and involves the cycling of nutrients. Nutrients are "any chemical element or compound an organism must take in to live, grow, or reproduce" (Miller, 1996, p. 92). Examples of common nutrients include oxygen, carbon and hydrogen. Miller (1996) explains that in terms of matter, the earth is a closed system and therefore the fixed amounts of nutrients must continually move from organisms to the non-living environment and back, as influenced by solar energy and gravity. A large number of important nutrients actually cycle in this manner with the most widely recognizable ones being carbon, phosphorus, nitrogen, water, and oxygen (Miller, 1996; Nebel & Wright, 1996).

Gravity may not frequently be thought of as being an important ecosystem process. Miller (1996), however, identifies that it is central to the non-living environment in two ways. First, gravity permits the earth to hold or maintain its atmosphere. This insures that sufficient heat is retained and that protection is afforded from the harmful rays of the sun. Second, gravity has a downward effect on the movement of matter and nutrient cycles. Without gravity neither the sun's energy nor essential chemicals would be able to function.

Ecosystem Interactions

In reality the three basic components of ecosystems are constantly interacting to produce specific conditions at a given geographical location which may or may not be conducive to any given species (it should be noted that species may also influence these conditions). This relationship is expressed in the law of tolerance, which states "the existence, abundance, and distribution of a species in an ecosystem are determined by whether the levels of one or more physical or chemical factors fall within the range tolerated by that species" (Miller, 1996, p. 104). Nebel and Wright (1996) broaden this concept by recognizing that for each species an optimal range of factors exist at which they flourish, a zone of stress occurs as they move towards their limits of their tolerance, and death occurs after that limit has been exceeded. It is also possible for organisms to adapt and change their level of tolerance (Miller, 1996).

Each species has a specific biotic potential which is the maximum number of possible offspring under optimal conditions (Miller, 1996). Working against this biotic potential is environmental resistance which combines all living and non-living factors which may limit the population (Marsh & Grossa, 2002; Miller, 1996). Many factors may constitute

environmental resistance including the availability of food and nutrients, disease, predators and habitat alteration (Marsh & Grossa, 2002; Nebel & Wright, 1996). Nebel and
Wright (1996) emphasize that the balance between biotic potential and environmental
resistance is dynamic. Fluctuations depend on the particular population in question and
vary from relatively stable to considerably abrupt changes. If the total number of individuals of a population drops below a minimum (critical) number upon which survival is
dependent a particular species may be classified as threatened or endangered (Nebel &
Wright, 1996).

Ecosystems have many natural (living and non-living) mechanisms for maintaining
balance. The best known of these mechanisms are predatory interactions between the
various trophic levels (Arms, 1990). Predation may take many forms including: herbivory
in which green plants are preyed upon although not necessarily killed; parasitism in which
one species feeds on another usually larger species without killing it; carnivory where the
predator kills and eats the prey; and, cannibalism in which a single species is both prey and
predator (Caughley & Sinclair, 1994; Enger & Smith, 1995).

Carnivory is the classic form of predation and has been researched extensively. One of
the best examples studied is on Isle Royale in Lake Superior (Caughley & Sinclair, 1994;
Nebel & Wright, 1996). Moose crossed from the mainland to the island in the winter
around 1900 where they avoided predators until 1948 when a pair of wolves also reached
the island. Biologists have closely monitored this unique situation and have observed a
correspondence between the two species over time as illustrated in Figure 3.1. With little
environmental resistance (low wolf population) the moose population increased. As the
wolf population increased the numbers of moose decreased. A decline in the moose

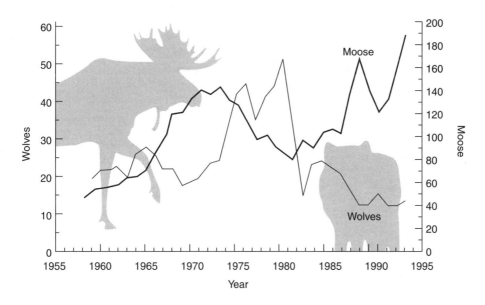

Figure 3.1 Moose and Wolves at Isle Royale.
Source: R.O. Peterson, in Nebel & Wright, 1996.

population, followed by a decline in the wolf population, further illustrates the related nature of these populations (Nebel & Wright, 1996). Recent data from research on Isle Royale indicates that this ecological relationship is very complex with predators only acting in a dispensatory way by preying on sick or weak moose (Caughley & Sinclair, 1994; Nebel & Wright, 1996).

The concept of balance underlies the widely held idea of carrying capacity. Caughley and Sinclair (1994) define ecological carrying capacity as the "natural limit of a population set by resources in a particular environment. It is one of the equilibrium points that a population tends toward through density-dependent effects from lack of food, space (e.g., territoriality), cover or other resources" (p. 117). Simply put, carrying capacity is the population of a species that "an ecosystem can support indefinitely" (Arms, 1990, p. 130). This is graphically illustrated by the logistical growth equation in Figure 3.2. It demonstrates the natural tendency for any given species for exponential growth unless some form of environmental resistance is encountered. Environmental resistance keeps the population size in balance so that the ecosystem does not become degraded and unable to support the population (Marsh & Grossa, 2002).

While ecologists have documented the pattern of exponential growth and environmental resistance to maintain balance in many populations, this issue remains critical for the human population. As shown in Figure 3.3 the human population clearly demonstrates a pattern of exponential growth pattern with relatively little environmental resistance. The concept of the earth's carrying capacity, the point of equilibrium for the human population, is an important and persistent question (Arms, 1990; Marsh & Grossa, 2002).

Although natural ecosystems tend towards balance, as graphically illustrated by the concept of carrying capacity, it is critical to recognize that ecosystems are also dynamic. Change is a normal course for ecosystems. Nebel and Wright explain that:

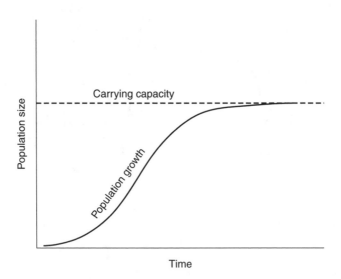

Figure 3.2 The Ecological Concept of Carrying Capacity.

74

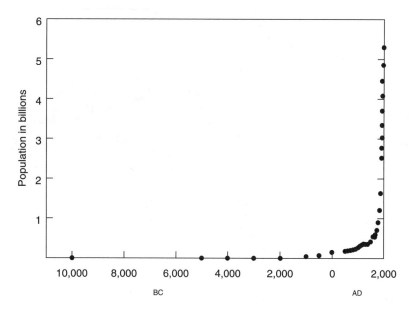

Figure 3.3 Human Population Growth.

this phenomenon of orderly transition from one biotic community to another is called ecological, or natural, succession. Natural succession occurs because the physical environment may be gradually modified by the growth of biotic community itself, such that the area becomes more favorable to the present occupants.

(1996, p. 97)

The process of succession may occur in areas not previously occupied (primary succession), in areas which have experienced disturbances such as fire (secondary succession), and in aquatic environments (aquatic succession) (Enger & Smith, 1995; Nebel & Wright, 1996). The progressive changes associated with succession leads to formation of a climax community for the particular ecosystem (Arms, 1990). Underlying the various types of ecological succession is the importance of biodiversity. As an ecosystem changes conditions may become optimal for other species to flourish. Limiting biological diversity and restricting natural processes raises concerns about naturalness as well as long-term environmental consequences.

RECREATIONAL RESOURCES

The concept of resources was briefly mentioned at the beginning of this chapter in association with the western paradigm or worldview. Specific parts of the environment become regarded as resources when they are of use to humans (Mitchell, 1989; Zimmerman, 1951). As Mitchell observes, "attributes of nature are no more than "neutral stuff" until man is able to perceive their presence, to recognize their capacity to satisfy human wants, and to devise means to utilize them" (1989, p. 2). Figure 3.4 illustrates the interplay of man, culture and nature by which attributes of the environment (neutral stuff) become resources. The

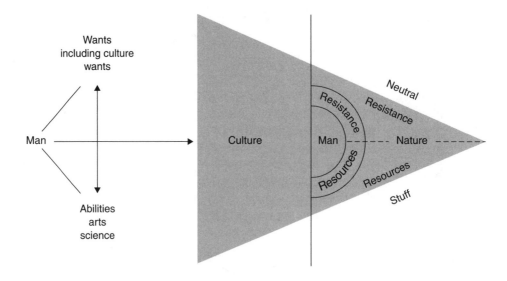

Figure 3.4 Man, Culture, and Nature.

Source: Zimmerman, 1951.

cultural component is especially important because it recognizes that resources are subjective and contextually defined. As Mitchell observes, "what is a natural resource in one culture may be 'neutral stuff' in another" (1989, p. 2).

In this book specific attention is focused on the concept of outdoor recreation resources. Consistent with the above understanding of resources, Clawson and Knetsch state that:

> there is nothing in the physical landscape or features of any particular piece of land or body of water that makes it a recreation resource; it is the combination of natural qualities and the ability and desire of man to use it, that makes a resource out of what otherwise may be a more or less meaningless combination of rocks, soil, and trees.

> (1966, p. 7)

Consequently, outdoor recreation resources are often not easily identifiable. At some point most environments may be considered recreational and therefore these resources cover a diverse range of settings, including areas that are typically viewed as inhospitable and/or difficult to access (Pigram & Jenkins, 1999). Recreational resources should also be understood within the cultural context, which itself may change over time and be subject to multiple perspectives (Pigram & Jenkins, 1999). The change in attitude towards wilderness in America, as discussed in Chapter 2, provides an excellent example of how resources are dynamic and how they may gain recreational attributes. Pioneers to America generally viewed the wilderness as a forbidding place and as an adversary that needed to be overcome. Contemporary perspectives have changed considerably with wilderness now being considered an important part of the American identity, worthy of preservation and a desirable setting for recreation pursuits (Nash, 1982).

Recreational resources, however, are not limited to natural environments. Kreutzwiser defines recreational resources as "an element of the natural or man-modified environment which provides an opportunity to satisfy recreational wants" (1989, p. 22). In broadening the concept of recreational resources, Kreutzwiser (1989) suggests that these resources exist on a continuum, with biophysical or natural resources on one end and human-constructed resources on the other. As shown in Figure 3.5 outdoor recreational resources are located along the full range of this continuum. An example of a biophysical outdoor recreational resource is an unaltered free-flowing river. A ski resort is an example of a human-modified recreational resource.

Outdoor recreation is a unique form of resource use because it does not usually obliterate the resource and may occur with other uses. Pigram and Jenkins observe that "outdoor recreation often imposes relatively non-aggressive and benign claims on the resource base, so that it is possible to envisage and actually plan for situations of multiple use" (1999, p. 61). Multiple-use approaches to managing resources gained popularity in the United States in the 1960s with the passing of the Multiple-Use Sustained-Yield Act. In this context "multiple use means that the management of all renewable surface resources are directed to meet the multiple needs of the American people" (Ibrahim & Cordes, 1993, p. 244). Managers attempt to realize greater economic and social benefits by expanding the range of potential uses of a resource such as forests, lakes and rivers. Although multiple use has been a dominant strategy in the United States other countries such as Australia have been somewhat reluctant to pursue such approaches (Pigram & Jenkins, 1999).

Supply of Outdoor Recreation Resources

The third section of this chapter explores the supply of resources for outdoor recreation. Supply "refers to the recreational resources, both natural and man-made, which provide opportunities for recreation. It is a complex concept influenced by numerous factors and subject to changing interpretations" (Kreutzwiser, 1989, p. 21). As the desire and ability to use attributes of the natural environment changes, specific features of the environment are classified as recreational resources. The task of classifying, or creating an inventory of such resources, is challenging because it has less to do with physical attributes and more to so with social ones. As Clawson and Knetsch observe "it is particularly hard to identify potential outdoor recreation areas because it is not the observable natural qualities that make an

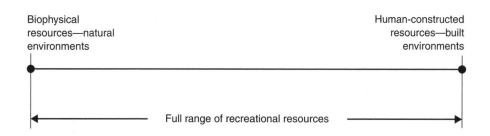

Figure 3.5 Continuum of Recreational Resources.

Plate 3.1 A Free-flowing River is an Example of a Resource Located at the Biophysical or Natural Environment End of the Continuum of Recreational Resources.

Plate 3.2 The Presence of Resource Users, Technological Innovations, and Lack of Alternatives Make Sand Dunes a Recreational Resource for Sandboarding.

area suitable or desirable for outdoor recreation, but the presence or absence of users and the availability or lack of better alternative areas" (1966, p. 146). Therefore, inherent technical challenges exist in attempting to quantify a subjective entity such as outdoor recreation resources. Classification schemes utilized to identify outdoor recreation resources are presented. Attributes common to many of the classification schemes are synthesized and evaluative issues are examined. The section culminates with a general discussion of recreational resource supply.

Classifying Resources for Outdoor Recreation

Areas with unique landscape features were initially classified as parks and protected areas. These areas were recognized in both the United States and Canada to ensure, in part, continued opportunities for outdoor recreation (Cordell & Betz, 2000; McNamee, 1993). Interest in inventorying and determining the supply of outdoor recreation resources began in earnest after World War II. As outdoor activities have continued to increase in popularity so have the values associated with resources that provide opportunities to satisfy outdoor recreational desires. The development of schemes to categorize resources for their recreational resource values follow. They reflect the continued search to refine classifications and ultimately provide commentary on the quality and quantity of recreational resources.

One of the first resource classification schemes to include outdoor recreation and have an enduring influence on future efforts was derived by Clawson, Held and Stoddard in 1960 (Pigram & Jenkins, 1999). This early classification scheme defines three types of recreation areas: user-oriented, resource based, and intermediate (Clawson, Held & Stoddard, 1960). User-oriented recreation areas are typically characterized by their close proximity to the user. Resource based areas are characterized by their outstanding natural features. Intermediate recreation areas tend to be a mix of the two as they are close to the user in some degree (usually no further than two hours' distance) and the natural features and recreation opportunities they afford are the "best" available within that distance (Clawson et al., 1960). The five items used to determine the type of area present include: general location, major types of activity, timing of major use, typical size of the area, and types of agency responsibility (federal, provincial/state, municipal or private) (Clawson et al., 1960). The three types of recreation areas can further be subdivided and classified according to the "intensity of use," ranging from very heavy to light. A neighborhood park used by very few people, for example, would be considered a user-oriented area with light intensity of use.

At the same time, the bipartisan Outdoor Recreation Resources Review Commission (ORRRC) also recommended a classification system. The concern at the time was not a lack of land area, but rather a lack of proper management of recreational resources (Brockman & Merriam, 1979). This classification system aimed to identify recreation needs and resources for the public and ensure a high level of quality, quantity and distribution of recreational opportunities, both for the present and the future (Brockman & Merriam, 1979). The ORRRC scheme consists of six classes in which lands used for recreation were organized according to their associated description. These classes and potential activities which may occur in each of the classes are shown in Table 3.1.

The ORRRC classification process occurred through the designated commission, under the authority of the Outdoor Recreation Resources Review Act, established in 1958. Recreation areas in the United States are zoned under this classification scheme in order to ensure consistency and adequate planning (Brockman & Merriam, 1979). As a consequence, the ORRRC classification scheme provides managers with guidelines to place limits on certain recreational activities that occur once land has been classified. The ORRRC also provided

Table 3.1 ORRRC Land Classification

Class	Examples	Activities
1. High-density recreation areas	Coulter Bay in Grand Teton National Park	Sports, games, sightseeing; use of many man-made facilities, marinas, etc.
		Yosemite Valley Huntington Beach, CA Jones Beach, NY
2. General outdoor recreation areas	State parks County parks Large city parks	Picnicking, camping, hiking, biking, skiing, water sports, fishing, ball playing, many man-made facilities
3. Natural environment areas	parts of: National Forests National Parks large land holdings	Hiking, camping, boating, fishing, hunting, almost exclusively; many trails, some picnic facilities, some pit privies
4. Unique natural areas	Old Faithful Yosemite Falls Bristle Cone Natural Area (in the Inyo National Forest)	Sightseeing, nature study
5. Primitive areas	Legally designated wilderness areas (Boundary Waters Canoe Area, Lostine Wilderness) roadless areas primitive areas	Canoeing, hiking, climbing; some trails, no other man-made amenities
6. Historic or cultural sites	Valley Forge Casa Grande Ruins Mesa Verde	Sightseeing, history or cultural study

grants to states in order to ensure maintenance of recreation resources (Brockman & Merriam, 1979). Ford and Blanchard (1993) view the classification scheme very positively and as a notable advancement. They assert that "this system has now been adopted world wide and has become the single land classification system of value in understanding the recreational uses of large areas that often serve other purposes" (Ford & Blanchard, 1993, p. 16). Others have been more critical of the ORRRC classification scheme because it is primarily descriptive, lacks capacity measures, and is generally a subjective classification process (Kreutzwiser, 1989).

The Canadian Land Inventory (CLI) is recognized as "the most ambitious and exhaustive scheme for classification of recreation potential" (Pigram & Jenkins, 1999, p. 68). The CLI originated in 1965 with the purpose of generating data regarding natural resources used for outdoor recreational pursuits (Canada Land Inventory, 2000). This involved developing an overview of the nature of outdoor recreation in Canada (quality, quantity, distribution), identifying outstanding natural features or values associated with recreation areas, and providing governments with assistance in forming policies regarding areas of recreation resources (Canada Land Inventory, 2000). Today, the CLI has covered over 2.5 million square kilometers of Canada's rural landscape (Canada Land Inventory, 2000, online).

The CLI uses biophysical attributes to classify land areas into one of seven classes, based on the accommodation and attraction of users (Kreutzwiser, 1989). These seven main classes are distinguished based on the capability of the land area to support recreation; the classes range from very high capability to very low capability (Canada Land Inventory, 2000). Assumptions of preference, again based on biophysical attributes, are used to designate subcategories. Comparisons between resource sectors are subsequently available to land managers that indicate both potential conflicts and opportunities.

While CLI has a long history and offers land managers valuable insight on some aspects required for recreation planning, it also has specific limitations. Exclusive reliance on biophysical attributes negates many other factors essential in determining supply of outdoor recreation resources and in this way it fails to address the quality of the recreation experience (Pigram & Jenkins, 1999). The CLI also relies heavily on assumptions regarding user preferences and demand (Kreutzwiser, 1989). Finally, the CLI does not accommodate or consider new or modified outdoor recreation pursuits which have emerged since its creation (Pigram & Jenkins, 1999). Although identified as one of the most ambitious classification schemes of outdoor recreation resources, the CLI ceased in 1994 and attention from federal resource agencies has subsequently been directed to modernizing the data base (Canadian Land Inventory, 2000).

Although discussed more fully in Chapter 6 as a framework for site-specific management, the Recreation Opportunity Spectrum (ROS) represents the incorporation of experiential elements into the classification of outdoor recreation resources (Driver, Brown, Stankey & Gregorie, 1987; Kreutzwiser, 1989; Ibrahim & Cordes, 1993; Pigram & Jenkins, 1999). Impetus for ROS came from deficiencies in previous classification schemes to conceive of a system of recreation opportunities as well as an intensifying need for land use planning (Driver et al., 1987). Central to ROS is the conceptualization of recreation opportunities which permit articulation of supply (Driver & Brown, 1978). A recreation opportunity is understood to involve:

> the combination of physical, biological, social and managerial conditions that give value to a place. Thus, an opportunity includes qualities provided by nature (vegetation, landscape, topography, scenery), qualities associated with recreation use (levels and types of use), and conditions provided by management (developments, roads, regulations). By combining variations of these qualities and conditions, management can provide a variety of opportunities for recreationists.
>
> (Clark & Stankey, 1979, p. 1)

Detailed tenets upon which ROS is based have been made operational by dividing the spectrum of potential opportunity settings into classes with the number of potential settings varying upon how ROS has been adapted. Clark and Stankey (1979) emphasize the

81

importance of access, non-recreational resource uses, extent of modification, nature of social interaction, acceptability of visitor impacts, and acceptability of regimentation as factors which influence opportunities. In this manner indicators or standards are generated for possible opportunities for recreation which may subsequently be classified according to specific classes.

The relative simplicity of ROS and managerial implications has prompted implementation by management agencies in the United States, Canada, and Australia (Driver et al., 1987). The ability to expand the framework from its original form to reflect potential complexity is identified by Pigram and Jenkins (1999) as a benefit. Despite widespread adoption, critical questions resonate regarding ROS including applicability in diverse cultural and geographic settings as well as quality measures of the experience (Driver et al., 1987). The ability of ROS to respond to diversity or individuals facing constraints has been raised as an important issue by Pigram and Jenkins (1999). The emphasis on manipulating biophysical settings as well as failing to acknowledge the presence of intrinsic biophysical attributes to opportunity settings are serious shortcomings identified by Pigram and Jenkins (1999) and Kreutzwiser (1989).

The above discussion of schemes to classify outdoor recreation resources noted limitation of each of the approaches. A significant challenge facing those attempting to inventory outdoor recreation resources is how to expand the scope of classification schemes with accuracy while at the same time being able to manage large amounts of data. The release of the Renewable Resources Planning Act (RPA) Assessment in the United States prompted the United States Forest Service (USFS) to develop the National Outdoor Recreation Supply Information System (NORSIS) (Cordell & Betz, 2000). This information system utilizes secondary sources of information to consider more than 400 supply elements, including all levels of government as well as information from owners of private resources. Such an approach may provide a more comprehensive means to inventory potential outdoor recreation resources than was previously possible.

Attributes of Recreational Resources

The approaches to classify outdoor recreation resources emphasize particular attributes. In a general sense, the ORRRC classification scheme focuses on biophysical attributes, the CLI emphasizes the biophysical suitability of landscapes, and the ROS considers experience in addition to rudimentary biophysical attributes (Kreutzwiser, 1989). Development of a comprehensive classification system for outdoor recreation is challenging because of the complex and dynamic nature of resources as well as the subjective elements associated with the outdoor recreation experience. Nonetheless, three attributes (capability, suitability, consistency with activity requirements) are central to gauging the appropriateness of a resource for recreation.

Classification systems essentially assess the quantity and quality of a particular resource. At a more refined level, foremost attention should specifically be given to the capability and suitability of a particular resource (Pigram & Jenkins, 1999). Resource capability is defined as "a measure of the feasibility of allowing a range of specified resource uses on an area of land, reflecting both the likely productivity and resilience of the site" (Pigram & Jenkins,

1999, p. 70). Capability considerations for terrestrial and aquatic resources direct attention to biophysical attributes such as size of the area, geological composition, vegetative composition, climate, and water depth.

While interrelated with the capability of a resource, suitability focuses attention on the potential desirability of land and/or water for outdoor recreation. Suitability involves four basic components of economic efficiency, social equity, community acceptability and administrative practicality (Pigram & Jenkins, 1999). Examples of resource attributes associated with suitability include: accessibility, ownership, potential management, amount of modification, social interactions, and visitor impacts.

Considering capability and suitability attributes are essential when determining the potential of a landscape to be a recreational resource. It is also important to bear in mind the intended form of outdoor recreation activity. Some landscapes have biophysical and suitability attributes that make them highly conducive to one outdoor pursuit and not others. A mountain slope that is owned by a private ski company during the winter may be conducive to mountain-biking in the summer. The same resource may be ill-suited for use by the general public for camping, due to its relatively small area, hill-slope, lack of vegetation, limited access, and ownership. As illustrated in this example, it is impossible to homogeneously address outdoor recreation resources.

Supply of Outdoor Recreation Resources

Many challenges are evident when attempting to determine the supply of recreational resources. Technical issues associated with particular classification schemes are further complicated by the considerations of capacity, suitability, and appropriateness or fit. In acknowledgment of these difficulties, a general discussion follows to illustrate the breadth of recreational resources in both terrestrial and aquatic settings, the influences of climate on these resources, and emerging trends in the supply of resources.

Terrestrial Recreational Resources

At the broadest level the natural environment is often categorized into regions called biomes. Biomes are relatively large in size and are "characterized by particular climate, soil, plants and animals, regardless of where it occurs on earth" (Raven et al., 1995, p. 94). All terrestrial biomes are made distinguishable by their land basis, which accounts for approximately 29% of the earth's surface (Hamblin, 1989). The three major types of terrestrial biomes found throughout the world include deserts and semi-deserts, grasslands and forests. Uniqueness within each biome comes from the types of landforms, climate, soil, vegetation and native species present. Specific examples of features desirable for outdoor recreation and their supply follow.

Outdoor recreation that occurs in the backcountry often relies on wilderness resources. Wilderness refers to vast expanses of land where human influence is minimal and natural processes dominate (Hendee, Stankey & Lucas, 1990). As legally defined by the Wilderness Act (1964) in the United States, wilderness is constituted by an area of 5,000 acres or enough size to make sustained preservation possible (Hendee et al., 1990). A more thorough discussion of the meaning of wilderness is discussed in Chapter 7. The United States, for example, boasts an extensive supply of wilderness resources. The National Wilderness Preservation System (NWPS) currently holds over 103.5 million acres of wilderness, approximately 57.4 million acres is located in Alaska (Betz, English & Cordell, 1999). These 630 wilderness areas are almost exclusively (96%) found in the western regions of the United States (including Alaska).

Mountains are "a topographic feature with an elevation of 600m above sea level, local relief of $200m/km^2$ and slope angles of 10–30°" (Slaymaker, 1999, p. 413). While most people exclusively think of mountains as high and rugged features, many different types of mountain exist in linear zones (mountain belts) with varying degrees of ruggedness caused by motion of the earth's crust and wear (Hamblin, 1989). Mountains are often classified according to a number of physical attributes such as tectonic framework, hydrology and geomorphology (Slaymaker, 1999). As a landscape feature, mountains cover approximately 24% of the globe and provide goods and services for more than one billion people world-wide (IUCN, 2006). Mountains are also an iconic example of a recreational resource which can broadly be found throughout the world. Some mountain ranges have gained particular recognition for recreation activities (e.g., climbing, skiing) such as the European Alps, Rocky Mountains and the Sierra Nevada range.

Forests are another important landscape feature and recreational resource. Many different types of forest exist (e.g., tropical rainforests, temperate forests, boreal forests), but these biomes commonly have a relatively high amount of precipitation that in turn supports growth of tree vegetation (Arms, 1990; Miller, 1996). The types and abundance of species found in different types of forests varies considerably with temperature, the amount of precipitation, and location. Substantial alterations have also occurred in forests. In North America, for example, all but 0.1% of original temperate deciduous forests remain and most large predators have been eliminated or displaced (Miller, 1996). Although the supply of original forest has been decimated, forests still constitute a considerable portion of the landscape in many countries. In Canada, for example, approximately 417.6 million hectares is forest cover which constitutes 45% of the land area (Natural Resources Canada, 2007, online). The ownership of forest resources is also important for outdoor recreation as 94% of Canadian forests are publicly owned, with 23% under federal jurisdiction and 71% controlled by the provinces and territories (Natural Resources Canada, 2007, online). Therefore the onus for management of forests largely resides with the provinces and territories and each has set specific guidelines, policies and management strategies related to their respective forest regions. Canadian forests provide considerable resources for recreation, employment and the commercial sector. Such ownership highlights the issue of resource suitability, particularly in the more densely populated southern part of the country.

Greenways or other open areas in the countryside are an important landscape feature for outdoor recreation. Smith explains that "a greenway is, in simplest terms, a linear open space. It is a corridor composed of natural vegetation or at least vegetation that is more natural than in surrounding area" (1993, p. xi). The concept of the countryside has been utilized in a similar way. Countryside conveys a sense of open green space and tends to focus on the physical and aesthetic aspects of general landscapes (Seabrooke & Miles, 1993). A number of specific areas may be associated with the countryside, including parks, heritage coasts, trails, picnic areas, and open access lands (Natural England, 2007a). The countryside concept is perhaps most dominant in the United Kingdom where legislation was introduced to safeguard it in 1949. The more recent Countryside and Right of Way Act of 2000 allows public access to open areas and requires conservation (Curry, 2004; Torkildsen, 2005). In 2005 the Countryside Agency completed mapping open access lands, which encompass 940,000 hectares or 7.1% of England's land mass (The Countryside Agency, 2005).

Trails are paths that may be followed (Bell, 1997). Their supply is neither simple nor straightforward due to their diversity of forms, route design, and construction. Trails take a diversity of forms (e.g., unimproved routes, surfaced footpaths, tours) and lead people to experience a variety of subjects (e.g., educational points of interest, scenic features, specific places, waypoints). The purpose of developing a trail (e.g., prevent environmental degradation, control access, enhance visitor experience) must be weighed against changing the character of the place, disturbing habitat, and concentrating users (Bell, 1997). Numerous excellent resources exist that cover all aspects of trail development from design through to construction (see Bell, 1997; Hultsman et al., 1998). Many countries now boast extensive supplies of trail and/or pathways. In the United Kingdom trails and/or pathways are often incorporated into green spaces or the countryside. The supply of trails in the United Kingdom, for example, includes: 15 National Trails (4,000 km) which link other pathways and are intended for multiple uses (National Trails, 2007); 17,000 km of greenways that are non-highway routes (Natural England, 2007b); 190,000 km of bridleways or walking paths (Torkildsen, 2005); 16,093 km of cycling trails (National Cycle Network, 2007); and, open access to the countryside as outlined above.

Aquatic Recreational Resources

Water is a common feature in the natural environment and the basis for all aquatic biomes. The importance of water to the earth and to humans cannot be overstated. Approximately 71% of the earth's surface is covered by water (Hamblin, 1989). Freshwater is critical as organisms, including humans, require it to live. Oceans are equally important as they absorb and distribute solar energy, influence climate, and facilitate the cycling of essential nutrients (Miller, 1996). Water also acts as a resource for recreation and is discussed in terms of freshwater (rivers and lakes) as marine environments. Specific examples of supply are included for each category.

Freshwater comes from either precipitation and/or the earth and these biomes are characterized by a relative absence of salt. The total amount of the earth's surface that is covered by freshwater is approximately 2%, and the amount readily available in lakes and rivers is 0.2% (Brewer, 1988). Freshwater biomes discussed include river systems and lakes as together they contribute to the functioning of the hydrological cycle.

Rosgen asserts "it has been said that the rivers are the life blood of civilization. At no other time in the history of modern man have the cumulative impacts associated with development along the river had a greater impact on water resource values" (1996, p. 1). The characteristics and behavior of water systems are of interest and concern to scientists, engineers, ecologists, citizens, and those undertaking outdoor recreation activities. Anything produced by the action of rivers as well as organisms found within them are generally

85

referred to as fluvial (Robert, 2003). Schumm (1977) suggests that a systems approach is useful and considers fluvial systems to consist of a production zone, transfer zone, and deposition zone. The production zone encompasses the area from which water and sediment is gathered, the transfer zone moves the collection of water and sediment, and the deposition zone releases the water and sediment into deeper water (Robert, 2003; Schumm, 1977). Rivers dominate the second zone in most fluvial systems and have received much attention. Rosgen (1996), for example, provides a classification typology for streams consisting of geomorphic (landscape forms), morphological (river forms) and condition variables.

Lakes form when water, through either runoff or the ground, fill depressions in the earth caused by glaciation, crustal displacement, and/or volcanic activity (Miller, 1996). Water may come to fill these depressions through either natural processes (e.g., glacial advance) or by human modification and impoundments (e.g., dams) (Brewer, 1988). Lakes vary considerably in terms of size. The Great Lakes of North America, for example, hold a surface area of 94,000 square miles, with a total watershed surface area of 201,000 square miles (The Nature Conservancy, 1994). Overall, this works out to be roughly 20% of the world's available freshwater (Tovell, 1979).

Like terrestrial biomes, lakes can be separated into specific regions. The littoral zone consists of the relatively shallow area around the edge of the lake in which rooted vegetation occurs; the limnetic zone which encompasses the open water portion of the lake; and the profundal zone which includes the near-bottom and bottom of the lake (Brewer, 1988). There are a number of specific features which influence the type of habitat the lakes provide including energy, oxygen and temperature (Brewer, 1988). Lakes can also be classified as to the amount of nutrients they contain, which generally corresponds to their age. New lakes with clear blue water, steep banks and relatively few nutrients are referred to as oligotrophic; as the amount of sediment and nutrients increase the lake becomes classified as mesotrophic; and lakes with a high amount of nutrients which support a large amount of biotic organisms are called eutrophic lakes (Miller, 1996).

Canada serves as an illustrative example of the supply of freshwater as it has approximately 20% of the world's available supply, 7% of which is renewable (Environment Canada, 2003, online). Water resources in Canada are managed through various federal, provincial and local institutions as well as non-governmental organizations. Opportunities for outdoor recreation from this supply of freshwater take multiple forms (e.g., ice in the winter, water during other times of the year) and encompass both rivers and lakes. Rivers and river systems have played an important role in the development of Canada due to the exploration for furs and minerals (Outwater, 1996). Some of the longest rivers in the world occur in Canada including the MacKenzie, the St Lawrence, the Nelson, the Yukon and the Columbia (Bryan, 1972). Many of these sizeable river systems occur in the northern portions of Canada and, consequently, almost 60% of Canada's freshwater drains north while 85% of population lives in the south along the Canada–United States border (Environment Canada, 2003, online). Major rivers flowing through populated areas present different challenges.

Canada is also fortunate to have an abundance of lakes (approximately two million in total) which cover 7.6% of the entire country (Teaching and Learning About Canada, 2007). Considerable attention from both Canadians and Americans has been directed to the

Great Lakes of North America. The four Great Lakes (Erie, Ontario, Huron and Superior) hold a surface area of 94,000 square miles, with a total watershed surface area of 201,000 square miles (The Nature Conservancy, 1994). These four lakes alone contain approximately 20% of the world's available freshwater (Tovell, 1979). Canada has many other lakes of substantial size, including: Great Bear, Great Slave, Winnipeg, Athabasca, and Reindeer (Teaching and Learning About Canada, 2007).

Marine biomes are typically distinguished by the level of salinity (amount of dissolved salt) within the water network (Enger & Smith, 1995) as well as their considerable depth (Raven et al., 1995). According to Miller (1996) ocean environments can be classified into two zones—coastal and open sea. The coastal zone, located from the point of high-tide outward to the continental shelf, is relatively warm and nutrient rich. It accounts for 90% of all marine species (Miller, 1996). Estuaries, the confluence of rivers into the ocean, as well as coastal wetlands, areas which are covered by saltwater for a portion of the year, provide the interface between marine and terrestrial systems. These areas are typically shallow and somewhat enclosed (Enger & Smith, 1995). These zones act as buffers to the land from the ocean, provide protection for breeding and young creatures, act as a natural process of water treatment, and support a rich diversity of species (Miller, 1996).

Extending outward from the estuary area is the continental shelf which has the greatest abundance of nutrients, algal and fish species (Caughley & Sinclair, 1994). The continental shelf accounts for 7% of the ocean's surface area, or roughly 0.2% of the ocean's volume (Postma & Ziljstra, 1988). At the shelf break, the continental shelf drops off dramatically and the shelf gradually descends to join with the ocean floor (Postma & Ziljstra, 1988). The high degree of biodiversity results from constant intertidal mixing of sediments and nutrients between shorelines and ocean water. Productivity is so great that 90% of all marine species are found in this zone (Miller, 1996; Nebel & Wright, 1996). The open sea begins with the increased depth at the end of the continental shelf and zones within it can be further classified according to the amount of sunlight received.

The four oceans (Atlantic, Arctic, Indian and Pacific) cover approximately 71% of the earth's surface and account for 97% of all water (Bigg, 2003; Herbert, 1999). A substantial proportion of the human population (about 37%) resides within 100 km of the ocean coastline (Herbert, 1999). Although under considerable stress, the oceans are a vast recreational resource that supports a number of activities such as sailing, fishing, surfing, kayaking, cruising and diving. Australia, for example, has many locations that are well known for ocean-based recreation activities. The Great Barrier Reef Marine Park Authority manages activities which focus on the Great Barrier Reef including tours, diving adventures and whale-watching (Great Barrier Reef Marine Park Authority, 2007). The Victoria region also takes advantage of the opportunities afforded by the ocean through the development of the Great Ocean Road, which offers vantage points of the coastline and facilitates touring, surfing and fishing (The Great Ocean Road, n.d.).

Climate and Climate Change

Climate was identified earlier as an example to illustrate how chemical and physical components of the non-living environment shape ecosystems. Climate refers to "the average

87

long-term weather of an area; it is a region's general pattern of atmospheric or weather conditions, seasonal variations, and weather extremes (such as hurricanes, or prolonged drought or rain) averaged over a long period (at least 30 years)" (Miller, 1996, p. 129). Moderation of the earth's climate is the result of interactions among physical components (e.g., variations in solar energy striking the earth, properties of air and water) and chemical components (e.g., greenhouse gases) that play an instrumental role in moderating climate (Boeker, 1995; Miller, 1996). It is further shaped by other features (e.g., mountains, large areas of vegetation and cities) which sufficiently alter conditions to form microclimates or conditions specific to a particular locality (Nebel & Wright, 1996). Hence, climate in different regions and around specific features determines, to a considerable extent, the availability of recreation resources.

Depending on the climatic conditions of a particular area, recreational opportunities are expanded or restricted by seasonal variations and weather. Seasons are the outcomes of general variations of temperature and other conditions throughout the year while weather refers to immediate conditions such as visibility, precipitation, temperature and humidity (Kreutzwiser, 1989). The supply of recreation resources in countries experiencing four distinct seasons expands greatly as water changes to snow and ice which makes it possible to satisfy a number of winter outdoor pursuits. A single recreational resource, such as a lake, may therefore satisfy very different recreational opportunities during different seasons. Seasonality and weather also influence access to remote sites, satisfaction derived from an outdoor activity, and length of the tourist season (Kreutzwiser, 1989).

Variability is an accepted eventuality within healthy ecosystems as they move through natural stages of development. These natural stages of development can include succession, disturbance and evolution, all of which bring about a variety of changes to the ecosystem (Arms, 1990; Enger & Smith, 1995; Nebel & Wright, 1994). These changes, especially at a large scale, tend to occur over prolonged periods of time. The Swedish scientist Svante Arrhenius first called attention to the issue of global climate change more than a century ago (von Storch & Stehr, 2000). Eleven decades later, the unprecedented speed of global climate change and the contributions of "un-natural" (human-induced) causes are being realized. Kappelle, Van Vuuren and Baas write that "global climate change is one of the most contentious topics in environmentalism, ecology and politics" (1999, p. 1385).

Raschke clearly and concisely summarizes that the greenhouse effect

> is caused by all those atmospheric gases which are vary transparent to solar radiation but absorb very effectively the thermal infrared radiation and re-emit it at there own temperature. These are all minor constituents in the atmosphere—water vapor, carbon dioxide, methane, nitrous oxide, and several carbon fluorochlorides. There are now more than 30 gas species under consideration, most of which are entirely of anthropogenic origin.
>
> (2001, p. 794)

While these greenhouse gases (GHG) make possible the "warm" temperatures on earth, increasing the amount of GHG raises temperature of the earth by "enhancing" this greenhouse effect (Collins & Storfer, 2003; Karoly et al., 2003).

Two questions are front and center on the scientific debate of climate change—detection and attribution (Loehle, 2004). Unlike relatively straightforward instrumental measures, detection of behavioral changes in systems which have demonstrated variability across timescales is inherently challenging (Loehle, 2004). Investigations of climate change have utilized numerous indices and approaches in an attempt to detect changes in the climate of the earth. The second question of attribution is somewhat more vexing as it requires the establishment of alterations beyond "normal" climatic variability that are due to a specific cause. The sharp increase in emissions of GHG by the human population since industrialization has prompted many scientists to investigate human activities as the primary reason for global warming. While determining human responsibility for climate change with absolute certainty was contentious for some time, the most recent report by the Intergovernmental Panel on Climate Change (IPCC) asserts that system warming is unequivocal and very likely (more than a 90% chance) due to human activities (IPCC, 2007).

Determining precise consequences from such global hypotheses is difficult due to their inherent complexity, direct and indirect nature, and the considerable timespan over which the consequences may become manifest (Collins & Storfer, 2003). Collins and Storfer recognize that "global change may affect a region directly, or change in one region may initiate a string of events that alters habitats far from the source" (2003, p. 93). In broad terms, the effects of climate change are serious and future predictions of impacts range from interruption to catastrophic (United Nations Framework Convention on Climate Change, 2007). Projected potential impacts include: increases in temperature more than twice the amount in the last century; rises in sea levels; reduction and elimination of ice shields and glaciers; increases in severe storms and events; extinction of many endangered species due to habitat alterations; and, extension of some vector-borne diseases (United Nations Framework Convention on Climate Change, 2007). Box 3.1 explores the potential impacts of climate change on outdoor recreation.

BOX 3.1 CLIMATE CHANGE AND OUTDOOR RECREATION

Alterations to Earth's climate will have a profound effect on the resource base upon which outdoor recreation relies as well as directly influencing particular outdoor activities. It is important to acknowledge that "only limited understanding about potential climatic influences on outdoor recreation has emerged, and much of that is more accurately described as informed opinion than as science" (Irland et al., 2001, p. 758). With this caution in mind, the potential consequences of climate change in outdoor recreation are likely to be substantive. Given the increased frequency and magnitude of extreme events, Sasidharan, Yarnal, Yarnal and Godbey (2001) argue that climate will increase in importance to outdoor recreation. Irland et al. (2001) observe that the effect of climate on outdoor recreation will be both direct and indirect. The extension of season length is given as an example of a direct effect. Indirect effects change the resource base which, in turn, alters outdoor recreation activities. Changing water levels which affect the quality of boating are given as an example of an indirect effect.

The effects of climate change on outdoor recreation are also not universal as some outdoor recreation activities may benefit while others may be eliminated all together, as shown in Table 10.1. In investigating the implications of climate change on visitors' willingness to pay at Rocky Mountain National Park both temperature and precipitation were found to be significant determinants with recreation benefits under two scenarios (Ricaardson & Loomis, 2005). Activities most vulnerable are those which rely on "fragile" or specific resources such as the coral reefs. Irland et al. (2001) recognize that cold-water fisheries are a key issue as increasing temperatures will reduce both the required habitat for, and populations of, species such as trout. Although cold-water species are expected to experience the greatest amount of loss, other cool- and warm-water species (e.g., smallmouth bass) are also likely to be affected (Michaels, Humphrey, Bell, Camacho & Funk, 1995). In investigating the economic impact that climate change would have on freshwater recreational fishing it is estimated that 80–95 million dollars (USD) in damages will result (Michaels et al., 1995). The ski industry has been the most frequently investigated outdoor recreation activity in respect to climate change.

Studies have also attempted to determine the sensitivity of outdoor recreation to climate change as well as postulate potential coping responses. Loomis and Crespi (1999) have used various models to estimate the effects of climate change on recreational visits and values and found that some activities increased and others decreased. Irland et al. (2001) and Sasidharan et al. (2001) both observe that climate change will prompt shifts in some outdoor recreation activities, and that it is the manner in which adaptation to these circumstances occurs that is paramount. Sasidharan et al. stress that "most important, parks and recreation areas that lack experienced managers, who are aware of the range of negative and positive possibilities associated with climate and social change, will find it difficult to survive" (2001, p. 4).

The scope and severity of climate change has prompted cooperation among national governments. The United Nations Framework on Climate Change was initiated in 1994 and aims to share information among the 189 member countries, introduce national strategies and promote knowledge transfer, and prepare for adaptation (United Nations Framework Convention on Climate Change, 2006). In 1997 the first international treaty on curbing emissions was developed in Kyoto, Japan (the Kyoto Protocol). The most recent United Nations Climate Change Conference was held in Nairobi in 2006, where the Kyoto Protocol continues to be amended (Linkages, 2006; United Nations Framework Convention on Climate Change, 2006).

Trends in Outdoor Recreation Supply

While various landscape features were used to illustrate the supply of outdoor recreation resources, observations concerning changes over time are particularly informative and critical to the future of these resources. The NORSIS system in the United States has allowed Cordell and Betz (2000) to comment on supply trends. From their assessment, considerable increases in the supply of outdoor recreation resources occurred from the ORRRC initiatives in the 1960s and 1970s at the federal level until the 1980s and 1990s, at which time declining budgets have plateaued or decreased prompting uncertainty about service and inclusive accessibility.

Cordell and Betz (2000) also observe advances in supply at both the state and municipal levels, but contend that similar financial pressures are also appearing at these levels. Although the private sector has greatly increased the proportion of goods and services, the future trends in supply by this sector are highly dependent upon the continued provision of publicly supplied resources as well as needing to address accessibility issues on private lands (Cordell & Betz, 2000). This leads Cordell and Betz to state:

> our interpretation of the most salient trends in the US supply system leads us to conclude that its sustainability is stressed and in many ways threatened. Continuing but slow growth in the land and water area managed by federal, state and local government; flat budgets at all three levels to take care of existent and added land and water area and greater reliance on nonappropriated sources for funding and staffing the system's operation and maintenance are not characteristic of a vigorous and healthy system. In the face of continuing and, in some places, very rapid population expansion, these trends quickly translate into substantial decreases in the per capita capacity of the American outdoor recreation supply system.
>
> (2000, p. 89)

The supply of outdoor recreation is more broadly under pressure from the multitude of issues concerning the integrity of natural ecosystems. Considerable awareness of these issues was raised by the World Commission on Environment and Development (WCED) in 1987 with publication of *Our Common Future*. Despite ongoing attempts to reconcile sustainability with development, environmental dilemmas continue. Environmental impacts from leisure-related activities (e.g., outdoor recreation, tourism) are substantial and contribute to transformations in land cover and use, utilization of energy and development impacts, distribution and loss of species, spreading of diseases, and alterations in environmental perceptions (Gössling, 2002). Resource opportunities are further diminished by the widespread trend of privatization (Goldman, 1998). Climate change poses an additional challenge to the supply of outdoor recreation worldwide.

SUMMARY

The natural environment is an essential element for outdoor recreation. This chapter opened with a discussion of environmental philosophy and described some of the major perspectives towards the natural environment held by humans. Environmental philosophy is a cornerstone of outdoor recreation because it involves both the pursuit of knowledge regarding the environment as well as moral and ethical questions between humans and the environment. The second portion of the chapter developed knowledge about how the natural environment functions. Ecology was used as a central theme to discuss living elements, non-living elements, and ecological processes. The concept of a resource was utilized in the final portion of this chapter to direct attention to the subjective way in which assign elements of the environment are assigned merit. Resources that provide opportunities for outdoor recreation exhibit specific attributes, which can be conceptualized along a continuum of human modification. Classification schemes developed to inventory the supply of outdoor recreation resources were critically reviewed. A general discussion of important landscape features highlighted some of the extensive terrestrial and aquatic resources for outdoor recreation. Implications of climate change and emerging trends in supply are concerning for the future of outdoor recreational resources.

KEY CONCEPTS

Anthropocentric	Environmental philosophy
Climate change	Landscape features (terrestrial and aquatic)
Continuum of outdoor recreational resources	Recreational resources
Ecocentric	Resources
Ecology	Supply of recreational resources
Ecosystem	

SUGGESTED KEY SOURCES FOR MORE INFORMATION

Belshaw, C. (2001). *Environmental philosophy: Reason, nature and human concern.* Montreal: McGill-Queen's University Press.

Ecology and society http://www.ecologyandsociety.org

Intergovernmental panel on climate change http://www.ipcc.ch

Leopold, A. (1966) *A sand county almanac.* New York: Ballantine Books. (Original work published 1949.)

Loomis, J. & Crespi, J. (1999). Estimated effects of climate change on selected outdoor recreation activities in the United States. In R. Mendelsonn and J. E. Newman (Eds.), *The impact of climate change in the United States economy* (pp. 289–314). Cambridge: Cambridge University Press.

Miller, G. T., Jr. (1996). *Living in the environment: Principles, connections and solutions* (9th ed). Belmont: Wadsworth.

Mitchell, B. (1989). *Geography and resource analysis* (2nd ed.). London: Longman.

Society and natural resources www.tandf.co.uk

WCED (1987). *Our common future.* New York: Oxford University Press.

Worster, D. (1994). *Nature's economy: A history of ecological ideas* (2nd ed.). New York: The Press Syndicate of the University of Cambridge.

REVIEW QUESTIONS

1. What is environmental philosophy?
2. Compare and contrast anthropocentric and biocentric perspectives towards the environment.
3. Define the term outdoor recreation resource. Provide an example.
4. What is ecology?
5. Identify and describe the three basic components of all ecosystems.
6. Explain how ecosystems tend towards equilibrium and are dynamic.

7. Describe the challenges in identifying the supply of outdoor recreation resources.
8. What attributes are desirable for outdoor recreation resources?
9. How might climate change influence outdoor recreation?
10. Explain why the supply of outdoor recreation resources is coming under increasing pressure.

Chapter 4

Social Psychology and Outdoor Recreation

OBJECTIVES

This chapter will:

- introduce the social-psychology approach to studying leisure;
- examine individual cognitions that influence participation in outdoor recreation;
- explore the social setting in which outdoor recreation occurs;
- provide insights on how the natural environment influences human behavior;
- offer explanations for outdoor recreation behaviors;
- document benefits of participation.

INTRODUCTION

Outdoor recreation is first and foremost a feature of human societies and a form of behavior. Why do you participate in outdoor recreation? Why do you prefer one specific type of outdoor recreation activity? Why are outdoor recreation experiences sometimes not satisfying? Social psychology has emerged within social science as a way to examine leisure as a form of human behavior and answer such questions. This chapter begins with a succinct overview of the social psychology approach and subsequently explores three emerging themes. The first theme focuses on the individual or person and examines motivation, personality and satisfaction. The influence of social factors on participation in outdoor recreation follows at both individual and societal scales. It is acknowledged that including the latter crosses into the domain of sociology. Such inclusion is warranted due to the relative proximity of the perspectives and the amount of attention outdoor recreation has received at the societal level. The third theme explores how individuals interact with the environment. Theories that, to varying degrees, integrate the previous themes to explain important aspects of outdoor recreation behavior are subsequently presented. Benefits accrued from outdoor recreation participation are documented at the close of the chapter.

THE SOCIAL-PSYCHOLOGY APPROACH

French poet Paul Valéry wrote that "the purpose of psychology is to give us a completely different idea of the things we know best" (as cited in Goldstein, 1994, p. 4). Psychology emerged as a social science at the end of the nineteenth century and aims to go beyond the collection of facts to develop general explanations of behavior as well as to understand the influences which prompt individuals to act (Goldstein, 1994; Mannell & Kleiber, 1997). Leisure has garnered considerable attention from the discipline of psychology (e.g., Csikszentmihalyi, 1975, 1990; Piaget, 1951). Iso-Ahola makes clear this applicability when he argues that:

> to understand the essence of the true meaning of leisure is to understand why people participate (or fail to participate) and what they strive to get for their involvement. Because an individual is a psychological being, the ultimate explanation of leisure behaviour has to be psychological.
>
> (1999, p. 35)

Social psychology developed as a subfield of psychology during the early twentieth century due to the emerging interest in individual behaviors and social influences (Mannell & Kleiber, 1997). It shares psychology's aim to understand and develop theories of human behavior, yet it is also interested in social context. Social psychology therefore refers to "the scientific study of the way in which people's thoughts, feelings, and behaviours are influenced by the real or imagined presence of other people" (Aronson, Wilson, Akert & Fehr, 2001, p. 6).

Competing approaches have emerged within social-psychology that attempt to explain human behavior. Mannell and Kleiber (1997, pp. 19–25) identify and describe the following three general categories. The stimulus–response approach focuses on the situation or circumstances prompting the particular behavior. Behaviorism, the most extreme form of this approach, solely focuses on actual or observable behavior to the exclusion of other considerations. The organism–response approach focuses on characteristics that are internal (e.g., attitudes) to explain both the consistent behavior of individuals in various situations as well as differences among people. The third category is the stimulus–organism–response (or interactionism) which considers both the situation as well as the person. Acknowledging these categories is valuable to gain an appreciation for the diversity of approaches employed within a relatively well-defined area of knowledge.

Leisure has emerged as a relatively new and specialized subfield of social psychology (Mannell & Kleiber, 1997). Although application of social psychology to leisure behavior coincided with the origin of the subfield and there have been many studies of leisure behavior from this perspective, relatively few efforts have comprehensively and systematically addressed this knowledge area. Three contributions are noteworthy in this regard as they have greatly enhanced understanding of leisure behavior—*Psychology of Leisure: Research Approaches to the Study of Leisure* (Neulinger, 1981, 2nd ed.), *The Social Psychology of Leisure and Recreation* (Iso-Ahola, 1980), and *A social psychology of leisure* (Mannell & Kleiber, 1997).

Central to this chapter is the social-psychology approach to leisure. Mannell and Kleiber explain that "the social psychology of leisure is the scientific study of the leisure behaviour and experience of individuals in social situations" (1997, p. 25). Iso-Ahola was one of the first to apply this approach to leisure behavior. He observed that "social psychology examines leisure and recreation in terms of (1) an individual and his personal cognitions, (2) the social context where behaviour is observed, (3) the time at which the behaviour occurs, and (4) the physical environment where behaviour occurs" (Iso-Ahola, 1980, p. 275). The contemporary social-psychological approach to leisure builds upon these initial research directions and aims to: utilize the scientific method though systematic means; direct attention to the individual as a level of analysis and is therefore interested in social worlds as experienced by the individual; involve inquiries about the leisure experience and behavior as observed and subjectively defined; and, examine the social context in which leisure occurs including other people, larger society, and environmental influences (Mannell & Kleiber, 1997).

Further areas of focus are evident even within the already specialized area of social psychology of leisure. Attention is directed at specific forms of leisure behaviour such as serious leisure (e.g., Stebbins, 1999), women's leisure (e.g., Henderson, 1986), outdoor recreation (e.g., Manning, 1999). The findings of researchers utilizing a social-psychology perspective to examine outdoor recreation are highlighted throughout this chapter.

Outdoor Recreation and the Individual

Social psychology focuses attention on the individual as a level of analysis. It is particularly concerned with individual cognitions (thoughts, feelings and perceptions) that influence behavior. These cognitions largely cannot be observed because they occur inside the mind. Elements most closely aligned with these individual cognitions include attitudes and values, motivations, and satisfaction.

Attitude

If you are reading this book chances are fairly good that you have a positive attitude about outdoor recreation. Perhaps you are especially passionate about a particular activity or more generally feel positive about the opportunity to spend time outdoors. Such feelings may be referred to as attitude. Fishbein and Ajzen explain that "attitude can be described as a learned pre-disposition to respond in a consistently favourable or unfavourable manner with respect to a given object" (1975, p. 6). Important qualities of attitudes include consistency, predisposition or underlying features which guide behaviors, and learning (Fishbein & Ajzen, 1975). These feelings, consciously or subconsciously, represent an evaluation towards a situation. Attitudes may have a cognitive (weighting of factors based on beliefs), affective (emotions and values), and behavioral (observations of how you behave) basis and consequently produce a given feeling (positive, negative or neutral) about something (Aronson et al., 2001).

Participation in outdoor activities and knowledge of environmental issues play key roles in formulating attitudes about outdoor recreation. Participation in activities has been found to determine the likelihood that particular attitudes will be held by an individual. Daigle,

Hrubes and Ajzen (2002) focused on attitudes related to hunting as an outdoor recreation pursuit. Through questionnaires they examined how a variety of people (hunters, wildlife viewers and recreationists) felt about hunting and the perceived benefits from the activity. Their findings show that hunters held a positive attitude towards the perceived benefits of hunting, whereas wildlife viewers and recreationists did not have a positive attitude towards the perceived benefits (Daigle et al., 2002). Attitudes also affected participation in activities. Cordell, Green and Betz (2002) studied the connection between outdoor recreation participation and environmental attitudes of Americans. They found that "across the diversity of Americans a number of statistically significant associations may be observed between recreation activity choices and environmental attitudes" (Cordell et al., 2002, p. 36). Gaining knowledge about a particular subject has also been found to influence attitudes. In a study of university students, it was found that those enrolled in a recreation and park management course held more positive attitudes towards the environment than students registered in other disciplines (Thapa, 2001).

The relative strength with which an attitude is held is an important additional consideration. A number of factors determine the strength of an attitude including ambivalence, accessibility, ability to relate to the experience, and personal recall (Aronson et al., 2001). Strength is important because it is directly related to the attitude change—the weaker feelings are about the entity the easier the attitude can be changed. Take the example of a first-year university student who enrolls in an introductory outdoor recreation class because it fits into his/her schedule. In addition to being rather ambivalent about the subject of outdoor recreation, he/she does not have access or means to pursue outdoor recreation, doesn't really know much about what outdoor recreation involves and has no personal experience with outdoor recreation activities. Consequently, the experience in the course is more likely to shape his/her attitude (positively or negatively) about outdoor recreation than if he/she entered the course with an intense attitude about the subject. The correlation between knowledge and attitude is particularly interesting. Hanna (1995), for example, found that people with significant ecological knowledge were more likely to care about the wilderness than those with relatively little ecological knowledge. Such research has profound implications for outdoor educators and interpreters who strive to increase understanding of the natural environment.

Although an individual may have a particular feeling or attitude about an activity, it does not necessarily translate into participation or advocacy. Intervening factors may include subjective norms, perceived amount of control and lack of opportunity. The process by which feelings transfer into behavior and manner in which other factors intervene are presented later in the chapter.

Motivation

Motivation is an internal factor which prompts purposeful or goal-oriented action. An individual may experience numerous and mixed motivations which sometimes conflict. Motivations result from internal (e.g., memories) and external (e.g., physical environment such as a forest) stimuli and give direction (goals chosen to pursue), intensity (amount of effort exerted), and persistence (length of effort exerted) to an action (Iso-Ahola, 1999). Understanding motivations is inherently difficult. Iso-Ahola (1999) identifies that the greatest challenge to understanding motivations is that they cannot be observed. Researchers are therefore forced to rely upon individuals to report their motivations or to make inferences from observations of actual participation. The following paragraphs introduce approaches to understanding motivations for leisure and then focus on specific applications employed in outdoor recreation.

Early motivational theories were rooted in biology. Motivations were viewed as a consequence of genetic predisposition or deficiency within an organism. Although largely dismissed because this proposition failed to explain the behavior of particular people, Ellis (1973) employed the idea of instinct into leisure studies with the notion of play. The related idea of drive was also introduced in early motivational theories. Drive is "an internal state of tension that motivates behaviours capable of alleviating that tension" (Goldstein, 1994, p. 446). In this manner drive is associated with physiological responses as well as learning processes to satisfy the drive. Enduring questions remain from this approach as it failed to account for the continued presence of a drive after the action had occurred, the desire to go beyond drive satisfaction, and the explanation for people to work hard, rather than to just satisfy drives (Goldstein, 1994).

Unlike the biologically determined approaches to motivation, the humanistic approach involves the concept of human choice and desire for fulfillment (Goldstein, 1994). The humanistic approach is optimistic about human nature as it considers humans to be responsible for their own actions (present) while influenced by their past experiences (e.g., traumatic childhood experiences) (Baron, Earhard & Ozier, 1998). Carl Rogers, working from this tradition, viewed motivation according to positive personality characteristics and traits which humans demonstrated throughout their lives as they progressed towards being "fully functioning persons" (Baron et al., 1998, p. 500).

One of the most notable works from the humanistic perspective is Abraham Maslow's general theory of motivation. The basis for his theory is the concept of need fulfilment. Maslow (1970) identifies five basic human needs (physiological, safety, love, esteem, and self-actualization) and arranges them into a hierarchy, illustrated in Figure 4.1. Needs necessary for human survival are located towards the bottom of the pyramid while psychological needs are located in the upper portion. According to Maslow (1970), each level of need must, at least partially, be fulfilled before an individual attempts to fulfill the next level of needs. He further explains that physiological and safety needs (e.g., food, thirst, shelter) must be satisfied before an individual is motivated to search for belonging, esteem, and intellectual stimulation. This model has been utilized by leisure scholars to investigate the relative importance of leisure as well as to document opportunities that leisure provides for self-actualization (Mannell & Kleiber, 1997). Although such a general theory of motivation is intuitively appealing, many challenges have been identified. Critics of Maslow's work charge that empirical evidence fails to support the hierarchy claims because specific classification of achieving self-actualization is difficult (if not impossible) to measure, some people skip lower stages in the hierarchy and it fails to account for social influences (Goldstein, 1994; Iso-Ahola, 1980; Mannell & Kleiber, 1997).

Iso-Ahola (1980) focuses more specifically on motivation for leisure behavior and proposes a model which illustrates (Figure 4.2) multiple levels of causality and accounts for

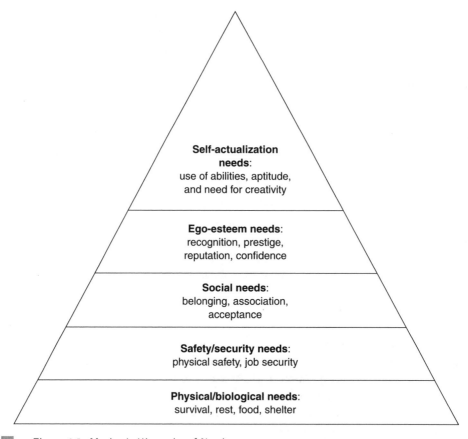

Figure 4.1 Maslow's Hierarchy of Needs.

influences from the general social environment as well as situational influences. Iso-Ahola (1980) likens motivation for leisure to that of an iceberg of which only the top portion is visible. He argues that motivations for leisure may be apparent at the upper levels, but these are a function of biological dispositions and socialization which shape personality and by extension future leisure activity. Biological disposition and socialization also influence the optimal amount of stimulation (arousal) which people seek and therefore diversity of leisure activities. The desire to realize intrinsic rewards is central to the third causal level as individuals seek behavior which is self-determined and provides an opportunity to realize competencies. Leisure needs are located at the pinnacle of the pyramid and constitute the reasons for which people have chosen to participate in a particular activity. By differentiating four causal levels for leisure Iso-Ahola (1980) recognizes that such behavior is complex, caused by both unconscious and conscious needs and requires various explanations. Mannell and Kleiber (1997) assert that this model explains why people may be unaware of their motivation to pursue particular activities. As a reflection of the social-psychological tradition, the model also accounts for the influence of social environments and situational factors. In a subsequent work Iso-Ahola (1999) explains that humans do not have a physio-

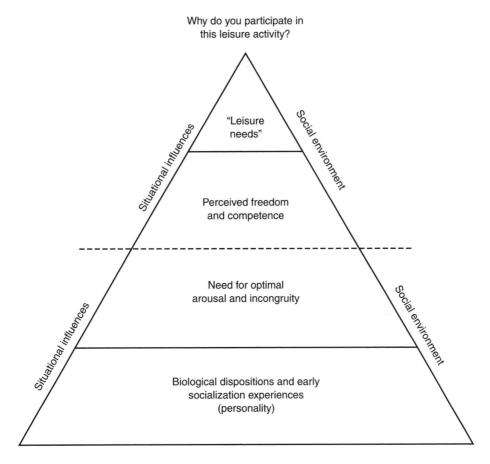

Figure 4.2 Levels of Causality of Leisure Behavior.

logical need for leisure in the same way as other basic requirements; however, he argues that leisure should be considered a social need of humans to achieve balance and quality of life.

Another theory that explains participation using motivation is expectancy theory. Expectancy theory (also termed "self-fulfilling prophecy") is the idea that certain behaviors will yield certain rewards (Quick, 1988; Solomon, 2002). It is premised on the assumption that a reward yielded by a particular behavior is of value and that the reward will be gained as an outcome of participation (Quick, 1988). Expectancy theory intuitively makes sense as a person engages in a behavior to achieve an expected outcome. Individuals may choose to run because they expect to gain better health. The self-fulfilling nature of expectancy theory stems from evidence that suggests if a certain reward is anticipated from a recreational activity the participant is more likely to exert effort to achieve the reward (Unger, Evans, Rourke & Levis, 2003). Expected outcomes also do not always have to be positive as behaviors can result from negative rewards as well. Unger et al. (2003) argue that is it possible to engage in a specific behavior in order to avoid an expected outcome.

There is relative agreement among leisure scholars that despite the large number of potential reasons or expectations reported to undertake leisure, a small number actually operate (Mannell & Kleiber, 1997). In this regard they recognize work by Iso-Ahola (1989) in which he reduces motivation for leisure behavior into two dimensions of seeking and escaping, as illustrated in Figure 4.3. Iso-Ahola (1989) contends that an individual's motivation to participate in a particular leisure activity may be simultaneously explained by the potential for both escape (change from both personal and interpersonal daily environments) and opportunities (search for optimal arousal). Iso-Ahola (1989) describes these opportunities as psychological satisfactions (intrapersonal or social) that people seek. Take the example of a business executive who participates in a backcountry hiking experience. Her motivation for participation may be explained as she wants to escape her personal (pressure from deadlines) and interpersonal (co-workers and constant meetings) environments while also intrinsically desiring to develop competence (personal reward) in backcountry travel with a few close friends (interpersonal reward). While considering motivation for leisure activities in such a way may be intuitively appealing, Mannell and Kleiber (1997) suggest that the utility of such an approach is limited because it fails to identify specific leisure needs and available need-satisfactions available.

Specific interest in determining motivations for outdoor recreation began to develop in the 1960s and has since progressed significantly (Manning, 1999). In outdoor recreation, a behavioral approach has received considerable attention. The behavioral approach builds upon earlier efforts in social psychology (e.g., Maslow's hierarchy of needs and expectancy theory) and outdoor recreation, which focused exclusively on activity and experience elements, to examine both why participation occurs as well as the potential benefits (Jackson, 1989; Manning, 1999). The basis of this approach was developed by Driver and Tocher (1970, p. 10) who describe the following five non-mutually exclusive postulates:

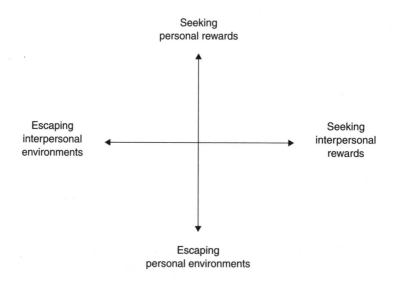

Figure 4.3 Seeking and Escaping Dimensions of Leisure Motivation.

Source: adapted from Iso-Ahola, 1989.

1. recreation is an experience that results from recreation engagements;
2. recreational engagements require a commitment by the recreationist;
3. recreation engagements are self-rewarding: the engagement finds pleasure in and of itself, and recreation is the experience;
4. recreation engagements require personal and free choice on the part of the recreationist;
5. recreational engagements occur during non-obligated time.

This shift in perspective is also important because it recognizes that the individual derives benefits from the experience and that outdoor recreation planners may influence the manner in which goals are achieved (Driver & Tocher, 1970). Driver (1972) subsequently identifies that psychologists have historically had limited involvement in recreation research and appeals for their greater involvement.

The behavioral approach contends that actions are specifically selected or directed by goals and/or expected outcomes (Jackson, 1989; Manning, 1999). Manning (1999) builds upon this central idea and the compendium of empirical studies undertaken. He identifies four levels or hierarchies of demand related to outdoor recreation, as illustrated in Table 4.1. Activities (level one) represent the traditional approach to understanding outdoor recreation and reveal little about why the activity was undertaken. Settings (level two) directly relate to motivations (level three) through expectancy theory. Settings are selected because it is perceived that they will facilitate the obtainment of goals (Manning, 1999). In the example (Table 4.1) an individual selects the activity of wilderness hiking. The setting in which this activity occurs is important as it relates directly to the motivation of obtaining the intended goals of challenge and risk taking. The final level considers the benefits from the experience, although Manning (1999) cautions that these are difficult to gauge as a direct consequence of outdoor recreation.

Table 4.1 Four Levels or Hierarchies of Demand for Outdoor Recreation

Level	Example 1	Example 2
1. Activities	Wilderness hiking	Family picnicking
2. Settings		
A. Environmental setting	Rugged terrain	Grass fields
B. Social setting	Few people	No boisterous teenagers
C. Managerial setting	No restrictions	Picnic tables
3. Motivations	Risk-taking challenge, physical exercise	In-group affiliation, change of pace
4. Benefits		
A. Personal	Enhanced self-esteem	Enhanced personal health
B. Social	Lower crime rate	Family solidarity
C. Economic	Lower health care costs	Increased work production
D. Environmental	Increased commitment to conservation	Higher quality environment

Source: adapted from Haas et al., 1980.

From his comprehensive review of studies of motivation in outdoor recreation, Manning observes that "motivations for outdoor recreation—indeed, motivations even within a single outdoor activity—are diverse and can be related to the attitude, preferences, and expectations of users" (1999, p. 162). The complex and inter-related nature of motivations in outdoor recreation continues to capture the interest of researchers. Specific investigation of response items used in the behavioral approach have isolated differences in motivations, identified specific motivation domains, and resulted in the development of the Recreation Experience Preference Scales and Domain (Manfredo, Driver & Tarrant, 1996). Additional attention has been directed at segmenting participants with similar motivations in an effort to understand the relationship between motivation and other user characteristics (Manning, 1999). Implications from such inquiries are important for resource managers concerned with individual satisfaction.

Satisfaction

The concept of satisfaction is closely associated with motivation in the social psychology approach to leisure studies as it can be addressed at multiple scales and as either a need or an evaluative item (Mannell & Kleiber, 1997). Satisfaction as a need has been introduced above. This section focuses on the concept of satisfaction as a source of evaluation in outdoor recreation. Satisfaction refers to the degree of congruency between the actual experience of individuals and their aspirations or expectations (Mannell & Kleiber, 1997; Manning, 1999).

Objective measures of quality do not exist in leisure studies (Mannell & Kleiber, 1997). Unlike other areas of study that have impartial measures (e.g., environmental integrity for ecologists) of success, both outdoor recreation participants and managers strive for quality experiences. Using satisfaction as an evaluative item is challenging because it depends on the expectations held by an individual prior to participation. Take the example of fishing. As an angler you may expect to catch fish. Are you still satisfied with your outdoor recreation experience if you do not catch fish? In one of the earliest motivation studies in outdoor recreation, Bultena and Taves (1961) found that angler satisfaction was actually linked to a diverse number of motivations.

The concept of satisfaction is particularly complex in outdoor recreation due to the number and diversity of potential influences and fluctuating environmental conditions. Manning (1999) has conceptualized overall satisfaction in outdoor recreation to be influenced by situational variables and mediated via subjective evaluations made by participants, as illustrated in Figure 4.4. This builds upon the work of Whisman and Hollenhurst (1998) who found that overall satisfaction by whitewater boaters was influenced directly by subjective factors and indirectly by situational factors. Situational variables encompass the various circumstances in which outdoor recreation occurs. Subjective factors are "affective" and pertain to how a participant views the relevant situational variables (e.g., perception of a social setting as crowded) (Manning, 1999; Whisman & Hollenhurst, 1998). In considering these variables together it is clear that satisfaction in outdoor recreation is a multi-dimensional concept.

Although satisfaction is important to both participants and managers of outdoor

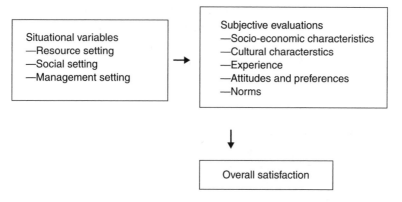

Figure 4.4 Model for Recreation Satisfaction.
Source: adapted from Whisman & Hollenhurst, 1998.

recreation, its complex and multi-dimensional nature raises many issues. Manning (1999) identifies that the concept of satisfaction itself is:

1. too general to be of use to outdoor recreation managers;
2. relative and open to considerable interpretation;
3. not alone an appropriate measure of quality as it may undermine resource and social integrity; and,
4. not measured in a standardized manner.

Despite these issues, outdoor recreation may contribute to the leisure satisfaction of an individual and in so doing enhance their quality of life. Leisure is optimally viewed when it is intrinsic, related to feelings of competency, and more likely to produce satisfaction if it is active (Iso-Ahola, 1980). These features are revisited later in the chapter in the discussion of flow.

Social Influences and Outdoor Recreation Behaviors

A second theme of the social psychology approach is the social setting in which behavior occurs. The importance of social influences on the leisure behavior of individuals is well-recognized (Ibrahim & Cordes, 2002; Iso-Ahola, 1980; Mannell & Kleiber, 1997; Manning, 1999). This section is divided into two parts—social influences on the individual and societal–individual influences.

Social Influences on the Individual

The first part of this section directs attention to social influences on individuals. Using the individual as a scale of analysis is consistent with the general social-psychology tradition and leisure studies (Mannell & Kleiber, 1997). Areas discussed include socialization, norms, and the life course. Investigations of these topics using the social-psychology approach have been fruitful for leisure study scholars in general, while some topics have received relatively little attention from those specifically interested in outdoor recreation. Inferences to outdoor recreation are consequently offered where appropriate in lieu of empirical research.

Socialization

Socialization focuses on the manner by which individuals learn (formally and informally) and the efforts by which social agents influence these processes (Miller, 1993). While socialization is of general interest, leisure studies scholars have recognized that:

> most variability in leisure behavior is attributable to how such inclinations are responded to and reinforced by the society in which children live. This process, by which children acquire motives, attitudes, values, and skills that affect their leisure choices, behavior and experiences throughout their lives, is referred to as socialization into leisure.
>
> (Mannell & Kleiber, 1997, p. 226)

Iso-Ahola (1980) specifically applies the process of socialization to leisure. The basic tenants of his conceptualization are illustrated in Figure 4.5. In this model the importance of social and cultural forces to socialization are recognized as boundaries to the entire process. These forces (discussed later under the heading of ethnicity) influence what experiences are available (repertoire of individual experiences) as well as societal norms regarding activities (via social agents). Social agents are particularly important because they further shape what experiences an individual is introduced to as well as his or her perceived competence in an activity. Ibrahim and Cordes (2002) classify groups of social agents as being either primary or secondary to this process. Primary groups include dyads (intimate relationship or friendships), family and peers. Secondary groups include schools, club/organizations, and other entities. Although the nature of the family is changing (see Godbey, 1999), it remains one of the most important agents for socialization as it provides both physical requirements as well as social space for outdoor recreation pursuits (Ibrahim & Cordes, 2002). Secondary groups of social agents are also critical as "there is sufficient evidence to conclude that outdoor/environmental education programs have the potential to produce benefits for both the participants and society" (Bammel & Burrus-Bammel, 1990, pp. 52–53). Participation (leisure involvement) in Iso-Ahola's (1980) model is the outcome of self-determination and perceived competence. Therefore, socialization represents an ongoing process by which feedback from involvement in a particular leisure activity further influences the social agents, the leisure repertoire, and the perceived competence. The nature of this relationship is indicated by the dashed lines in Figure 4.5. Iso-Ahola (1980) further asserts that the process of socialization is ongoing and ultimately leads to enhancement of an individual's social competence.

The influence of socialization is an important area of outdoor recreation research. In this regard, the specific role of socialization towards outdoor recreation in childhood has been investigated and found to be significantly related to participation in outdoor recreation in later life (Manning, 1999). Early-life experiences have also been found to be among several factors that contribute to environmental attitudes held by individuals (Ewert, Place &

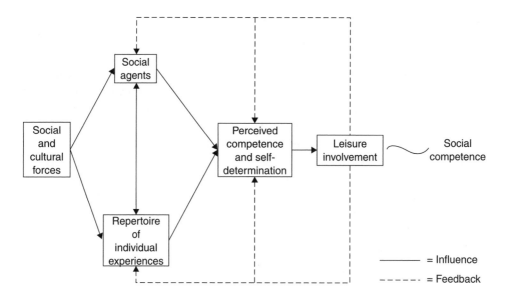

Figure 4.5 Process of Leisure Socialization.

Sibthorp, 2005). Specific investigations have also been conducted regarding how socialization relates to participation. In one of the more recent studies of the effects of socialization, Bixler and Morris (1998) found that those individuals who canoed and kayaked in their youth accumulated considerable outdoor capital (outdoor experiences) which positively influenced adoption of these specific activities as well as general backcountry experiences.

Norms

The influence of social agents on outdoor recreation extends beyond the process of socialization. Outdoor recreation behavior as a function of the social group in which one is a member was observed in the context of hunting by Burch (1964). The importance of social groups to outdoor recreation has changed very little since as "this finding has been consistently corroborated for most outdoor recreation areas and activities" (Manning, 1999, p. 32).

Social psychology has conceptualized such social influences on the individual using the idea of subjective norms. Subjective norms are considered to be "people's belief about how those they care about will view the behaviour in question" (Aronson et al., 2001, p. 245). This appears to be intuitively straightforward as subjective norms recognize the importance given to what an individual believes others think about his/her behavior. Subjective norms have been applied to a number of specific outdoor recreation behaviors. Daigle et al. (2002) have examined norms associated with hunting, wildlife viewing and other outdoor recreation activities. Their findings revealed that wildlife viewers and other outdoor recreationists felt that hunting was unacceptable and that people should not engage in such an activity, while hunters felt that the activity was a perfectly acceptable social norm (Daigle et al.,

2002). Subjective norms have also been demonstrated in less controversial activities by Heywood and Aas (1999). In their study of cross-country skiing in Norway there was a high level of support for controlling dogs while skiing. Subjective norms are also not limited to specific activities. Examination of littering studies by Heywood (2002) revealed that a majority of people who littered felt a high degree of guilt because such actions are considered to be unacceptable by the general public. Therefore, the obligation to not litter while outdoors can be considered a social norm.

Heywood, Manning and Vaske observe that "normative research has made important contributions to our understanding of outdoor recreation behavior and the social and environmental conditions of outdoor recreation settings" (2002, p. 251). This connection to behavior is important as social norms play an integral role in influencing behavior in outdoor recreation (Heywood et al., 2002; Manning, 1999). This influence and the relationship to other key social-psychology concepts (e.g., motivation, attitudes) is expanded using the theory of planned behavior in the final section of this chapter (Aronson et al., 2001; Fishbein & Ajzen, 1975; Manning, 1999).

The normative concept has an additional application or use in outdoor recreation. Manning explains that the norms in this context are understood as "standards that individuals use to evaluate recreation conditions. Personal norms can be aggregated to test for the existence of broader social norms" (1999, p. 152). Normative theory goes beyond the basic idea of subjective norms to actually make estimations or evaluations of acceptability regarding outdoor activities and has received considerable application in outdoor recreation (Heywood et al., 2002; McDonald, 1996; Manning, 1999). Manning (1999) has used the normative approach to establish an acceptable number of encounters among backcountry recreation users. He found that a relatively low number of encounters with other campers is a preferred condition and that backcountry users in general are more sensitive to many normative indicators when compared to their frontcountry counterparts. Manning, Newman, Valliere, Wang and Lawson (2001) have stressed the importance of gauging social norms of visitors and argue that quality standards should be based on these evaluations. This becomes challenging as there are many competing standards that may be used by managers such as legal mandates, agency policy and/or public opinion (Shelby & Vaske, 1991a).

Normative theory, especially as it has been modified to incorporate standards, has important practical implications for outdoor recreation management (Heywood et al., 2002). Methods for assessing norms typically involve asking participants to rate the acceptability of the variable in question. A hypothetical norm curve is illustrated in Figure 4.6. It consists of a line that represents a neutral position and then a range of potential conditions from those which are most acceptable or desired to those which are least acceptable or desired. The normative curve shows the acceptable level of conditions as well as the relative consistency or strength of the social norm. From such information managers are able to make appropriate responses, incorporate such information into future planning and maximize the potential for satisfaction (Manning, 1999; Manning et al., 2001). Despite the broad applications of normative research, conceptual and measurement questions have been raised by McDonald (1996). Stewart and Cole (2003) caution that clear distinctions are required between descriptive information (norms) and prescriptive decisions.

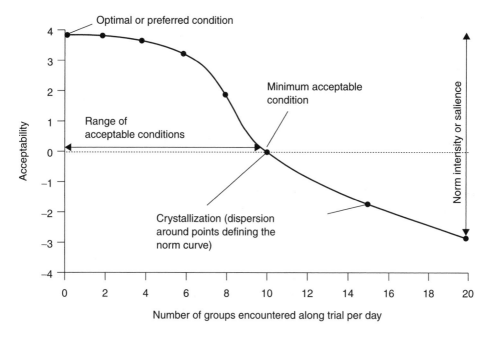

Figure 4.6 *Outdoor Recreation Norm Curve.*

Life Stages

Social psychologists are also interested in how leisure behavior changes with age (Mannell & Kleiber, 1997). This connection is particularly important because participation in some outdoor recreation activities has consistently been found to relate to age (Kelly, 1980; Manning, 1999). From the social-psychology perspective aging consists of a biological process and a changing social context which together influence an individual and his/her leisure behaviors (Mannell & Kleiber, 1997). The relationship between age and leisure is complex and inextricably connected to a host of factors such as motivations, preferences and constraints (Kelly & Freysinger, 2000).

The concept of life stages has been commonly used to approach the issues of participation and changes in leisure activities. Kelly and Freysinger assert that "research has shown that despite increasing expectations to age-graded roles, the vast majority of us continue to acquire, occupy, and leave social roles in a remarkably age-ordered way. Hence, the notion of sequential periods of life remains useful" (2000, p. 114). Discussion of these life stages and their accompanying implications to leisure studies are frequently presented or classified into three stages—the preparation stage, the establishment stage, and the culmination stage (Godbey, 1999; Kelly & Freysinger, 2000; Searle & Brayley, 2000).

The preparation stage includes children and adolescents. Within this stage considerable attention is directed at the universal concept of play as well as childhood influences. Play is recognized by Huizinga (1950) to involve voluntary behavior beyond "ordinary" life, which is bounded (time and space) yet absorbing for the participant. Childhood influences

109

regarding leisure are important because "many of the activities a child is exposed to in early life may be sustained throughout life, or even returned to at later periods" (Searle & Brayley, 2000, p. 228). In addition to broad factors that influence individuals throughout the life course (e.g., gender, culture, race), the maturation process during adolescence is important to identity formation (Kelly & Freysinger, 2000). Values, attitudes and beliefs that form during this time provide the basis upon which individuals generally operate and specifically shape their outlook towards recreation and leisure. Considerable constraints to participation may also be experienced during this life stage (Searle & Brayley, 2000). An individual may want to go skiing but is not yet of age to drive a vehicle and therefore experiences a constraint to participation. The role of leisure and recreation is regarded as significant in the preparation stage because individuals have considerable amounts of leisure time and such activities provide a means to form an identity, socialize and seek acceptance (Godbey, 1999; Searle & Brayley, 2000).

The establishment stage generally coincides with adulthood (around ages 18–21) and extends through until ages 50–55 (Searle & Brayley, 2000). This stage has further been classified to include young adulthood (approximately 20–45) and mid-life years (45–retirement) (Kelly & Freysinger, 2000). During young adulthood individuals attempt to establish themselves in terms of their employment, intimate relationships or families, and social identities (Kelly & Freysinger, 2000). Participation in leisure activities during young adulthood is largely contingent upon lifestyle changes (e.g., career, accommodations, parenthood) made during this time (Godbey, 1999). According to Kelly and Freysinger the shift to "middle adulthood is delineated from other age periods not so much by chronological age as by positions occupied within the different contexts of life—the body, the work career, and the family" (2000, p. 115). Individuals experience both physical and psychological changes in mid-life. Although some of these changes (physical) are unavoidable, evaluation and revision often occurs as a result of contextually based circumstances (e.g., achievement, additional caregiving responsibilities, blended families) (Kelly & Freysinger, 2000). Despite the recent preoccupation with the "mid-life crisis," mid-life is often a fulfilling time (Godbey, 1999).

Although traditionally associated with the retirement age of 65 and beyond, the culmination stage now encompasses periods ranging from pre-retirement to old age (Kelly & Freysinger, 2000; Searle and Brayley, 2000). During the culmination stage of life individuals may experience many demands such as their exit from the workforce, concerns about losses of income and health, and social and cultural beliefs about this stage of life (Kelly & Freysinger, 2000). Despite these challenges, this stage of life has received more attention than any other from leisure researchers. Changes in leisure participation during the culmination stage have been explained using the concepts of withdrawal, active involvement and continuity (Godbey, 1999; Searle & Brayley, 2000). The availability of time and amount of accumulated wealth at this life stage may result in the ability to pursue meaningful leisure activities. However, this trend may not continue in the future. Godbey (1999) observes that the "boomer" generation is unlikely to retire early and will continue to live and participate in the same leisure activities in retirement which they did while working. Many individuals in this stage of life also face considerable constraints as well as limited leisure choices.

The brief summary of changes in the three main stages of life provides a picture of some of the notable influences that individuals may experience. Although many general theories of aging exist, most leisure scholars (e.g., Edginton et al., 1995; Kelly & Freysinger, 2000; Searle & Brayley, 2000) recognize the importance of Iso-Ahola's (1980) work pertaining to changes in leisure that occur throughout the stages of life. Central to his understanding of leisure throughout the life span is the concept of the leisure repertoire. According to Iso-Ahola the "leisure repertoire can be both objective and subjective. The former refers to the quantity of leisure activities and the later to the quality of these pursuits" (1980, p. 174). As an individual progresses through various life stages from birth to mid-life the number of daily leisure activities increases. As a person continues to age their leisure repertoire tends to shrink. This theory of leisure changes throughout the life stages is illustrated in Figure 4.7. Iso-Ahola (1980) contends that this theory holds true for both the number and quality of leisure activities, although it may more accurately reflect the number of activities.

Iso-Ahola (1980) is similarly recognized for his contribution to understanding successful aging. He considers the role(s) of stability and change throughout the life span and illustrates the outcomes of seeking novel and familiar forms of leisure, as shown in Figure 4.8. The strong attachment for the familiar during infancy quickly alters in childhood as the individual starts to seek new experiences. This quest for novelty in leisure activities, as opposed to

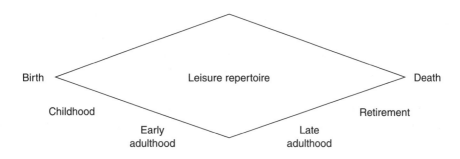

Figure 4.7 Leisure Repertoire.

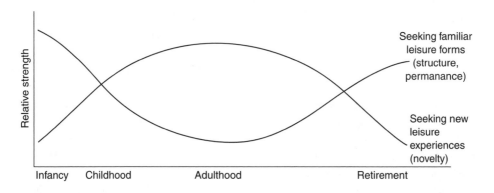

Figure 4.8 Leisure Novelty.

111

those which are familiar, increases in relative strength and broadly peaks at mid-life and then starts to decline. Prior to retirement a greater relative strength is again directed to familiar forms of leisure which offer both structure and permanence. He concludes that "the more a person neglects this aspect of optimal arousal (either for personality or social reasons), the less successful will be his adjustment to the aging process" (Iso-Ahola, 1980, p. 177).

Societal–Individual Influences

The second part of this section pushes the limit of social psychology and crosses into the domain of sociology as it explores societal–individual interactions. It is included here due to the relative proximity of the approach and the substantive amount of work conducted on how societal factors influence participation in outdoor recreation activities. Demographic, subculture and lifestyle considerations are discussed at a societal scale as they correspond to patterns of participation in outdoor recreation.

Demographics

According to Adam Foot, author of the best-selling book *Boom, Bust, or Echo* (1998), almost two-thirds of everything can be explained by the study of demographics. The study of demography uses statistics to examine the structure of a given population to ultimately better understand and/or predict behavior (Foot, 1996). Commonly recognized demographic variables include age, income, sex and occupation (Manning, 1999). Each of these variables is of interest here as they represent societal factors which influence individual behavior.

Interest in social (demographic) factors related to outdoor recreation can be traced back to the ORRRC reports of the 1960s in which "five socioeconomic variables were found to be related to outdoor recreation patterns: age, income, occupation, residence, and stage of family life cycle" (Manning, 1999, p. 25). Numerous studies have since explored the relationship between social characteristics and specific outdoor recreation activities. Hvenegaard (2002), for example, examined the popular activity of birding and found that age and income were directly related to birder specialization. Income is often considered a determining factor for participation in some outdoor recreation activities. More and Stevens (2000) examined changes in user fees for outdoor recreation areas. They found that 23% of low-income users altered their use habits as a result of fee increases, whereas few high-income users altered their participation. Such research reinforces the connection between income and/or wealth and participation. Lee, Scott and Floyd (2001) examined how a host of socio-economic variables affected participation in outdoor recreation activities, including state park visitation. Their findings showed that younger people, with more education and income, were more likely to participate in outdoor recreation. Older individuals, with less education and in a lower socio-economic bracket were less likely to participate (Lee et al., 2001).

Although considerable attention has been exerted to explain participation in outdoor recreation by demographic factors relatively few definitive conclusions can be offered. Demographic information has been used by Foot (1996) as a basis to predict broad changes in Canadian leisure patterns away from physically demanding activities towards more passive pursuits such as birding and gardening. Even in cases where some differences are evident, such as between men and women in traditionally "masculine" activities such as hunting, these differences are equally explained due to the influence of socialization (Kelly, 1980). Synthesizing the compendium of demographic research that has been conducted focusing on outdoor recreation leads Manning to conclude that:

> demographic and socioeconomic variables—for example, income, education, and occupation—are generally not powerful predictors of overall participation in outdoor recreation. However, such variables are often more strongly related to specific outdoor recreation activities. For example, age tends to be inversely related to recreation activities requiring physical strength and endurance while use of backcountry and wilderness areas is directly related to socioeconomic status, especially education.
>
> (1999, p. 46)

In light of the limited effectiveness of demographic variables it is appropriate to reiterate Burdge and Field's (1972) call for broader and more holistic approaches to understanding participation in outdoor recreation. Recent work by Cordell et al. (2002) indicates movement in this direction as they incorporate six socio-demographic factors to examine changing trends in outdoor recreation demand, environmental attitudes and demographics in the United States.

Ethnicity

Attention has also been directed at the coincidence of particular groups within society and participation in outdoor recreation. In this regard, Manning (1999) identifies frequent confusion and incorrect misuse of the terms race (genetic and biological differences), ethnicity (shared culture), and nationality (citizenship of a country). He observes that research in outdoor recreation has focused on differences in recreational patterns among racial or ethnic groups and has attempted to offer explanations for such differences. The term ethnicity best characterizes these studies and refers to "groups of people who share distinguishing characteristics such as religion, language, customs, and ancestry" (Manning, 1999, p. 36).

Inquiries about differences in recreational patterns among groups can again be traced back to the ORRRC studies, which first identified notable differences. Since these initial differences were identified "study findings have been nearly universal in their conclusion that whites participate more often than minority populations (particularly blacks and Hispanics) in traditional outdoor recreation activities" (Manning, 1999, p. 36). Research regarding ethnicity goes beyond the frequency of participation to also reveal differences in leisure preferences. Manning again provides a useful synthesis of existing research in writing that:

> Findings suggest that, compared to whites, minority subcultural groups tend to:
>
> 1. use and prefer "urban-oriented" recreation facilities and services;
> 2. participate in larger groups that often include extended family and friends and comprise more diverse age groups;

113

3. use and prefer more highly developed facilities;
4. participate in activities that are more fitness- and sports-oriented;
5. have a longer length of stay;
6. use areas that are closer to home;
7. use land-based rather than water-based areas;
8. make more intensive use of facilities and services.

(1999, p. 37)

The consistent and pervasive findings documented above establish that outdoor recreation participation occurs mainly by whites and that leisure preferences for many subculture groups do not include outdoor recreation. These findings beg the question as to why? Martin (2004) suggests the existence of a racialized outdoor identity. He bases this assertion on his content analysis of magazine advertisements from 1984 to 2000 which revealed that black models were rarely featured in outdoor settings while whites regularly were. Manning (1999) recognizes the importance of research conducted by Washburne (1978), who suggests that these differences were explained by the existing tension between theories of marginality and ethnicity. Together the theory of marginality, which asserts disadvantages that form barriers to participation (cost, transportation, location) are due to historic discrimination, and the theory of ethnicity, that asserts inherent subcultural values are distinct and therefore result in particular leisure preferences, combine to account for preference and participation in recreation activities. More recently, a third explanation has emerged using the theory of racism. From this perspective, subcultural groups experience discrimination that restricts their participation in outdoor recreation activities (West, 1993). While the more than 30 studies conducted on subcultural differences and outdoor recreation provide various support to each theory above, they more importantly shape the contemporary view that "the relationship between recreation behavior and subcultural factors is complex and can be understood only through consideration of multiple and possibly interrelated influences" (Manning, 1999, p. 39).

Lifestyles

The term lifestyle "refers to the generalized ways people act and consume, that is somewhat more fine grained than subcultures—but more general than specific groups or experiences" (Bradshaw, 1978, p. 2 as cited in Ibrahim & Cordes, 2002). While discussion thus far has addressed demographic factors and ethnic considerations, most individuals also identify with a particular societal belief system (Ibrahim, 1991). Identification with a particular belief system moves beyond a single variable to encompass gender, income, and psychographic variables which become manifest through dress, language, and actions (Edginton et al., 1995). The combination of all these factors is encompassed by the concept of lifestyle.

In their discussion of social factors influencing participation in outdoor recreation, Ibrahim and Cordes (2002) recognize the historical importance of Mitchell's (1983) work pertaining to lifestyles in the domain of outdoor recreation. Mitchell (1983) comprehensively studied Americans to arrive at four broad lifestyle groups and nine specific lifestyles. The battery of tests used included participation in leisure activities. Although the study is somewhat dated, it effectively illustrates another approach to understand leisure and outdoor recreation participation.

Mitchell (1983) identified the first lifestyle groups as being need-driven and constituted by survivor and sustainer lifestyles. These groups largely focus on requirements for daily living (see Maslow's hierarchy of needs). Survivors are further characterized by a lack of education and diminutive resources while sustainers, although on the edge of poverty, remain hopeful and work in manual and service occupations. In terms of leisure preference and participation, survivors avoid expenditure of energy and reported watching television while sustainers had the greatest attendance at horse races of any lifestyle, enjoyed fishing and watched nature on the television. Outer-directed groups are the second lifestyle group identified by Mitchell (1983). Three lifestyles were identified within outer-directed groups—belonger, emulator and achiever. Belongers are typified as "middle-class," have a strong desire to fit into society, and exhibited preferences for home-based outdoor activity such as gardening. Emulators are young in age, largely conforming in their behaviors, and enjoy activities such as bowling and nightclubs (Ibrahim & Cordes, 2002). Achievers are individuals typified as professionals with commensurate incomes and desires to pursue travel, refined activities, and sports such as golf. The inner-directed lifestyle group in Mitchell's (1983) typology consists of the I-am-me, experiential, and societally conscious lifestyles. This group is most concerned with their personal objectives, goals, and self-direction. Although relatively few individuals fit into the I-am-me lifestyle, these individuals actively participate in sports and other distinctive or specialized endeavors. Evidence also suggests that it is this particular lifestyle group which owns the most recreation paraphernalia, including outdoor recreation equipment. The experiential lifestyle concentrates efforts on realizing experiences and pursues outdoor activities including backpacking and cycling, they also own an abundance of outdoor recreation equipment (Ibrahim & Cordes, 2002). While the I-am-me and experiential lifestyles focus on the realization of goals and experiences, the societally conscious lifestyle includes individuals who have achieved affluence and are not concerned with publicly flaunting their success (Ibrahim & Cordes, 1993). Participation in outdoor pursuits is great within this group as well as viewing sport-related television programs. The final group in Mitchell's (1983) classification is the combined outer- and inner-directed group. This final group is constituted by individuals who exhibit an integrated lifestyle, characterized by balancing attempts to "fit in" or respond to societal pressures and respond to self-fulfillment. Integrated lifestyles represented the smallest amount of Mitchell's (1983) sample and were very diverse in their characteristics. While Mitchell's (1983) lifestyle segment relies upon what is now considerably dated empirical evidence, the work illustrates the manner in which understanding lifestyles may contribute to explaining participation, preferences and constraints among the general population.

Interacting with the Natural Environment

Chapter 3 extensively focused on the natural environment as an essential component of outdoor recreation. The environment in which human behaviors occur is also of interest to social psychologists (Iso-Ahola, 1980). In this section attention is directed towards the influence of settings, particularly natural ones, on human behavior. Ibrahim and Cordes provide the following overview:

> research conducted on the relationship between the individual and the setting can be roughly divided into three perspectives. The first approach, called experimental aesthetics, addresses the meaning of the setting in the person's experience. The second approach, environmental cognition, addresses the meaning of the setting in the experience, which is a reflection of one's perception of the setting. The third approach, called behavioural ecology, concentrates on directly observable behavioural patterns in the natural settings.
>
> (2002, p. 64)

Each of the three approaches to investigating the relationship between individuals and the natural environment are subsequently described and important insights gained from research conducted in each area is highlighted.

Experimental Aesthetics

Experimental aesthetics involves the manner in which an individual appreciates the structure and organization of an environment and the extent to which the environment elicits a response from the individual. Iso-Ahola (1980) identifies experimental aesthetics as a strong tradition of research in the 1970s as efforts were made to determine the perceived landscape qualities necessary for outdoor recreation and specific characteristics of landscapes that produced responses. This line of research found that more natural features are associated with settings appropriate for outdoor recreation, quality of an environment for outdoor recreation is directly related to perceived naturalness, and that characteristics of naturalness correspondingly increase to the degree of perceived wilderness (Iso-Ahola, 1980). In one example of such research, Shafer and Mietz (1969) examined the aesthetic and emotional experience rates in wilderness hikers in the White Mountains and Adirondacks. Results from this study indicated that aesthetic and emotional values were considerably more important than social values attributed to the experience.

More recently, research within experimental aesthetics has blurred with the study of environmental cognition. Environmental cognition involves the way people relate to the natural world around them—the larger environmental context (Craik, 1977). Within environmental cognition the concept of environmental mapping, whereby a person creates a mental image of the world through direct and indirect experiences, has gained currency (Matthews, 1986). The ways in which a person experiences his/her environment and comes into contact with information regarding the environment affects the way in which the individual understands and interprets the environment in a larger context (Matthews, 1986). This development of mental mapping and environmental conceptions begins at an early age. A study conducted by Palmer and Suggate (1996) found that children as young as four are able to visually identify things from distant environments. This shows that children begin to develop environmental cognition at a young age and can both interpret and represent the natural environment. Many variables can affect the development of environmental cognition. For example, Matthews (1986) found that gender differences and societal norms result in varying degrees of the development of environmental cognition between boys and girls.

Environmental Cognition

Research in the environmental cognition tradition focuses on how the individual perceives the natural environment and the role or meaning which he/she attaches to the environment within his/her overall outdoor recreation experience. In one such early study, Cicchetti (1972) explored wilderness preferences among students. Although it initially appeared that differences emerged due to education, further examination revealed a contrast effect; the environment provided a stark difference to built city environments and resulted in a stronger preference for wilderness by those dwelling in cities (Cicchetti, 1972).

Iso-Ahola (1980) contends that outdoor recreation environments are subjective and based upon the expectations which an individual has about the particular environment and the potential of those environmental features to satisfy his/her recreational needs. Iso-Ahola describes this approach:

> the perceived quality of a recreation environment (PQRE) amounts to the same as reporting whether a person derived from the recreation environment what was expected from it. When the individual has experienced ("observed") an outdoor recreation environment, the question then is whether that actual experience fulfills the preconceived environmental and psychological expectations. Thus, PQRE is defined by

Plate 4.1 Environmental Cognition is Concerned with the Perceptions and Meanings of the Environment.

117

comparing actual experiences over expected experiences, taking into account both environmental and psychological aspects of recreation experiences.

(1980, p. 278)

The importance and contribution of Iso-Ahola's (1980) concept of PQRE is that it brings together the aesthetic expectations of a particular setting with other psychological elements (values, attributes, beliefs, motivations) which shape a person's desire to participate.

Work by Kaplan and Kaplan (1989) has been particularly insightful in regard to the experience of nature. In a book entitled *The Experience of Nature*, Kaplan and Kaplan (1989) discuss preferences for natural settings. They argue that people have preferences to natural areas in which they think that they can thrive. This generally means areas that feel safe to the individual (orderly, easy to move through) and areas in which a person feels that his/her skills will be matched (competence) (Kaplan & Kaplan, 1989). The authors found that people overall generally have a low preference for industrial scenes and areas with "the clearest human influence" (Kaplan & Kaplan, 1989, p. 43). On the opposite end of the development continuum, people also apparently have a low preference for areas of "extreme openness" (Kaplan & Kaplan, 1989, p. 47). Overall, people have a strong preference to be close to water and areas which have trees, even if they must share in order to experience these natural elements.

Behavioral Ecology

Downes explains that "human behavioral ecology, or simply behavioral ecology, is a field that focuses on relations between ecological factors and adaptive behaviors" (2001, p. 579). In more general terms, behavioral ecology is a research approach interested in "how people behave in everyday settings, including natural settings" (Ibrahim & Cordes, 2002, p. 65). Natural settings can help to explain the behavior of people (including psychological and social aspects) as well as be useful for managers who may gain knowledge on the services needed in a given area (Ibrahim & Cordes, 2002).

The behavior of people in the outdoors is a subject of general interest and academic study. Whitman's (2000) article in the *U.S. News & World Report* documented the "foolish" behaviors of tourists and outdoor recreationists. For example he observed that:

At Yellowstone, visitors often fail to realize that the 2,000-pound bison amiably chewing cud by the roadside can outsprint Olympic 100-meter champion Carl Lewis. Despite park rules requiring visitors to stay 100 yards away from bears, some tourists will get up close to pet or photograph one anyway. A couple of years ago, a tourist got out of his car to pat a grizzly cub on the rump, only to be charged by the sow, who halted within 3 feet of the man, woofing and growling. After the shaken tourist returned to his car, he explained that he thought he was "exempt" from the 100-yard rule because the grizzlies had been near the road.

(2000, p. 48)

From an academic perspective, Kaplan and Kaplan (1989) recognize the relationship between environmental cognition and the approach of behavioral ecology. Returning to their work briefly, it was found that individuals have preferences for certain kinds of areas and that such preferences also influence behaviors in certain settings. Interactions among environmental and social factors have also been explored by Minnegal (1996). She concludes that ecological and social constraints are both causes and effects of subsistence behaviors and therefore it is necessary to understand the relational aspects of these variables.

Given the central role of natural resources to outdoor recreation, the manner in which people behave or utilize "common" resources has been of particular interest to behavioral ecologists. These common property resources characteristically are open access so exclusion is difficult and with use comes a reduction in the amount of resources available (Berkes & Farvar, 1989). Given the characteristics of these resources, concern has been expressed about the tendency of individuals towards exploitation for immediate personal gain at the expense of the environment and other humans. The need to limit self-interested behavior in the commons was popularized by Garett Hardin's (1968) article "Tragedy of the commons" (1968). Although his argument remains the subject of much debate, the behavior of people in such environments remains an important consideration in decision-making about resources such as fisheries (Guest, 2003; Ostrom, 1990).

Explanations for Outdoor Recreation Behavior

Three major themes of the social-psychology approach have been considered as they relate to outdoor recreation in this chapter. A more holistic approach (aligned with the interactional mode of social psychology) is taken in this section to probe explanations for outdoor recreation behaviors. The section opens with a discussion of factors that lead to or prohibit participation in outdoor recreation—a general model of motivation is presented and the more refined theory of planned behavior is discussed. Constraints and substitutability are discussed as variables that mediate between intention and actions. The concept of flow is introduced as an explanation of the leisure experience and recreational specialization is presented as a way to account for changes in outdoor behaviors. The chapter closes with a discussion of potential benefits received by participants in outdoor recreation.

Why Participate in Outdoor Recreation?

As an entry point to answering this pressing question, attention is focused on how the concepts of motivation and satisfaction can work together to enrich understanding why people participate in behaviors, such as outdoor recreation. These concepts were introduced earlier in this chapter and initial connections between them were made as satisfaction was recognized as a form of motivation as well as an outcome of behavior. The relationship between motivation and satisfaction provides a basis from which a general model of motivation is developed. According to Mannell and Kleiber "the basic components of a general model of motivation are: (1) needs or motives, (2) behavior or activity, (3) goals or satisfactions, and (4) feedback" (1997, p. 188). This general model of motivation is illustrated in Figure 4.9. A need or motive arises with the accompanying belief that a particular form of behavior will meet this need so action is undertaken. For example, a person may feel the "need" for a breath of fresh air, so his/her first thought is to step outside. Such activity may lead to

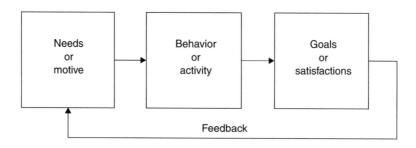

Figure 4.9 General Theory of Motivation.

satisfaction if the expectation is met. Feelings of refreshment may further reinforce the "need" for contact with the outdoors and thereby influence future motives. The general model of motivation is useful to highlight the important relationship among motivation, behaviors and satisfactions.

While the general model of motivation is useful to illustrate relatively spontaneous behaviors (Aronson et al., 2001), behaviors such as outdoor recreation are often undertaken with a great deal of deliberation, intent and planning. The theory of planned behavior is the outcome of a series of works by Martin Fishbein and Icek Ajzen (Ajzen, 1985; Ajzen & Fishbein, 1980; Fishbein & Ajzen, 1975). It is recognized as the best-known explanation of how deliberate behavior occurs (Aronson et al., 2001; Mannell & Kleiber, 1997; Manning, 1999).

Fishbein and Ajzen (1975) initially observed the strong connection between attitude, subjective norms and the intention of an individual to perform a particular behavior. Since attitude and subjective norms have been discussed earlier in the chapter they will not be pursued further here. A third element of perceived behavioral control was identified as an additional influence. This element refers to the manner in which an individual cognitively matches his/her abilities with an activity (Aronson et al., 2001). Perceived behavioral control reflects the "perceived ease or difficulty of performing the behaviour" and is related to the likelihood of participation (Hrubes, Ajzen & Daigle, 2001, p. 166). If, for example, someone watches a movie in which rock-climbing occurs and perceives it to be very difficult, it is less likely that this will result in a strong intention to pursue rock-climbing. By contrast, if an individual watches the same movie, but perceives that there is a high degree of control in rock-climbing, it is more likely to result in an intention to try rock-climbing.

According to the theory of planned behavior, "the best predictors of a person's planned, deliberate behaviours are the person's attitudes toward specific behaviours, subjective norms, and perceived behavioural controls" (Aronson et al., 2001, p. 244). A visual depiction of this concept is given in Figure 4.10. The theory of planned behavior makes clear the complexity involved in understanding how individuals come to actual participation in outdoor recreation. They are influenced by: their own feelings about the particular behavior (perhaps they are intrigued by the idea of canoeing); their perception of how the behavior will be accepted by social significant actors (their friends may think canoeing is a waste of time); and, the extent to which control is perceived (an individual believes he/she can canoe).

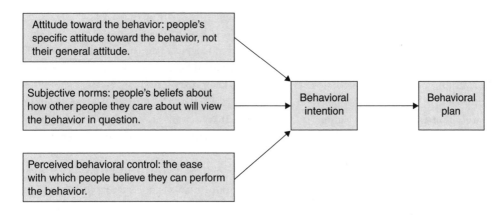

Figure 4.10 Theory of Planned Behavior.
Source: adapted from Ajzen, 1985.

One of the most important contributions made by the theory of planned behavior is the distinction between intention and actual behavior. Searle and Brayley (2000) suggest that for this reason differentiation is required among the concept of participation, repertoire and favorite. Participation refers to engagement in the actual activity. Favorite leisure activities are those which individuals, if asked, would prefer to participate in as a consequence of their attitudes. Repertoire, although traditionally associated with research regarding older adults, refers to the number and diversity of activities in which an individual participates and potential changes associated with this range (Searle & Brayley, 2000). These three concepts are important because they recognize and prompt research regarding the dissonance between intention and participation.

Constraints and Substitutability

Mannell and Kleiber (1997) identify the Outdoor Recreation Review Commission (ORRRC) in the United States as the origin of research on leisure constraints. During the 1960s researchers sought to explore both the demand for outdoor recreation and identify associated barriers. Godbey (1999) recognizes that all humans face constraints or barriers to their involvement in leisure activities.

Crawford and Godbey (1987) have classified constraints as being intrapersonal, interpersonal and structural. Intrapersonal constraints are psychological in nature and include the way a person feels about participation. Interpersonal constraints are those barriers involving other individuals and human interactions. Structural constraints are barriers that prevent individuals from participation although they want to do so. According to Godbey (1999) constrains create distinct challenges and must sequentially be overcome if a person is to participate in an outdoor recreation activity. Individuals must initially overcome intrapersonal barriers, then interpersonal barriers, and finally structural barriers. Consider the example of a university student who wants to go paddling. Perhaps the individual is watching television and views a program about canoeing and wants to try the activity. Despite having a positive attitude about the activity, the student is also studying for her final examinations and experiencing high levels of anxiety and stress. Eventually she overcomes these intrapersonal barriers and decides that she would study better after a break. One of her friends is both an expert paddler as well as having finished his exams, but she hesitates to ask him to join her because she is not sure if she can keep up. Upon realizing that she has no other choice, she overcomes this interpersonal barrier and asks him to go. He agrees immediately, but when getting ready to go they realize that he took his personal flotation device (PFD) home. They decide to rent PFDs from a local outfitter to overcome this final structural barrier and actually go canoeing.

Continuing with this example, what would happen if the two individuals could not overcome the structural constraints? They may decide not to participate in any outdoor activity or they may substitute another outdoor activity for their preferred choice of canoeing. Brunson and Shelby understand the term recreation substitutability to refer to "the interchangeability of recreation experiences such that acceptably equivalent outcomes can be achieved by varying one or more of the following: the time of the experience, the means of gaining access, the setting, and the activity" (1993, p. 69).

Hendee and Burdge (1974) introduced the theory of recreation substitutability from studying the displacement of individuals while participating in outdoor recreation. The results of their research indicated that people substitute activities which they anticipate to result in similar consequences (experiences, satisfaction and benefits) (Hendee & Burdge, 1974). If an individual, for example, wanted to go backcountry camping to be with his/her friends and all of the permits had been reserved, he/she may substitute a frontcountry camping experience.

Manning (1999) broadly classifies subsequent outdoor recreation research investigations of substitutability into two distinct types. The first type of substitutability research in outdoor recreation focuses on activity types and the extent to which activities within types, containing similar characteristics and traits, can be substituted. The second type of substitutability research involves direct questioning and behavioral observations. Shelby and Vaske (1991b) expanded the depth of the substitutability context with the findings of their study of salmon-fishing in New Zealand. As a consequence of their work a typology of substitutability was proposed which incorporates both activity and resource substitutability.

Substitutability of outdoor recreation activities is both a personal issue as well as a managerial opportunity. Substitutability is recognized as a complex concept spanning activity, resource, and temporal dimensions. Despite this complexity, substitutability is important for outdoor recreation managers to provide opportunities which are in short supply, relieve pressure from stressed resources, and mitigate important issues such as crowding and conflict (Manning, 1999).

Flow

In addition to understanding why people participate in outdoor recreation, it is important to recognize that participation forms a feedback loop with important implications on future involvement. In 1975 Csikszentmihalyi introduced the concept of flow. Csikszentmihalyi (1975) derived the concept of flow from interviews with individuals who concentrated considerable effort on activities which appeared to offer few extrinsic rewards (e.g., artists, amateur athletes, rock-climbers). From these interviews Csikszentmihalyi (1990) determined that it was the quality of the experience which caused the activity to be intrinsically rewarding, as opposed to other routine events in the daily life of the individuals. Csikszentmihalyi labeled this experience as flow and describes the term as:

> Flow refers to the holistic sensation present when we act with total involvement. It is a kind of feeling after which one nostalgically says: "that was fun," or "that was enjoyable." It is the state in which action follows upon action according to an internal logic which seems to need no conscious intervention on our part. We experience it as a unified flowing from one moment to the next in which we are in control of our actions, and in which there is little distinction between self and environment; between stimulus and response; or between past, present, and future.
>
> (1975, p. 58)

In subsequent work Csikszentmihalyi (1990) further develops the concept of flow. The main tenets of his theory of flow are illustrated in Figure 4.11. Challenges, located on the vertical axis, refer to provocation or nature of the specific task/activity. Skills, located on the horizontal axis, refer to the abilities of an individual pertaining to the specific skill or task. As shown in Figure 4.11, both the degree of challenge and level of skill exist on a continuum ranging from low to high. Csikszentmihalyi (1975, 1990) asserts that: anxiety is produced in situations with a high degree of challenge and low degree of skill by the participant; boredom results in a situation where an individual has a high degree of skill and the

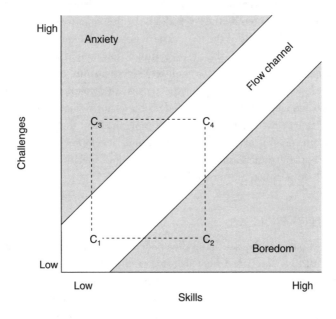

Figure 4.11 Model of Optimal Experience or Flow.
Source: Csikszentmihalyi, 1990.

task provides little challenge; and flow is achieved if the amount of challenge in an activity is commensurate with the amount of skill held by the individual. This state of flow depends on the perception of the individual (both of the challenges and the environment), is dynamic and complex, and it ultimately provides for opportunities of personal growth and discovery (Csikszentmihalyi, 1990).

The ability of the flow concept to capture the essence of the outdoor recreation experience is demonstrated through an example. Bob is just learning how to canoe. Upon starting the activity of canoeing, indicated as C1 in Figure 4.11, Bob perceives the activity to be very challenging. Canoes appear to be very unstable and he has heard many stories about canoes tipping. His canoeing skills are low as he has never been in a canoe before. Therefore upon starting the activity of canoeing, Bob may quickly achieve flow while canoeing in a relatively safe environment. Bob learns how to paddle as well as stern the canoe. He is no longer worried about upsetting the craft and as his skills improve he becomes bored (C2) with the current activity of canoeing on a flat pond. Recognizing that the class is ready for a greater challenge, his instructor takes the class to a river with moving water and rapids. Bob watches some of his friends upset their canoes and realizes that the skills he developed in the pond offer him little assistance in whitewater. He becomes very anxious about attempting this new task. Despite successfully launching his canoe into the river and negotiating an initial set of rapids, thoughts of upsetting his canoe remain and as a consequence he feels very anxious about the activity. In this instance, the challenges presented by the environment have increased and Bob perceives these challenges to be greater than his abilities or skills thereby resulting in a feeling of anxiety (C3). A few more canoe lessons help Bob further develop his skills and abilities. He returns to the same river later in the summer with the new skills he has acquired and has a very different experience. His abilities now correspond to the challenge presented by the river and Bob consequently experiences flow (C4).

Many important implications of the flow experience have been recognized and the idea of optimal experiences has provided the basis for much subsequent research. Apparent from the initial conceptualization of flow, as well as evident in our example with Bob, is the important fact that leisure and recreation experiences are dynamic. According to Csikszentmihalyi (1990) the concept of flow acknowledges the changing nature of these experiences, the tendency for these activities to increase in complexity, and the potential for these activities to provide meaningful avenues for growth and development. Flow is important in modern life as people are increasingly attempting to find meaning in activities that are of their choice and hold personal meaning (Csikszentmihalyi, 1988).

Recreation Specialization

The importance of outdoor recreation on the concept of self and an individual's social world has been of interest to leisure scholars. This topic can be broadly connected to many parts of this chapter including the influence of social settings and social agents, theories of motivation and satisfactions, and concept of flow. Recreation specialization provides specific insights about how individuals advance within an activity as well as how a particular outdoor recreation activity may gain a central place in an individual's life.

Research pertaining to self-concept and the construction of social worlds based on leisure experiences led Bryan (1977) to extensively study trout fishermen. From this research he analytically constructed a typology of anglers based on the notion of specialization. Recreation specialization is defined as "a continuum of behaviour from the general to the particular, reflected by equipment and skills used in the sport and in the activity setting preferences" (Bryan, 1977, p. 175). Based on extensive on-site interviews he proposed the following typology consisting of four ideal types:

> Occasional Fisherman—those who fish infrequently because they are new to the activity and have not established it as part of their leisure, or because it simply has not become a regular part of their leisure, or because it simply has not become a major interest.
>
> Generalists—fishermen who have established the sport as a regular leisure activity and use a variety of techniques.
>
> Technique Specialists—anglers who specialize in a particular method, largely to the exclusion of other techniques.
>
> Technique-Setting Specialists—highly committed anglers who specialize in method and have distinct preferences for specific water types on which to practice the activity.
>
> (1977, p. 178)

According to Bryan (1977) motivations changed as anglers progressed through these ideal types (from catching fish to the experience and setting) and these changes could be observed in equipment preference, setting preference, experience, and especially commitment. Bryan's (1977, 1979) work is "generally recognized as a useful, easily understood framework for guiding management decision-making" (McIntyre & Pigram, 1992, p. 3). It has also provided the basis for a considerable amount of outdoor recreation research.

Reflecting upon over 20 years of outdoor recreation experience research, Manning asserts that "the concept of recreation specialization expands on the notion of experience to

Plate 4.2 Fly-Fishing for Trout Typifies Technique-Setting Specialists Associated with Recreation Specialization.

include cognitive, behavioural, and psychological components in an effort to distinguish and define among types of recreationists" (1999, p. 223). In this manner specialization represents an opportunity to accurately capture the various dimensions of outdoor recreation experiences as well as recognizing the interconnected nature of these elements. These dimensions of the outdoor recreation experience are shown in Figure 4.12. As knowledge and skills (cognitive component) are enhanced through taking courses or reading publications, it is likely the behavioral and psychological components will change. The centrality of the activity and involvement of the pursuit is also likely to increase as is the desire for particular settings, advanced equipment and elements of the experience itself (Manning, 1999).

As the concept of recreation specialization has developed it has been both challenged and held up. It is criticized for, in some instances, being a tautology or using circular reasoning if elements are used to both define specialization and measure its influence on the same variable (e.g., involvement) (Ditton, Loomis & Choi, 1992; Manning, 1999). Progression through a continuum based on multiple dimensions has also been identified as being relatively simplistic and unilaterally interpreted (Manning, 1999). Notwithstanding these and other criticisms, recreation specialization is an important concept in capturing the experience of outdoor recreation. Acknowledgment and incorporation of multiple

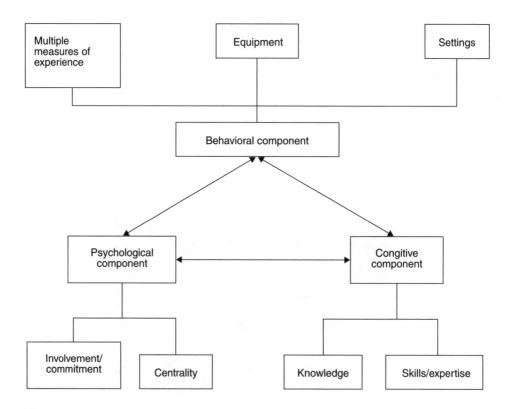

Figure 4.12 Recreation Specialization.

Source: adapted from Little, 1976; McIntyre & Pigram, 1992.

dimensions are particularly noteworthy. Recreation specialization also serves as a useful construct to investigate the sense of place as well as providing a basis for comparisons among activities (Donnelly, Vaske & Graefe, 1986; Manning, 1999).

BENEFITS FROM PARTICIPATION IN OUTDOOR RECREATION

The social-psychology approach illuminates the many benefits that may be realized from participating in outdoor recreation activities Brown's (1981) work synthesized experiences which were valued by individuals participating in outdoor recreation activities. He found that "the specific experiences identified for different activities lead to first order or immediate benefits, which in turn lead to second order longer-term benefits" (Brown, 1981, p. 16). Garst, Schneider and Baker (2001) confirm the immediate and latent nature of these benefits. They studied adolescents participating in outdoor recreational activities (this particular study focused on adventure trips) and found that individuals received positive impacts on their self-perception. Many participants on the trip altered their behavioral conduct and these alterations lasted for four months after the trip in many cases (Garst et al., 2001).

Benefits to individuals are also directly related to environmental settings. People participating in outdoor recreation activities may develop a sense of place or attachment to a particular area. Bricker and Kerstetter (2002) studied the sense of place gained by whitewater boaters and was found to create feelings of meaning and belonging. Natural settings in which outdoor recreation occurs can also have a cognitively calming effect, which can in turn reduce physiological symptoms of negative health. Ulrich et al. found that viewing outdoor scenes produced positive feelings and reduced symptoms related to stress, including "blood pressure, skin conductance, muscle tension" (1991; as cited in Mace, Bell & Loomis, 2004, p. 8).

Finally, outdoor recreation can also impact a person's self-efficacy over the short and long-term. Self-efficacy is the conviction an individual has in him or herself to undertake actions to produce a given outcome (Bandura, 1998). In the context of outdoor recreation, self-efficacy has been defined as "one's capability to act in specific situations that may contain novel, unpredictable and potentially stressful encounters" (Propst & Koesler, 1998, p. 321). Research has established the positive relationship between adventure recreation and self-efficacy (Jones & Hinton, 2007). For example, Propst and Koesler (1998) studied National Outdoor Leadership School (NOLS) participants (both prospective and current) across a variety of courses. They found that participation in an outdoor-leadership activity increased the level of self-efficacy immediately after the experience, and remained quite high a year later.

SUMMARY

This chapter employed the social-psychology approach to understanding outdoor recreation as a form of human behavior. It began with a general overview of social psychology and discussed the manner in which it has been applied to leisure studies. The individual and outdoor recreation behavior was explored through a discussion of attitudes, motivation, and satisfaction. Social influences on the individual were highlighted through the process of socialization, the influence of social norms and social settings that correspond to various life stages. The importance of early involvement in outdoor activities was recognized as being directly related to undertaking similar pursuits later in life. Societal factors (e.g., demographics, ethnicity, lifestyle) which correlate to outdoor recreation participation were also presented. Explanations for various aspects of outdoor recreation behavior were pursued by exploring theories which integrate many of the concepts highlighted earlier. The chapter concluded with a succinct discussion of benefits an individual may receive from participating in outdoor recreation activities.

KEY CONCEPTS

Attitude	Life stages
Behavioral ecology	Lifestyles
Benefits	Maslow's hierarchy of needs
Constraints	Motivation
Demographics	Recreation specialization
Environmental cognition	Satisfaction
Ethnicity	Socialization
Experimental aesthetics	Substitutability
Flow	Theory of planned behavior
Hierarchies of demand in outdoor recreation	The social-psychology approach

SUGGESTED KEY SOURCES FOR MORE INFORMATION

Csikszentmihalyi, M. (1990). *Flow: The psychology of optimal experience.* New York: Harper & Row.
Iso-Ahola, S. E. (1980). *The social psychology of leisure and recreation.* Dubuque, Iowa: Wm. C. Brown Company.
Kaplan, R. & Kaplan, S. (1989). *The experience of nature: A psychological perspective.* Cambridge and New York: Cambridge University Press.
Mannell, R. C. & Kleiber, D. A. (1997). *The social psychology of leisure.* State College, PA: Venture.

REVIEW QUESTIONS

1. How does social psychology approach the study of leisure?
2. Define the term motivation.
3. Explain why you participate in an outdoor recreation activity using Iso-Ahola's (1980) causes of leisure behavior model.
4. How do the dimensions of seeking and escaping explain participation in leisure behavior?
5. Identify and describe the two approaches used to explain participation in outdoor recreation behavior.
6. Explain the theory of planned behavior and apply it to an example.

7. Identify and describe three types of constraints which must be overcome in order to participate in an outdoor recreation activity.
8. The concept of flow was introduced to explain the experience of recreation. Illustrate and explain the concept of flow.
9. Explain three changes in outdoor recreation participation as an individual moves through life stages using the concepts of familiarity and novelty.
10. How does leisure repertoire change over the course of the life span?
11. How can differences between outdoor recreation participation by ethnic groups be explained?
12. Identify and describe three benefits of outdoor recreation to the individual.

Chapter 5

Economics and Outdoor Recreation

OBJECTIVES

This chapter will:

- explore the relevance of economic analysis to outdoor recreation;
- present concepts central to economic analysis and describe their applicability;
- consider the economic impacts related to outdoor recreation;
- gauge the demand for outdoor recreation;
- examine how outdoor recreation opportunities are provided.

INTRODUCTION

The association between economics and outdoor recreation has been longstanding as early interest in the subject matter came from this knowledge area. Economic analysis broadly considers values based upon human evaluations. This chapter begins by documenting the appropriateness and challenges of applying economic analysis to outdoor recreation. Central concepts of economics (e.g., demand, cost, pricing, valuation and impacts) applicable to outdoor recreation are discussed. Current participation rates for outdoor recreation activities are presented and future projections of demand are contemplated. The final portion of the chapter explores the outdoor recreation delivery system that provides opportunities (meets the demand) for outdoor recreation. Economic analysis of outdoor recreation makes clear the substantive values assigned to both activities and resources as well as illustrates the magnitude of the associated delivery system.

ECONOMIC ANALYSIS AND OUTDOOR RECREATION

Why has an economics of outdoor recreation emerged? Hanley, Shaw and Wright (2003) recently answered this question. They recognize that the interest in and relevance of economics regarding outdoor recreation largely came about due to increasing popularization of such activities, accompanying conflicts with other land uses (e.g., forestry), and attention by resource agencies to derive broader benefits from a single resource (e.g., multiple use). Consequently, economists realized the possibility of integrating recreation demand with welfare economics and thereby linking people and the environment (Hanley et al., 2003).

Economic analysis is both relevant and important to understanding outdoor recreation. In their seminal work, *Economics of Outdoor Recreation*, Clawson and Knetsch (1966) established the bearing of economic analysis to outdoor recreation. They state that:

> economic analysis is of particular applicability here, as it is largely a study of human reactions, actions, and choices. It deals with the implications of subjective evaluations and intrinsic characteristics of recreation sites and experiences, not as such, but in terms of how such things affect what man does or is willing to do. Economic comparisons deal with physical and other characteristics of goods and services only to the extent that these affect human decisions.
>
> (1966, p. 45)

The above quotation acknowledges the full breadth of the economic perspective, which goes well beyond the issues of cost and pricing to essentially examine the issue of human values.

Economic concerns in outdoor recreation are generally consistent with the goals of economics in general. Krutilla and Knetsch (1974) succinctly explain how economic analysis in outdoor recreation is reconciled within the larger goals of economics. They observe:

> the essential concerns in the economics of outdoor recreation differ little from those of economic concerns generally. We are faced with demands on scarce resources which can be used for recreational purposes, and also, in most cases, for alternative purposes, and we desire to allocate or use these productive resources in the ways that are most beneficial. All this is part of the larger problem of maximizing the *net* benefit from all potential combinations of goods, services, and leisure within the economy is capable of producing, given the resources with which it is endowed, the level of technology available, and the preferences of members of society with respect to alternative goods, services, and leisure.
>
> (1974, p. 168)

Economic analysis also offers specific insights and benefits to understanding outdoor recreation. In this regard it provides a convincing "picture" of an impact from outdoor recreation. Concepts such as demand, for example, are useful to explain many central concerns of outdoor recreation such as the relationship between consumption and price, the nature of participation in specific activities, and future trends.

The general merits of employing economic analysis to outdoor recreation have changed relatively little over time. Many years ago economics was recognized as being a "particularly useful vehicle for focusing on two important aspects of outdoor recreation: the question of worth or values, and the determination of patterns and regularities" (Clawson & Knetsch, 1966, p. 46). Economics remains essential to focusing on these aspects more than 40 years later. Not only do these issues remain just as relevant today, they may actually be accentuated by the increased interest in assessment of resource damage (Hanley et al., 2003).

Despite economic analysis being a well-established and pervasive research tradition in outdoor recreation, it faces many inherent challenges when compared with applications to other goods and services. While the fact that people are willing to pay for goods and services associated with outdoor recreation is consistent with a market-based system, the nature of outdoor recreation challenges the conventional assumptions that:

1   the economic value of outdoor recreation is comparable to other resource uses; and
2   socially sanctioned income distribution which permits efficient resource allocation exists (Krutilla & Knetsch, 1974).

Krutilla and Knetsch (1974) suggest that imagining a continuum of recreation resources is useful to making this distinction. At one end of the spectrum are outdoor recreation activities that rely heavily on immobile resources such as lakes, mountains, rivers and forests. At the other end of the continuum are recreational activities which take place near populated areas and are not site-specific such as playgrounds, recreation facilities, and recreation programs. Outdoor recreation is therefore viewed to be resource oriented while other forms of recreation are more market oriented.

Three other attributes of outdoor recreation present specific challenges to the application of economic analysis. The first relates to the clear estimation of values. Traditionally, "the value of outdoor recreation is simply the individual user's willingness to pay for the use of resources rather than go without the opportunity" (Krutilla & Knetsch, 1974, p. 168). This concept of value makes sense for goods and services where "price" is easily measured in terms of dollars. However, the demand for outdoor recreation is often not registered on a market (Clawson & Knetsch, 1966; Krutilla & Knetsch, 1974; Smith, 1989). In this way outdoor recreation is also unique among resources such as timber products, mineral resources and/or agriculture. The second relates to the very nature of the outdoor recreation experience, as described in Chapter 1 to involve five phases. Consequently, outdoor recreation is different than other goods and services because multiple costs are incurred during the experience. Clawson and Knetsch (1966) recognize that outdoor recreation involves costs of money, time and travel. While most other goods and services subsume or ignore these additional costs they represent a considerable challenge for outdoor recreation (Clawson & Knetsch, 1966). Finally, traditional economic analysis in outdoor recreation is confounded by a complex range of variables. Clawson and Knetsch (1966) recognize three categories of factors which ultimately affect demand: the potential recreation users themselves; the characteristics of the recreation area or resource; and the relationship between the first and second factor. Although challenges are evident in applying traditional economic analysis, it does not negate the importance of attempting to ascertain the value of outdoor recreation.

CENTRAL CONCEPTS OF ECONOMIC ANALYSIS IN OUTDOOR RECREATION

The preceding section scoped the appropriateness and challenges of economic analysis to outdoor recreation. In this section key central concepts to economic analysis are introduced as they have been applied in the context of outdoor recreation.

Demand

The concept of demand is central to economic analysis. Clawson and Knetsch (1966) assert that it is, without doubt, the most useful and important tool from this tradition. Notwithstanding its importance, the term demand is variously understood and applied (Clawson & Knetsch, 1966; Smith, 1989). In this section the concept of demand is used to explore the relationship between consumption and price, current participation (consumption) in outdoor recreation, and forecasts of future outdoor recreation participation.

Three basic considerations offered by Clawson and Knetsch (1966) should be kept in mind before entering the discussion on demand. First, the notion of demand actually represents human choice. Second, demand is a relevant concept which depends on association with price and/or relevant costs, but it is also influenced by societal forces such as buying habits, competition and changing tastes. Third, the notion of price should more accurately be broadened to the concept of cost. Willingness to pay for a particular good or service represents one measure of cost, but many others may hold significant value (e.g., time, travel).

Neoclassical Economic Use of Demand

In essence, the concept of demand is used to identify the existence of a relationship between a good or service which would be consumed at a particular time for a specified price. Clawson and Knetsch (1966) identify that such information can be simply presented in a two-column table relating quantity to various prices, as illustrated in Table 5.1. Smith identifies this as the traditional neoclassical economic definition in which "demand is a schedule of the quantities of some commodity that will be consumed at various prices" (1989, p. 46). Although this schedule may be described in a table, it is most frequently presented graphically as a demand curve. Smith's (1989) illustration of hypothetical demand curves (Figure 5.1) is helpful to conceptualize and subsequently discuss the neoclassical concept of demand.

The typical demand curve for most goods/services has a downward trend slope from left to right. This is shown in Figure 5.1 in the slope from D to D'. The example of tickets to a ski hill will be used to illustrate the concept represented by this "typical" demand curve. The uppermost point of the demand curve (point D) corresponds to greatest ticket price

Table 5.1 Demand as a Schedule of Visits, Costs per Visit, and Total Expenditure, Hypothetical Recreation Area

Cost per visit ($)	Number of visits	Total expenditures (1,000)
25.00	0	0
20.25	5,000	101
16.00	10,000	160
9.00	20,000	180
6.25	25,000	156
4.00	30,000	120
1.00	40,000	40
0.00	50,000	0

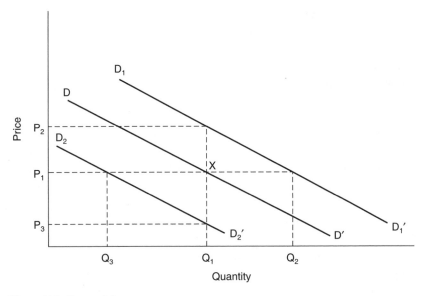

Figure 5.1 Demand Curves.

and the least amount of consumption (quantity). If ski tickets are really expensive few will be sold. Moving from left to right, the demand curve reveals that as the price for ski tickets is reduced the amount of consumption (quantity) increases. The end of the demand curve (point D') corresponds to the greatest amount of consumption as well as the lowest price. If ski tickets are really cheap more will be sold. With all other forces remaining constant, the neoclassical use of demand is a reflection of scarcity.

Although the fundamental concept of demand in the neoclassical sense is relatively straightforward, the concept is typically broadened to reflect a host of other variables. In reality, many factors influence demand. Examples include a change in societal preferences or taste, change (positive or negative) in the actual individual towards the item, introduction of new/alternative opportunities, and the long-term effects of socio-economic change (age, income, amount of free time) (Clawson & Knetsch, 1966; Pigram & Jenkins, 1999; Smith, 1989). These factors, referred to as demand shifters, are recognized for "their effect on a plot of the demand curve under specific conditions" (Smith, 1989, p. 48). The potential effect of demand shifters is illustrated again using the example of ski tickets. Slope DD' in Figure 5.1 represents the demand curve for ski tickets at a hypothetical ski resort. Although not previously described in depth, consider that the hypothetical ski resort is publicly owned. It is relatively small in size and offers only three runs of moderate difficulty. The ski hill has a single lift which is always up to standard and is reliable, but very slow. The ski hill also has relatively few amenities. An old residential building is used as a clubhouse which offers a limited menu from a small canteen. Consider a scenario in which the park and recreation director expanded the budget for the facility. Additional funds result in the creation of two additional runs, a new high-speed lift, a new promotional campaign, and a contract with a private business to operate a full-scale restaurant. As a consequence of these new developments (demand shifters), the demand curve DD' would move or shift up and to

135

the right. This is represented by the new demand curve D_1D_1'. When considering the relationship of price and quantity using this new demand curve, it is evident that:

1 people are willing to pay more ($P_2 > P_1$) for the same ticket (quantity) due to the recent improvements at the ski hill; and
2 people are willing to purchase more tickets ($Q_2 > Q_1$) for the same price.

In a second scenario a budgetary freeze is introduced and the hypothetical ski hill receives no new funding. As maintenance costs rise, the overall condition of the ski hill declines. The floors of the clubhouse are only cleaned once a week and the canteen is only open for a limited number of hours. Staff are reduced to a minimum number and as a result it takes even longer to use the single chair lift. In a further effort to save money lights are no longer used and consequently night skiing is no longer available. These demand shifters cause the original demand curve (DD') to shift to the left and downward, resulting in the demand curve (D_2D_2'). As illustrated in Figure 5.1 a constant price (P_1) in this scenario results in fewer people willing to purchase ski tickets. Conversely, to sell the same quantity (Q_1) the price must be lowered considerably ($P_3 < P_1$). This is intuitively understandable as people don't want to pay the same amount for an inferior product.

Although the neoclassical concept of demand was explained using a hypothetical example, it has been employed in numerous studies of outdoor recreation. Huhtala (2004) conducted a study examining outdoor recreation economics in Finland. The purpose of the study was to determine the willingness to pay for services and outdoor experiences. The rates that people are willing to pay were found to vary according to individual preferences, services offered and experiences afforded. Huhtala found that 50% of the study participants were willing to pay to participate in outdoor activities in Finnish recreation areas and supported a "recreation payment system" (2004, p. 40). Natural resources also have a significant economic value in the context of recreation. A study conducted by Holgen, Mattsson and Li (2000) investigated boreal forests with various amounts of timber harvested in an attempt to determine which types of area would be most valued for recreation. They found that the most highly valued types were shelterwood forests in which regeneration occurs under older trees (Holgen et al., 2000).

The Demand for Outdoor Recreation

The concept of demand is used here to direct attention to participation in outdoor recreation activities. In this way demand is considered to involve consumption (participation) at a particular price (Smith, 1989). Demand in this application is usually treated more broadly to simply refer to current participation. While a comprehensive global assessment is beyond the scope of this book, a succinct overview of participation in outdoor recreation in particular countries is valuable to convey its magnitude. The demand for outdoor recreation is summarized in the following paragraphs for Australia, Canada, the United Kingdom, and the United States. Notwithstanding the importance of participation in outdoor recreation in all countries, these are profiled because of the longstanding popularity of such activities and the systematic collection of information on participation.

Participation in Outdoor Recreation in Australia

Collection of information on various facets of Australian life is the responsibility of the Australian Bureau of Statistics. In 1991 the Australian Bureau of Statistics formed the National Centre for Culture and Recreation Statistics (NCCRS), a jointly funded initiative to facilitate the collection and analysis of information related to this topic (Australian Bureau of Statistics, 2002). Information on sport, recreation and culture is systematically collected as part of the General Social Survey and reported on as a specific theme (see Australian Bureau of Statistics, 2002). It is also collected monthly to provide annual insights through the Multi-Purpose Household Survey (MPHS) (Australian Bureau of Statistics, 2007). These efforts are building a robust understanding of participation in leisure related activities.

Drawing upon the most recent (2005–2006) survey, 66% of Australians participate in sports and physical recreation annually, with 29% doing so at least twice per week (Australian Bureau of Statistics, 2007). It should be noted in interpreting these statistics that a distinction is not made between sport, physical recreation, and recreation. In the category of physical recreation, walking was the most popular with 25% (four million people) participation (Australian Bureau of Statistics, 2007). Participation in other outdoor recreation activities included swimming (9%), cycling (6%), bushwalking (3%), canoeing/kayaking (0.4%) and scuba-diving (0.2%) (Australian Bureau of Statistics, 2007).

Participation in Outdoor Recreation in Canada

The most comprehensive and systematic attempt to gain information about participation in outdoor recreation activities in Canada occurs through the Survey on the Importance of Nature to Canadians (SINC) (Environment Canada, 1999; Gray, Duwors, Villeneuve, Boyd & Legg, 2003). Based on results from the SINC survey, approximately 84.6% of Canadians (19.9 million) over 15 years of age participated in activities related to nature. Participation in nature-based activities varies across provinces and territories with Alberta having the greatest rate of participation at 88.9% (Environment Canada, 1999).

The SINC survey measures participation in four main activity types. The first is outdoor activities in natural areas which consisted of 17 specific recreational activities. The percentage of Canadians responding in each of these activities is summarized in Figure 5.2. The second, third and fourth types of activities (wildlife-related, recreational fishing, and hunting) were considered separately because comparisons could be made to previous studies in 1991. Notwithstanding the caution by Environment Canada (1999) that changes may be partially due to modifications in survey design, it appears that the level of non-consumptive wildlife-related trips has increased (from 18% in 1991 to 18.6% in 1996) while both angling and hunting have decreased (from 26.2% and 7.3% in 1991 to 17.7% and 5.1% in 1996).

Information was also gathered on the general interest in the natural environment by the public. This was done by considering indirect participation in nature-related activities. General interest in nature by Canadians was gauged to be high as an estimated 17.6 million people indirectly participated in some form of nature-related activity. While activities such as watching films or television as well as reading demonstrate an interest in nature, the

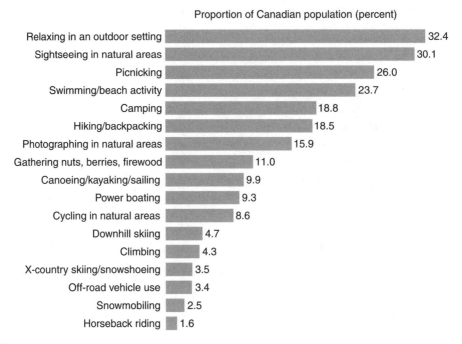

Figure 5.2 *Percentage of Canadians Participating in Outdoor Activities in Natural Areas in 1996.*

maintenance, restoration, and/or purchase of land reported by approximately 760,000 Canadians shows considerable commitment.

Participation in Outdoor Recreation in the United Kingdom

Knowledge regarding leisure and outdoor recreation in the United Kingdom is evident from a few sources. At a national level, statistical information is collected to provide insights into many aspects of daily life. For example, the average expenditure by a household on recreation and culture between 2003 and 2006 was £57.90, with expenditures being the greatest in this category (£65.50) in the eastern portion of the country (National Statistics, 2007).

The most specific source for information on participation in outdoor recreation activities comes from the England Leisure Visits Survey (ELVS). The ELVS is carried out by Natural England and is supported through a compendium of agencies with an interest in the natural environment and recreation and aims to determine the amount of leisure visits, their value and related trip characteristics (Natural England, 2005). Results of the 2005 survey indicate that during the past year:

> 64% of adults had visited a town/city with 62% visiting a seaside town/city, 59% visited the countryside and 37% had visited the seaside coast. Across England as a whole, 40% had visited a wood/forest in the past year. A quarter (25%) of people had

visited a stretch of inland "water with boats" whilst just under a fifth (18%) had taken a trip to "water without boats."

(Natural England, 2005, p. 8)

The total volume of annual leisure visits continued to decline from 5.2 billion trips in 1998 to 3.6 billion trips in 2005 while expenditures made during these visits remained almost constant from 2003 to 2005 (Natural England, 2005).

Participation in Outdoor Recreation in the United States

Information has been collected about participation in outdoor recreation in the United States since the 1960s with the ORRRC. Most recently this has occurred through the National Survey on Recreation and the Environment (NSRE) as well as the federal assessment of outdoor recreation and wilderness as required by the Renewable Resources Planning Act (see Cordell, 1999; Cordell, Lewis & McDonald, 1995; Cordell & Super, 2000). These surveys are routinely conducted and provide the most up-to-date and comprehensive assessment of current participation as well as revealing emerging longitudinal trends. Information from the most recent 2005/2006 NSRE has yet to be released. Although it is beyond the scope of this book, very detailed information on specific activity types is available from government agencies and industry organizations.

How many people actually participate in outdoor recreation in the United States? An estimated 94.5% of people in the United States reported participating in an outdoor recreation activity at least once during the past year (Cordell et al., 1999). Viewing and learning opportunities were the activities in which people most frequently participated, while other activities associated with little cost, minimal physical expenditure, and low levels of specialization were also popular (Cordell et al., 1999). Adventure or risk-based activities which focus on physical challenge and occur in more remote locations also received considerable involvement with an estimated 74 million Americans participating.

Cordell et al. (1999) have classified activities into three categories according to attributes of the recreational resource (land-based, water-based, and snow- and ice-based) upon which the activity depends to provide a more refined understanding of participation. Land-based activities are the largest category and constituted by many diverse forms, as shown in Table 5.2. Most popular among the specific activities was walking. Water-based activities are a second category used in the NSRE and include a diverse range of outdoor activities as shown in Table 5.3. While fishing remains popular, the proportion of people who angle in the most recent study declined (Cordell et al., 1999). The final category of participation information collected by the NSRE is for activities based on snow or ice, as shown in Table 5.4. Sledding, downhill skiing, and ice-skating are activities with the greatest amount of participation in this category.

The Future of Outdoor Recreation Participation

Demand may also be used to focus on unmet and future needs. Latent demand captures the difference between current and potential levels of consumption or participation due to the

139

Table 5.2 Percent and Number of People 16 Years and Older in the US Participating in Land-Resource-Based Outdoor Activities, 1994–1995

Type of outdoor activity	Percent of population 16 or older	Number in millions
Trail/street/road activities		
Running/jogging	26.2	52.5
Biking	28.6	57.4
Long-distance biking	3.2	6.4
Walking	66.7	133.7
Viewing/learning activities		
Visiting a nature center	46.4	93.1
Visiting a visitor center	34.6	69.4
Visit a prehistoric site	17.4	34.9
Visit a historic site	44.1	88.4
Bird-watching	27.0	54.1
Wildlife viewing	31.2	62.6
Other wildlife viewing	13.8	27.5
Sightseeing	56.6	113.4
Camping		
Developed area	20.7	41.5
RV developed camping	8.6	17.3
Tent developed camping	14.6	29.4
Primitive area	14.0	28.0
RV primitive camping	3.5	7.1
Tent primitive camping	10.7	21.5
Other camping	2.1	4.2
Hunting		
Big game	7.1	14.2
Small game	6.5	13.0
Migratory bird	2.1	4.3
Outdoor adventure		
Hiking	23.8	47.8
Hiking to a summit	8.3	16.6
Orienteering	2.4	4.8

presence of barriers (Smith, 1989). This relates to the discussion of constraints and barriers (Chapter 4). It also highlights the implications for technology (Chapter 10), which may influence the realization of this demand. Potential consumption considers the possibility (option) or using a resource in the future and/or merit in knowing that it exists. Option and existence values are expressions of worth for natural environments even though the individual may never actually use the good or service and can be incorporated into forecasts of participation related to a broad level of factors (Smith, 1989).

Forecasting future participation is an additional use of the demand function. Technical aspects of making such predictions and well-documented challenges of anticipating change lead Wall (1989) to be skeptical of forecasting future outdoor recreation participation. Notwithstanding these caveats, both Wall (1989) and Foot (1996) consider broad societal changes in Canada and assert that they bode well for future participation. Foot (1996) uses demography to make more specific predications that as Canada's population ages participation in skiing, tennis and attendance at sporting events will decline and participation in

Table 5.3 Percent and Number of People 16 Years and Older in the US Participating in Water-Resource-Based Outdoor Activities, 1994–1995

Type of outdoor activity	Percent of population 16 or older	Number in millions
Boating/floating		
Sailing	4.8	9.6
Canoeing	7.0	14.1
Open-top canoeing	6.8	13.5
Closed-top canoeing	0.4	0.8
Kayaking	1.3	2.6
Rowing	4.2	8.4
Floating, rafting	7.6	15.2
Motor-boating	23.5	47.0
Water skiing	8.9	17.9
Jet skiing	4.7	9.5
Sailboarding/windsurfing	1.1	2.2
Fishing		
Freshwater	24.4	48.8
Saltwater	9.5	19.0
Warmwater	20.4	40.8
Coldwater	10.4	20.8
Ice	2.0	4.0
Anadromous	4.5	9.1
Catch-and-release	7.7	15.4
Swimming		
Surfing	1.3	2.6
Swimming/pool	44.2	88.5
Swimming/non-pool	39.0	78.1
Snorkeling/scuba	7.2	14.5
Viewing activities		
Fish viewing	13.7	27.4
Visiting a beach or waterside	62.1	124.4
Studying nature near water	27.6	55.4

Source: 1994–1995 National Survey on Recreation and the Environment, USDA Forest Service and the University of Georgia, Athens, Georgia. The NSRE is the most recent of the series of National Recreation Surveys begun nationally in 1960.

walking, curling, swimming and birding will increase. Cordell et al. (2002) explore outdoor recreation demand, environmental attitudes and demographic changes in the United States. In establishing connections among these elements they demonstrate the tremendous potential of demographics to shape participation in outdoor recreation activities as well as environmental opinions. Beyond the demographic factors specific to any one nation are more widespread changes. Globalization and movement towards a market orientation are influencing policy and consumers' experience (Curry, 2004; Karlis, 2006).

One of the most recent and ambitious efforts of forecasting in outdoor recreation occurred with *Projections of Outdoor Recreation Participation to 2050* (Bowker, English & Cordell, 1999b). This initiative estimates future participation through models using present behavior, with acknowledgment that many variables (e.g., changes in real income, supply of opportunities) pose considerable challenges. Bowker et al. forecast that:

Table 5.4 Percent and Number of People 16 Years and Older in the US Participating in Snow- and Ice-Based Outdoor Activities, 1994–1995

Type of outdoor activity	Percent of population 16 or older	Number in millions
Downhill skiing		
Snowboarding	2.3	4.5
Sledding	10.2	20.5
Downhill skiing	8.4	16.8
Cross-country skiing		
On groomed trails	2.7	5.4
On ungroomed trails	2.8	5.7
Backcountry	1.9	3.7
All forms	3.3	6.5
Ice skating	5.2	10.5
Snowmobiling	3.6	7.1

Source: 1994–1995 National Survey on Recreation and the Environment, USDA Forest Service and the University of Georgia, Athens, Georgia. The NSRE is the most recent of the series of National Recreation Surveys begun nationally in 1960.

the five fastest growing outdoor recreation activities through the year 2050 as measured by number of participants are projected to be: cross-country skiing (95% growth), downhill skiing (93% growth), visiting historical places (76% growth), sightseeing (71% growth), and biking (70% growth). The five slowest growing outdoor recreation activities as measured by the number of participants are projected to be: rafting (26% growth), backpacking (26% growth), off-road vehicle driving (16% growth), primitive camping (10% growth), and hunting (minus 11% growth).

(1999b, p. 349)

Overall, participation in outdoor recreation activities that are winter-based, water-based, and development-based will exceed the growth rate of the American population while dispersed activities such as hunting are not expected to keep pace with the general population (Bowker et al., 1999).

Cost of Outdoor Recreation

Imagine a relatively simple form of outdoor recreation such as going for a walk in your local woodland or park. Upon arrival you park in a graveled lot and are greeted by interpretive signs. You also notice the provision of garbage cans, picnic tables and trail markers. Although walking in the park may appear to be free as you are permitted access to the outdoor recreation experience without directly paying for the privilege, there are costs associated with the provision of such an experience.

Although in many cases outdoor recreation may appear to be free, it is more accurate to assume that the real costs to provide the service have been realized elsewhere (Clawson & Knetsch, 1966). Clawson and Knetsch (1966) classify these into three specific categories of capital, management and maintenance. Capital costs incurred represent the resource value, either at market price of acquisition or the opportunity costs for using the resource for recreation as compared to something else. Managerial costs include the expenses associated with trained personnel. Maintenance costs refer to ongoing expenses related to the upkeep and continued operation of the recreational opportunity. Reflecting upon the example of going for a walk in a park, it is apparent that the land area of the park has a value that others are willing to pay, as indicated by the real estate market. The same piece of land could have other potential values (e.g., timber harvesting, mineral extraction) which would illustrate a cost in utilizing the park for outdoor recreation. The salary and vehicle expenses of the park ranger who periodically hikes the trail to insure safety and proper etiquette provide an example of managerial costs. Fixing a walking bridge that has become unstable due to wear and emptying of trash cans represent ongoing maintenance costs.

Who is responsible for the costs associated with outdoor recreation? Costs related to the provision of outdoor recreation opportunities are addressed through the leisure delivery system. The leisure delivery system consists of the various levels of government, private enterprises, and non-governmental organizations. These three components are addressed later in the chapter in terms of their respective philosophy, administrative structure and finances. While the leisure delivery system provides opportunities for outdoor recreation, the participant is often required to meet a proportion of the cost. Clawson and Knetsch (1966) argue that private individuals do this by paying the capital and ongoing costs for a particular opportunity (e.g., purchasing a cottage and paying property taxes), a fee to use a private recreation area (e.g., buying the privilege to hunt on private land), and/or the cost for transportation to and from the activity site (e.g., bus-pass, fuel for car).

Although participation in many outdoor recreation activities may appear to be "free," considerable costs are accrued in the provision of every outdoor recreation experience. No studies, to the author's knowledge, have been conducted on the total cost of outdoor recreation. The following approximations for segments of the delivery system in the United States illustrates the potential magnitude of these costs. Ibrahim and Cordes (2002, p. 110) estimate that together the 50 states spend almost one billion dollars (US) on the provision of outdoor recreation opportunities. They also recognize work by Jensen (1995), who estimates that 2.3% of local government expenditures (almost two billion US dollars) are towards parks and recreation.

Values

The term cost was used above to refer to the amount of expenditure required in dollars to realize an outdoor recreation experience. There are certainly many other non-monetary expenses associated with outdoor recreation such as time, social relationships, foregoing other opportunities. The willingness to make expenditures (in this broader sense) represents the importance or value a person assigns to outdoor recreation. Going for a walk in the woods may cost you one hour of time from work. Choosing to go for the walk represents the value you place on the activity.

Although it is possible to describe the importance or value of outdoor recreation in many different ways, it is often expressed in terms of dollars. Using money to represent value is of particular interest because it provides a basis for comparison between outdoor recreation (non-market good/service) and other goods and services that are exchanged on markets (Smith, 1989). Differentiation is thus warranted between the focus of recreation economists and those interested in regional economic development. Hanley et al. make this distinction clear as they instruct:

> To begin, for the uninitiated, we want to dispel the notion that recreation economists wish to value coca-colas, sandwiches, sun hats, and locally purchased gasoline. Many, many times we recreation economists have had to spend time convincing the public that expenditures in areas where recreation destinations are located is *not* our primary focus. Their mistake is in thinking that more local expenditures means a highly valued recreation destination, and such may not be the case. It is the job of the regional economist to ascertain what impact, if any, recreational visitors have on local areas when they visit. But recreational and environmental economists are more interested in the value of a lake itself, which does not include the value of the soft drinks purchased while there.
>
> (2003, p. 6)

Many different techniques have been developed and utilized to estimate the value of outdoor recreation and tourism. Tourism is included here as a shared body of common knowledge and application has emerged. Although a comprehensive review is beyond the scope of this book, two frequently used methods to estimate the value of outdoor recreation and tourism are discussed. An alternative method of considering value is also included which may be of future interest to the reader.

Consumer Surplus

The concept of demand is central to estimating the economic value of goods and services which are not exchanged on a market (Smith, 1989). Shadow pricing or consumer surplus estimate the value of a particular area for a particular purpose, in this case recreation. Consumer surplus refers to the added value received beyond the amount paid for a particular experience (Loomis, 2005; Smith, 1989). Smith (1989) uses the following example of a recreation site to explain the consumer surplus model. In this example a demand curve is illustrated for a recreation area, as shown in Figure 5.3. The demand curve shows the relationship between the current admission fee of $2.50 and the quantity of 500,000 user days. We can assume that the recreation area is designed in such a way that collection of the admission fee does not present undue difficulty. Further examination of the demand curve reveals that many individuals would have paid more than $2.50 for admission to the recreation area. Anyone who indicated a willingness to pay more than $2.50 receives a consumer surplus. For the individual who was willing to pay $5 for admission to the recreation area he/she receives a consumer surplus of $2.50. The sum of all individual consumer surpluses may then be aggregated to produce a total for the particular recreation site (A in Figure 5.3).

Central to the consumer surplus model is the idea of willingness to pay. Willingness to pay is an estimate used by researchers when they ask individuals to indicate a monetary amount they would be willing to pay for a particular experience or to use a specific site.

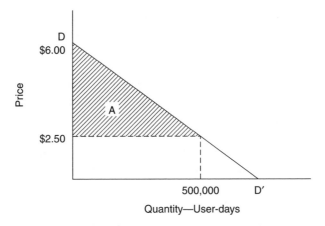

Figure 5.3 Consumer Surplus Model.

This approach has been extensively used in outdoor recreation to determine value associated with resources. In one of the most comprehensive such efforts to date, Loomis (2005) compiled 1,239 observations (studies) of consumer surplus in outdoor recreation from 1967 to 2003 in the United States and Canada. In focusing upon the Pacific Northwest region in particular, he was able to determine the average per day value of hunting ($35), fishing ($42), wildlife viewing ($35) and hiking ($24).

Although this approach provides a way to conceptualize the value of specific areas and activities, there are some inherent difficulties with the consumer surplus model (Smith, 1989). Willingness-to-pay studies based on hypothetical situations are often subject to errors and biases (Kim & Crompton, 2001). Study participants may engage in "strategic behavior" or "gaming responses" recognizing that the responses they provide may be used as a means to increase prices and consequently may report a lower willingness to pay (Kim & Crompton, 2001; Smith, 1989). Interpretation of such studies is also critical. As noted in the work of Richer and Christensen (1999) price adjustments to the willingness to pay without consideration of other factors (e.g., equity) may result in an "unacceptable" loss of visitors to a public area. Consequently, Loomis (2005) suggests that it is always preferable to use data from the particular site in question than broad averages.

Travel Cost Method (TCM)

Many of the shortcomings associated with the consumer surplus model relate to accuracy. In this regard, the travel cost method has received considerable attention (Ibrahim & Cordes, 2002; Loomis, 2005; Smith, 1989). Clawson and Knetsch explain that:

> we need a range in the observations in order to trace out a significant portion of the curve. For this purpose, we rely primarily upon geographic analysis, using differences in numbers of visits and in cost per visit from different areas or distance zones to estimate the basic relationship.

(1966, p. 64)

145

They subsequently utilize these variables (cost per visit zone versus number of visits from each zone) to produce the demand curve. From the demand curve generated using TCM it is then possible to determine the total economic value or consumer surplus by calculating the area under the curve (Smith, 1989).

The TCM is advantageous because it reflects the five phases of the outdoor recreation experience, is based on actual behavior, or revealed preference (as opposed to what individuals report a willingness to pay), and is effective in the absence of admission fees (Hanley et al., 2003; Smith, 1989). Notwithstanding these merits, limitations of the initial TCM technique have also been recognized. Clawson and Knetsch (1966) themselves recognize that the TCM method is limited due to the presence of additional constraints (e.g., time), the cost associated with time, and potential intervening or alternative outdoor recreation opportunities. They also acknowledge that travel and money are only indirect measures of what individuals may be willing to pay to use a recreation area. Calculation of the TCM protocol is also debated. Smith (1989) explains that the actual "costs" of travel are under scrutiny as non-basic costs (e.g., food, accommodation, equipment) may or may not be considered.

The travel cost method has been extensively adapted and refined since Clawson and Knetsch's (1966) initial foray based on count models. Siderelis, Moore and Lee (2000), for example, used this approach to study demand for North Carolina trails. Their random survey of North Carolina residents showed the importance of perceived quality of trails and their incorporation into travel cost models. Another adaptation identified by Hanley et al. (2003) is based on Random Utility Models (RUMs). RUMs are forecasting tools that consider changes in the quality of site attributes. They also identify the possibility of combining the revealed preference choice with other survey-based willingness-to-pay methods in an effort to estimate the affect of changes. More generally, the travel cost method has increased in sophistication as an individual is now recognized as the correct scale of application, trips have been identified as having multiple destinations, site characteristics have been incorporated, and analytical devices themselves have been advanced (Hanley et al., 2003).

In summarizing their initial experience with the travel cost method Clawson and Knetsch state:

> At this point, a non-economist might well exclaim: "If you must so carefully qualify your already somewhat novel approach to the estimation of demand for outdoor recreation, is the whole procedure too complicated and too arbitrary to be useful in practice?" While this reaction might be natural enough, it misses the main point. It is not the procedure as such that needs qualification and caution, but rather the basic recreation experience and the available data about it which are complicated and not easily interpreted. Anyone attempting to analyze the same basic experience and same data by any less rigorous or superficially simpler method would encounter the same problems of interpretation and analysis; moreover, he might more easily be led astray by a less adequate method and thus reach a less dependable conclusion.
>
> (1966, p. 89)

The above quotation raises an important consideration that is equally relevant today as when it was first written. Determining the value of outdoor recreation is very difficult.

Alternative Ways to Determine Value

Many alternative approaches to determining value of the natural environment and/or outdoor recreation are evident that may be of interest to readers. These approaches may be broadly classified into those which utilize a monetary basis and those which present a fundamentally different valuation scheme

Monetary-based approaches are often labeled as Contingent Valuation Method (CVM). Venkatachalam observes that CVM "is a simple, flexible nonmarket valuation method that is widely used in cost–benefit analysis and environmental impact assessment" (2004, p. 89). Hanley et al. (2003), in their historical review of economics and outdoor recreation, trace such an approach back to Ciriacy-Wantrup in 1949. The CVM method is usually applied by surveying individuals about their willingness to pay for, or to avoid, a particular condition. For example, anglers may be asked how much they would be willing to pay to have parking access adjacent to a particular river. The outcome of the survey thus provides a measure of intention based on (contingent) proposed actions. Hanley et al. (2003) state that the CVM method has been positively received and applied in both academic and policy circles because it is broadly applicable and simple.

The CVM has been applied in studies of both the natural environment and outdoor recreation. Loomis (1990), for example, employed the CVM in a study of 100 California households to determine value of Mono Lake. Results from his study indicate that reliable estimates of total willingness to pay for preservation of resources were gained from the general population and that recreation options and existence values are good predictors of values (Loomis, 1990). Hanley and Wright (2003) use a CVM to investigate mountaineering in Scotland as free access to climbing in the UK is increasingly popular. In this study a number of choices were presented to technical climbers in a survey from which they had to select their preferred alternative. The results of this study provided the obtainment of implicit prices for particular site attributes; such knowledge has application to evaluations of land use changes as well as site attributions that managers can potentially influence (Hanley & Wright, 2003). The CVM has also received critical attention. Venkatachalam writes that "the criticism revolves mainly around two aspects, namely, the validity and the reliability of the results, and the effects of various biases and errors" (2004, p. 89; Jorgensen, Syme, Smith & Bishop, 2004). Stemming from such criticism, Venkatachalam (2004) concludes that CVM has much to offer in the domain of public policy but should not be used indiscriminately.

A second way to capture the value of the natural environment and spaces conducive for outdoor recreation is through hedonic valuation. Unlike the willingness-to-pay approach discussed earlier, hedonic valuation is based on actual conduct (Luttik, 2000). In the standard form of this approach, the price of a house is a function of the structural features, location and environmental characteristics (Anderson & West, 2006; Bolitzer & Netusil, 2000; Loomis, Rameker & Seidl, 2004). Hedonic valuation has been used extensively to demonstrate the positive impact of open or green spaces, water and trees (e.g., Loomis et al., 2004; Luttik, 2000). The technique has also been employed to demonstrate the influence of environmental disamenities, such as brownfields (Kaufman & Cloutier, 2006).

Other approaches to determining value reject using money as the basis of exchange.

147

Rudolf deGroot (1992), for example, has developed an alternative value system based on the concept of functions. deGroot writes that "environmental functions are defined as the capacity of natural processes and components to provide goods and services that satisfy human needs (directly and/or indirectly)" (1992, p. 7). In this manner, the system of values becomes extended and the depth of "functions" provided by the natural environment more adequately recognized. This "function" scheme explicitly recognizes many of the values that monetary-based approaches attempt to proxy. Functions also make clear the contributions of the natural environment that are not recognized or conveyed by economic-based approaches (deGroot, 1992). This is imperative for resource attributes that influence the experience of outdoor recreation (e.g., landscape quality). deGroot (1992) accomplishes this by assigning specific values to aesthetic and carrier functions so they are considered the same as resource production (typical types of resource development such as timber harvesting) functions of the natural environment.

Price

Price specifically refers to the amount charged for something—in this case an outdoor recreation opportunity. Think of your arrival at a national park. Upon entering the main office to register one of the first things you see is a price schedule. Various prices are posted for different outdoor recreation opportunities. One price may be for day use, another for overnight camping and another for additional amenities such as electric and water services.

Prior to investigating the specific issues of pricing in outdoor recreation, a more general understanding of price is required. According to Howard and Crompton "we may normally think of price as the amount of money we must sacrifice to acquire a unit of service we desire" (1980, p. 406). They argue that such consideration of price is too narrow and that it should more accurately reflect both monetary and non-monetary costs. Hence, there is a clear relationship between price and the previously discussed concept of cost. It is important to reiterate that to arrive at participation in outdoor recreation an individual must make choices among goods and services in general, alternative recreation opportunities, and even among types of outdoor pursuits. Starting from this broader perspective:

> if total costs are high, relatively few people can afford them or will choose to give up the comparatively large amounts of goods and services that could be bought with the same money; if costs of the whole recreation experience are lower, time and other factors will be more important constraints than costs.
>
> (Clawson & Knetsch, 1966, p. 273)

The mechanism of price is integral to dictating allocation (resources, capital, labour) among activities and prompting consumer choice among alternatives, which can subsequently be expressed through a market to suppliers (Clawson & Knetsch, 1966).

Applying the concept of price to outdoor recreation is neither simple nor straightforward. Outdoor recreation is a modified case of pricing because the resource can co-exist with other types of resource use (Clawson & Knetsch, 1966). This indeed has been an important feature in the United States as multiple-use management strategies have been vigorously pursued. Ibrahim and Cordes explain that "multiple-use management takes advantage of the resource's ability to provide a bundle of uses and benefits from the same land" (2002, p. 131). In the context of outdoor recreation, price has many important implications. If price fails to reflect cost or is regarded as nominal resource use will be greater (Clawson & Knetsch, 1966). Outdoor recreation provides a classical example in which costs are significant and yet opportunities are often regarded as free. Price may effectively distribute use, negatively affect private competition in a situation where public pricing is near zero, and adversely influence decisions pertaining to private investments (Clawson & Knetsch, 1966; Howard & Crompton, 1980). The discussion of price above assumes that it is related to costs and therefore is beneficial for decision-makers. Clawson and Knetsch (1966) caution that specific attention is warranted if price is arbitrarily set because it then does not reflect costs and fails to effectively allocate resources. If these are underestimated, as is typically the case in outdoor recreation, price promotes both the undervaluing of the resource and encourages waste (Clawson & Knetsch, 1966).

The collection of fees in outdoor settings further poses significant challenges to administrators. Clawson and Knetsch (1966) recognize that attempting to collect user fees in situations of open access or remoteness may exceed the total revenue. Attempts have been made to formulate systems that reduce administrative collection duties while retaining revenues. Voluntary pay (honour system or donation) or automated systems have been tried in outdoor recreation areas (Clawson & Knetsch, 1966; Ham, 1992; Howard & Crompton, 1980). Spot checks have been feasibly used in association with specific activities, such as fishing (Clawson & Knetsch, 1966). Anglers, for example, are responsible for purchasing fishing licenses and may get asked by a conservation officer/ranger to show their license.

Howard and Crompton (1980) extend the discussion of challenges associated with pricing by presenting five arguments against establishing user prices, as shown in Figure 5.4. From a philosophical perspective, they argue that opportunities for recreation ought to be regarded as a basic "need" for everyone and that imposing user fees creates the greatest hardships for those of lower socio-economic status. From an administrative perspective they argue that legal restrictions may actually prevent the levying of charges; the lack of controlled access to many recreational resources may prevent collection; and sometimes the cost of collection is greater than the revenue gained (see the preceding discussion).

Stemming from their thought-provoking arguments against charging fees, Howard and Crompton write that:

> There are two kinds of pricing questions which the recreation and park manager has to answer. The first is, "What are my objectives in pricing this program?" The objectives will serve as guidelines in establishing a specific price. The second question is "What method should be used to set a specific price for a program in accordance with those guidelines?"
>
> (1980, p. 418)

As made clear in the above quotation, the amount to charge for outdoor recreation should be connected to agency/programmatic objectives. Providing outdoor recreation experiences for free still represents a pricing decision—the choice has been made to charge

149

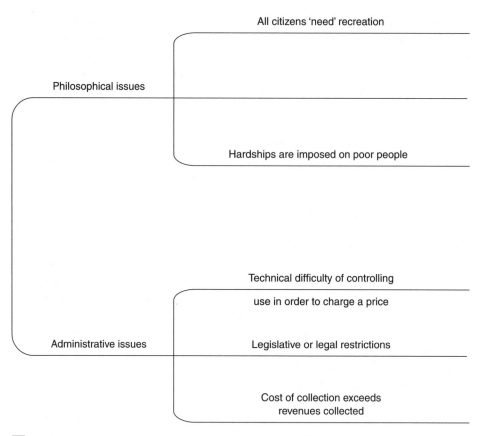

All citizens 'need' recreation

Philosophical issues

Hardships are imposed on poor people

Technical difficulty of controlling
use in order to charge a price

Administrative issues

Legislative or legal restrictions

Cost of collection exceeds
revenues collected

Figure 5.4 Arguments Against User Fees.

nothing for the experience (Clawson & Knetsch, 1966). In an attempt to answer their first question, Howard and Crompton (1980) discuss six "typical" objectives associated with pricing. These objectives and their potential outcomes are shown in Figure 5.5. Visualizing pricing in this way is helpful because it highlights the intended reason that an agency or organization is charging a fee. These objectives are not expanded here as they are visited extensively in the final portion of this chapter as well as considered as a part of outdoor recreation management. While clear definition of why an organization or agency is charging a fee ought to be a priority, Howard and Crompton observe that "unfortunately, very few agencies consciously establish pricing objectives or clearly state their specific price policy" (1980, p. 418).

Methods of setting prices in outdoor recreation remain somewhat of a quandary. Recreation economists have proposed competing theories as to where the price limits ought to be set. Clawson and Knetsch (1966) assert that the added cost of both facilities and services is most relevant. This added cost is broadly interpreted to include not only monetary costs, such as maintenance, but also experience costs realized by other resource users from increased participation.

Ibrahim and Cordes (2002) recognize the influence of government. They contend that

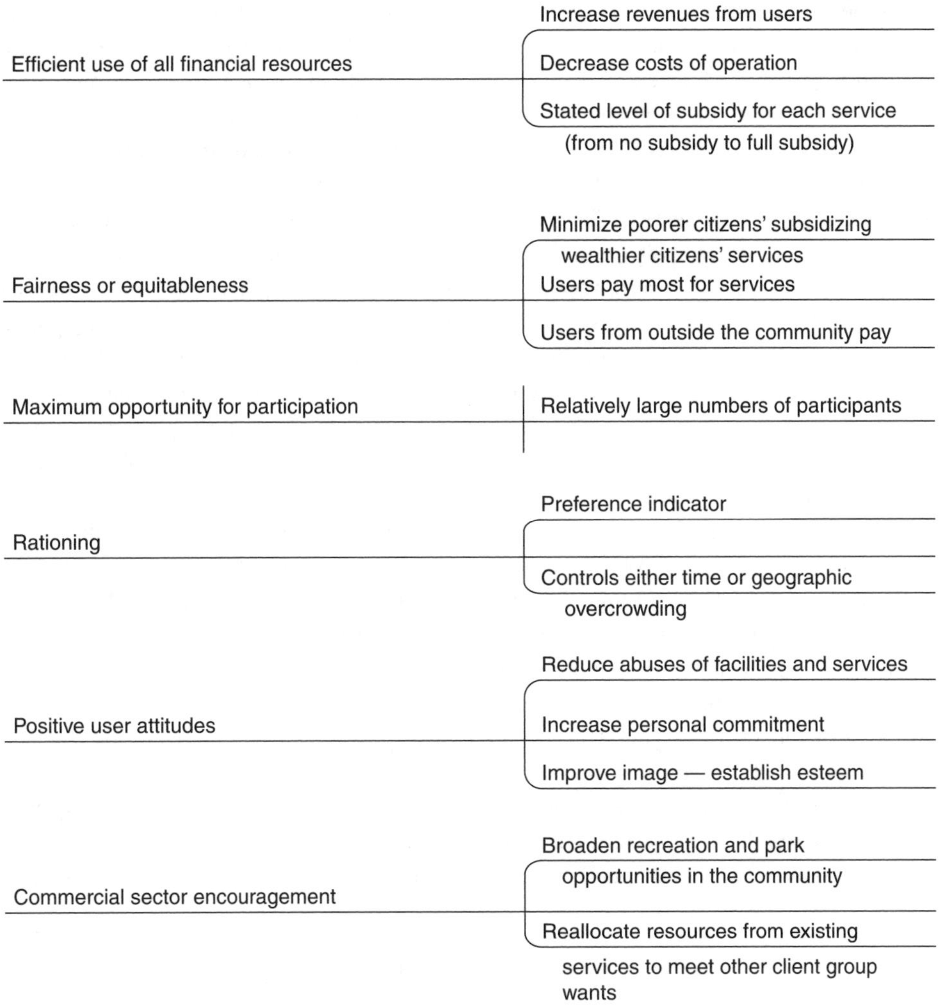

	Increase revenues from users
Efficient use of all financial resources	Decrease costs of operation
	Stated level of subsidy for each service (from no subsidy to full subsidy)
	Minimize poorer citizens' subsidizing wealthier citizens' services
Fairness or equitableness	Users pay most for services
	Users from outside the community pay
Maximum opportunity for participation	Relatively large numbers of participants
	Preference indicator
Rationing	Controls either time or geographic overcrowding
	Reduce abuses of facilities and services
Positive user attitudes	Increase personal commitment
	Improve image — establish esteem
	Broaden recreation and park opportunities in the community
Commercial sector encouragement	Reallocate resources from existing services to meet other client group wants

Figure 5.5 Objectives of Pricing in Recreation.

determining price is difficult in situations where competitive options are relatively scarce. While undoubtedly some alternatives exist, many settings for outdoor recreation (e.g., wilderness) are owned and operated by government. Given this situation, they believe it appropriate for managers to adopt a correct least-cost orientation. Ibrahim and Cordes state that "the user fee should be set at the intersection of the demand curve with the marginal cost and average cost curve" (2002, p. 111). In this approach, the average cost (cost for investment and cost for operation) is used and marginal costs are considered as the difference between demand and supply. They also recognize the importance of intervening variables. For example, distance creates an inverse relationship for outdoor recreation as greater concentrations of people (demand) are located at some distance from many outdoor recreation opportunities (supply).

Another important element in the scheme of pricing outdoor recreation is the attitude held by the public and resource users. If fees are viewed as reasonable they will be more readily paid (Clawson & Knetsch, 1966). The acceptability of moving towards a "user pay" orientation was reflected by public opinion in the United States as early as 1980. The Heritage Conservation and Recreation Service study found that "respondents typically accepted user fees as a reasonable method for paying for outdoor recreation activities. Most citizens also feel that recreation services should be on more of a pay-as-you-go basis. This attitude was shared by all demographic groups, for all regions of the country" (as cited in Howard & Crompton, 1980, p. 411). More recently, Bowker, Cordell and Johnson (1999a) utilized a portion of the National Survey on Recreation and the Environment concerning public opinion of user fees as a funding mechanism for public outdoor recreation-related services. The results of their study "suggest a receptiveness by the public for recreation fees, as indicated by the fact that over 95% of the respondents in our sample supported either user fees or a combination of user fees and taxes to fund at least one recreation service on public land" (Bowker et al., 1999a, p. 11).

A succinct but comprehensive summary of methods used to establish price is offered by Howard and Crompton (1980). Two main approaches are used to determine price, as shown in Figure 5.6. The first approach encompasses methods that do not directly consider costs of providing the opportunity. Demand-oriented pricing is given as a familiar example of this approach. The popularity of undertaking a float trip down the Grand Canyon permits setting prices at how much people are willing to pay. A second approach involves pricing methods that reflect, to varying degrees, the cost of providing such opportunities. Specific methods identified by Howard and Crompton (1980) are further distinguished by the manner in which they address fixed costs (constant regardless of the amount of participants) and variable costs (fluctuate with the number of participants). A residential camp is illustrative as the buildings and insurance represent fixed costs while food represents a variable

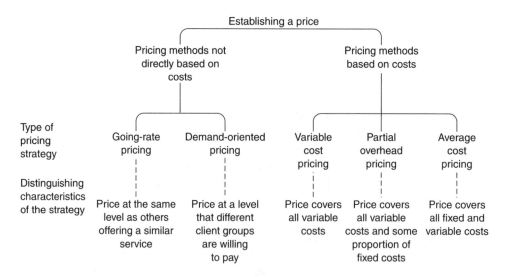

Figure 5.6 Approaches and Methods of Pricing.

cost. Although understanding such pricing methods is of assistance to administrators of outdoor recreation areas and activities, the previously identified characteristics remain noteworthy challenges.

This section on pricing does not provide a definitive answer as to how outdoor recreation activities should be priced. The complexity, administrative considerations and varying levels of use across outdoor recreation areas and activities make pricing an inherently difficult task. Recognizing the increasing importance of pricing in outdoor recreation in the early 1960s, the following five principles were advanced for levying user charges:

1. Avoid user charges which are administratively unworkable or unsound. If costs would be out of proportion to results, if widespread evasion is probable, or if collection would present unusual administrative difficulties or have undesired other effects, user charges should not be levied.
2. Define carefully the purpose to be achieved by the collection of user charges. Is it to raise revenue, to increase efficiency in allocation of resources as between recreation and other uses, to change user attitudes towards the resource, to accomplish certain management goals, or for other reasons?
3. Choose the method or methods of levying charges which are appropriate to the goal. If the objective is to shift use from one area to another, the difference in charge is perhaps more important than the level of either charge; if the objective is to raise maximum revenue, then the maximum revenue fee as estimated from the demand curve for the resource is the proper criterion; if the objective is to raise revenues sufficient to meet annual management costs, then the necessary fee can be estimated from the demand curve; and so on.
4. Tell the recreation users, frankly and fully, why a charge is imposed and what will be done with the funds; management must certainly work with recreationists, not against them.
5. Consider carefully the equity considerations in any proposed fee schedule; try to anticipate the side-effects, and eliminate the undesired ones (Clawson & Knetsch, 1966, p. 284).

More than 40 years later these remain relevant guides as they bring together much of the information presented in this section. Administrative considerations which should accompany the collection and charge of user fees are highlighted. Above all else, these principles recognize the potential of user fees to be a powerful management tool through the allocation of resources, distribution of users and influence of participation.

ECONOMIC IMPACTS FROM OUTDOOR RECREATION

Earlier in this chapter a quotation by Hanley et al. (2003) was used to differentiate the interests of recreation economists and regional economists. Recreation economists are interested in the value of a particular resource while regional economists are concerned about ascertaining the economic impacts from those participating in outdoor recreation. Attention here is directed at economic impacts from outdoor recreation which includes the benefits received from outdoor recreation-related expenditures. It is again important to recognize the close connection between outdoor recreation and nature-based tourism research in terms of economic development.

Interest in generating economic impacts from outdoor recreation as well as nature-based tourism activities has occurred for some time. The quest for economic advantages drove development of both the Canadian and American park systems. The interest in such development increased in the 1960s because it tended to expose goods and services to people from outside the area, increase economic support for the local area, and increase the economic profile of rural areas which may be economically depressed or not well suited for other forms of economic development (Clawson & Knetsch, 1966).

The development and promotion of outdoor recreation and tourism opportunities was historically assumed to be inherently beneficial to the local geographic region. In the contemporary context a more critical perspective on the full range of potential impacts has emerged, as summarized in Table 5.5. Although often lauded for economic benefits, the impacts from outdoor recreation and tourism are now recognized to have positive and negative consequences on local economies, socio-cultural milieu, and environmental settings, as illustrated in Table 5.5 and discussed later in Chapter 10. Focusing specifically on the economic impacts from outdoor recreation, it is probable that expenditures will be made by participants and that additional benefits (e.g., new employment, investments) may be realized (Hall & Page, 1999; Rollins & Robinson, 2002). Table 5.5 summarizes some of the potential negative economic impacts which may also occur. Rollins and Robinson further caution that:

> the presumed economic benefits sometimes are not what has been anticipated. Perhaps tourism revenues only benefit some community residents, who are employed in services that tourists require; while other residents in the community may not receive such benefits and may in fact resent the benefits that other residents receive from tourism. Sometimes the jobs created by tourism go to non-residents, such as students, who are hired from urban areas to provide summer help for tourism operators. The tourism operators may not be local either, adding an additional drain of economic benefits away from host communities.
>
> (2002, p. 140)

It is also necessary to acknowledge the host of other variables that influence the extent to which economic benefits or costs are realized. These include the extent or ability of a local area to actually attract people to an outdoor recreation/tourism attraction, the seasonal and discretionary nature of recreation/tourism-based industry, and the ability of the local tax base to support necessary development (Clawson & Knetsch, 1966). Realistic expectations and appropriate considerations are therefore required prior to actively developing outdoor recreation opportunities.

Notwithstanding the benefit/cost debate to local communities, considerable interest has been expressed in determining the amount of economic impact from outdoor recreation or nature-based tourism on a particular area. Gaining expenditure information from individuals is challenging because money is spent at various locations (e.g., home, traveling to

Table 5.5 Positive and Negative Dimensions of the Impacts of Tourism on Host Communities

Type of impact	Positive	Negative
Economic dimensions		
Economic	• Increased expenditures • Creation of employment • Increase in labor supply • Increase in standard of living • Increase in investment	• Local inflation • Real estate speculation • Failure to attract tourists • Better alternative investments • Capital outflows • Inadequate estimation of costs of tourism development • Undesirable costs including transfer of funds from health and education
Tourism/commercial	• Increased awareness of the region as a travel/tourism destination • Increased knowledge concerning the potential for investment and commercial activity in the region • Creation of new facilities, attractions and infrastructure • Increase in accessibility	• Acquisition of a poor reputation as a result of inadequate facilities, improper practices or inflated prices • Negative reactions from existing enterprises due to the accessibility of new competition for local manpower and government assistance
Socio-cultural impacts		
Social/cultural	• Increase in permanent level of local interest and participation in types of activity associated with event • Strengthening of regional values and traditions	• Commercialization of activities which may be of a personal or private nature • Modification of nature of event or activity to accommodate tourism • Potential increase in crime • Changes in community structure • Social dislocation
Psychological	• Increased local pride and community spirit • Increased awareness of non-local perceptions	• Tendency toward defensive attitudes concerning host regions • High possibility of misunderstandings leading to varying degrees of host–visitor hostility
Political/administrative	• Enhanced international recognition of region and values • Development of skills among planners	• Economic exploitation of local population to satisfy ambitions of political elite • Distortion of true nature of event to reflect values of political system • Failure to cope • Inability to achieve aims • Increase in administrative costs

Table 5.5 continued

Type of impact	Positive	Negative
		• Use of tourism to legitimize unpopular decisions • Legitimation of ideology of local elite
Environmental impacts Physical/environmental	• Development of new facilities • Improvement of local infrastructure • Conservation of heritage • Visitor management strategies	• Environmental damage • Changes in natural processes • Architectural pollution • Destruction of heritage • Overcrowding • Changed feeding and breeding habits of wildlife

Source: After Getz (1977); Mathieson and Wall (1982); Ritchie (1984); Hall (1992).

and from the site, at the site), items include consumable and durable items (e.g., a sandwich versus a pair of hiking boots), and a single item may serve multiple purposes (e.g., a car). The total amount of expenditures, the specific type of expenditures, the destination or actual site of the outdoor recreation activity, and any specific recreation-related expenditures are of particular concern when gauging economic impacts (Clawson & Knetsch, 1966).

Archer's (1982) classification scheme is helpful to distinguish the different types of economic impacts from outdoor recreation. He classifies economic impacts as being either primary or secondary. Hall and Page (1999) expand on these terms and describe primary impacts, also frequently referred to as direct impacts, as those which result from spending by the individual participating in the activity. The purchase of a coffee by an individual while at a canoe launch is an example of primary impact. Secondary impacts require further elaboration as they may be either indirect or induced (Hall & Page, 1999). Indirect impacts occur in response to money spent by an individual during participation and result in a change of local business transactions (Hall & Page, 1999). A campground owner who builds new facilities and invests in rental equipment is an example of an indirect impact. Induced impacts relate to both direct and indirect economic impacts. Hall and Page describe induced impacts as:

> those arising from the additional income generated by further consumer spending, e.g. the purchase of goods and services by hotel employees. For each round of spending per unit of initial visitor expenditure leakage will occur from the regional economy until little or no further re-spending is possible.

> (1999, p. 123)

The amount of money spent at the site of the outdoor recreation activity (direct expenditures) only reveals a portion of its economic impact. For this reason, the multiplier effect has been of particular interest to those interested in economic impacts (Clawson & Knetsch, 1966; Hall & Page, 1999; Ibrahim & Cordes, 2002). The "multiplier effect is a term used to indicate that the effect of one dollar spent at one point will be more than merely one dollar" (Ibrahim & Cordes 2002, p. 117; Smith, 1997). Total economic impact from a particular site or activity is therefore the combination of direct impacts and secondary impacts. Hall and Page (1999) recognize that multipliers vary considerably; depending upon the size of the region, rate of circulation, type of spending, and pattern of economic behaviors. Although capturing the total economic impact from an outdoor recreation site or activity to a community or regional economy is a daunting task, many advanced modeling techniques have been developed to do so. One such example identified as being particularly relevant to outdoor recreation is the Impact Analysis for Planning (IMPLAN) (Johnson & Moore, 1993). The IMPLAN model has extensively been applied in investigations of sport fisheries. In one such application in Pennsylvania, the total economic impact from sport fishing resources ($3.98 billion) was more than three times direct expenditures ($1.26 billion) (Upneja, Shafer, Seo & Yoon, 2001)

Despite the intense interest in determining the amount of economic impact from outdoor recreation activities, shortcomings of the multiplier approach have increasingly been recognized. The multiplier effect has, in many cases, contributed to the presumption and overestimation of economic benefits (Hall & Page, 1999; Rollins & Robinson, 2002). Archer (1982) observes that often the assumptions upon which multipliers are based are "unrealistic." Hall and Page (1999) assert that considerable caution should be exercised in the use of economic multiplier studies, especially when used as a basis to justify policy and development decisions. They express support for Murphy's (1985) assertion that such efforts should be treated as case studies which reveal little about the actual costs and benefits of development.

Thus far economic impacts have been discussed largely from a regional perspective. Such a perspective assumes that much, or at least some, of the economic impact occurs locally to the actual site of the outdoor recreation activity. In many instances relatively little monetary expenditures are actually made near the site of the activity. Consider the example of a person from Boston who wishes to go climbing in Canada's Rocky Mountains. He may buy all of his equipment, including a majority of his foodstuffs, at a local outdoor store in Boston. He may also hire a company from Boston to guide him on his excursion and pay for his flight to Calgary in Boston. Although he may pay for ground transportation, a few meals, and a park pass while in Canada, much of his expenditure has actually occurred in the United States. As demonstrated in this example, spatial considerations of potential expenditures related to outdoor recreation and tourism are important. Stevens and Rose (1985) have developed a hierarchy that reflects such spatial considerations, as illustrated in Figure 5.7. According to Stevens and Rose (1985) the actual site where outdoor recreation occurs is the smallest sphere in the hierarchy. Most direct expenditures take place in the second (support) area which emphasizes the selling of goods and services immediately required by the participants. Expenditures in the remainder of the spheres (travel corridors, consumer residence area, and extended region) more vaguely connect to areas in which participation may occur. Hall and Page (1999) also direct attention to the consumer's place of residence as an extended region with the potential to contribute to national economies. They also raise the important issue of foreign and international capital investments in the context of globalization which may distribute/redistribute wealth.

157

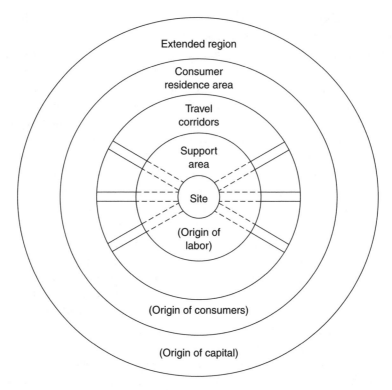

Figure 5.7 Spatial Considerations for Expenditures.

Source: Stevens & Rose, 1985.

Further adding to the complexity of determining economic impacts is the fact that expenditures for recreation are diverse and come from individuals, governments, and industry. Using the example of the United States, it is estimated that personal expenditures (by individuals, households, and groups) on outdoor recreation total $500 billion (Ibrahim & Cordes, 2002, p. 108). While difficult to gauge the exact amount spent at the national level, Ibrahim and Cordes (2002) estimate that expenditures made by the 50 states to be in the range of $1 billion and local government expenditures are estimated at $2 billion. These expenditures fail to encompass spending on recreation activities by private businesses, organizations and non-profit entities. Making reference to the previous workings of the economic systems, Ibrahim and Cordes write that "spending on, and for, leisure pursuits is only half of the total picture, the other half being the incomes accrued from these activities" (2002, p. 110). When considering both sides of the equation, as well as accounting for the close connection to tourism, leisure is one of the largest industries in the world (Godbey, 1999; Hall & Page, 1999). Outdoor recreation is an important part of the leisure industry.

THE PROVISION OF OUTDOOR RECREATION OPPORTUNITIES

The first two parts of this chapter clearly established that outdoor recreation has considerable value and that participation in outdoor activities is very popular. The insatiable demand for outdoor recreation opportunities is fulfilled by the leisure delivery system. Searle and Brayley identify that the "leisure delivery system serves two major functions with respect to outdoor recreation: the protection, development, enhancement and management of natural areas, and the development and management of outdoor recreation leadership and pro-grams" (2000, p. 193). The leisure delivery system consists of three inter-related sectors—government, non-governmental organizations and commercial/private enterprise. Each is subsequently discussed in terms of their rationale or mandate; potential forms or structures and related functions; and accompanying finances. The chapter closes with a brief discussion of the manner in which integration occurs among the three sectors.

The Public Provision of Outdoor Recreation

Rational and Mandate

Governments have been involved (often taken a leading role) in the provision of recreation services and environmental protection. Sessoms explains that "because democratic govern-ment is concerned with the well-being of its citizens, and because recreation experiences contribute to that well-being, organized park and recreation services became a respons-ibility and function of government" (1984, p. 118). It is appropriate for government to provide such opportunities because they serve all facets (e.g., age, race, sex) of the popu-lation; have the resources, authority and continuity to meet the needs of the public; and are able to realize efficiencies of service volume without exclusiveness (Sessoms, 1984).

Government involvement in environmental management is perhaps even better estab-lished. Governments generally share (in various configurations) jurisdictional authority for natural resources. Pertinent legislation and management efforts may therefore be found across scales of administrative structures, as described below. Real property may also be owned and managed on behalf of citizens. It is appropriate that government takes an important role in meeting environmental challenges because it can respond at scales com-mensurate with such problems (e.g., global); ideally consider cumulative effects from a systems perspective; and extend interest to flow resources which flow across boundaries (e.g., water) and/or may not have local management (e.g., space) (Plummer, 2005).

Administrative Structures and Functions

Delivery or administration of recreation opportunities and management of natural resources occurs through a complex web of institutional interactions. These institutional arrange-ments are complicated by the multiple levels of government (national/federal, state/provincial/territory, regional, municipal/county/local) which share (sometimes overlap-ping and frequently changing) jurisdictional responsibilities. The following examples are selected to illustrate the scope and nature of government involvement across these various scales.

The national government of many countries fulfills their mandate for recreation and the environment through one or more agencies. As expected, the name and organizational structure of these agencies varies considerably. The breadth and complexity of outdoor

159

recreation and the natural environment typically results in multiple agencies having purview over specific aspects. Chapter 2 describes the circumstances leading to federal government involvement in the United States, the administrative structures and functions are described here as an example of how this occurs at a national scale. The federal government administers a total of 650 million acres or approximately 28% of the entire United States (Betz et al., 1999). This is accomplished through seven main agencies (Cordell & Betz, 2000), as shown in Table 5.6. The USDA Forest Service and Bureau of Land Management are examples of agencies concerned with multiple-use management; they specifically develop sites, collect fees, and maintain access on federal land in which outdoor recreation is possible (Betz et al., 1999). A second group of federal agencies (National Park Service, US Fish and Wildlife Service, Department of the Interior) have a primary duty to protect/allocate the natural environment and a secondary administrative role in outdoor recreation (Betz et al., 1999). It is important to recognize that other agencies in the United States also impact opportunities for outdoor recreation. The Bureau of Indian Affairs, for example, has promoted opportunities for outdoor recreation as a means of economic development and tourism (Rankel, 1999).

Government involvement also takes place at the state/provincial/territorial level. The manner in which this involvement occurs is illustrated by presenting a few examples within

Table 5.6 Land and Water Area[a] Administered by Federal Land-Managing Agencies by Agency and Region, 1995

Agency	Region (1,000 acres)				
	North	South	Rocky Mountains	Pacific Coast[b]	US total
USDA Forest Service	11,957	12,900	100,093	66,665	191,615
National Park Service	1,882	5,412	10,830	65,072	83,196
Fish & Wildlife Service[c]	1,209	3,809	7,193	78,239	90,450
Bureau of Land Management	388	796	144,237	122,219	267,640
US Army Corps of Engineers	2,907	5,634	2,475	540	11,556
Tennessee Valley Authority	0	1,032	0	0	1,032
Bureau of Reclamation	0	197	5,470	854	6,521
All Agencies	18,343	29,780	270,298	333,589	652,010

Sources: Land Areas of the National Forest System, as of September 1995; National Park Service, Master Deed Listing. State and County Report by State. As of October 31, 1995; US Army Corps of Engineers Natural Resource Management System (NRMS). 1994; Bureau of Land Management. Public Land Statistics. 1993; Annual Report of Lands Under Control of the US Fish and Wildlife Service. As of September 30, 1995; Bureau of Reclamation. Recreation Areas on Bureau Projects. 1992; Development of TVA Recreation Facilities Cumulative Through September 30, 1992; TVA Areas Above Full Pool Level, By County, September 30, 1987.

Notes
a   Numbers may not sum exactly to totals because of rounding. Table does not include Department of Defense land or other miscellaneous Federal agencies with minor land holdings.
b   Alaska accounts for 242.4 million of the Pacific Coast's 333.6 million acres. Agency breakdown is: FS, 22.0 million; NPS, 54.7 million; FWS, 76.8 million; BLM, 88.9 million. There is one COE project in Alaska with 19,709 acres.
c   US Fish and Wildlife Service acreage includes National Wildlife Refuges and Waterfowl Production Areas. About 23.6 million acres of the 90.5 million acres of FWS managed land are not open for recreational use.

Australia, where agencies exist at the state level to address specific aspects of outdoor recreation. In New South Wales (NSW), the NSW Department of Primary Industries, Fishing, and Aquaculture has purview over commercial and recreational fishing, which involves the provision of information (e.g., guidebooks) for angling within the region and the collection of fees for recreational angling (NSW Department of Primary Industries, 2005). In the state of Tasmania services related to outdoor recreation are provided by the Tasmania Parks and Wildlife Service. The Tasmania Parks and Wildlife Service provides sites for camping, maintains accessible parks and implements outdoor education (Tasmania Parks and Wildlife Service, 2007).

Government provision of outdoor recreation and protection of the natural environment also occurs at a local level, focusing on relatively small geographic areas by regional governments, municipal governments, and city governments. The scope of local governments is extensive; Beeler (1999) estimates that there are approximately 4,300 such agencies in the United States. The capital city of Fredericton, New Brunswick, Canada provides an illustrative example of how a city government provides for such opportunities. Nestled along the banks of the St John River, the city has established and maintains a green space adjacent to the river for the entire length of the city. The provision of natural spaces for recreation is a priority with many forests, gardens and trails (City of Fredericton, 2004). Regardless of the form they take, Searle and Brayley stress that "local or municipal governments are often overlooked in discussions of the outdoor recreation delivery system, yet they play an extremely important role in promoting and facilitating outdoor recreation" (2000, p. 193).

Finances

Several mechanisms are used by governments to garner the resources required to meet the demand of outdoor recreation. Levying various forms of taxes has been the dominant way of generating the required revenue by governments. Allocation of such revenues from the general coffers to the agencies with a specific mandate for outdoor recreation and natural resource protection remains an important issue (Cordell & Betz, 2000).

Each level of governments may also levy fees for permits, licenses, and other regulatory matters. The sale of fishing and hunting licenses is an excellent example of a fee generation technique used by all levels of governments. In Canada, for example, the federal government issues permits to hunt migratory waterfowl; the provincial government allocates licenses for game and recreational fisheries; and townships have the ability to issue licenses for particular species. Despite the transfer of taxes and/or levies for specific permits, budget restrictions combined with increasing costs have forced government (at all levels) to increasingly rely on volunteers and alternative funding structures to provide services (Cordell & Betz, 2000).

Provision by Volunteer Organizations

Rationale and Mandate

Numerous organizations have long been committed to the provision of outdoor recreation opportunities and/or protection of resources. As service provision increasingly relies upon volunteers their prevalence and significance has increased. These organizations are known by many names including the third sector, volunteer groups and non-governmental organizations.

The sheer number of people that volunteer is impressive as approximately 50% of Americans (Silverberg, Backman & Backman, 2000), 27% of Canadians (Hall, McKeowan & Roberts, 2001), 41% of Australians (Australian Government Department of Family and Community Services, 2005) and 48% of people in the United Kingdom (Institute for Volunteering Research, 1997). Although the concept of volunteering may initially conjure notions of benevolent giving, and indeed it may be, it is more accurately understood to involve dimensions of free choice, reward (low remuneration), context (formal to informal) and identified beneficiary (Arai, 2000). With President Clinton's proclamation for the role of citizens, "volunteerism has become the cornerstone for a new American agenda" (Silverberg et al., 2000, p. 454). The roles between government and volunteers (non-governmental organizations) are becoming closely linked, as signaled in the recent dialogue around co-production of recreation services in which a need exists to assist governments as well as oneself in order for complete provision of public services (Backman, Wicks and Silverberg, 1997).

Volunteer and non-governmental organizations also aim to provide services to their members. Searle and Brayley (2000) identify a number of such organizations including: sectarian and non-sectarian, sport and recreation, cultural organizations, private clubs, employee organizations, and other groups. Members of a boat club may "volunteer" time to do landscaping as part of their commitment to the club. The link between public good and personal benefits is complicated in the context of outdoor recreation. Dennis and Zube (1987) conducted one of the few studies to specifically examine voluntary association membership and outdoor recreation. They found that "group members appear to view their associational memberships as a means to obtain public goods that enhance environmental quality and opportunities for outdoor recreation" (Dennis & Zube, 1987, p. 242).

Administrative Structures and Functions

Volunteer or non-governmental organizations may employ a diverse range of administrative structures including highly structured organizations (incorporated with an executive), loosely affiliated groups or coalitions, membership-based organizations and grassroot organizations (Arai, 2000). At the more formal end of the continuum these organizations have some similarities with government agencies and businesses with bylaws, complex hierarchical structures and specific roles and responsibilities. At the informal end of the continuum such organizations may lack structure and share most functions. Leadership roles between those who are paid in such organizations and those who are not require careful consideration and may be a source of tension (Catano, Pond & Kelloway, 2001).

These organizations play three particular roles in meeting the demand for outdoor recreation. The first role is advocacy. The coalition of non-governmental organizations and First Nations groups who joined together to halt logging on South Morseby Island in British Columbia, Canada (despite economic pressures valued at 100 million dollars CDN) is an ideal example of the potential power of such grassroots organizations (Searle & Brayley,

2000). The second role is the provision of programs and projects. Organizations in this sector are playing an increasingly important role in both direct service delivery as well as raising funds to support services which they believe to be important (LaPage, 2000; Propst, Wellman, Campa III & McDonough, 2000; Searle & Brayley, 2000). The proliferation of "Friends of . . ." organizations is indicative of the increasing reliance on these organizations. For example, Friends of Algonquin Provincial Park consists of a variety of volunteers who want to contribute to the welfare of the park. They offer interpretive and education experiences for visitors as well as providing publication materials and donations to fund park services (Friends of Algonquin Provincial Park, 2007). Direct service provision is especially important for organizations that primarily serve the interests of their members. The Victorian Climbing Association in Australia is an example of an organization that exists to serve its members through protecting climbing environments, organizing outings, and sharing information (Victorian Climbing Association, 2007). The third role of organizations in this sector is to act as a liaison between government and private interests (Searle & Brayley, 2000). Ducks Unlimited is an example of an organization which combines the advocacy function and acts as a liaison between government agencies and private interests.

Finances

Despite the various roles and interests of organizations in this sector, they generally share a non-profit philosophy. Non-profit does not mean that such organizations lack monetary resources or do not emphasize the ability to generate funds. Rather, non-profit signals that profit motivation is not central to their mandate and that someone (individual, organization, shareholders) does not realize a gain.

Non-governmental organizations and volunteer-based organizations have traditionally raised funds required to support their organizations through their membership, sometimes in the form of a membership fee. The ability to garner gifts and donations from philanthropic individuals with similar interests is noteworthy. Generating funds has become increasingly important for many of these organizations and consequently a concerted effort is often made to raise money by applying for government grants, selling products and/or charging fees.

Commercial/Private Provision of Outdoor Recreation

Rationale and Mandate

This chapter focuses on the economic impacts of outdoor recreation and documents considerable demand for outdoor recreation pursuits. The commercial sector is motivated by potential profits from meeting the demand for outdoor recreation. Unlike those who identify themselves as park and recreation professionals, "those involved with it [commercial sector] are generally known as business people, not recreation and park professionals. They provide goods and services, attend their own trade meetings, and judge success on the basis of their profit/loss statements" (Sessoms, 1984, p. 107).

Administration Structure and Functions

Forms of administration in the commercial sector are distinct from both the public and volunteer sectors. Outdoor recreation enterprises of a commercial nature vary in size from those which are very small (e.g., local fishing pond) to those which are multinational entertainment corporations such as Disney (Ibrahim & Cordes, 2002). It is possible to think of numerous businesses which are either directly (e.g., backcountry guiding service) or indirectly (e.g., airline which provides travel) involved with the delivery of outdoor recreation goods and services. While it is difficult to get an accurate count, it is estimated that there are more than 130,000 private outdoor recreation businesses in the United States alone (Ibrahim & Cordes, 2002).

Organizational structures in the commercial delivery system are usefully grouped by Searle and Brayley (2000) into four categories. The first and most prevalent types are small businesses. Small businesses are flexible and adaptable to change, but are also prone to failure due to capital costs and increasing specialization. An example of such an outdoor recreation business may be a family-run fly-shop and guiding service. Large businesses (differentiated by having more than $250,000 CDN in capital assets) are a second category that typically consists of corporations or franchises. An example of a large outdoor recreation business would be an educational provider such as Outward Bound. The third type of commercial service provider is large conglomerates or "big ones" (assets over 25 million dollars CDN). These are governed by boards of directors, and attract customers from broad markets. Searle and Brayley (2000) use Canadian Pacific Resorts as an example in this regard. The final category is concessionaires who operate independently, but whose business is linked to a particular market and operates under some form of agreement. Concessions are popular within parks and provide an array of services to campers including boat rentals, groceries and guiding.

Given the amount of small businesses, entrepreneurship is particularly important in outdoor recreation. Entrepreneurship focuses on meeting emerging trends, anticipating the direction of these trends, and pursuing innovation. Entrepreneurs typically explore or offer services that appear to be risky or edgy, to which a certain percentage of the population is not yet accustomed. Searle and Brayley offer that, in reality:

> the true entrepreneur is, in fact, less of a risk-taker because of his or her careful attention to staying in tune with market conditions than is the "comfortable tenured" recreation practitioner who flirts with professional redundancy and market irrelevancy by ignoring consumption trends, environmental changes, and opportunities to adjust product and service offerings accordingly.
>
> (2000, p. 127)

Snowboarding provides an excellent example of an outdoor pursuit which was initially promoted by entrepreneurs and has since gained popularity (2.2 million people in 1995) and has now become incorporated into more mainstream ventures of the ski industry.

164

Finances

Profit motivation is central to the philosophy of the commercial sector and influences finances. Funding for the commercial sector comes from the owners or promoters who expect a return on their capital investment by levying user charges or fees (Searle and Brayley, 2000). The commercial sector generally seeks and provides opportunities which they believe will provide a considerable rate of return, although this does not always occur in reality.

Specific data regarding investments in private outdoor recreation ventures and market capture is difficult to gain on an aggregate level. This is challenging because it largely depends on what statistics are included (e.g., including travel to and from the site changes the picture dramatically). With this caveat in mind, an estimated $300 billion is spent by Americans on leisure, with $83 billion stemming from the outdoor recreation system (Bullaro & Edginton 1986, as cited in Ibrahim & Cordes, 2002).

Relationship among Sectors of the Delivery System

The delivery system for outdoor recreation has been described in terms of public, volunteer and commercial sectors. It is important to recognize that in reality the three sectors are not mutually exclusive and should be considered as overlapping spheres of interest, as shown in Figure 5.8. The point of intersection between these spheres highlights their relationships through service delivery, funding and policy.

At times the sectors may be in competition as they provide similar services (e.g., public golf courses compared to private golf courses). Notwithstanding these relatively few areas of overlap, the commercial and public sector are complementary. Private businesses provide services which the government is unable to and the public sector extends incentives to such enterprises (Searle & Brayley, 2000). The relationship among the three sectors since the 1990s has become even more interconnected. Kooiman describes this as an era of change in which governments are interested in "governing in terms of 'co' such as co-steering, co-managing, co-producing and co-allocating" (1993, p. 2). Co-production of recreation services was introduced above as a means of continuing program delivery in light of budgetary restrictions.

Policy is another element which interconnects the three sectors. Various levels of government have the purview to make laws regarding both business practices and the industry as a whole (e.g., free trade) (Searle & Brayley, 2000). Policy is particularly of interest in outdoor recreation because governments are largely responsible for land use and natural resource allocation. These concerns are likely to increase in the future as:

> the challenge for recreation will be gaining a fair share of resources and just treatment against other interests on the national scene in an era of greater challenges. The private policy component, industry's role, may prove critically important in the next century by shaping trends in demand through new activities, equipment, and venues; public policy may be faced with the task of keeping up with these changes if a closer working relationship is not formed between all of recreation's players.
>
> (Siehl, 2000, p. 101)

165

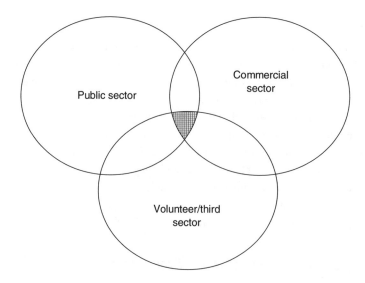

Figure 5.8 *Outdoor Recreation Service Delivery System.*
Source: adapted from Searle & Brayley, 2000.

A final player in the provision of outdoor recreation opportunities which does not specifically fit within any of the three categories is private property owners. The supply of outdoor recreation opportunities provided by this group and the ability to meet demand is somewhat unique as owners have sole discretion over the use of their property for recreation. According to the National Private Landowners Survey (NPLOS) in 1995–1996 approximately 70% of private landowners recreate on their own lands and almost half of those surveyed permit access to persons outside their family for the purpose of outdoor recreation (Teasley, Bergstrom, Cordell, Zarnoch & Gentle, 1999). Growing concerns of liability as well as the potential to lease land for recreation purposes were identified as important trends (Teasley et al., 1999).

SUMMARY

This chapter began by exploring the appropriateness and challenges of economic analysis to outdoor recreation. Initial scoping of economic analysis makes clear that the interest in outdoor recreation fits well within the purview of economic analysis as it considers both resource scarcity and resource allocation. Key concepts associated with economics that have been applied to outdoor recreation were subsequently discussed. Demand was initially examined in the neoclassical sense to highlight the schedule or relationship between the supply and call for a particular outdoor recreation good or service. Costs of providing outdoor recreation opportunities, challenges of setting prices and the fundamental nature of values were each presented as they applied to outdoor recreation. Economic impacts were distinguished as a separate class of values from outdoor recreation which concerned the benefits accrued as a consequence of expenditures related to activities. The second portion

Table. 5.7 Key Features of the Leisure Services Delivery System

Leisure service delivery sector	Philosophy	Administration	Finances
Public/government	Enrichment of society in "worthwhile" pursuits	Government agencies	Taxes
Commercial/private	Satisfy demand by the public to gain profit	Corporations, private business and entrepreneurs	Owners through capital investments and users through service charges
Volunteer/non-government	Augment public services and/or provide services to members with an emphasis on particular groups and individuals	Non-profit (formal and informal) organizations, non-governmental organizations	Gifts, fundraising, grants and membership fees

Source: adapted from Searle and Brayley, 2000.

of the chapter documented demand for outdoor recreation, understood as participation in activities. In reviewing data from several countries it is possible to conclude that outdoor recreation activities are immensely popular. The final portion of the chapter explored the delivery service which makes outdoor recreation opportunities possible as well as protects resources. The distinguishing characteristics of each sector are summarized in Table 5.7. The chapter concluded with a brief discussion of the interconnections among the three sectors and their relationship through the delivery of programs, funding, and policy.

KEY CONCEPTS

Commercial sector

Consumer surplus

Contingent valuation method

Cost

Direct economic impact

Economic analysis

Impacts from outdoor recreation

Latent demand

Multiplier effect

Neoclassical demand

Price

Public sector

Recreation service delivery

Travel cost method

Value

Volunteer sector

SUGGESTED KEY SOURCES FOR MORE INFORMATION

Bowker, J. M., English, D. B. K. & Cordell, H. K. (1999b). Projections of outdoor recreation participation to 2050. In H. K. Cordell, B. L. McDonald, R. J. Teasley, J. C. Bergstrom, J. Marti, J. Bason & V. R. Leeworthy (Eds.), *Outdoor recreation in American literature: A national assessment of demand and supply trends* (pp. 223–350).

Clawson, M. & Knetsch, J. L. (1966). *Economics of outdoor recreation*. Baltimore: The Johns Hopkins Press.

deGroot, R. S. (1992). *Functions of nature*. Amsterdam: Wolters-Noordhoff.

Ecological economics www.elsevier.com

Hanley, N., Shaw, W. D. & Wright, R. E. (Eds.). (2003). *The new economics of outdoor recreation*. Cheltenham: Edward Elgar.

REVIEW QUESTIONS

 1. Identify and describe different types of demand.
 2. Explain the neoclassical economic concept of demand using the example of a campground.
 3. Why are economists interested in outdoor recreation?
 4. Identify and describe challenges to studying the economics of outdoor recreation.
 5. What sector has traditionally absorbed a significant amount of the costs associated with outdoor recreation? Why?
 6. Explain the Travel Cost Method.
 7. Identify the five principles of pricing outdoor recreation and apply them to an example.
 8. Discuss two different types of impacts from outdoor recreation.
 9. What is an economic multiplier?
10. The recreation service delivery system is paramount to the provision of recreational opportunities and protection of natural resources.

    a Name each of the sectors involved in the delivery of outdoor recreation.
    b Explain how they are different in terms of philosophy, administration and financing.
    c Explain three ways in which they are inter-related.

Chapter 6

Management of Outdoor Recreation

OBJECTIVES

This chapter will:

- critically assess the impacts from outdoor recreation;
- introduce the field of recreation ecology;
- explore the process of outdoor recreation management;
- appraise techniques and tools utilized by outdoor management;
- consider strategies for visitor and site management.

INTRODUCTION

Outdoor recreation was traditionally thought of as a benign form of land use (Pigram & Jenkins, 1999), and when compared to some competing uses of the natural environment (e.g., forestry, mining, livestock grazing, urban development) it may be less severe. However, the impacts of outdoor recreation are increasingly being realized and are anticipated to expand with increased participation. This chapter begins with an overview of the consequences or impacts from outdoor recreation activities. Recreation ecology is introduced as an area of research which has specifically focused on the biophysical consequences of outdoor recreation. Salient social impacts from outdoor recreation are also explored. The second part of the chapter explores the enterprise of outdoor recreation management in terms of its history, mandate, functions and principles. This background provides the foundation to examine key concepts that inform the practice of outdoor recreation management. Carrying capacity and recreational opportunities are highlighted as pervasive ideas which provide a conceptual basis for more specific managerial tools such as pre-formed management frameworks.

The chapter closes with a description of the roles and responsibilities of outdoor recreation managers. Influencing people undertaking outdoor recreation may ultimately resolve both degradation of the natural environment (caused by outdoor recreation) as well as negative influences on visitor experiences.

IMPACTS FROM OUTDOOR RECREATION

The popularity of outdoor recreation and participation in related activities is considerable, as documented in Chapter 5. In the first book solely dedicated to the issue of impacts from outdoor recreation, Michael Liddle (1997) is clear and unequivocal in assessing the implications of this popularity. He asserts that in the contemporary situation "the impacts of outdoor recreation, including ecotourism, are extensive and increasing, focusing more and more on the world's remaining natural areas" (Liddle, 1997, p. 1).

At this point it is important to define the term impact as it pertains to outdoor recreation. According to Hammitt and Cole, the "disturbance to natural areas as a result of recreational use has typically been defined as *resource* or *ecological* impact" (1998, p. 5). Yet impacts do not just occur to the natural environment. They are also frequently experienced by people who are participating in an outdoor recreation activity. Hall and Page write that "the social impact of tourism refers to the manner in which tourism and travel effects changes in collective and individual value systems, behaviour patterns, community structures, lifestyle and the quality of life" (1999, p. 126). Hall and Page (1999) also recognize that significant contributions have been made in social impacts by those studying outdoor recreation.

An impact, in and of itself, is neutral of value (Hammitt & Cole, 1998). This means that the term impact indicates a change caused by something but does inherently attach a value to it. Construction of a new trail, for example, may result in different behavior patterns for whitetail deer. The change in behavior patterns is an impact from trail development, but it does not specify if the change is positive or negative. In the context of wildland recreation, the term impact usually has negative connotations and is used to signal changes in the environment which are undesirable, including degradation to any parts of the ecosystem. The term impact is used here to signify negative changes in both natural ecosystems and social experiences.

Impacts on the Natural Environment

All outdoor recreation and ecotourism activities have an impact on ecological integrity or disturb the environment (Hammitt & Cole, 1988). Even activities that appear to be relatively harmless, such as walking through the woods, have an impact. In this example vegetation becomes trampled, litter (the uppermost part of soil consisting of leaves) becomes displaced, and wildlife may become disturbed. There is also no fundamental difference between impacts from activities classified as outdoor recreation and those considered as tourism (Hall & Page, 1999). Studies of ecological impacts provide another important area of overlap between those interested in recreation and tourism.

Impacts from outdoor recreation and ecotourism can generally be classified into four broad categories. Direct impacts are those which are the immediate result of a particular activity. The death of a pheasant as a consequence of being shot by a hunter is an example of a direct impact. Indirect impacts are negative changes to the natural environment which have come about through circuitous means. Take for example the development of a new trail which attracts a considerable amount of hikers. In addition to the direct impact of cutting down trees, development of the trail may also have an indirect affect on the composition of the surrounding habitat as the removal of taller trees permits more light-seeking vegetation species to flourish. Impacts from outdoor recreation and tourism also may be synergistic or compensatory in nature. Synergistic impacts are those in which a change in one element of the natural environment causes a corresponding and similar change in another element. The relationship between trampling of vegetation and soil erosion provides a good example. According to Liddle, "experiments have shown that by the time vegetation wear becomes visible, erosion is well under way and the land is already adjusting to conditions of greater soil loss" (1997, p. 339). Compensatory impacts refer to a situation where a change in one element of the environment prompts an offsetting change in another element. The predator–prey relationship between snowshoe hares and wolves illustrates a compensatory impact. If hunting pressure reduces the number of hares available a corresponding reduction in the population of wolves will occur (Caughley & Sinclair, 1994).

Recreation Ecology

Concern about impacts on the natural environment from recreation and tourism activities began in the 1970s and coincided with the growing public concern for the natural integrity (Hall & Page, 1999; Hammitt & Cole, 1998; Manning, 1999). Although the interest in impacts from these particular types of activities initially appears to be relatively recent, Liddle contends that:

> recreation ecology is in a sense a redefining of an age-old activity. Doubtless, humans moving through the wilderness or bush have always observed the impacts of others who may have gone before them. So, as with many areas of enquiry, it is hard to give a date when recreation ecology began.
>
> (1997, p. 3)

Liddle's (1997) seminal work entitled *Recreation Ecology* provides one of the most extensive and well-respected reviews of early efforts in this regard (Hamitt & Cole, 1998). He identifies the systematic investigation on the growth of meadowgrass on footpaths in the Malvern Hills, England by Stillingfleet in 1759 as the earliest formal study of recreation ecology. Although a few studies occurred in England and the United States in the 1920s and 1930s regarding trampling, it was after the 1960s that interest by ecologists increased exponentially in the subject (Liddle, 1997).

This brief background brings attention to the term recreation ecology. A relatively broad definition is offered by Liddle who explains that "recreation ecology deals with the impact of wildland-outdoor recreation on natural or semi-natural environments" (1991, p. 13). While this definition captures the comprehensive nature of recreation ecology, it is possible to be more explicit about the particular interests of recreational ecologists. Hammitt and Cole (1998) explain that, unlike early studies which particularly focused on vegetation and trampling, all resources and all forms of disturbance are of interest to researchers and students of recreation ecology.

Wall and Wright (1977) have synthesized impacts from outdoor recreation and ecotourism, as shown in Figure 6.1. The arrows illustrate both known and potential (questionable) relationships between a recreational activity and one of the four main divisions of concern to recreation ecologists (soil, vegetation, wildlife and water). Wall and Wright (1977) explain that impacts from recreational activities may be either positive and/or negative. Hiking for example causes vegetation to become trampled which negatively impacts the percentage of ground cover due to plant loss but may also have a positive affect on the growth rate of other species.

This disciplinary orientation presents considerable challenges to recreation ecologists as knowledge pertaining to any one area is increasingly specialized and continues to be explored from that particular perspective. Soil science is an excellent example of an area of study which has important links to the larger ecosystem impacts. The following section briefly explores the nature of recreation impacts in the four main areas of soil, vegetation, water and wildlife. Each element is introduced, potential impacts are identified, and an example of related research is provided. This approach gives structure to the areas of inquiry within recreation ecology. Subsequently, the interactions among these four main areas are discussed to capture the holistic effects on the natural environment, as recognized by Liddle (1997). Therefore, a discussion of interactions among the four main areas of recreation ecology is also included.

Soil

Soil is a critical element of ecosystems upon which outdoor recreation has considerable affects. Although fundamental to many outdoor recreation pursuits soil is not commonly associated with outdoor recreation. Hammitt and Cole assert that "soil, the basis of all ter-

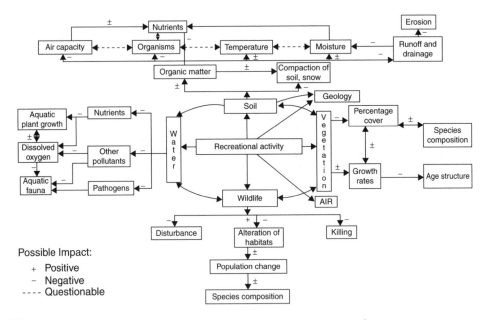

Figure 6.1 *Impacts from Outdoor Recreation.*

Source: Wall & Wright, 1977.

restrial life, is commonly misunderstood. Much more than just inert dirt, soil is alive—produced and maintained by interactions between living organisms, rock, air, water, and sunlight" (1998, p. 23). Although the composition of soil varies, it generally consists of layers of organic forms, mineral soils, accumulated oxides, clays, and organic/mineral substrate (Hammitt & Cole, 1998; Liddle, 1997). Considerable interaction occurs between soil layers with a general downward movement as organic materials decompose. Key features of concern to soil scientists and considerations with important implications for outdoor recreation managers include texture (size of particles which constitute the soil), structure (how the particles combine), and pore space (distance between the particles) (Hammitt & Cole, 1998).

Compaction is the most apparent impact on soil from outdoor recreation (Hammitt & Cole, 1998; Liddle, 1997). It arises from a diverse range of activities from those which are relatively simple or primitive (e.g., hiking) through to the use of mechanized transportation (e.g., all-terrain vehicles) in the backcountry. The most visible impact related to soil is removal of the top layer of litter (organic matter) which directly exposes soil to the elements and results in erosion (Liddle, 1997). Hammitt and Cole (1998) observe that erosion is the most serious of soil-related impacts because it is permanent and will continue even if use stops. While outdoor recreation tends not to continually directly impact soil, "recreation can therefore set in train a series of processes leading to, at best, a more vigorous growing environment for plants and, at worst, ugly scars on a previously natural and undisturbed landscape" (Liddle, 1997, p. 212). Other specific changes include shifts in soil moisture, loss of organic matter, reductions in pore space, and reduced infiltration rates (Hammitt & Cole, 1998).

The relationship between outdoor recreation and soil impacts is well documented by empirical research. The bulk density of soil (amount of air pockets within soil), was found to be low when an area was unused and to increase significantly when used by more than 1,000 people (Liddle & Greig-Smith, 1973). High bulk density increases the likelihood of erosion (Liddle, 1997). Intensive recreation at campsites in the Eagle Cap Wilderness in Oregon was found to be related to lower levels of essential nutrients (Zabinski, DeLuca, Cole and Moynahan, 2002). Such research has important implications for managers working to restore the functional capabilities of the soil, as using compost on disturbed campsites was identified as a potential way to increase the levels of missing nutrients (Zabinski et al., 2002).

Vegetation

Vegetation encompasses all plants including mosses and lichens, groundcovers, grasses, shrubs and trees. In addition to providing critical ecological functions, vegetation also contributes to outdoor recreation experience. Hammitt and Cole observe that "along with water, vegetation is probably the most important resource component affecting visitor selection of recreation sites. Vegetation adds to site desirably by providing shade, screening for campsite privacy, and attractiveness" (1998, p. 49).

Impacts from outdoor recreation on vegetation may be more obvious from visual inspection than on soil. Trampling, through its many forms, is an immediate and direct impact. Liddle (1997) observes that changes in the quantity and size of plants are common in areas in which recreation occurs. Composition may also be impacted as a result of trampling or the direct removal of species (Liddle, 1997). The variety of species in a particular area is of interest because it has implications for the structure of the environmental community (Hammitt & Cole, 1998). Contact with vegetation, sometimes even encouraged through interpretation and outdoor education (Chapter 8) has an impact on plants. Liddle (1997) contends that plants have specific physiological and morphological (more general forms) reactions to touching, shaking, bending, abrasion, wounding, defoliation and breakage which often occur during recreation. In this respect managers are concerned with the resistance, resilience and regeneration of particular species in an effort to maintain vegetation in areas of high recreation use (Liddle, 1997).

Research illustrates just how sensitive some vegetation is to outdoor recreation and how long restoration may take once sites have become impacted. Scott, Bayfield, Cernusca and Elston (2002) studied the impacts of trampling on vegetation and found that the rate of evapotranspiration (loss of moisture) for plants directly increased. After 75 passes on a vegetative area evapotranspiration became higher than normal and after 500 passes this increase became extensive (Scott et al., 2002). In studying the vegetative impacts at campsites, Cole and Monz (2004) showed that even after camping in an area ceased, impacts on vegetation were sustained. In some cases these impacts continued for more than three years (Cole & Monz, 2004).

Water

> Water is among the most essential requisites that nature provides to sustain life for plants, animals and humans. The total quantity of fresh water on earth could satisfy all the needs of the human population if it were evenly distributed and accessible.
>
> (Stumm, 1986, p. 201)

Water was also recognized above as the component of the natural environment that most influences site selection in outdoor recreation. Despite its importance, the impacts of outdoor recreation "on aquatic ecosystems is seldom mentioned or understood, yet water quality is a major concern in recreation areas. It serves as a medium for water-based activities, including body contact sports, and a drinking source for users" (Hammitt & Cole, 1998, p. 93). Water ecology is generally concerned with parameters pertaining to water quality. Some common parameters of concern include: chemical composition, suspended solids, temperature/flow, alkalinity, and bacteria (Hammitt & Cole, 1998, p. 93). Relationships among elements in aquatic systems are also important as they encompass forms of plant and animal life.

Outdoor recreation activities impact water resources in many ways. Recreation can result in pollution (e.g., oil from boats and human waste) entering the water network, loss of aquatic vegetation (from boats and trampling) as well as direct and indirect impacts on aquatic wildlife (Hammitt & Cole, 1998; Liddle, 1997). According to Hammitt and Cole "the major controversy over recreational use of water is based on a sanitation concern. Many studies suggest that recreational activity is a significant source of bacterial contamination" (1998, p. 99). Although this is typically associated with frontcountry or higher use areas, bacteria have also been problematic in wilderness areas such as the White Mountains (Hammitt & Cole, 1998). Other forms of contamination are also concerning. Anderson, Stewart, Yates and Gerba (1998) studied the impacts of swimming on pathogen and disease levels in water systems. They found that all swimmers introduced pathogens into the water, the majority of pathogen introduction occurred during the first 15–30 minutes, and the majority of pathogens were introduced by participants under the age of 18. These pathogens can affect water quality, and often end up in drinking water (Anderson et al., 1999).

Wildlife

Outdoor recreation often impacts wildlife. These impacts can be either purposefully or inadvertent, depending on the nature of the particular activity. Liddle (1997) provides a typology of disturbance to describe the nature of wildlife–recreation interactions. Type one disturbances are situations in which the animal is aware of the recreationist. Type two disturbances includes situations in which habitat is altered or which wildlife adapts to a new situation. The final type of disturbance, type three, is the most extreme. In the third disturbance type, there is "direct and damaging contact with the animal" (Liddle, 1997, p. 347).

A multitude of variables influence the response of wildlife to disturbances. These include: frequency of the disturbance, magnitude of the disturbance, type of species, time of year, and other situation variables (Hammitt & Cole, 1998; Liddle, 1997). Liddle (1997) observes that responses to type one or type two may be positive or negative, largely depending on the species in question and the amount of habituation that has occurred. While positive responses tend to be associated with acute feeding opportunities or habitat changes more suited to a particular niche, negative consequences largely relate to stresses caused by the encounter. The third type of disturbance particularly affects large mammals. Even if the disturbance between recreationists and wildlife does not lead to death, wildlife may be displaced and reproduction levels may decrease which ultimately results in a change of species composition and structure (Hammitt & Cole, 1998).

Relatively few investigations have systematically studied the relationship between outdoor recreation activities and impacts on wildlife and therefore knowledge about this relationship is limited (Hammitt & Cole, 1998). In one of the few volumes specifically dedicated to the interactions between wildlife and recreationists, *Wildlife and Recreationists: Coexistence Through Management and Research*, Knight and Gutzwiller (1995) discuss the idea of humans living in a utilitarian society and the need to recognize the effects we are having on wildlife. They highlight various ways in which recreationists impact wildlife, from direct disturbances (wildlife–human encounters) to indirect disturbances (loss of habitat through recreational exploitation of resources). Their work provides a basis for understanding how humans affect wildlife through recreational pursuits, a concept that now is emerging in various studies. For example, Reimers, Eftestol and Coleman (2003) examined changes in behavior in wild reindeer, resulting from direct disturbance from skiers and snowmobilers. The study found that when reindeer encountered recreationists (either on snowmobile or foot) they elicit a flight response, thus decreasing their energy levels. These disturbances may also lead to loss of habitat, as reindeer may begin to avoid areas in which recreationists are present (Reimers et al., 2003). Mammals are not the only form of wildlife directly affected by recreationists as birds may also be impacted. In a study of waterbirds, Schummer and Eddleman (2003) found that recreational disturbances (e.g., boating, fishing and vehicle use) affected migratory patterns by causing higher than necessary amounts of energy to be expended and increasing the overall amount of time for migration.

175

Interactions among the Four Components

Interactions also occur between the four main areas of recreation ecology, as illustrated by the arrows in Figure 6.1. As ecology stresses the interconnections between organisms, it is important to recognize that impacts from recreation not only have an affect on a particular component of nature, but also may impact the entire ecosystem. An ecosystem is described by Costanza and Folke as "plants, animals, and microorganisms which live in biological communities and which interact with each other and with the physical and chemical environment, with adjacent ecosystems, and with the atmospheres" (1996, p. 13).

Although Figure 6.1 is very informative as to impacts from recreation and their relationships, it is less effective in conveying other pertinent management considerations. Managers should recognize that impacts from outdoor recreation are rarely isolated as "single activities cause multiple impacts, and each impact tends to exacerbate or compensate for other changes" (Hammitt & Cole, 1998, p. 6). Impacts may also not be easily distinguishable by visual inspection. Hall and Page (1999) provide the example of New Zealand which relies on "clean, green" images; although in reality many of these locations exhibit low biodiversity and have limited indigenous species. Additional persistent challenges associated with considering impacts include:

a   the difficulty of distinguishing between changes induced by tourism and those induced by other activities;

b   the lack of information concerning conditions prior to the advent of tourism, and hence, the lack of baseline against which change can be measured;

c   the paucity of information on the numbers, types and tolerance levels of different species of flora and fauna; and,

d   the concentration of researchers upon particular primary resources, such as beaches and mountains, which are ecologically sensitive.

(Mathieson & Wall, 1982, p. 94)

Despite the growing knowledge about ecological degradation stemming from outdoor recreation and tourism, attributing degradation to specific activities is very difficult. These impacts may have cumulative consequences throughout the ecosystem which remain undetectable for considerable time periods.

Social Impacts from Outdoor Recreation

The increasing number of participants in outdoor activities in the 1950s and 1960s not only brought attention to impacts on the natural environment, it also prompted concern about the "quality" of the outdoor recreation experience (Manning, 1999). Both social and psychological dimensions of outdoor recreation have been of considerable interest, as explored in Chapter 4.

Simply, "outdoor recreation involves people, and the social environment in which recreation takes place has a good deal to do with the level of satisfaction experienced" (Pigram & Jenkins, 1999, p. 93). Research and knowledge of social impacts from outdoor recreation has largely occurred on the subjects of crowding, conflict, and visitor use.

Crowding

Crowding emerged as an issue in the early 1960s, was specifically investigated in the ORRRC review, and early crowding research focused on wilderness or remote natural areas (Manning, 1999). In one of the best known early studies of crowding, Lucas (1964) investigated the perception of crowding in the Boundary Waters Canoe Area which borders Minnesota and Ontario. In this study participants in outdoor recreation activities were asked about crowding concerns or the degree of bother when they encountered others. Results clearly illustrate the significance of social impacts on the outdoor recreation experience as canoeists reported a low desire to see others while those who used motorized means of travel, either canoe or boat, were less disturbed by encounters. From these initial studies, the topic of crowding has received continued attention from both researchers and managers. In his recent review of outdoor recreation research, Manning (1999) identified crowding as one of the most investigated issues. Researchers are not alone in their interest in crowding. Managers in the United States National Park Service reported that in a high propensity of areas capacity was exceeded (Manning, 1999). Crowding in the Canadian context is less clear. In a recent study of Ontario Provincial Park managers, crowding was not reported to be of significant concern s (Spiers & Plummer, 2005).

Crowding is distinct from the level of use at a site. Manning explains that:

> use level is a physical concept relating number of people per unit of space; it is strictly neutral and suggests no psychological or experiential evaluation or interpretation. Crowding, on the other hand, has a psychological meaning, it is a negative and subjective evaluation of a use level. Thus, use level may increase to a point where it is perceived to interfere with one's activities or intentions, but only at this point does crowding occur.
>
> (1999, p. 94)

Crowding is a judgment by a person of a specific use level. Pigram and Jenkins (1999) observe that crowding is influenced by psychological, social, and site-specific factors. They specifically note the connection to motivations and values held by the participants as identified in the theory of planned behavior as well as the homogeneity of the group (social status, behavior, composition). Site characteristics found to particularly influence the perception of crowding includes the size of the area, type of terrain, and density of vegetation. Pigram and Jenkins (1999) explain that these landscape features "absorb" or limit the perception of crowding despite the actual level of use so an area appears to be less crowded.

Crowding is a concern for managers because it has been shown to directly relate to decreased satisfaction in wilderness settings (see Manning, 1999; Pigram & Jenkins, 1999). The inverse relationship between crowding and satisfaction is different from many other recreational activities in which crowding or high numbers of people are actually desirable such as musical concerts, festivals and dances. Figure 6.2 illustrates the distinction between the two situations as well as the relationship between crowding and satisfaction.

In addition to decreased satisfaction, the perception of crowding often prompts individuals to engage various forms of coping behaviors. From his synthesis of crowding

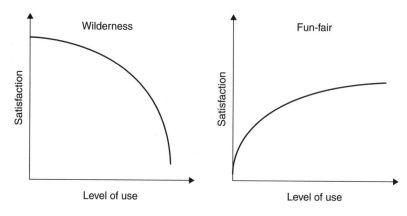

Figure 6.2 Crowding and Satisfaction.
Source: adapted from Brotherton, 1973.

research in outdoor recreation, Manning (1999) identifies three responses to crowding—displacement, rationalization and product shift. Displacement involves those participating in a particular area/activity changing location. Manning identifies that:

> it is important to note that displacement does not have to involve a shift from one recreation area to another—intersite displacement—but can involve shifts within a recreation area—intrasite displacement—and shifts from one time period to another—temporal displacement.
>
> (1999, p. 95)

Rationalization involves individuals altering their perception of the situation and therefore potential satisfaction. The theory of cognitive dissonance, in which people aim to reduce internal cognitive inconsistencies, is employed by Manning (1999) to explain why individuals who have made substantial investments are likely to positively make sense of the experience. For example, if a group was seeking solitude in a wilderness setting and instead encountered numerous people, they may alter their perception to highlight the benefits of making new acquaintances. Product shift relates to the concept of substitutability, introduced in Chapter 4. Under this form of coping behavior, an individual experiencing crowding changes their perception of the opportunity and/or activities. They may actually participate in a different activity, which they perceive to be less crowded. Each of the above responses to crowding presents a specific challenge to managers concerned with the quality of the experience as such perceptions may lead to reduced satisfaction or leaving the area/facility.

Conflict

Concern and interest regarding conflict in outdoor recreation also emerged during the 1950s and 1960s. Since drawing initial attention, conflict in recreational settings can be categorized into four management eras:

- User activity–space allocation era (1950s–1960s)—conflict in recreation settings becomes apparent and focus is directed at multiple activities attempting to use the physical space for different activities.
- Perception cause era (1970s)—the presence of conflict in situations where activities were not in direct competition as well as individual and group differences prompted attention on psychological dimensions with particular emphasis on motivation and perceptions. The Recreation Opportunity Spectrum (ROS) was a dominant management strategy to mitigate conflict.
- Institutional–public involvement era (1980s)—public interest and perception was formally incorporated into the decision-making process so attention shifted to public values. This new relationship between the public and managers resulted in tension with the public input potentially being marginalized.
- Coping–resolution era (1990–)—conflict in recreational settings is accepted as inevitable. Attention is directed at resolution strategies, individual coping responses, and collaborative management strategies (Hammitt & Schneider, 2000, p. 348).

In the contemporary context, conflict is understood as "a condition that exists when one person, or group of people, experience or perceive an interference of goals or the likelihood of incompatible goals, as the result of another person's or group's actions, threat of action, or personal/group attributes" (Ewert, Dieser & Voight, 1999, p. 337). Cross-country skiers and snowmobilers provide an illustrative example. Assume skiers have a trail for their exclusive use which is located some distance apart from the snowmobile trail, which is specifically restricted for snowmobiling purposes. Although the two groups do not compete for space or come into physical contact with each other, the noise and pollution from the snowmobiles may interfere with the goals of quiet nature experience of the skiers.

The above example demonstrates that understanding conflict in recreational settings must continue to become more comprehensive and diverse as conflict extends well beyond face-to-face disputes. Schneider (2000a) recognizes that conflict may be intrapersonal, interpersonal and/or organizational. It is evident that participants themselves, other outdoor recreation participants (either in the same activity or in a different activity) as well as managers may be involved in conflict.

Interest has been directly focused on how individuals respond to conflict. Lazarus and Folkman (1984) have found that conflict produces a stress response, which prompts adaptation on the part of the individual. Over a decade later, Rasmussen and Brunson (1996) proposed that conflict should be modeled as being multi-dimensional, involving both intensity and the resolution process. Participants in outdoor recreation experiencing conflict have also been observed to exhibit similar responses to those experiencing crowding (Schneider, 2000b). Management is often involved in recreation conflict, both as an intermediary between individuals and sometimes even as a causal agent.

As managers are increasingly being called upon to resolve conflict, the diverse nature of these conflicts poses new challenges. Ewert et al. (1999) identify that managers require additional information and solutions to address conflict. Hammitt and Schneider (2000) have proposed a model of the conflict resolution process for managers involving the three steps of analysis, confrontation and resolution. In response to the need for additional information and to assist managers with negotiating the increasingly diverse forms of conflict, Spiers and Plummer (2005) have created a conflict typology for outdoor recreation and park managers. This typology connects each type of conflict (intrapersonal, interpersonal, organizational) to key considerations synthesized from the literature, information requirements, and managerial actions. Such a typology encourages comprehensive thinking about conflict.

Visitor Use

While crowding and conflict are perennial issues receiving considerable attention and research, a host of other considerations are captured under the term visitor use. These considerations impact both the ecological and social experience of outdoor recreation and include (Hammitt & Cole, 1998, pp. 181–198):

- Use distribution—closely linked to the issue of crowding, visitor use is typically concentrated along trails, at campsites, and adjacent to lakes and streams.
- Types of user groups—individuals participating in overnight stays tend to have greater impacts and destination patterns in the form of nodes.
- Party size—groups in excess of 8–10 people tend to have a greater spatial impact, particularly on vegetative communities.
- User behavior—the manner in which people act while in the backcountry directly relates to both ecological and social impacts. Knowledge of minimum impact and/or leave no trace principles, which educates users about how to minimize impacts, specifically address campfires, noise, tent colour, litter and waste. The greater amount of experience a user has the more sensitive he/she is to both social and ecological impacts and the more seasoned the campers are the more likely they will recognize such impacts. Coincidentally, user motivations, or the reasons why individuals are participating in the particular activity, have been shown to relate to impacts. For example, if an individual going cross-country skiing is motivated by the aesthetics and quietness of the forest, they are unlikely to produce either considerable social or ecological impacts.
- Social group and place attachment—relatively few individuals actually participate in outdoor recreation alone and therefore the nature of the group may greatly influence both ecological and social impacts. In addition to the social nature of the outdoor recreation experience, individuals and groups develop deep attachments to the location/environment in which they participate in outdoor recreation. Place attachment, and the strong emotional responses with ecological changes and/or other users who encroach on these areas potentially results in significant social impacts.
- Mode of travel—the manner by which people traverse the backcountry is a key variable in influencing vegetative and social impacts from outdoor recreation. Mode of travel can be generally classified as being motorized (snowmobiles/off road vehicles/motorized boats), assisted or mechanized (stock, mountain bikes) and human powered (walking). The potential for impact is highest among motorized means of travel as

180

noise, pollution and transfer of power is most pronounced; assisted or mechanized also present considerable impacts as, for example, horse travel, causes considerable ecological damage and the speed of mountain bikes may pose a considerable safety hazard. Even human-powered travel is not immune to causing some ecological damage, although it is considerably less than that by either motorized or mechanized forms of travel.

The above visitor use considerations illustrate the breadth of variables which the outdoor recreation manager must consider. Further complexity comes from the fact that these visitor use considerations influence the other ecological and social impacts from outdoor recreation. Therefore, it is this web of considerations which confront outdoor recreation managers.

OUTDOOR RECREATION MANAGEMENT

Outdoor recreation managers face a vexing conundrum. Participants in outdoor recreation pursuits impact the natural environment and may also cause social impacts which detract from the experience of others. Managers of outdoor recreation areas/facilities are charged with the task of protecting the natural environment while maintaining/promoting quality outdoor recreation experiences.

Outdoor recreation management was given an intermediate position between the second and third levels in the conceptual framework (Figure I.2) because it constitutes both an area of knowledge and application. Understanding management and related issues is critical for three reasons. First, many students of outdoor recreation will, at some point in their career, likely be involved with management. These opportunities include: managing resource areas such as parks, conservation lands, waterways and forests; owning/managing an outdoor recreation service provision business or facility; and having to work for an outdoor recreation manager. Second, participants in outdoor pursuits will interact or frequently encounter management as well as managerial decisions (e.g., regulations). Third, it is through outdoor recreation management that impacts, both environmental and social, can be minimized. While both knowledge and practice are discussed, the emphasis here is to present information on the enterprise of management which the reader can relate to the subsequent three chapters on parks and protected areas, outdoor education and interpretation, and adventure.

The importance of outdoor recreation management cannot be overstated: without such management the natural environments which provide settings for outdoor experiences may become degraded and/or the socio-economic qualities which make outdoor recreation desirable may become compromised. As both the number of participants increase and the diversity of activities expand (Cordell & Super, 2000) the role of managers will also increase in importance.

The Tradition of Outdoor Recreation Management

The tradition of outdoor recreation management is inextricably linked to the broader evolution of outdoor recreation, presented in Chapter 2. Jubenville and Twight (1993) categorize the history of outdoor recreation into three management eras. The custodial era began with concerns about the natural environment and the need to provide quality opportunities to experience wilderness. These came from influential individuals (e.g., Muir & Leopold) and organizations (e.g., the Sierra Club). Passionate expressions and popularization gave rise to greater public concern and ultimately translated into greater government involvement on behalf of all citizens. During this initial era, most resource areas were held by the government with relatively little access or facility development.

Socio-economic forces and the increased demand for outdoor recreation at the end of World War II prompted a change to the era of extensive management. Government agencies directly responded to the increased demand for outdoor recreation. The hallmarks of this era are the increased provision of general supply (e.g., access roads, logging and facility development) and the development of specific outdoor recreation related initiatives (e.g., visitor management, interpretation and site protection) (Jubenville & Twight, 1993). Satisfaction played a central role to all concerned with outdoor recreation. As Manning explains:

> managers want to provide high-quality outdoor recreation opportunities, and visitors want to have high-quality outdoor experiences. Researchers want to understand what contributes to and detracts from high-quality outdoor recreation experiences. As a consequence, the concept of quality is contained, explicitly or implicitly, in the goals and policies governing most outdoor recreation areas and is an underlying objective of most outdoor recreation research.
>
> (1999, p. 8)

Referring back to the model of recreation satisfaction in Chapter 4 (Figure 4.5.), it is immediately evident that managers exert considerable influence over the three situational variables (resource setting, social setting, and managerial setting).

Intensive management characterizes the third management era. Although the exact time at which the third era began is debatable, "emphasis seems to be the need for developing and updating baseline data on both the effect of visitor participation in a particular area, including the visitor's perceptions of quality recreation experiences" (Jubenville & Twight, 1993, p. 7). Attention focused on objectives, the need to refine models, and the continual search for innovative managerial practices.

In the 1990s considerable attention was directed towards cooperative models of governance in which people from many spheres of life come together to manage resources. Declining government investments and interest in innovative administrative structures (from the intensive era) resulted in downsizing, deregulation, and the devolution of responsibilities (Meadowcroft, 1998). Kooiman describes this as an era of change in which governments are interested in "governing in terms of 'co' such as co-steering, co-managing, co-producing and co-allocating" (1993, p. 2). Hence, the current situation represents a fourth era of outdoor recreation management. An example of this co-management approach is provided by Stankey, McCool, Clark and Brown (1999) who describe the transactive approach employed in the development of the Bob Marshall Wilderness Complex plan.

The Process of Outdoor Recreation Management

Management, in the broadest sense, is "the process of reaching organizational goals by working with and through people and other organizational resources" (Certo, Appelbaum & Shapiro, 1993, p. 8). This broad definition is useful to illustrate the main elements of management, prior to exploring it more specifically in the context of outdoor recreation. Certo et al. (1993) assert that management is analogous to a house and is constituted by four main components, as illustrated in Figure 6.3. Goals/objectives towards which management is orientated are located at the apex of Figure 6.3. The foundation of this process is the activity of planning, located at the base of Figure 6.3. Planning itself is a term that is variously employed. Here it is used to convey a preconceived notion or course of actions rationally determined in advance, to move towards organizational goals and objectives. From the base of planning, managers move towards the achievement of goals and objectives through organizing, influencing and controlling. Organizing involves assigning tasks to individuals and allocating sufficient resources so tasks may be achieved. Managers must also ensure that actions and people move the organization towards its goals and objectives. This pillar is referred to as influencing as both activities and people are guided in appropriate directions. The final pillar in the concept of management is controlling. Controlling involves feedback from the other components in the model by which actions are monitored and modifications are made to plans and actions. Controlling is particularly important as changes occur within organizations, outside of organizations and to organizational goals and objectives.

Resource management is a specific application of the general concept of management. Resource management is understood by O'Riordan as:

> a process of decision making whereby resources are allocated over space and time according to the needs, aspirations, and desires of man within the framework of his

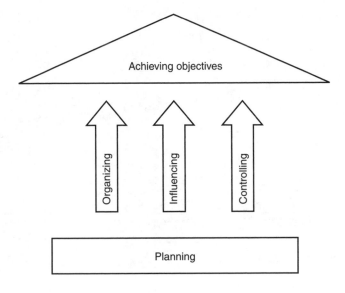

Figure 6.3 The General Components of Management.

technological inventiveness, his political and social institutions, and his legal and administrative arrangements. Resource management should be visualized as a conscious process of decision involving judgment, preference and commitment, whereby certain desired resource outputs are sought from certain perceived resource combinations through the choice among various managerial, technical and administrative alternatives.

(1971, p. 19)

The process of resource allocation is complicated as it involves multiple perspectives and spans temporal and spatial dimensions (Mitchell, 1989). Once the decision is made to allocate a particular resource for outdoor recreation, or a portion of a particular resource in the case of multiple use management, goals and objectives can more clearly emerge.

Outdoor recreation management is a process by which purposeful actions are undertaken to ensure ecological integrity while concomitantly providing opportunities for experiences that are personally meaningful and intuitively worthwhile. Reflecting the general idea of management, this is accomplished through planning, organizing, influencing and controlling. Although management in the context of outdoor recreation certainly resembles the general management model, it is distinguished by its associated goals and objectives as well as its emphasis on planning.

Returning briefly to the earlier satisfaction model, outdoor recreation management is oriented towards three complementary objectives. Manning recognizes that "outdoor recre-

Plate 6.1 How can Outdoor Recreation Managers Strive to Protect the Natural Environment and Provide Opportunities for Meaningful Experiences?

Plate 6.2 *Providing a Rope Bridge is Sometimes the Best Option to Protect the Environment and to Facilitate Travel.*

ation should be considered within a three-fold framework of concerns: the natural environment, the social environment, and the management environment" (1999, p. 278). This "framework" represents the objectives for outdoor recreation management. Although initially these objectives appear relatively straightforward, they are more accurately conceptualized as a series of continuums that act in some combination to guide management. Figure 6.4 illustrates the potential range of positions associated with each general objective. For example, a wilderness situation may be guided by positions which are located at one extreme of the three objectives (high environmental integrity, social solitude, few management interventions). Conversely, objectives for a community park would be located at the opposite end (manicured or altered natural environment, encounters desired, management intervention expected). Indeed, a similar notion is at the heart of the Recreation Opportunity Spectrum (ROS), presented later in the chapter.

Although not mutually exclusive, management should also be distinguished from other aspects of the decision-making process related to outdoor recreation. Driver and Brown (1983) make clear this distinction, stating that:

> policy issues relate to the establishment of decision guidelines, including budgetary guidelines, within an organization. Management decisions must be made within these guidelines and generally relate to the production of some type of good or service, Outdoor-recreation policy decisions, therefore, are made at all levels of a recreation agency, while management decisions are made only at those levels that actually "manipulate" the environment to provide recreation opportunities.

185

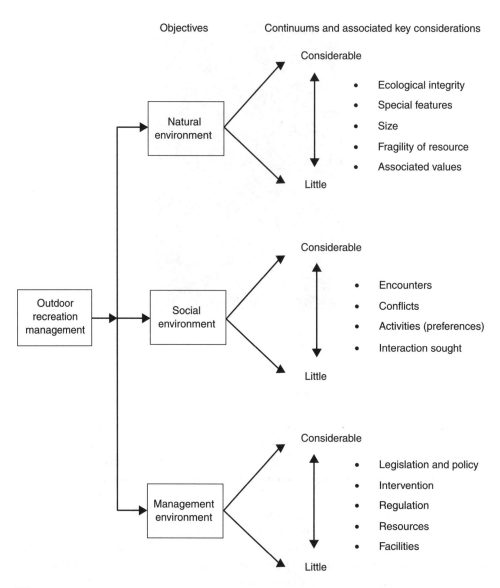

Figure 6.4 *Objectives of Outdoor Recreation Management.*
Source: adapted from Manning, 1999.

Policies providing guidance to those managing outdoor recreation areas have been discussed in Chapter 2 and are therefore not reviewed here. Given the geographic scope and multiple scales considered, a plethora of governmental agencies, commercial organizations and non-governmental organizations all maintain policies as to how outdoor recreation management ought to occur. They take varied positions along the three outdoor recreation objectives presented earlier.

The applied perspective offered by Driver and Brown (1983) and the theoretical view offered by Jubenville and Twight (1993) provide helpful insights into the management of outdoor recreation. Outdoor recreation may be viewed as a production process which converts natural resources into recreation benefits/impacts for which both managers and users play important roles, as illustrated in Figure 6.5. According to Driver and Brown (1983) there are three processes which actually constitute the recreation production process. The first starts with the natural environment being viewed as a resource that can be used to satisfy the human desire for outdoor recreation. It is through managerial actions (e.g., providing access, developing sites, constructing trails) that opportunities for outdoor recreation are developed. Jubenville and Twight (1993) emphasize this distinction as the manager may only provide the opportunity for outdoor recreation to occur. The second production process, distinguishable from the first because it focuses on the participant, begins with an individual deciding (seeking satisfaction) to participate in a particular recreation opportunity. It is the participant, not the manager, who actually creates the recreation experience. The final process, comprised of the recreation experience, involves the generation of benefits and/or adverse impacts (Driver & Brown, 1983; Manning, 1999).

Jubenville and Twight (1993) further describe the outdoor recreation management model as a system. They explain that:

> a system is a set of interrelated and independent parts, or subsystems, which can react as a total organism resides in an environment which sustains the organism. The "organism" or system exists because of demands for its products or services from elements of its environment, and it produces outputs of products or services which it exchanges with the environment in return for social support.
>
> (1993, p. 13)

A systems perspective acknowledges forces (e.g., political, economic) which influence government policy and, in turn, provide direction to outdoor recreation managers. Following Jubenville and Twight's (1993) systems model, three interrelated inputs are identified as

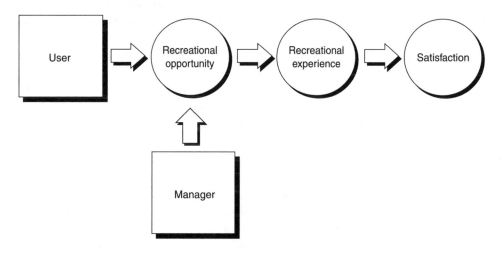

Figure 6.5 Outdoor Recreation as a Production Process.

primary to the outdoor recreation management system—the visitor or recreationist, the natural resource base or environment, and management. Building upon these components (which Manning (1999) similarly identifies), outdoor recreation managers act to produce recreation opportunities. Primary functions of outdoor recreation managers are therefore conceived as specific subsystems: visitor management involves the social elements that influence recreationists' experiences (e.g., crowding); resource management entails manipulation or activities that prevent alterations of the natural environment; and service management involves facility/amenity provision to users.

In order for managers to effectively and efficiently perform their functions, particular knowledge, skills and abilities are required. Reading a book such as this or enrolling in outdoor recreation courses are excellent first steps to developing an understanding of outdoor recreation. Specific knowledge and skills are also necessary for outdoor recreation managers as they have the following general responsibilities:

1. to determine how many scarce public resources (e.g., land, labor, and capital) will be allocated to outdoor-recreation programs, when, where, for whom, and at what price to the users;
2. to provide appropriate, high-quality recreation opportunities once basic allocations have been made;
3. to protect the biophysical and cultural–historic recreation resources from unacceptable change or damage;
4. to reasonably protect the users from harm;
5. to evaluate the effectiveness of the results of the above actions (Driver & Brown, 1983, p. 309).

In addition to these general responsibilities, the role of outdoor recreation managers has changed considerably over the past 50 years. In the 1950s managers decided what recreational opportunities should be provided and set out to provide them (Jubenville & Twight, 1993). This clearly reflects the view that outdoor recreation management is a production process. More recently, Manning (1999) has urged that the "commodity" approach should be replaced with a more "transactive" approach, which emphasizes the fundamental nature of the participant in constructing the experience. Stankey et al. (1999) reinforce this shift towards a collaborative or transactive direction.

In the contemporary context, outdoor recreation managers are confronted with the challenge of incorporating participation and interaction (i.e., transactive approach), while doing so in a systematic and structured way. Manning's (1999) outdoor recreation management framework fulfills this need as it emphasizes the process qualities of management and permits the incorporation of specific tools, which are explored later in this chapter.

Manning's (1999) outdoor recreation management framework involves four steps, as illustrated in Figure 6.6. The first step involves inventorying existing conditions along environmental, social and managerial dimensions. It should be recognized that these correspond to the three goals set out at the start of this section. The second step involves determining specific objectives associated with each of the aforementioned dimensions,

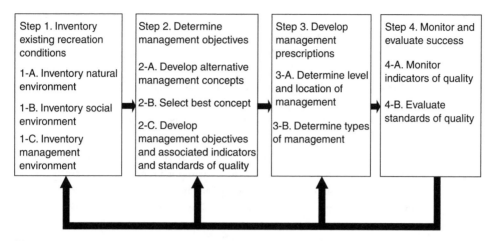

Figure 6.6 Outdoor Recreation Management Framework.

considering input from participants and the public, and formulating specific indicators/ standards for selected management actions. The third step involves moving from the existing conditions to the specific objectives. Developing management prescriptions involves formulating and implementing specific actions as well as detailing the level/type of management required (e.g., direct and/or indirect techniques). Monitoring and evaluating success is the final step. Information collected during the initial inventory as baseline information is evaluated in light of current conditions to gauge the effectiveness of managerial actions and progress toward the objectives specified. The feedback arrows that accompany each step of the management framework are important because outdoor recreation management is rarely linear or straightforward.

Outdoor Recreation Techniques and Tools

In this section the reader is introduced to specific concepts and tools employed by outdoor recreation managers, which fit within the general outdoor recreation management framework. Concepts covered include: carrying capacity, the recreation opportunity spectrum, limits of acceptable change, visitor activity management protocol, visitor impact management, and visitor experience and resource protection. These planning concepts are complemented by an overview of specific techniques for visitor and site management.

Carrying Capacity

The general concept of carrying capacity builds upon the idea of balance in natural ecosystems and the definition of ecological carrying capacity, introduced in Chapter 3. From a geography/resource analyst perspective, Mitchell (1989) observes that this idea of carrying capacity has been used broadly and applied to a number of situations including the earth, the human population, agriculture, and wilderness. As the concept has been applied to each of these situations, the importance of the theoretical model has been recognized (Jubenville & Twight, 1993).

The idea of carrying capacity was readily adapted to outdoor recreation from the rangeland management tradition (Pigram & Jenkins, 1999; Shelby & Herberlin, 1986). Pigram and Jenkins explain that "most definitions of recreation carrying capacity attempt to combine [the] notion of protection of the resource base from overuse with, simultaneously, the assurance of enjoyment and satisfaction for participants" (1999, p. 90). Carrying capacity in outdoor recreation refers to "the level of use beyond which impacts exceed levels specified by evaluative standards" (Shelby and Herberlin, 1986, p. 18).

Shelby and Herberlin (1986) have developed a conceptual framework of carrying capacity (illustrated in Figure 6.7) for outdoor recreation research and management. It consists of descriptive and evaluative components. The descriptive component involves objectively describing the management parameters (elements of the system that management can influence) and impact parameters (elements affected by use and type of capacity in question). The evaluative component prompts outdoor recreation managers to consider the manner in which an area should be managed. It consists of the desired type of experience or outcome from a particular opportunity as well as the evaluative standards which articulate quality judgments (minimum, maximum or optimum) regarding the acceptability of particular impacts. The model highlights the importance of: determining elements that can be manipulated by managers; objectively gauging use/impacts; and recognizing the need to combine objective and subjective dimensions.

Many different types of carrying capacity (e.g., physical, facility, economic, ecological, social) are pertinent to outdoor recreation managers (Jubenville & Twight, 1993; Payne & Nilsen, 2002; Pigram & Jenkins, 1999; Shelby & Herberlin, 1986). Physical and/or facility carrying capacity are used to indicate capacities related to space (Pigram & Jenkins, 1999; Shelby & Herberlin, 1986). This form of carrying capacity is particularly important for design considerations regarding safety. The maximum number of people allowed in an amphitheater as per the fire code is an example of facility capacity. The maximum number

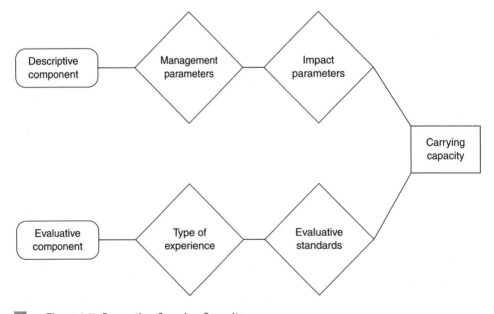

Figure 6.7 Recreation Carrying Capacity.

of vehicles that can park at a scenic vista is an example of a physical capacity upon which the maximum cannot be exceeded as it is only physically possible to park a given number of cars in a parking lot. Minimum capacities are also of interest as there may be a minimum number of resource users required for an outdoor area to remain viable.

Ecological and social carrying capacities are of the greatest relevance to outdoor recreation (Payne & Nilsen, 2002; Pigram & Jenkins, 1999). Ecological carrying capacity "is concerned with the maximum level of recreational use, in terms of numbers and activities, that can be accommodated by an area or ecosystem before an unacceptable or irreversible decline in ecological values occur" (Pigram & Jenkins, 1999, p. 91). The characteristics of natural ecosystems and the cause(s) of the impacts considerably influence the ecological capacities of each site. While ecological concerns historically took precedence, social impacts are demanding increasing attention from outdoor recreation managers. How a manager can effectively discern evaluative standards which are subjective or personal is a pressing issue.

Adding further complexity to carrying capacity is the interrelated nature of the various types. For example, ecological carrying capacity can be related to the social carrying capacity for a particular campsite. Consequently linkages need to be made between social and ecological dimensions as knowledge of both are required by managers (Payne & Nilsen, 2002). It is the responsibility, and to a large extent the judgment of the outdoor recreation manager, to balance these capacities. Pigram and Jenkins observe that "both resources and people must be taken into account when considering carrying capacity. It is important for decision-makers to be aware of the dynamic, multidimensional nature of the capacity concept, in order to adopt a balanced approach to managerial responsibilities" (1999, p. 95).

Despite the conceptual development and potential managerial applications of carrying capacity in outdoor recreation, the concept has been sharply criticized. In their research note, *Rethinking Carrying Capacity*, Lindenberg, McCool and Stankey (1997) assert that: definitions of carrying capacity lack the specificity/workability to guide pragmatic implementation as they rely on subjective values rather than explicit criteria; perception of the approach as objective/scientific is misleading managers to assume criteria exist which can or should be applied between sites; and the approach promotes confusion as the concept stresses levels of use whereas managers are concerned about conditions. Consequently, Lindenberg et al. (1997) suggest that the traditional notion of carrying capacity should be replaced in favor of alternative planning/management frameworks, because they shift focus to the conditions desired. Mitchell (1989) raises ethical issues for managers associated with gathering information on the use and/or experience of those while participating in outdoor recreation activities.

Alternative Planning and Management Frameworks

Even if carrying capacities for outdoor recreation are established "they are not the key to management for which some have been looking. The key to management, in recreation as in range and wildlife management, is specifying management objectives and monitoring conditions" (Hammitt & Cole, 1998, p. 15). Experience and research associated with recreation carrying capacity has provided the basis for many of the alternative planning and management approaches (Hammitt & Cole, 1998; Lindenberg et al., 1997; Mitchell, 1989; Pigram & Jenkins, 1999).

191

Recreation Opportunity Spectrum

The Recreation Opportunity Spectrum (ROS) was one of the first alternative planning/management frameworks to emerge from the concept of recreation carrying (Mitchell, 1989). It was developed by the United States Forest Service (USFS) and the Bureau of Land Management (BLM) in the late 1970s and early 1980s. As these agencies sought ways to enhance their ability for integrated resource planning as well as the need to provide diverse opportunities the ROS structure was proposed (Driver et al., 1987). Driver et al. explain that ROS:

> involves specifying recreational goals in terms of broad classes of recreation opportunity, identifying specific indicators of these opportunities that permit their operational definition and defining specific standards for each indicator that make distinctions among the opportunities possible. The result is a clear definition of recreation opportunities as both the products of management and the services desired by recreationists. These opportunities, with their explicit specification of appropriate conditions for each indicator, can be incorporated into a land use planning process and used to provide guidance for on-the-ground recreation management.
>
> (1987, p. 204)

Central to ROS is the notion of recreational opportunity. A recreational opportunity involves a threefold relationship among activity opportunities, setting opportunities, and experience opportunities (Driver et al., 1987). Attention is directed at the attributes of the physical setting (biophysical elements of the natural environment), social setting (human dimensions or users involved at the site), and managerial setting (amount of regimentation observed) (Driver et al., 1987; Hammitt & Cole, 1998).

Although specific forms of the ROS structure have varied, implementation usually involves classifying large land areas into classes according to the specific setting attributes. The USFS and BLM have prescriptive approaches to applying ROS (see Hammitt & Cole, 1998) which use six opportunity classes. These opportunity classes represent the continuum or recreation resources from the most primitive to the most urban, as illustrated in Table 6.1. Setting attributes and associated indicators assist in differentiating among the potential opportunity classes.

Initial excitement regarding ROS was considerable. Driver et al. capture the early optimism associated with the approach in stating that "the ROS framework has caught the attention of recreation resource administrators in Asia, northern Europe, North America and the South Pacific" (1987, p. 210). Early enthusiasm about ROS has not translated into universal adoption. However, its utility is recognized for:

1   inventorying available recreational opportunities;
2   developing prescriptions (objectives and standards) for management which are associated with the respective classes;
3   clarifying the challenges for managers interested in the primitive end of the spectrum as impacts are less acceptable and management less desirable (Hammitt & Cole, 1998).

Table 6.1 Appropriate Setting Descriptions for Each of the Six Classes in the Recreational Opportunity Spectrum

Recreational opportunity spectrum class

Primitive	Semi-primitive non-motorized	Semi-primitive motorized	Roaded natural	Rural	Urban
Area is characterized by essentially unmodified natural environment of fairly large size. Interaction between users is very low and evidence of other users is minimal. The area is managed to be essentially free from evidence of human-induced restrictions and controls. Motorized use within the area is not permitted.	Area is characterized by a predominantly natural or natural-appearing environment of moderate-to-large size. Interaction between users is low, but there is often evidence of other users. The area is managed in such a way that minimum on-site controls and restrictions may be present, but are subtle. Motorized use is not permitted.	Area is characterized by a predominantly natural-appearing environment of moderate-to-large size. Concentration of users is low, but there is often evidence of other users. The area is managed in such a way that minimum on-site controls and restrictions may be present, but are subtle. Motorized use is permitted.	Area is characterized by predominantly natural-appearing environments with moderate evidences of the sights and sounds of humans. Such evidences usually harmonize with the natural environment. Interaction between users may be low to moderate, but with evidence of other users prevalent. Resource modification and utilization practices are evident, but harmonize with the natural environment. Conventional motorized use is provided for in construction standards and design of facilities.	Area is characterized by a substantially modified natural environment. Resource modification and utilization practices are to enhance specific recreation activities and to maintain vegetative cover and soil. Sights and sounds of humans are readily evident, and the interaction between users is often moderate to high. A considerable number of facilities are designed for use by a large number of people. Facilities are often provided for special activities. Moderate densities are provided far away from developed sites. Facilities for intensified motorized use and parking are available.	Area is characterized by a substantially urbanized environment, although the background may have natural-appearing elements. Renewable resource modification and utilization practices are to enhance specific recreation activities. Vegetative cover is often exotic and manicured. Sights and sounds of humans, on-site, are predominant. Large numbers of users can be expected, both on-site and in nearby areas. Facilities for highly intensified motor use and parking are available, with forms of mass transit often available to carry people throughout the site.

Source: USDA Forest Service, 1982, ROS Users Guide.

The spirit of ROS is also reflected in other zoning processes, such as those employed in Canada's National Parks (Payne & Nilsen, 2002). It has also served as a basis for subsequent framework development. For example, Boyd and Butler (1996) have modified ROS and the Tourism Opportunity Spectrum (TOS) to create the Ecotourism Opportunity Spectrum (ECOS) as a conceptual guide for managing ecotourism destinations.

Many pertinent questions and challenges have been raised regarding ROS. Driver et al. (1987) note that further research is required to determine the relationship among experiences received, activity, and settings; applicability of ROS to diverse situations and scales; and importance about quality aspects of opportunities afforded. The absence of explicit ecological factors or inputs in ROS is a pervasive criticism (Jubenville & Twight, 1993; Payne & Nilsen, 2002). Although ROS specifies benefits from resource allocation decisions to local communities, ROS is primarily driven by rational planning theory, dependent upon technical data, and not conducive to public input (Payne & Graham, 1993). These challenges are amplified by the recent trend towards transactive decision-making, value of pluralistic inputs, and increasing importance being placed on public involvement.

Limits of Acceptable Change

A second alternative planning/management framework is the Limits of Acceptable Change (LAC). This approach was introduced in the 1960s and is traced to work by Frissell in the Boundary Waters Canoe Area Wilderness (Hammitt & Cole, 1998). Others (see Jubenville & Twight, 1993; Payne & Nilsen, 1993; Pigram & Jenkins, 1999) have explicitly traced the heritage of LAC to the concept of recreation carrying capacity. LAC is "a reformulation of the recreational carrying capacity concept, with the primary emphasis now on the conditions desired in the area rather than on how much use an area can tolerate" (Stankey, Cole, Lucas, Peterson & Frissell, 1985, p. 1). Important and distinctive qualities of this approach are that it prompts managers to focus on desired conditions, includes elements of the natural environment and embraces change as an anticipated and "normal" fact (Pigram & Jenkins, 1999).

A model illustrating the acceptability of ecological change is shown in Figure 6.8. The gray or shaded area indicates that change is a natural and expected part of ecological systems. Ecological change increasing beyond this natural level is induced by humans and can further be distinguished between those which are acceptable or unacceptable (Pigram & Jenkins, 1999). The LAC process has advanced from this basic idea into a systematic approach by which managers:

1. determine acceptable/achievable conditions for both ecological resources and social situations as well as detailing operational parameters;
2. determine the existing environmental and social conditions and analyze the congruency between these baseline conditions and the acceptable standards established in step one;
3. identify and implement actions that bring social conditions in line with the standards defined, if the conditions are beyond the standards specified;
4. evaluate the effectiveness of actions undertaken, change in environmental and social conditions, and appropriateness of accept standards (Stankey et al., 1985).

The basic components above have lead to the development of a nine-step planning process for wilderness areas, as illustrated in Figure 6.9 (see Hendee et al., 1990; Stankey et al., 1985). ROS is immediately identifiable in the nine-step process as opportunity classes are defined and described in step two and used to identify alternative allocations in step six. In this manner, the LAC approach builds upon ROS and attempts to overcome some of the associated shortcomings.

Researchers and managers have recognized positive aspects with the LAC approach. Jubenville and Twight (1993) lend support to the basic concepts upon which LAC is based. The inclusion of stakeholders and the problem orientation in the approach is a welcome and noteworthy addition for Payne and Nilsen (2002). Perhaps the most positive review of LAC was by Knopf (1990), who revealed 20 strengths and a single weakness. Managerial experiences with LAC go back to the USFS who employed the approach to create a viable plan for the Bob Marshall Wilderness Complex (Jubenville & Twight, 1993). It has received limited use in the United States, compared to ROS, because the approach necessitates considerable risk from agencies (Payne & Graham, 1993). In Canada the LAC approach has also been sparingly applied. Payne and Nilsen (2002) document the attempt to apply LAC in Yoho National Park in response to issues caused by access controls in Yoho Valley. Managers outside of North America have expressed some interest in applying LAC. For example, there is increasing interest in LAC in Australia where the approach has been applied to diverse resources including wild and scenic rivers as well as public lands (Pigram & Jenkins, 1999).

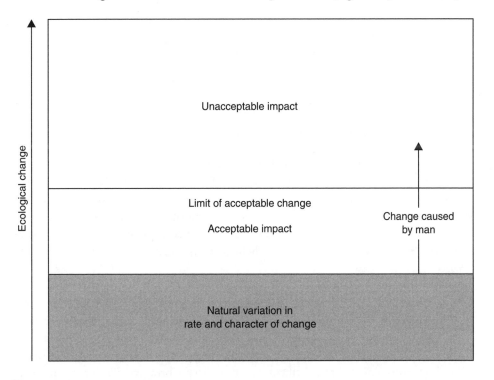

Figure 6.8 *Limits of Acceptable Ecological Change.*
Source: Hammitt, 1990.

195

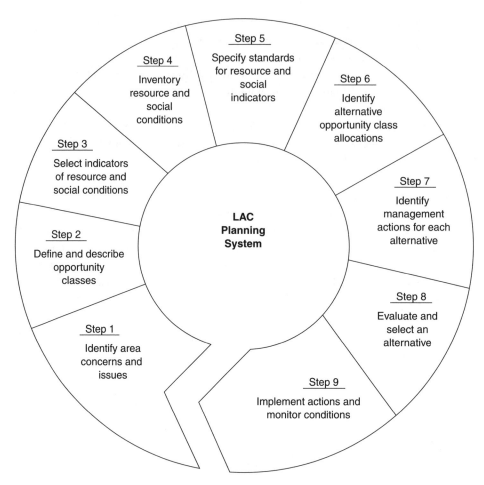

Figure 6.9 Limits of Acceptable Change Planning System.

Challenges with LAC have also been recognized. Timing of the LAC process poses a challenge as it must occur in conjunction with plan formulation, rather than after such plans have been developed (Jubenville & Twight, 1993). Other persistent concerns with LAC involve the subjective selection of indicators and determination of what is acceptable change and the difficulty associated with uncertainty surrounding environmental conditions (Pigram & Jenkins, 1999). Even Knopf, who overwhelmingly identified many positive aspects of the approach, expressed that:

> it seems that the LAC framework has the potential for feeding a certain kind of negative disposition that abounds in outdoor recreation management ... that disposition has to do with an attitude that the primary goal of resource management is to arrest the deterioration of environmental quality ... people being construed as objects that impede quality environmental management ... that litter, form crowds, create noise ... trample vegetation ... pests ... messing things up.
>
> (1990, pp. 207–208)

Visitor Impact Management

Although the LAC approach, along with the incorporation of ROS, represents considerable advancement from the basic conception of recreation carrying capacity, the above critiques offer potential areas for refinement. The creation of the Visitor Impact Management Framework (VIM) responds to these challenges by recognizing that outdoor recreation management is inherently complex (more than setting levels or capacities) and that managers must combine technical competencies with sound judgment (Pigram & Jenkins, 1999). The VIM framework was developed by a consortium of researchers, the National Parks and Conservation Association, and an American NGO (Payne & Nilsen, 2002). This consortium sought to review/synthesize antecedent literature and formulate a framework with broad applicability throughout the National Park System in the United States (Pigram & Jenkins, 1999).

The resulting VIM framework reflects the idea of recreation carrying capacity, specifically focuses on impacts (both ecological and social), and is intended to be applied to parks and protected areas. One of the architects of the VIM framework, Alan Graefe, summarizes that the VIM framework is designed to:

> facilitate dealing with three basic issues that are inherent to impact management: (1) the identification of problem conditions (or unacceptable visitor impacts); (2) the determination of potential causal factors affecting the occurrence and severity of the unacceptable impacts; and (3) the selection of potential management strategies for ameliorating the unacceptable impacts.
>
> (1990, p. 216)

The complete version of the VIM framework is illustrated in Figure 6.10. It consists of eight sequential steps, which place considerable technical/scientific demands on managers. The multiple feedback loops inherent in the framework direct attention to the need for continuous monitoring, which is unlike the previous approaches (Graefe, 1990).

The VIM framework has a level of flexibility not found in the other frameworks as it can be used as a stand-alone planning framework, be integrated with either pre-existing park planning procedures, and/or be incorporated into other alternative planning frameworks, such as LAC. As a spatial framework, VIM works well at a site scale but is less applicable when considering landscapes (Payne & Nilsen, 2002). VIM also retains a rational approach ("bounded" within the organization) and is the "least" concerned about external or community relations (Payne & Graham, 1993).

Despite the strengths and weaknesses identified with the VIM framework, it has drawn considerable international attention. It has been applied in:

> Australia (e.g., Jenolan Caves), Canada (e.g., Prince Edward Island), and in the US (e.g., Icewater Spring Shelter, Great Smokey Mountains National Parks; Logan Pass/Hidden Lake Trail, Glacier National Park; Florida Key National Marine Sanctuary, Florida; Buck Island Reef National Monument, Virgin Islands; and the Youghiogheny River, Western Maryland).
>
> (Pigram & Jenkins, 1999, p. 122)

197

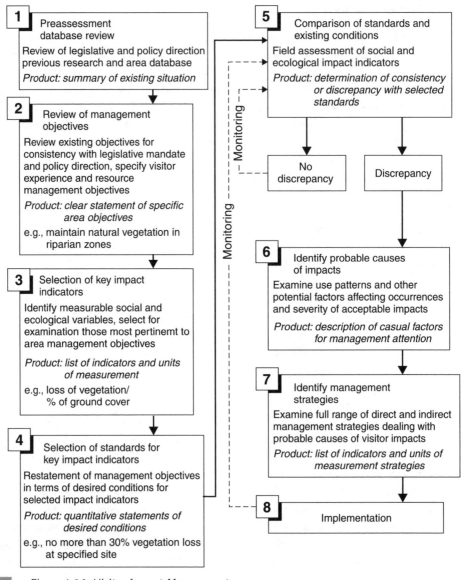

Figure 6.10 Visitor Impact Management.

Source: Graefe, 1990.

Visitor Activity Management Protocol

The Visitor Activity Management Protocol (VAMP) is a clear response to many of the emerging trends in management, discussed earlier in this chapter. More specifically VAMP arose from the need to balance resource protection with visitor use as well as make the managerial shift from production process to market orientation (Pigram & Jenkins, 1999). Unlike the other frameworks which originate in the United States, VAMP was developed in Canada by Parks Canada.

198

Although the VAMP framework shifts managerial orientation, it is designed to comple-ment the resource management functions of the agency and be integrated into the overall parks planning process within Parks Canada (Payne & Nilsen, 2002). Figure 6.11 illustrates how VAMP is integrated within the park planning process and complements other functions required by managers, such as resource management. Set in this context, VAMP is:

> a pro-active, flexible, conceptual framework that contributes to decision-building related to planning, development and operation of park-related services and facilities. It includes an assessment of regional integration of a park or heritage site, systematic identification of visitors, evaluation of visitor market potential, and identification of interpretive and educational opportunities for the public to understand, safely enjoy and appreciate heritage. The framework was developed to contribute to all five park management contexts: park establishment; new park management planning; established park planning and plan review; facility development and operation.
>
> (Graham, 1990, p. 279)

The visitor activity profile is at the heart of the VAMP framework (shown in Figure 6.11). It focuses on an activity and makes connections with the characteristics of those participating, the setting needed, and trends influencing the activity (Payne & Graham, 1993; Payne & Nilsen, 2002). These authors use the activity of cross-country skiing to illustrate the visitor activity profile concept. Within the particular activity of cross-country skiing it is possible to identify four activity subcategories (recreation/day-use, fitness, competition, and backcoun-try). The distinct characteristics of the individuals participating in each subactivity and setting requirements (e.g., backcountry skiing requires little modification and few services where competitive skiing may require considerable facility construction and habitat alter-ation), once identified, are integrated into the park management plan and services may be appropriately detailed (Payne & Nilsen, 2002, pp. 160–162).

The strength of the VAMP framework resides in its ability to focus on actual activities, facilitate the evaluation of these against managerial/park objectives and specifically address/integrated visitor considerations into the management of parks (Payne & Graham, 1993; Payne & Nilsen, 2002). VAMP also has the potential to incorporate elements of transactive planning and consider communities close to parks (Payne & Graham, 1993). The VAMP framework also faces challenges as a supportive organizational culture is required to experience success, a considerable challenge under the priority of efficiency (Graham, 1990). Consequently, VAMP represents a new way to plan (Payne & Graham, 1993). Despite the merits of VAMP, implementation has almost exclusively occurred in Canada (e.g., Pukaswa National Park, Glacier National Parks, Kejimkujik National Park) and is not prevalent in other parts of the world (Pigram & Jenkins, 1999).

Visitor Experience and Resource Protection

The Visitor Experience and Resource Protection framework (VERP) is the most recent alternative planning/management framework and was developed in the mid to late 1990s. The VERP framework was developed by the National Park Service (NPS) in the United

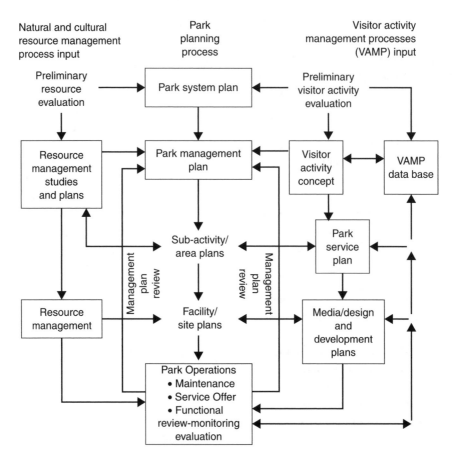

Figure 6.11 Visitor Activity Management Process.

Source: Parks Canada, 1994a.

States to assist managers in addressing carrying capacity in national parks (Manning, 2001). This connection is important as the NPS requires general management plans to address carrying capacity (social and ecological) according to zones (Payne & Nilsen, 2002).

The VERP framework is highly structured and consists of nine steps. A summary of each step in the VERP approach is shown in Table 6.2. Comparisons are made to LAC and VIM to recognize similarities as well as specific innovative features. Similarities include the use of zones, indicators, standards, management actions, and monitoring. The explicit interdisciplinary nature and team orientation taken within VERP (step one) is innovative and clearly consistent with the concept of pluralism. Early public involvement (step two) by establishing potential rapport/support is critical for implementation and reflects the social/political context in which VERP was developed.

Experiences with VERP and critical assessments of the framework are starting to emerge. Implementation has occurred throughout the United States at some recognizable parks, including: Aches National Park, Grand Canyon National Park, Yellowstone National

Table 6.2 Nine Steps of VERP

Step 1.	Assemble a project team, consisting of planners, managers and researchers.
Step 2.	Develop a public involvement strategy.
Step 3.	Develop clear statements of park purposes, significance and primary interpretive themes. This step sets the stage for the rest of the process.
Step 4.	Map and analyze the park's important resources and potential visitor experiences.
Step 5.	Identify potential management zones that cover the range of desired resource and social conditions consistent with the park's purpose.
Step 6.	Apply the potential management zones on the ground to identify a proposed plan and alternatives. The park's purpose, significant resources, and existing infrastructure are included at this stage of analysis.
Step 7.	Select indicators of quality and associated standards for each zone. A monitoring plan is developed at this stage.
Step 8.	Park staff compares desired conditions with existing conditions to address discrepancies.
Step 9.	Identify management strategies to address discrepancies.

Park, and Yosemite National Park (Manning, 2001). VERP has also been utilized to investigate specific issues such as conflict between horse riders and mountain-bike riders in Acadia National Park (Jacobi & Manning, 1999). The approach has not been applied outside the United States (Payne & Nilsen, 2002).

From the initial steps in the process, managers applying the VERP framework are to actively seek out "the public." This positions the VERP approach well in terms of both transactive planning and community involvement, which have received increasing attention. The incorporation of social and ecological information, especially with the explicit mention of carrying capacity, also bodes well for the approach. Despite these positive features, "applying VERP, however, has been proven to be difficult, primarily because managers find it taxing to identify both social and ecological park zones" (Payne & Nilsen, 2002, p. 169).

Visitor and Site Management

Many commonalities are evident among the planning/management frameworks presented above. Hammitt and Cole (1998) have advanced a simplified planning framework which highlights these similarities. It consists of setting objectives, inventorying conditions, determining if objectives are being met, undertaking management actions if required, and monitoring the situation (Hammitt & Cole, 1998). This planning process reinforces that it is the responsibility of the manager to undertake deliberate actions which bring conditions (environmental and social) in line with the set objectives. Managers may either influence the visitor or address the site of the activity. A succinct overview of visitor management strategies and site management alternatives follows. Its aim is to introduce readers to a few of the major strategies and alternatives available to managers.

Visitor Management Strategies

Frustration associated with the increasing (mis- and over-) use of natural resources may lead some managers to conclude that eliminating use is desirable. Hammitt and Cole (1998) stress that this is seldom a desirable approach as there are many variables (e.g., amount of use, concentration of use, type of use, user behavior, size of group) which may influence use without completely eliminating it. Visitor management involves "regulation, information, and education designed to influence the amount, type, and timing of use, visitor behaviour, and the extent to which use is dispersed or concentrated" (Hammitt & Cole, 1998, p. 255). Visitor management requires careful consideration among all possible alternative actions within the larger outdoor recreation management process. Regulatory means of visitor management are presented in the following paragraphs. Information and education methods as well as the related notion of service provision are discussed in the subsequent chapter on outdoor education and interpretation.

The relationship between the amount of use and impact is subject to many intervening variables. However, use and related variables remain one of the most important elements of visitor management. Jubenville and Twight (1993) suggest that managers should initially attempt to promote voluntary dispersal, prior to either limiting, or as a last resort, closing the area. Communication and education in this regard are critical as individuals may be quite willing to redistribute use. The many different forms of dispersal are illustrated by Hammitt and Cole who write:

> Think about camping, for example. Dispersal could involve (1) spreading people out on the same number of campsites but with greater distances between parties, (2) spreading people out on more sites with or without increasing distances between parties, or (3) spreading people out in time (increasing off season use) with or without changing spatial distribution.
>
> (1998, p. 266)

Notwithstanding the complexity of ecological and social impacts associated with each of these forms of dispersal, they may do more to achieve social objectives than ecological goals (Hammitt & Cole, 1998). Concentrating use, the opposite of user dispersal, is also a frequently employed technique in areas which are popular and therefore substantial ecological impacts are possible (Hammitt & Cole, 1998).

Placing limitations (amount of people that can access the area, length of stay, type of activities) is ultimately a managerial decision; but such decisions should be undertaken in consultation with stakeholders. Such consultation may result in more support for the decision as users come to understand the importance of resource protection (Hammitt & Cole, 1998). Jubenville and Twight (1993) distinguish restrictions from predicting carrying capacity as the latter occurs when the actual impact has exceeded some acceptable level. Significant challenges are posed to managers who must subsequently set these limits and determine allocation processes.

The first challenge faced by managers is to determine where and what limits should be placed on visitor use. Hammitt and Cole observe that "there is substantial controversy over the extent to which empirical data can be directly translated into use limits" (1998, p. 257). In the absence of clear empirical evidence and faced with multiple and competing interests, the subjective and judgmental nature of these decisions are well established (see Hammitt & Cole, 1998; Jubenville & Twight, 1993). Once the decision has been made to set limits on visitor use, the secondary, and perhaps more perplexing, question of allocation arises.

202

The allocation question is difficult for managers, especially when moving to a situation in which some users and/or uses must be precluded. Jubenville and Twight (1993) argue that one of the most appropriate methods is to create zones that place limits upon particular uses. They suggest the following four types of potential zoning rationale:

- zoning based on the type of activities—zones are created within the area being managed and complementary activities, those with similar attributes, are permitted within a particular zone. E.g., separate zone for motorized and non-motorized forms of water-based recreation;
- zoning based on time—different activities are permitted at different times (daily, weekly, seasonally) depending on the nature of use, concentration, and redistribution sought. E.g., walking may be permitted on a trail on Monday, Wednesday, Friday and Sunday, while all other days of the week mountain biking is permitted;
- zones based on space—zones are created based on density in remote areas to insure wilderness opportunities. E.g., one person per 10 square mile density;
- zones based on quota—zones are limited by the maximum capacity of people that can be supported. E.g., a developed campsite may only have 50 possible sites (Jubenville & Twight, 1993, pp. 202–203).

Creating zones to limit visitor use only partially solves the challenge. Once the capacity of the area, either physically or set by a manager, is reached, it is up to the manager to determine the process to allocate or ration the available spots. Dustin, McAvoy and Schultz recognize this is a fundamental challenge when they write "this time the commons is a public recreation setting. And the tragedy is allowed to occur because park and recreation professionals are reluctant to exclude anyone from visiting what lawfully belongs to everyone" (1996, p. 11).

Particular allocation mechanisms or means of rationing may be more acceptable than others under certain circumstances. Hammitt and Cole (1998) advance the following types of rationing systems frequently employed by outdoor recreation managers:

- request—reservations are made in advance and accompanied with a monetary deposit. E.g., reservations for a camping site made in advance over the telephone with a credit card deposit;
- lottery—all persons desiring an experience have an equal change of being selected. E.g., random draw for deer tags;
- queuing—first come first serve basis. E.g., snowboarding half-pipe is full and you can wait in line until someone leaves;
- pricing or fee—a monetary fee is associated with participation and those willing/able to pay the most take priority. E.g., climbing Mt. Everest;
- merit—must demonstrate adequate skills and knowledge of activity to be granted a permit. E.g., boating operator card and subsequent Captain's papers.

Each of the above allocation systems has specific advantages and disadvantages and no allocation system will work under all conditions. Associated side-effects and enforcement costs are important additional considerations that will be discussed more fully in Chapter 7.

Site Management Alternatives

A second alternative for managers to curb impacts from visitor use is to change the site itself. While site management techniques are differentiated from visitor management techniques, the two are complementary and should be utilized in concert to achieve management objectives. The ability to direct visitors to more durable sites is one of the best ways to limit impacts from outdoor recreation (Hammitt & Cole, 1998).

Manipulating sites to increase their durability or resistance to impact is a foremost strategy of site management. After sites have been located properly:

> the major means of increasing the durability of camp and picnic areas are to surface areas that receive concentrated use and to construct facilities that shield the resource, such as tent pads, shelters, fire grates, and toilets. In heavy-use areas, it is possible to minimize compaction, improve drainage, and avoid the creation of muddy, wet areas by surfacing tent sites, eating areas, and trails between facilities with gravel or wood chips.
>
> (Hammitt & Cole, 1998, p. 310)

The above quotation illustrates many of the specific actions that managers may undertake to manipulate site conditions to reduce impacts. In the situation of a developed campground, for example, campers are assigned a specific site number and must locate their tent in the place provided, often a raised and well-drained tent platform. A single campfire ring, with a grate for cooking, is well established so campfire impacts do not spread. Washroom facilities are provided in centralized locations to avoid unnecessary deposit of waste. Garbage facilities, for both recyclable and non-recyclable materials, assist in reducing litter. Site manipulation is equally applicable to backcountry or primitive situations where site location and provision of pit toilets or "thunder boxes" concentrate impacts and minimize resource damage.

Site manipulation extends beyond the actual location of use and includes the manner in which people travel to the location. Erosion on trails frequently requires an engineering-based solution and techniques often employed to control water include: outsloping, drainage dips, water bars, steps and sediment traps (Hammitt & Cole, 1998). Trails can also be hardened or engineered with natural materials (stones, logs, woodchips) to promote drainage and avoid negative impacts. Trail construction, especially paving, is contentious because it promotes universal access and greatly reduces the potential for impacts while detracting from the "natural" experience (Pigram & Jenkins, 1999).

Site manipulation and design can also "naturally" direct participants. Hammitt and Cole recognize "three primary means of affecting visitor use are manipulation of ease of access, development of facilities in some places and not in others, and design of concentrated-use sites, such that traffic flow is contained" (1998, p. 302). Participants are likely to take a path of least resistance when undertaking an activity so if an easy walking trail takes them directly to a washroom facility they are likely to follow it. Vegetation which is not managed discourages use; it is unlikely that someone will fight through a patch of brambles to take a shortcut to the washroom. Basic principles of site design are critical to both limit impacts, direct

204

users, and attract participants. Comprehensive resources on site design are available which extensively deal with this topic (see Bell, 1997; Hultsman et al., 1998).

Differing Perceptions

Differing perceptions of the outdoor recreation experience is an additional challenge for outdoor recreation managers. Hammitt and Cole (1998) recognize distinctions between ecologists, managers and participants. In their comparison of these views they assert that ecologists are most concerned about the health/functioning of ecosystems; managers have an interest in providing quality opportunities while minimizing impacts and face constraints by agency guidelines; and recreationists are most concerned about impacts that reduce functionality and enjoyment.

Although the above perceptions may initially appear to be broad generalizations, studies have consistently found differences between managers and participants in outdoor recreation. Studies have found that managers are more perceptive of impacts in all types of areas and that they believe them to be greater problems than participants do (Manning, 1999). Speculated reasons for these differences include: professional training and affiliation of managers with natural sciences; continual reinforcement of preconceived notions; and their own subjective views of what ought to happen (Manning, 1999). It is critical for managers to be cognizant of potential reasons for their perceptions as well as how they are distinct from participants.

SUMMARY

This chapter established that impacts are inevitable from every type of outdoor recreation activity. Recreation ecologists seek to understand these impacts on wildland areas by investigating consequences on particular elements (e.g., soil, vegetation, wildlife and water) of the natural environment. Social impacts (e.g., crowding, conflict and visitor use) which detract from the desired experience were also examined. Outdoor recreation managers face the challenging task of fostering opportunities for meaningful outdoor experiences while concomitantly insuring ecological integrity. Reflecting upon the tradition of outdoor recreation management revealed a transition from a production process to a transaction approach. Manning's (1999) model was used to synthesize key aspects of the outdoor recreation management process. Key concepts and tools (e.g., carrying capacity, alternative planning and management frameworks) were discussed. Visitor and site management considerations were also presented. The overarching message from this chapter is that outdoor recreation management is difficult and fraught with challenges. The complexity and magnitude of the challenges facing outdoor recreation managers will increase in the future (see McCool & Patterson, 1999; Manning, 1999).

KEY CONCEPTS

Allocation mechanisms

Conflict

Crowding

Differing perceptions

Impact

Impacts from outdoor recreation on the
 natural environment

Limits of acceptable change

Management

Objective of outdoor recreation management

Outdoor recreation management framework

Production process

Recreation ecology

Recreation Opportunity Spectrum

Recreational carrying capacity

Resource management

Social impacts

Transactive approach

Visitor activity management protocol

Visitor Experience and Resource Protection

Visitor impact management

Visitor use

SUGGESTED KEY SOURCES FOR MORE INFORMATION

Bell, S. (1997). *Design for outdoor recreation*. London: Spon Press.

Hammitt, W. E. & Cole, D. N. (1998). *Wildland recreation: Ecology and management* (2nd ed.). New York: John Wiley and Sons.

Hultsman, J., Cottrell, R. L. & Hultsman, W. Z. (1998). *Planning parks for people* (2nd ed.). State College, PA: Venture.

Jubenville, A. & Twight, B. W. (1993). *Outdoor recreation management: Theory and application* (3rd ed.). State College, PA: Venture.

Jenkins, J. & Pigram, J. (2005). *Outdoor recreation management*. London: Routledge.

REVIEW QUESTIONS

1. Define the term recreation ecology.
2. Identify and describe four types of ecological impacts from outdoor recreation.
3. Identify and describe three types of social impacts from outdoor recreation.
4. How might participants in outdoor recreation activities respond to crowding?
5. Explain the three objectives for outdoor recreation managers.
6. Identify and describe the main steps in Manning's (1999) general model for outdoor recreation management.
7. Define and apply the term recreational carrying capacity.
8. How is the limits of acceptable change approach an extension of the carrying capacity concept?
9. How are visitor and site management similar and different?
10. Explain the major difference in perception between managers and participants in outdoor recreation.

Chapter 7

Parks and Protected Areas

OBJECTIVES

This chapter will:

- introduce the idea of a park;
- explore the development of park systems in North America and their influence;
- discuss key aspects of park planning and management;
- consider the concept of wilderness and associated management systems;
- critically assess the international situation of parks and protected areas;
- reflect upon the future of parks and protected areas.

INTRODUCTION

Efforts to protect the natural environment through parks and protected areas are a major influence on the history of outdoor recreation. This chapter begins by exploring the concept of parks. Development of parks in North America is chronicled as they have had notable influence throughout the world. Attention is subsequently directed to the task of park management. This includes the vision associated with parks, systems of management, and the mechanisms in place to realize these goals. While many parks purport to protect or promote wilderness, it is independently considered. The meaning of wilderness is probed, associated values are explored, and its prevalence in North America is discussed. A broader international perspective is subsequently taken to consider the global importance of parks and protected areas as well as their future.

A BASIS FOR PARKS

One of the earliest definitions of "park" comes from the *Oxford English Dictionary*, where it is considered:

> an enclosed piece of ground, of considerable extent, usually within or adjoining a city or town, ornamentally laid out and devoted to public recreation; a "public park" as the

various "parks" in and around London, and other cities and towns. Also, an enclosed piece of ground, of considerable extent, where animals are exhibited to the public (either as a primary function of that "park" or as a secondary attraction).

(as cited in Eagles & McCool, 2002, p. 2)

According to this definition many of the early examples of outdoor recreation described in Chapter 2 (e.g., gardens of King Gudea, hunting preserves) could be connected with "parks."

However, parks are much more than just an enclosed area of land. Eagles and McCool observe that "all parks are created by society for a purpose, which has varied across time and geography. Each park emerged within a particular societal ethos and organization" (2002, p. 1). Their statement raises three important points. First, it makes clear that parks are a human construct and are designed to suit or achieve a particular aspiration. Second, any discussion of parks must acknowledge the accompanying context. Third, parks represent a tangible manifestation of societal or collective values. Dearden and Rollins go further and explain that "parks are not an end in and of themselves but rather a means towards an end" (2002, p. 9). Parks, in this broader sense, represent considerably more than just the natural features within their boundaries. Parks represent societal views towards the natural environment and the human relationship with it.

The paragraph above makes the point that parks are a reflection of values. In this way parks "represent a rich and complicated suite of ideas. Park managers must fully be aware of the history of meanings contained in one site, as well as the changes in emphasis over time" (Dearden & Rollins, 2002, p. 15). To illustrate how meanings associated with parks have changed, the development of park systems in Canada and the United States follow. The development of these systems is significant because the formation of parks and park systems in North America have served as a source of innovation and influence worldwide (Boyd & Butler, 2000; Hales, 1989).

DEVELOPMENT OF PARK SYSTEMS IN NORTH AMERICA

Canada

Kevin McNamee, in his comprehensive and well-articulated chapter, *From wild places to endangered spaces: A history of Canada's national parks*, states that "the evolution of the national parks system since its inception in 1885 has been influenced more by the nation's focus on economic development and prevailing social values, and less on the need to preserve wilderness" (1993, 2002a, p. 21). While constructing the railway across Canada, employees of the Canadian Pacific Railway (CPR) found the cave and basin hotsprings, near what is now Banff National Park. The potential commercial value of this find, as hotsprings were all the rage in Europe and the United States as healthful forms of recreation, propelled the workers to make claim to the property. This claim caused concern for the government, which in turn established a federal reserve around Banff Hot Springs. This subsequently became Canada's first national park in 1885 for the purpose of economic development in partnership with the railway (Boyd & Butler, 2000).

The Rocky Mountain Park Act greatly expanded the initial boundaries of the Banff National Park. Between 1885 and 1911, the Government of Canada formed a total of five parks and forest preserves (Rocky Mountain Park, Yoho and Glacier Park Reserves, Waterton Lakes, and Jasper Forest Parks). The motivation and rationale for forming parks remained contested as "these areas were multiple use parks, inspired by a profit motive and were not founded in any environmental ethic" (McNamee, 2002a, p. 28). According to Boyd and Butler (2000) expansion under the Rocky Mountain Parks Act placed strong emphasis on both recreation and public enjoyment.

The early part of the twentieth century provided the foundation upon which the current system of national parks in Canada has been built. In 1911 the Dominion Forest Reserves and Park Act was passed. The act provided a twofold classification of reserves and parks, activities permitted within parks were restricted while those within reserves were more liberal; the Dominion Park Branch was formed; and existing parks were reclassified as reserves reducing the amount of land given park status (McNamee, 2002a). James Harkin, the commissioner of the Dominion Park Branch from 1911 until 1936, "brought a philosophy to the position that was a mixture of reverence for the power of nature, and a pragmatic view of the economic value of nature and the parks to society" (McNamee, 2002a, p. 29). Harkin combined a passion for natural areas with the practicality (political astuteness) of his position and left an indelible mark on Canadian parks. He was instrumental in the advancement and passing of the National Parks Act in 1930 which stated that: "The National Parks of Canada are hereby dedicated to the people of Canada for their benefit, education and enjoyment . . . and shall be maintained and made use of so as to leave them unimpaired for the enjoyment of future generations" (as cited in Eagles, 1993, p. 58). This legislation is of critical importance because it formally prohibited certain uses (e.g., mining) from within parks and established the term "national parks." This legislation provided considerable momentum and acted as a catalyst for the creation of more parks in central and eastern Canada (McNamee, 2002a).

The policy of expropriation was critical in the establishment of several national parks, including Forillion, Kouchibougac, and Gros Morne (McNamee, 1993). In these instances the parks branch selected desirable land for a park and the provinces annexed the landowners (MacEachern, 2001). Expropriation met with strong civil resistance in the 1960s during the formation of Kouchibougac National Park in New Brunswick. A commission was launched to investigate the controversy and as a result the expropriation policy was altered and extended to include both consideration and sensitivity to local communities in the formation of parks (McNamee, 1993).

Environmental awareness and active citizenship were hallmarks of the 1960s and in Canada this enthusiasm included advocacy for parks. The National and Provincial Parks Association, forerunner of the Canadian Parks and Wilderness Society, was formed in 1963 (McNamee, 2002a). The most important outcome of this advocacy was the adoption of a systematic approach to park planning and management which placed emphasis on the need for ecological protection (McNamee, 2002a). As part of this systematic approach to planning, representing unique features (physical, biological, geographical) of Canada's 39 natural regions became a goal of the park system (McNamee, 2002a). This approach to planning, accompanied by the urgency to protect wilderness due to resource developments

209

in northern Canada, brought attention to and development of 13 parks and 64,000 sq. km of protected land from 1968–1984 (McNamee, 2002a). Despite steadily progressing toward the goal of forming a representative park system, the centennial of parks in Canada (1985) "proved to be a low point in their history" (McNamee, 2002a, p. 41). Political changes and an economic recession shifted focus temporarily away from parks. Despite this, policy developments within this time period are important as they signify important changes in thinking. Boyd and Butler (2000) identify that amendments in 1979 placed emphasis on ecological integrity; associated planning processes in 1985 stressed the need to involve people early in the development process; and amendments in 1989 directed attention to an ecosystem-based approach.

The notion of advocacy and the concept of representing unique ecological features came together in the Endangered Spaces Campaign launched by the World Wildlife Fund Canada (WWF) during September 1989 (Hummel & Hackman, 1995). The purpose of the campaign was to increase protection of Canada's ecosystems. Since 1989 more than 600,000 citizens have signed the Canadian Wilderness Charter and over 300 organizations have indicated their overwhelming support for protecting Canada's ecosystems (Hummel & Hackman, 1995). McNamee describes the essence of this campaign, which dominated the parks and protected areas agenda for the next ten years, in writing the:

> WWF challenged Canada's federal, provincial, and territorial governments to protect a representative sample of each of Canada's 486 terrestrial natural regions by the year 2000, and each of its marine regions by the year 2010.... Just declaring an area as a park or ecological reserve was not enough. The Campaign set the following standard: "an area had to be permanently protected (usually through legislation) and prohibit industrial uses, including logging, mining, hydro-electric and oil and gas development. For a marine area, a qualifying protected area must prohibit oil and gas drilling, dumping, dredging, bottom trawling and dragging, along with other non-renewable resource exploration and extractive activities."
>
> (2002b, pp. 51–53)

At its conception, the Endangered Spaces Campaign indicated that 12% of the lands and waters of Canada would be protected (Hummel & Hackman, 1995). This 12% was consistent with the target set in 1987 by the World Commission on Environment and Development. Overall, the primary focus was on representing all of the natural regions in Canada.

The campaign was well timed and coincided with the introduction and popularization of sustainable development through the Government of Canada's *Green Plan* (1990). The endangered spaces campaign received broad-based support/involvement from: politicians at all levels of government who worked towards setting objectives in a concerted fashion; industry which moved forward on some fronts in crafting more environmentally sensitive practices (e.g., certification for the forestry industry); aboriginal support through land claims which secured their rights and responsibilities; and, conservation groups that spearheaded the initiative (McNamee, 2002b). By the end of the endangered spaces campaign in 2000 both successes and challenges had been experienced. In his critical assessment of the campaign, McNamee (2002b) observes that the 3.89% increase in protected Canadian lands (total of 6.84% or 389,025 sq. km) through establishing 1,000 new protected areas is an important achievement; however, the challenge of representation remains as only 132 of the 486 natural regions identified are protected which is a far cry from the goal of establishing a systems which is ecologically representative.

Despite this challenge, recent legislation has clearly established ecological integrity as the central management focus of Parks Canada (Parks Canada, 2006). In an effort to capture information regarding existing ecological conditions and better understand implications of management, Parks Canada has developed an ecological monitoring framework. The ecological monitoring framework encompasses biotic diversity, ecosystem processes, and stressors (Parks Canada, 2006). While requiring reports on ecological integrity in each park will reveal considerable information, many additional challenges have emerged around the usage of indicators, data complexity, and cross-scale considerations (Parks Canada, 2006).

The contemporary situation of Canadian Parks reflects its past and is a call to action. There are currently 42 national parks in Canada (Parks Canada, 2007). These parks protect approximately 250,000 sq. km or 2.5% of federal lands. Protected areas expand the amount of land protected in Canada and as of 2001 amounted to about 10.45% of Canada's landmass (Environment Canada, 2007). Despite political commitments to complete the national park system in Canada, the government failed to meet its obligations and the related goals of the endangered spaces campaign. At the start of the new millennium, considerable gaps remained in the parks system in terms of both quantity and representation. At a federal level, and even if all protection initiatives in Canada are included, minimum targets associated with parks and protected internationally, discussed later in this chapter, have not been met. With a total of 14 natural regions still not represented and only 30% of all unique ecological features reflected in the system of protected areas important gaps remain.

The United States

Early conservation and protection initiatives that gave rise to the parks system in the United States are closely tied to exploration of the west and formulation of the American identity, associated with independence (Ibrahim & Cordes, 2002). George Catlin advanced an early conceptualization of a "park" in 1832 as he traveled through Sioux territory and sought protection for the unique culture and lands (Ibrahim & Codes, 2002). Yosemite Valley was found as a consequence of this westward expansion. With a population of giant Sierra redwood trees the aesthetic beauty and grandeur of this valley prompted the government of the United States to cede the territory to California in 1864, under the provision that the land be for public use and recreation in perpetuity (Ibrahim & Cordes, 2002). The impetus for other parks can also be traced to wilderness expeditions. In 1870 Washburn and Doane ventured into the area of Yellowstone and, while there, initiated a critical discussion with Hedges and Langford around a campfire which prompted the idea of making the area a park (Nash, 1982). Railroad interests combined with political publicity causing Congress to consider formation of a park bill in 1871, which, after much debate, was passed on March 1, 1872. This established Yellowstone as the first national park in the United States (Nash, 1982).

John Muir played a pivotal role in the early development of parks in the United States, as mentioned in Chapter 2. Muir's eloquent writing, combined with Johnson's political lobbying, succeeded in the formation of Yosemite National Park in 1890. This was the first park consciously undertaken for values specifically associated with wilderness (Nash, 1982). Although these values provided the impetus for the park, there was little doubt about the view in Congress regarding these lands. Ibrahim and Cordes observe that:

> during these early years a policy had evolved in Congress that only "worthless" lands could be set aside as national parks. This meant that it was necessary to first demonstrate there was no possibility of economic viability before Congress could be set aside for national parks.
>
> (2002, p. 147)

Although other areas of federal land are not the focus of this chapter, it is important to recognize that in 1891 the Forest Reserve Act was passed which afforded some protection to forests, although the parameters were not specified at the time (see Nash, 1982).

At the turn of the century legislative changes significantly altered the potential for park creation and administration. The Antiquities Act of 1906 provided the president with the ability to protect land in federal ownership if deemed of historic or scientific importance (Ibrahim & Cordes, 2002). Passing of the Organic Act in 1916 was particularly important as it created the National Park Service. Little time was lost by Steven Mather, the first director, who prompted a successful campaign which led to the National Park Service Act of 1916. Direction was given to this agency to protect nature and promote enjoyment (Nash, 1982). Research into ecological features (resulting in materials provided for education and protection) also became important at this time (Albright, 1933; as cited in National Park Service, n.d.a, online).

Demands by visitors to parks in the United States increased significantly at the conclusion of World War II as 33 million visitors in 1950 quickly grew to 72 million visitors in 1960 (Ibrahim & Cordes, 2002). The 1960s were a time of great change for the park service. The increased numbers of visitors demanded more services and the role of interpretation was greatly expanded under The National Historic Preservation Act of 1966 (Ibrahim & Cordes, 2002). More fundamentally, the orientation of the National Park Service began to shift during this time. Nash observes that:

> in general before 1960 the national parks leaned toward anthropocentrism. Hotels were built, roads extended, trails improved, toilets provided and lakes stocked with fish—all in the name of aiding the recreating public. . . . A seminal document in the difficult struggle of biocentrism for parity with anthropocentrism in national park policy was the 1963 report from an advisory board on wildlife to Secretary of the Interior Stewart Udall.
>
> (1982, pp. 325–327)

This important document directed attention towards ecological considerations.

From the early 1970s to the 1990s approximately 97 new parks were formally established with a substantial emphasis on historical aspects (Zinser, 1995). The formal incorporation of Alaska into the system is particularly substantive. Nash conveys the magnitude of this event in writing:

212

On December 2, 1980, President Jimmy Carter consummated the greatest single act of wilderness preservation in world history. In signing the Alaska National Interests Lands Conservation Act, Carter protected 104 million acres of federal land, or 28% of the state, an area larger than California. Of this total the National Wilderness Preservation System received 56 million acres which more than tripled its size. The National Park Service doubled the area it administered.

(1982, p. 272)

The incorporation of Alaska actually "diluted" the amount of natural units as it accounted for 17 of the 29 parks added during this time (Boyd & Butler, 2000; Zinser, 1995). Addition of various sites continued and by 1995 the system consisted of 357 units (80,155,984 acres) among 20 different types of classifications ranging from national battlefield parks to national sea shores.

The 1990s were also a period of change for the National Park Service. In commemoration of their 75th anniversary a major conference was held in Vail, Colorado which sought to examine environmental leadership (Sellars, 1997). Sellars observes that "in truth, the leadership culture of the Park Service has been defined largely by the demands of recreational and tourism management and the desire for the public to enjoy the scenic parks" (1997, p. 283). The "Vail Agenda" focused attention on the need for the park service to bolster efforts towards ecological science (Sellars, 1997). In 1994 efforts were initiated under the Clinton administration to reduce federal administration and the park service was restructured into clusters with park employees gaining additional responsibilities (Sellars, 1997; Zinser, 1995).

The National Park System of the United States is recognized for serving as a model for other park systems throughout the world (Boyd & Butler, 2000). The National Park System consists of 391 areas and protects 83.6 million acres (National Park Service, 2007). It is important to note that national parks are not uniformly distributed with greater amounts in the western portion and Alaska. There are also a number of challenges confronting the formation of parks and protected areas in the United States. The enduring influence of tourism and sheer numbers of visitors to particular parks presents considerable managerial challenges (Butler, 2000). Brennan and Miles (2003) recognize that it may be difficult to maintain support in light of more restrictive regulations. The National Park Service's shift towards a "moving picture" of landscapes brings with it considerable problems from influences outside of the parks themselves (e.g., communities, pollution) (Brennan & Miles, 2003).

PARK PLANNING AND MANAGEMENT

The development of parks and protected areas in Canada and the United States illustrates how values have changed over time. Although not mutually exclusive, the emphasis on parks in North America has shifted from economics and resource protection to enjoyment and use and to ecological integrity. Consequently, considerable tension exists between the enjoyment people derive from parks and the need to protect ecological integrity (Eagles, 2002; Hultsman et al., 1998).

Park planning and management are inherently messy, yet essential to ensure that a desired future condition will be reached (Eagles & McCool, 2002). As a more specific form of outdoor recreation management, many of the concepts introduced in Chapter 6 are directly applicable to parks. This section on park planning and management focuses specifically on the desired condition (the vision), the mechanism in place to achieve this future condition (planning systems), and the means by which it is achieved (park management).

The Vision

Societal values become manifest through the political process via legislation and policy, which provide guidance for parks and park managers. Legislation consists of "acts or laws and is approved by legislature and must be followed by the government, by its citizens, and is enforced by the court systems" (Wright & Rollins, 2002, p. 208). Legislation, by its very nature, is closely tied to the political process and frequently results in broad statements of intent. Legislation also has an important enabling function (Wright & Rollins, 2002). In this regard it provides guidance for the formulation of both policies and practices through which it is interpreted. Wright and Rollins explain that "policies are statements of intent for management and are usually much more detailed and explicit than legislation. Although policy direction should be followed by the bureaucracy, it is not directly enforceable in the courts" (2002, p. 213).

The National Parks Act of Canada (1930) provides both an example of legislation and illustrates how legislation may change with time. The purpose of Canada's National Parks is situated at the heart of this legislation as "parks are hereby dedicated to the people of Canada for their benefit, education, and enjoyment . . . and shall be maintained and made use of so as to leave them unimpaired for the enjoyment of future generations" (as cited in Eagles, 1993, p. 58). Changes over time have specifically aimed to clarify the priority of ecological integrity and what activities should constitute use. The most recent amendment leaves little room for misinterpretation as it specifies "maintenance or restoration of ecological integrity, through the protection of natural resources and natural processes, shall be the first priority of the Minister when considering park zoning and visitor use in a management plan" (National Parks Act, as cited in Eagles, 1993, p. 58). In terms of policy direction, the mandate for Parks Canada is to "protect and present nationally significant examples of Canada's natural and cultural heritage and foster public understanding, appreciation and enjoyment in ways that ensure their ecological and commemorative integrity for present and future generations" (Parks Canada, 2007, online).

A slightly different experience with legislation is evident in the United States regarding parks. The direction for the National Park Service stems from the National Park Services Act. President Wilson signed the act in 1916 which established:

the service thus established shall promote and regulate the use of the Federal areas known as national parks, monuments and reservations hereinafter specifies by such means and measures as conform to the fundamental purpose of the said parks, monuments and reservations, which purpose is to conserve the scenery and the natural land and historic objects and the wildlife therein and to provide for the enjoyment of the same in such manner by such means as will leave them unimpaired for the enjoyment of future generations.

(as cited in Zinser, 1995, p. 72)

This initial legislation, combined with the need to bolster support for parks clearly gave priority to enjoyment and tourism.

Legislative developments regarding parks in the United States have been characterized as being filled with uneasy tensions (Sellars, 1997). Sellars writes that "much of the history of the National Park Service from the George Wright era on involved conflict not between 'good' intentions and 'bad' intentions, but between two idealistic factions—each well-meaning but committed to different perceptions of the basic purpose of national parks" (Sellars, 1997, p. 204). This tension hinges on the issue of enjoyment of parks versus protection of them in an unimpaired condition. The following mission statement conveys this dual purpose:

The National Park Service preserves unimpaired the natural and cultural resources and values of the national park system for the enjoyment, education, and inspiration of this and future generations. The Park Service cooperates with partners to extend the benefits of natural and cultural resource conservation and outdoor recreation throughout this country and the world.

(National Park Service, n.d.a, online)

A Systems Approach

While parks in North America were initially created as opportunities presented themselves, the formation and advancement of a park system subsequently emerged. A system is:

a set of interrelated and interdependent parts or subsystems, which can react as a total organism under given situations, and this so-called organism resides in an environment which sustains the organism. The "organism" or system exists because of demands for its products or services from elements of its environment, and it produces outputs of products or services which it exchanges with the environment in return for social support.

(Jubenville & Twight, 1993, p. 13)

The environment in which the system operates is particularly elucidating when applying this systems definition to parks in North America and highlights the importance of context. From 1934 to 1972 expansion in the United States was constant and fueled by the demands for use while the Canadian system was more sporadic (Boyd & Butler, 2000). During this period of time in Canada it was the general notion or rationale that each province and/or region should have a park which characterized the geographic area (Wright & Rollins, 2002).

As a reflection of the change in vision significant changes have occurred in the Canadian and American park systems. In Canada a plan for the park system based on natural landscapes was advanced (Wright & Rollins, 2002). The rationale behind this approach was furthered in the 1980s through the use of an eco-region approach and today Parks Canada is committed to ecological integrity and sustainable development (Wright & Rollins, 2002). Management statements are similarly required for all national parks in the United States and are revised bi-annually (Zinser, 1995).

Theory associated with the systematic planning for parks has advanced well beyond current practice. In a generic sense, an optimal park system:

> should include, as far as possible, representative samples of biological regions, ecosystems, natural communities, and species. Parks should protect a nation's ecological diversity, its genetic wealth, and its wildland life-support systems and processes. And even though self-contained ecosystems are difficult to establish and maintain today, it is necessary to begin biological restoration as soon as possible.... An optimal parks system must strive to save all parts without exception.... An optimal parks system should be planned and managed comprehensively, which entails plans for each park, a national systems plan, and its integration into the country's overall development planning process.
>
> (Ugalde, 1989, p. 146)

In the above description of an "optimal" parks system innovation is increasing predicated upon ecological principles. On a broad scale, these ecological principles are the concern of conservation biologists.

Conservation biology is primarily concerned with scarcity and diversity under which fall the themes of endangered species, ecosystems, reserve design, and environmental impacts (Braithwaite, 1998). Each of these topics has received considerable attention, but two particularly relevant to parks will be discussed here. Biodiversity encompasses the richness (among other measures) of life in the three hierarchies of genes, species and ecosystems for any set area (WRI, IUCN & UNEP, 1992). Relatively little information actually exists about the biodiversity of earth. However, the causes or mechanism by which biodiversity is lost are well established and include habitat loss and fragmentation, introduced species, over-exploitation, pollution and climate change (WRI et al., 1992). Parks, if designed under particular ecological principles offer a way to reduce the loss of biodiversity. Parks and protected areas are generally becoming increasingly fragmented and isolated due to growing development pressures and other activities occurring outside their boundaries, which lead to reductions in biodiversity and a host of other related issues (Shafer, 1990). This has prompted attention to reserve design. The theory of island biogeography has been specifically examined with regard to these habitats and species islands. This approach, which is supported to varying degrees, focuses extensively on the size and design of parks and protected areas and their influence on species increases and richness (Shafer, 1990).

Managerial Functions

Building upon the concepts presented in Chapter 6, park planning and management is guided by specific legislation and accompanying comprehensive policies. Although the functions of management have remained somewhat consistent over time in parks and protected areas, the emphasis placed on an ecosystem approach has increasingly been recognized during the past 15 years (Slocombe and Dearden, 2002).

Ecosystem management "integrates scientific knowledge of ecological relationships within a complex sociopolitical and values framework towards the general goal of protecting native ecosystem integrity over the long-term" (Grumbine, 1994, p. 35). Slocombe and Dearden (2002) characterize an ecosystem approach to management as one that is holistic, inclusive of people, based on natural boundaries, acknowledges dynamism at multiple scales, and has active management. They also note that such a systems approach is adaptive in nature and ought to expand parks and protected areas beyond arbitrarily set boundaries. One of the best examples of applying these ecosystem principles in parks and protected areas in North America is the Yellowstone to Yukon (Y2Y) initiative as described in Box 7.1.

BOX 7.1 YELLOWSTONE TO YUKON INITIATIVE

Yellowstone to Yukon
  Huge conservation initiative aims to maintain biological connectivity in the wild heart of North America

JEFF GAILUS

It was not far away, at least in continental terms, that Harvey Locke began to dream the Yellowstone to Yukon dream. Two thousand kilometers north of Yellowstone, by a campfire above Keilly Creek in one of the most remote parts of BC's Northern Rocky Mountains, Locke conceived of a matrix of wilderness areas that would allow grizzly bears, caribou and other wide-ranging species to survive in the wild heart of North America forever. He told some like-minded people of his dream and discovered they had a similar one of their own.

"The bottom line is that our protected areas simply aren't big enough," says Locke, an environmental lawyer and long-time conservationist from Alberta who now resides in Boston, Massachusetts. "If we want to maintain biological diversity and ensure the long-term survival of grizzly bears and wild salmon in the Rocky Mountains, we've got to change the way we manage this landscape."

A few years later, in 1997, many of these dreamers, including scientists and other interested citizens from Canada and the US, convened in Waterton Lakes National Park to breathe some life into the Yellowstone to Yukon concept. Now, with over 150 supporting organizations, eight full-time employees, and a budget exceeding one million dollars, Y2Y and its network members are working hand-in-hand to define and design a network of protected areas in the Yellowstone to Yukon ecoregion.

The idea isn't unique. Before and since, conservationists have proposed similar initiatives for other parts of North America: the Yukon Wildlands Project, the central coast of British Columbia, the Nova Scotia Wildlands Vision, southwest Colorado's Wild San Juans

Network, and the Sky Islands Wildlands Network for southwestern Arizona and New Mexico and northern Mexico. Perhaps the most recognizable one to central and eastern Canadians is the Algonquin to Adirondack Conservation Initiative, an attempt to maintain ecological connectivity between Ontario's Algonquin Park and Adirondack Park in northern New York State.

But none is as big and as bold as the Yellowstone to Yukon Conservation Initiative, which spans two Canadian territories, two Canadian provinces, five US states, and the traditional territories of 31 indigenous peoples, roughly 1.2 million square kilometers of mountains, valleys and foothills between west-central Wyoming and the Yukon's Mackenzie Mountains. It ranges from 200 kilometers wide at its midriff east of Prince George to 800 kilometers wide in the north, where it bulges out to encompass portions of the Yukon and Northwest territories, and in the south, where it takes in parts of Idaho, Montana, Oregon, Washington and Wyoming.

It is conservation on a scale most North Americans have never considered, and the necessary adjustments to current protected areas systems will require substantial attitudinal, social and policy changes. But as Locke says, "science has shown us that it's the only way to maintain biological diversity over the long term."

Like most tenable place-based conservation initiatives of the new millennium, Yellowstone to Yukon is steeped in the principles of conservation biology. The first step is to synthesize all the research being conducted in the Yellowstone to Yukon ecoregion study area to begin to understand what kind of habitat the region's indigenous plants and animals need to persist. Then it should be possible to map out what additional lands need to be protected outright, and where other approaches to respecting wildlife needs should be applied. The challenge will be to design and designate a socially and politically acceptable habitat network that will ensure wildlife survival over the long term.

Looking at the habitat needs of the grizzly bear is not enough. Y2Y's scientific model will also take into account the needs of avian species that use the region for migration and breeding, as well as the integrity of watersheds integral to the survival of everything from spawning salmon to long-toed salamanders. And, of course, there are the other terrestrial carnivores, the wolves and cougars and marten and lynx and fisher that help to regulate the health of a very complex ecosystem like a loose-knit government—from the top down. (Wolves, for instance, keep the number of deer and moose at a reasonable level, so they don't over-browse the understory, kill the trees, and starve during the winter. And when a harsh winter causes prey populations to dwindle, so too do the number of wolves.)

Many communities that rely on timber and coal to fuel their economies are suspicious of initiatives like Yellowstone to Yukon, fearing that this new wave of conservation will put them out of business. Hinton, Alberta, Mayor Ross Risvold, for instance, expressed concern about how Yellowstone to Yukon would affect the local economy and the bank accounts of his constituents. And he is not alone.

"If science is moving toward a concept of connectivity, then we should go there," said Jack Munro, chair of the Forestry Alliance of British Columbia, in a Prince George

Free Press article about Y2Y. "But we should be up front about what it's going to cost us."

Yellowstone to Yukon's Pissot maintains that we may be "years away" from an accurate analysis of how effectual, landscape-based conservation will benefit the economies of the two provinces, two territories, and five states that make up the region, and he is quick to suggest that economy and ecology are mutually inclusive. In fact, he sees Y2Y as an opportunity to improve on both accounts.

"We have maintained all along that we are very aware, and very concerned, about the needs of the people that reside in the region," says Pissot. "But history has shown us over and over again that the boom-and-bust nature of resource-based economies is not always the best way to meet the needs of natural or human communities. We're simply inviting people to join us to find a better way."

Pissot says the First Nations and ranchers and loggers and hunters in the Yellowstone to Yukon region need to be part of the process by which the network is identified, defined, designated and managed. "We need not only their buy-in but their support to make this vision an on-the-ground reality. Without it, we're just going through the motions."

Jeff Gailus (jeff@y2y.net) is a writer and conservationist living in Canmore, Alberta, on the eastern edge of Banff National Park. For more information see (www.y2y.net).

Caution is also required when using an ecosystem-based approach to orientate the functions of park mangers. Slocombe and Dearden (2002) recognize the need to acknowledge: that management often focuses on human activities; limitations are associated with complexity and uncertainty; and, pragmatic challenges exist to applying the approach across jurisdictions. Walton (1998) recognizes the critical issue of time between ecological processes, which tend to be considerable, and political decision-makers, which tend to have, by comparison, limited terms.

Management Plans

Notwithstanding the vision for parks and the broad orientation taken, "at the individual park level, the park management plan is the primary tool for directing management" (Wright & Rollins, 2002, p. 211). Management plans essentially translate the legislative direction and comprehensive policy statements into specific tactics that can be implemented at a site. Although different agencies provide specific guidelines for the development of such plans, and indeed have specific planning branches or departments within their agencies, there is a core set of issues addressed across most jurisdictions. Table 7.1 gives an example of the "typical" content of a management plan for a national park in Canada. Most management plans begin by addressing the manner in which the specific park "fits" within the larger system. This is typically accomplished using a classification system which serves a dual purpose in providing direction for the specific park as well as detailing how the specific park contributes to achieving the goals and objectives of the overall system.

Table 7.1 Contents of a National Park Management Plan

1.	Foreword
2.	Recommendation Statement
3.	Executive Summary
4.	Table of Contents
5.	Introduction
6.	Role of National Park in the National Park System
7.	Planning Context
8.	Vision and Strategic Goals
9.	Managing for Ecological Integrity
10.	Protection of Cultural Resources
11.	Heritage Presentation
12.	Visitor Use and Services
13.	Park Communities
14.	Transportation and Utilities
15.	Administration and Operations
16.	Partnerships and Public Involvement
17.	Park Zoning and Wilderness Area Declaration
18.	Summary of Environmental Assessment
19.	List of Contributors
20.	References

Most park plans focus on human use; even objectives which emphasize protection of ecological integrity often require managers to address human actions (Wright & Rollins, 2002). Rather than try to change human use, managers should:

> accept the principle that recreational use can occur in wildlands, and that no matter how small, will produce an impact of some type. Management's role, in general, is not to halt change within wildland areas, but to manage for acceptable levels of environmental change.
>
> (Hammitt & Cole, 1998, p. 13)

Park management plans follow the broad objectives set for the park and describe how human activities will be reconciled with the natural environment. This is typically addressed through zoning, visitor use, and service provision. Most park plans also contain information relating to the administrative structure and operation procedures of the park. More recently, park plans are also encompassing relevant issues (e.g., partnerships, "friends of" organizations, relationships with communities) which are beyond their boundaries.

Many other types of plans (e.g., business plans, visitor management plans, development plans, operation plans) are also being incorporated into park management. Wright and Rollins observe that:

> this wealth of plans or strategic documents has emerged based often on good rationale. Since the early 1980s with an increased emphasis on ecosystem-based management and ecological integrity, a series of plans or strategic documents including ecosystem conservation plans, ecological integrity statements, and vegetation and aquatic management plans have arrived on the scene. Similarly, at various times there has been an

increased focus on human use—from marketing, to communications, to community outreach, to visitor activity management. Often the response has been that each component has been afforded separate plans.

(2002, p. 221)

This proliferation of plans comes with pragmatic challenges. Charron (1999) is critical of Parks Canada in this regard, explaining the inherent challenges in finding coherent linkages between the different plans. Developing plans for each new direction has also been criticized for leading to planning in perpetuity, an overall lack of action by the agency, and confusion from the public (Wright & Rollins, 2002). The lack of monitoring, evaluation, and accountability are identified as shortcomings within the Canadian system (Wright & Rollins, 2002) as well as more broadly of park and outdoor recreation management (Pigram & Jenkins, 1999). Despite the importance placed on developing them, a plan, no matter how well conceptualized and presented, is of little value if it is not implemented or has little pragmatic value (Pigram & Jenkins, 1999).

Zoning

Zoning is a common technique employed by park managers and appears in most park management plans. Zoning is a prescriptive management tool that "involves the allocation of differing recreation opportunities, biophysical conditions and management actions to different places within a park. Each zone represents a different land use or recreation opportunity" (Eagles & McCool, 2002, p. 107). Through zoning managers influence what activities will occur in specific areas of the park and under what conditions, or range of conditions, impacts from such uses will be accepted. Areas within a park which are zoned or designated for particular use(s) should be consistent with the overall objectives of the park.

While a universally agreed upon system of zoning for parks does not exist, most schemes employed are relatively similar and consist of a range of zones, from those which emphasize ecological integrity and prohibit most activities to those that acknowledge extensive development and permit many uses. Specific park systems or agencies tend to employ their own zoning schemes. Within the National Park Service in the United States, for example, Zone I is considered to be a wilderness area (National Park Service, n.d.a, online). Areas designated with this zone across the park system are very much natural and unobstructed by human use, with a high degree of biological integrity. An example of such a zone would be the South Fork of the Merced Wild and Scenic River in California (National Park Service, n.d.a, online).

The concept of zoning is versatile. Zoning has been incorporated into management frameworks (e.g., ROS) which have been applied to parks and protected areas. Zoning has also been applied outside of parks and protected areas as a tool for wilderness management. Using a core/buffer concept, a wilderness area is surrounded by a managed zone so that "the protective function is two-way—to protect the wilderness, and to protect adjacent land from disturbances such as wildfires which might originate in the wilderness" (Pigram & Jenkins, 1999, p. 200). Despite the broad applications of zoning, few inquiries have been made of its use or effectiveness (Nelson, 1993).

221

Visitors, Sites and Services

The topics of visitor and site management were described in Chapter 6 and many of the concepts presented earlier are equally applicable to management of parks and protected areas. Because parks often emphasize human use, managers may require additional specialization in the area of design and service provision. All too often in practice "the responsibility for planning falls to the person who is the 'least unqualified'" (Hultsman et al., 1998, p. 11). This challenge is somewhat explained by the initial absence of attention to human needs and overemphasis on technical elements and subsequent extensive training in "people skills" which left technical competencies required to plan and design park services (e.g., campgrounds) wanting (Hultsman et al., 1998).

Visitor management, as it specifically applies to parks, refers to the procedures employed by park administration to alter the experience of individuals attending the park in an attempt to meet the goals and objectives set forth in the park plan. Eagles and McCool suggest the following principles for visitor management in parks:

> Understanding park visitor characteristics, motivations and expectations is key to effective management policies.
>
> Visitor-related developments generally represent both the best opportunity for appreciation of the park and the key internal threats to its biophysical or cultural integrity.
>
> While tourism is a market-driven industry, the management of national parks and protected areas is determined by legislative mandates.
>
> Negative impacts from visitor use follow predictable patterns that can be used to structure management systems and actions.
>
> (2002, pp. 99–101)

As made clear from the above principles, visitor management in parks and protected areas is conceptually and pragmatically similar to outdoor recreation management. In terms of visitor management, it should also specifically be noted that many of the frameworks for planning and management covered in Chapter 6 (ROS, LAC, VIM, VAMP, VERP) were developed, applied, and/or are utilized in parks and protected areas (Eagles & McCool, 2002; Payne & Graham, 1993; Payne & Nilsen, 2002). The manner and techniques that managers employ to limit and/or influence visitors to the park is critical.

The issue of allocation tends to be accentuated in parks because of the tremendous demand by people to use some parks. For example, it is estimated that more than 3.5 million people visit Yosemite National Park annually (National Park Service, 2006). Parks also clearly illustrate the allocation dilemma because they tend to have more clearly defined boundaries (e.g., an entrance gate) and typically have staff present. Ford and Blanchard (1993) recognize that park managers need to exercise considerable forethought before employing any rationing system. They provide an excellent critical assessment of common rationing systems, including request, lottery, queuing, pricing and merit. Table 7.2 summarizes difficulties for administrators posed by each approach, efficiency and visitor use implications, and potential effect on visitor use behaviors.

It is also common for allocation systems to combine multiple types of rationing.

Table 7.2 Administrative Evaluation Criteria

Rationing system	Difficulty for administrators	Efficiency—extent to which system can minimize problems of sub-optimization	Principal way in which use impact is controlled	How system affects user behavior
Request (reservation)	Moderately difficult. Requires extra staffing, expanded hours. Record-keeping can be substantial.	Low to moderate. Under-utilization can occur because of no shows, thus denying entry to others. Allocation of permits to applicants has little relationship to value of the experience as judged by the applicant.	Reducing visitor numbers. Controlling distribution of use in space and time by varying number of permits available at different trailheads or at different times.	Affects both spatial and temporal behavior.
Lottery (chance)	Difficult to moderately difficult. Allocating permits over an entire use season could be very cumbersome.	Low. Because permits are assigned randomly, persons who place little value on wilderness stand equal chance of gaining entry with those who place high value on the opportunity.	Reducing visitor numbers. Controlling distribution of use in space and time by number of permits available at different places or times.	Affects both spatial and temporal behavior.
Queuing (first-come, first-served)	Difficulty low to moderate. Could require development of facilities to support visitors waiting in line.	Moderate. Because system rations primarily through a cost of time, it requires some measures of worth by participants.	Reducing visitor numbers. Controlling distribution of use in space and time by number of persons permitted to enter at different places or times.	Affects both spatial and temporal behavior. User must consider cost of time and of waiting in line.
Pricing (fee)	Moderate difficulty. Possibly some legal questions about imposing a fee for wilderness entry.	Moderate to high. Imposing a fee requires user to judge value of experience against cost. Uncertain as to how well use could be fine tuned with price.	Reducing visitor numbers. Controlling distribution of use in space and time by using differential prices.	Affects both temporal and spatial behavior. User most consider cost in dollars.
Merit (skill and knowledge)	Difficult to moderately difficult. Initial investments to establish licensing program could be substantial.	Moderate to high. Requires users to make expenditures of time and effort (maybe dollars) to gain entry.	Some reduction in numbers as well as shifts in time and space. Major reduction in per capita impact.	Affects style of camping behavior.

Information technology systems have permitted request (reservation), pricing (fee), and queuing techniques to be applied to an entire parks system. Ontario Parks, for example, has a system by which reservations may be made either over the telephone or the Internet up to three months in advance of the visit. Fees are associated with making the reservation and the site that is being booked. A certain amount of sites are also made available on a first-come, first-served basis and cannot be booked in advance. For example, backcountry sites in Algonquin Park may not be reserved after the month of October.

Beyond the general demand for parks are expectations about site attributes and associated services. Within parks that emphasize use, site and service tools and techniques have become increasingly important. Administration should ideally be considered prior to site design as it can enhance the ability of administration (e.g., facilitate the control of traffic) or create systemic problems (e.g., safety concerns) (Hultsman et al., 1998). Successful planning in parks requires technical knowledge, common sense and a certain amount of creativity (Hultsman et al., 1998). While it is beyond the scope of this text to comprehensively cover these three ingredients, typical site considerations facing park managers are introduced and the accompanying skills required to effectively address them are presented.

Planning in parks focuses on key features such as trails, boat ramps, visitor centers, campsites, play areas, washroom facilities, and maintenance/service requirements. Within each of these areas the three ingredients for park planning can be employed. Take the example of trails. It is possible to think of many different types of trail (e.g., single use, multiple use) that serve very different purposes. Once a manager has decided on the purpose of the trail, they are immediately confronted by a host of design options and specifications. Implementation or construction of these trails requires engineering knowledge and construction experience using natural or semi-natural materials. The trail is intended to be used by people and therefore design psychology is an important aspect of directing individuals as well as protecting both users and the natural environment. While the example of a trail has been used to illustrate a few of the many considerations, site management becomes increasingly complex when multiple features must work together within a park.

In addition to considering physical aspects of the site, park managers must also deal with people. These considerations were introduced in Chapter 6 within the service management system that includes facilities, services and related programs (Jubenville & Twight, 1993). The design, construction and administration of parks are all critical services that enhance the experience of visiting parks. One of the most important service functions of parks has been in the development and delivery of programs. The earliest park program and interpretive book is *The Yosemite Guidebook* developed by J. D. Whitney in 1869 (Butler & Hvenegaard, 2002). Interpretation of park features has advanced considerably and significantly contributes towards the education and appreciation mandate associated with most parks (Butler & Hvenegaard, 2002). The critical role of providing outdoor education as well as interpretation programs are the focus of Chapter 8.

Park managers may also have to provide additional services to meet the needs of visitors. Concession management "is directed toward providing specialized facilities/services in order for the visitor to enjoy a particular setting" (Jubenville & Twight, 1993, p. 21). Concessions have been increasingly contracted out to private service providers. Maintenance is one such important example which is often contracted out to a private business. Types of maintenance, often in parks, may be categorized into ongoing maintenance (e.g., garbage collection every day), long-term maintenance (e.g., replacement of built structures as they age) and preventative maintenance (e.g., replacing the sides of trails before they start to erode).

WILDERNESS

Throughout the above discussion it is evident that parks are located in many different locations, receive varying amounts of visitors, and require different forms of management. In this section focus is directed to parks and other geographic areas associated with wilderness. A working definition of wilderness is pursued and values associated with it are discussed. The situation of wilderness is subsequently explored in North America and internationally.

In the prologue to *Wilderness and the American Mind*, Nash (1982) provides one of the most succinct yet thorough examinations of the term wilderness. He writes that:

> "wilderness" has a deceptive concreteness at first glance. The difficulty is that while the word is a noun it acts like an adjective. There is no specific material object that is wilderness. The term designates a quality (as the "-ness" suggests) that produces a certain mood or feeling in a given individual and, as a consequence, may be assigned by that person to a specific place. Because of this subjectivity a universally acceptable definition of wilderness is elusive.
>
> (1982, p. 1)

Although a single definition of wilderness may be elusive, it has not stopped advocates of wilderness and scholars from attempting to document its origins or delineate the concept. The word wilderness can be traced back to the Norse language meaning uncontrollable as well as the Old English term for "weald" or "woeld," noting the importance of biblical influences and translations (Nash, 1982). Beyond these initial formulations of the term wilderness, the term has evolved via lexicographers who suggest that:

> Wildis has a twofold emotional tone. On the one hand it is inhospitable, alien, mysterious, and threatening; on the other, beautiful, friendly, and capable of elevating and delighting the beholder. Involved, too, in this second conception is the value of wild country as a sanctuary in which those in need of consolidation can find respite from the pressures of civilization.
>
> (Nash, 1982, p. 4)

Hendee et al. (1990) assert that there are two different perspectives from which the term wilderness can be understood. The first is a legal perspective as instructed by the Wilderness Act passed in the United States in 1964. In the Wilderness Act:

> A wilderness, in contrast with those areas where man and his own works dominate the landscape, is hereby recognized as an area where the earth and its community of life are untrampled by man, where man himself is a visitor who does not remain. An area of wilderness is further defined to mean in this Act an area of undeveloped Federal land

retaining its primeval character and influence, without permanent improvements or human habitation, which is protected and managed so as to preserve its natural conditions and which (1) generally appears to have been affected primarily by the forces of nature, with the imprint of man's work substantially unnoticeable; (2) has outstanding opportunities for solitude or a primitive and unconfined type of recreation (3) has at least five thousand acres of land or is a sufficient size as to make practicable its preservation and use in an unimpaired condition and (4) may also contain ecological, geological, or other features of scientific, educational, scenic, or historic value.

(1964, Sec 2 (c); as cited in Hendee et al., 1990, p. 505)

The legal definition of wilderness adds considerable precision as to what constitutes wilderness and emphasizes experiential qualities.

The sociological definition of wilderness provides an additional perspective in which wilderness is what people think it is (Hendee et al., 1990). Nash (1982) refers to this perspective as understanding wilderness as a state of mind and cautions that it has the potential to render the term meaningless beyond an individual. A more constructive way to understanding wilderness is "the conception of a spectrum of conditions or environments ranging from the purely wild on one end to the purely civilized on the other—from the primeval to the paved" (Nash, 1982, p. 6).

The term wilderness is also inconsistent with some cultures. For example, the indigenous people of North America generally considered themselves as one with the environment and therefore it was incompatible to distinguish wilderness (Hendee et al., 1990). In other regions of the world (e.g., Africa) wilderness has little if any significance as people have lived with wilderness for centuries and have little if any conception of why, therefore, it should be preserved. Many places which purport to have wilderness areas frequently do not reflect or coincide with the legal definition of wilderness, as these areas may be relatively small, contain a number of individuals and built structures, and permit multiple uses such as hunting and motorized vehicle access (Hendee et al., 1990). These different cultural perspectives have important implications. Hendee et al. observe that "this difference in perceptions and attitude has created a sort of 'cultural blockage' to further adoption of the wilderness concept, especially in developing countries and, because wilderness is so heavily tied to cultural significance, this will always remain a major factor" (1990, p. 49).

Wilderness Values

Values associated with wilderness have inspired numerous individuals to pursue its preservation. Wilderness is often coveted for the experience it affords. Nash (1982) focuses on how the experience of wilderness has shaped and/or influenced the national character and ideology of America. He explains that:

seizing on this distinction and adding to it deistic and Romantic assumptions about the value of wild country, nationalists argued that far from being a liability, wilderness was actually an American asset. Of course, pride continued to stem from the conquest of wild country, but by the middle decades of the nineteenth century wilderness was recognized as a cultural and moral resource and a basis for national self-esteem.

(1982, p. 67)

Yet the value of experiences afforded by wilderness goes beyond the influence on a national identity. Individuals continue to actively seek wilderness experiences (Hendee et al., 1990).

Scientific values are also frequently associated with wilderness. Early proponents of wilderness, who were responsible for forming the Wilderness Society in the United States, saw scientific values related to ecological functioning as an important reason to advocate conservation of wilderness (Hendee et al., 1990). Wilderness is appreciated for three specific scientific values. First, wilderness provides a relatively undisturbed example of natural processes which can be used as a baseline for ecological information (Hendee et al., 1990). Second, important discoveries may be found in wilderness that solve problems that humans have not yet even realized (Hendee et al., 1990). Wilderness, in this manner, acts as a genetic reservoir. As it disappears so does the potential to realize any of these benefits. Wilson makes the following plea to illustrate this concept:

> Natural products have been called the sleeping giants of the pharmaceutical industry. One in every ten plant species contains compounds with some anticancer activity. Among the leading successes from the screening conducted thus far is the rosy periwinkle, a native plant of the West Indies. It is the very paradigm of a previously minor species, with pretty five-petaled blossoms but otherwise rather ordinary in appearance, a roadside casual, the kind of inconspicuous flowering plant that might otherwise have been unknowingly consigned to extinction by the growth of sugarcane plantations and parking lots. But it also happens to produce two alkaloids, vincristine and vinblastine, that achieve 80 percent remission from Hodgkins' disease, a cancer of the lymphatic system, as well as 99 percent remission from acute lymphocytic leukemia. Annual sales of the two drugs reached $100 million in 1980.
>
> (1984; as cited in Hendee et al., 1990, p. 9)

A final scientific value of wilderness is their benefit to some species of flora and fauna as they are typically large in size and have little human presence. This value relates to the importance of ecological functioning and the need for protection of large areas or ecosystems to maintain ecological integrity (Slocombe & Dearden, 2002). It is only wilderness areas that provide adequate habitat for large wildlife species (e.g., grizzly bears, wolves, wolverines) (Eagles, 2002) and protection of this habitat is necessary for rejuvenation of wilderness-dependent species that are threatened (Hendee et al., 1990). Although such protection is critical, many questions are raised when human–wildlife interactions cause adverse affects. Box 7.2 documents the example of human–wildlife interactions in and around Banff National Park in Canada.

Wilderness also holds considerable aesthetic and spiritual values (Hendee et al., 1990; Nash, 1982). It was the aesthetic values and inspiration associated with the wilderness that captured the early imagination of America (Nash, 1982). In the United States considerable markets exist for works of literature and art involving wilderness scenery. Works by Buel (e.g., *America's Wonderlands: Pictorial Descriptive History of our Country's Scenic Marvels* and *Delineated by Pen and Camera*) fed the ready market for such materials (Nash, 1982). One of the

227

BOX 7.2 BANFF NATIONAL PARK

ELK OUT OF BOUNDS ON GOLF COURSE

For decades, elk at the Banff Springs Golf Club have freely puttered around greens, munched on manicured fairways and drunk from pristine ponds. But the free range is coming to an end—Parks Canada is running about 200 lollgagging elk off the 27-hole golf course into the wild. "Next summer we are going to try to keep the golf course elk-free," says park warden David Norcross. "Then we don't have to worry about golfers getting ambushed."

Removing the elk is the latest in a long-running battle between commercial developers and environmentalists over wildlife in federal parks. In Banff, it's a fight that has seen wardens and locals use slingshots, rubber bullets and border collies to run the elk out of town. Parks Canada and many of the 8,000 Banff townsite residents want the elk removed because of vicious attacks and, they say, it just isn't natural for such animals to live on pavement. But wildlife protectors say the elk have a right to live wherever they choose in federal parks. "That's their habitat and we are taking it away," said Liz White of Animal Alliance of Canada. "You have to ask the government every time you build another recreational golf course or hotel in the park and the animals intrude on the territory, is the end result going to be trapping and moving?"

Parks Canada moved 150 elk from the centre of town last year because officials said it was too dangerous for them there. The number of aggressive elk cases in Banff soared to 109 in 1999 from 42 in 1993. Each year the habituated beasts hurt several people—locals and tourists who often require stitches. Many tourists believe the elk are cute, docile animals; some feed the animals in town and take pictures. But the wild animals can be unpredictable, particularly when their hormones are raging and parenting instincts kick in. Bulls get into a flap in October during rutting season; cows become protective of their little ones after calving in April and May.

Earlier this year Parks Canada officials and locals ran hundreds of urban elk out of town by harassing them with loud pistol shots and stinging them with rocks from rubber bullets from shotguns. Then they brought in more effective artillery—two border collies. The little black and white dogs, bred for herding sheep, were dispatched to nudge and push the elks' hooves to the town limits.

The golf course wasn't a priority last year for clearing the four-legged beasts from town.

"It's more open, most people are using carts and you don't have children playing and getting ambushed," said Norcross. Besides, he noted, golfers carry weapons—a bag full of clubs.

Park wardens plan to trap elk in pens on the golf course, using alfalfa as bait, then truck the animals beyond park boundaries. White calls that cruel. "They are all of a sudden being displaced into a territory that has already been established and a pecking order has to reoccur."

But all elk may not have to be transported. A pack of eight wolves, living three kilometers away from the golf course, is expected to consume one elk every ten days. In hopes of encouraging more predators to the golf course to eat stray elk, the area is closed this winter to cross-country skiiers and snowshoers, said chief park warden Ian Syme. "This pack of wolves, we expect, will be very active in there this winter," Syme said.

Victoria Times Colonist, December 11, 2000

most recognizable artistic expressions of the Canadian wilderness came from the Group of Seven. This collection of artists concentrated on painting the northern landscape of Ontario and in so doing both made people of that time aware of the beauty contained in wilderness as well as left an enduring legacy of wilderness impressions. At the time that the group was painting, Canadian painters typically followed European traditions; the Group of Seven broke out of this traditional style to create a truly unique form of Canadian art (Town & Silcox, 1977).

Spiritual values associated with wilderness often prompted the outward expression of aesthetic values. At the core of these spiritual values is reverence for wilderness and the natural environment. Early Transcendentalists (e.g., Emerson and Thoreau) clearly connected God, the natural environment, and the individual. Nash explains that "the concept of wilderness as a church, as a place to find and worship God, help launch the intellectual revolution that led to wilderness appreciation" (1982, p. 268). The importance of such values continues to be explored in the context of spiritual enlightenment. Wilderness offers solitude, a sense of tranquility and a chance for people to share experiences; all factors which can lead to spiritual enlightenment (Heintzman, 2003). These experiences can also contribute to the overall "spiritual growth" and can last well beyond the wilderness experience itself (Heintzman, 2003, p. 30).

Wilderness also has value as it challenges the way in which humans think and act. Evernden notes that:

> the action that is being asked of environmentalists today is to recognize this paradox and publicly to decline to use the old map. Instead of accepting beliefs that trivialize the experience of living and assert the reality of a valueless world, the environmentalist is urged to attest to his own experience of a meaningful, valuable, colourful world. Environmentalism, like Romanticism before it, is essentially "a protest on behalf of value."
>
> (1993, p. 33)

To this extent, wilderness values pose an important mandate to those who profoundly care for the perpetuation of such special places. The eloquent writing of Whitehead synthesizes the values of wilderness. He writes that:

> Remembering the poetic rendering of our concrete experience, we see at once that the element of value, of being valuable, of having value, of being an end in itself, of being something which is for its own sake, must not be omitted in any account of an event as the most concrete actual something. "Value" is the word I use for the intrinsic reality of an event. Value is an element which permeates through and through the poetic view of nature.
>
> (1967; as cited in Evernden, 1993, pp. 33–34)

229

Wilderness in North America

Although the history of parks and development of parks systems in North America share many similarities, the cultural context within which wilderness is defined makes an interesting point of comparison between Canada and the United States. The cultural context, legislative basis and management systems between the two countries are compared in this section.

The interplay between culture and the American identity has been established above. McCloskey (1966) recognizes that "two conditions as necessary for developing a consensus that wilderness warranted preservation: (1) a society with highly educated leaders and with economic surpluses, and (2) an increasing scarcity of wilderness areas" (as cited in Hendee et al., 1990, p. 48). America clearly met the conditions required to preserve wilderness as a country with economic prosperity and whose leaders recognized the increasing scarcity of wilderness. In bringing these elements together, the "response to the vanishing frontier was the rise of popular interest in preserving portions of the American wilderness" (Nash, 1982, p. 149).

The Canadian experience with wilderness has been very different. Canada is the second largest country in the world (9,976,140 sq. km), has a low population density, and has a distribution of that population that is primarily located along a 8,890 km wide stretch with the American border (Atlas of Canada, 2007). Of Canada's population, 80% is further concentrated in 25 metropolitan areas (Atlas of Canada, 2007). Dooling writes that "wilderness preservation, because of a smaller population, large amounts of public land, and a perception of still relatively large unexploited forest wealth has scarcely raised a tremor in Canada compared with that of the United States" (1985, p. 322). It is important to keep in mind that such observations are comparative in nature and do not negate the foresight and actions of protection by Canadians. Feher explains that "the idea and value of an un-peopled landscape is a kind of Canadian cultural phenomenon. The idea of wilderness has driven much of what can be called the Canadian identity" (2005, p. 2). He connects this identity to early exhibitions by the Group of Seven as well as Harkin's efforts with national parks. The endangered spaces campaign was in part an emotional appeal to Canadians to protect natural areas (McNamee, 2002b). However, the Canadian experience does illustrate the wilderness paradox. Hendee et al. observe that "the Canadian experience furnishes added evidence for the paradox that the possession of wilderness is a disadvantage in the preservation of wilderness. In Canada's case it is the north country—unbelievably huge and empty, a continuing frontier that elicits frontier attitudes towards the land" (1990, p. 68).

Legislative differences are an outward manifestation of these cultural distinctions. The concern for legislation pertaining to wilderness conservation in the United States was first introduced by Zahniser in 1956. During the eight years in which the bill was refined and negotiated significant changes occurred. Notable changes included:

1. the exclusion of the Bureau of Indian Affairs;
2. the National Wilderness Advisory Council included in the original notion was dropped;
3. primitive areas within the United Forest Service were not included within the bill; and,
4. restrictions on actions within wilderness areas (e.g., mining) were much more liberal (Hendee et al., 1990, pp. 105–106).

230

These changes led Nash (1982) to conclude that in many respects the wilderness bill was a disappointment, when compared to the manner in which it was originally envisioned. Although it was a compromise, the Wilderness Act was passed in the United States in 1964. This initial statement of policy read:

> In order to assure that an increasing population, accompanied by expanding settlement and growing mechanization, does not occupy and modify all areas within the United States and its possessions, leaving no lands designated for preservation and protection in their natural condition, is hereby declared to be the policy of the Congress to secure for the American people of present and future generations the benefits of an enduring resource of wilderness.
>
> (1964, Sec. 2 (a); as cited in Hendee et al., 1990, p. 505)

Canada does not have equivalent legislation that is either national in scope or prescriptive in formulating a system of wilderness. The closest approximation of legislation for wilderness in Canada is the National Parks Act, discussed earlier in this chapter. Within this legislation, the primary mechanism for conservation or preservation is zoning, which specifically limits the activities that may occur in designated areas. Amendments introduced in 1988 reflect similar ideas of the Wilderness Act in the United States (Hendee et al., 1990). This revision afforded areas designated as wilderness or special preservation some protection, while confirming the importance of ecological integrity for the first time (Woodley, 2002). At a provincial level, wilderness-related legislation varies significantly throughout Canada with Nova Scotia and Newfoundland being most progressive (Boyd, 2002). According to Boyd's (2002) report to the Canadian Parks and Wilderness Society all of the provinces and territories are greatly lacking in legislation to protect wilderness.

Partially as a consequence of the cultural differences and partially as an extension of the varied legislative backgrounds, two very different wilderness systems have emerged in North America. The passing of the Wilderness Act in the United States also established a National Wilderness Preservation System that immediately included some 54 areas totaling 9.1 million acres (Hendee et al., 1990). The Wilderness Act also provided a mechanism by which other lands could be considered. An example of this approach are the efforts of the United States Forest Service under the Roadless Area Review and Evaluation (RARE I and RARE II) process which aimed at obtaining and distributing wilderness ecosystems, including in relative proximity to urban areas (Hendee et al., 1990).

While a complete review of the development of the wilderness system in the United States is beyond the scope of this book, it is important to recognize the magnitude of the contribution made by Alaska. Nash asserts that "on December 2, 1980, President Jimmy Carter consummated the single greatest act of wilderness preservation in world history. In signing the Alaskan National Interest Lands Conservation Act, Carter protected 104 million acres of federal land, or 28% of the state, an area larger than California" (1982, p. 272). In the 1990s the National Wilderness Preservation System, under the administration of the United States Forest Services, the National Park Service, the Fish and Wildlife Service, and the Bureau of Land Management, reached a total of 490 units comprising some 90,760,106 acres (Hendee et al., 1990). The National Wilderness

Preservation system currently consists of 702,107,436,642 acres (Wilderness.net, n.d., online).

This national wilderness system is complemented by other federal conservation systems (e.g., the wild and scenic rivers systems) as well as nine states that have explicit measures in place to protect wilderness (Hendee et al., 1990).

The amount of federal land formally classified as wilderness in Canada is diminutive when compared to that of the United States. At the time of the 1988 revision to the National Parks Act in Canada, Parks Canada administered a total of 182,000 sq. km of park lands, of which 90% could be considered wilderness (Hendee et al., 1990). The endangered spaces campaign, discussed earlier in the chapter, affords the additional classification of areas as wilderness (Davis, 1995). In fact, the endangered spaces campaign resulted in the protection of more than 1,000 (390,000 sq. km) wilderness and natural areas, an increase in the amount of adequately or moderately representative natural areas across Canada to 27%, and the adoption of policy documents which established specific strategies within provinces (McNamee, 2002b). Despite the efforts of the endangered spaces campaign:

> the myth of Canada as one limitless tract of wild spaces left forever untouched is clearly just that—a myth.... Canada possesses 20 per cent of the world's remaining wilderness. Should another Endangered Spaces Campaign emerge in the coming decade, perhaps it will be founded not on national identity, but on the very survival of the human and wildlife species that call this planet home.
>
> (McNamee, 2002b, p. 66)

INTERNATIONAL SITUATION OF PARKS AND PROTECTED AREAS

This chapter has mainly focused on parks and protected areas in North America because of their influence around the world. Four particularly influential aspects of these systems include:

1. the overarching intent of scenic preservation and utilization of parks by people for enjoyment;
2. the concept of "setting aside" these places so as to avoid their use for other development purposes;
3. the strong emphasis on visitor enjoyment or satisfaction from using the parks; and,
4. recognition that preserving some of these places ought to be an important function of government (Hales, 1989).

Hales observes that "these aspects of early North American parks experience have served as centers around which the international dissemination and application of the parks concept have revolved" (1989, p. 140).

Experiences with parks and protected areas in Australia and New Zealand illustrate the extent of this influence. Hall explains that that "the evolution of wilderness preservation in

Australia has distinct parallels with North America and New Zealand and has been particularly influenced by developments in the USA" (2000a, p. 31). Early attitudes in Australia were ambivalent to positive about wilderness, which resulted in a receptive situation for the formation of parks which started in 1879 with Port Hacking (Hall, 2000a). Although the federative nature and historical development of Australia has resulted in somewhat less federal involvement than the individual states, a national park system was developed in the 1960s and 1970s.

North American and European influences similarly prompted the establishment of Tongariro National Park in New Zealand in 1894 (Booth & Simmons, 2000). Park development in New Zealand has moved through four phases of acquisition, maintenance, management and negotiation (Booth & Simmons, 2000). During this time the focus of parks has changed from mountainous areas to encompass a more diverse range of ecosystems as well as emphasizing the role of Maori peoples (Booth & Simmons, 2000; Hendee et al., 1990).

Formation of parks and wilderness protection has also occurred as the direct result of international interest. This is most evident between areas that are more developed and have a scarcity of wilderness (either within a country or among countries) and areas that tend to be less developed and have an abundance of wilderness. Nash (1982) draws upon the economic concept of marginal utility to visually illustrate this phenomenon, as shown in Figure 7.1. Initially the marginal value of civilization is much greater than wilderness because wilderness is abundant and civilization is scarce. As civilization intensifies and the amount of wilderness decreases, the marginal value attributed to wilderness increases.

Figure 7.1 also depicts the conditions under which emphasis is placed on either exporting or importing nature. In describing this import–export phenomena, Nash writes that "the

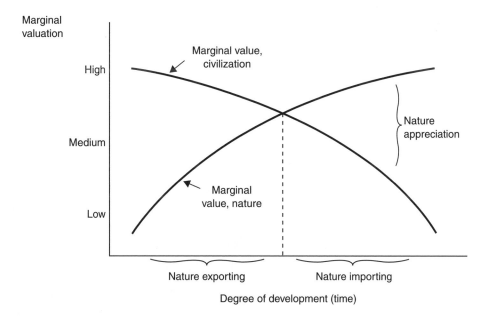

Figure 7.1 The Relationship Between Wilderness and Civilization.

233

export–import relationship underscores the irony inherent in the fact that the civilizing process which imperils wild nature is precisely that which creates the need for it" (1982, p. 343). In this manner, it is the experience associated with the natural environment that becomes the commodity of interest or value. Nash traces the history of this phenomenon to the early English interest in the Alps where "the natives feared and hated the high country, avoiding it whenever possible. Only when it became apparent that money was to be made by assisting foreigners climb did the legendary alpine guide stride forth with rope coiled and hand outstretched" (1982, p. 347).

Considerable tension frequently results between more developed and lesser developed areas of a country or between countries. This tension arises because the context of the latter is not sympathetic to the idea of parks. Yet, the former exerts considerable pressure to preserve or protect the environment in the form of potential income from tourists, economic incentives (e.g., debt reductions), and political pressures. Nash provides a pointed example:

> the tension between the nature exporters and the nature importers is historic and continuing. It should be noted that exporters do not as a rule recognize the marketability of their product. Africans, for example, have lived with wild animals as long as they can remember. You cannot interest a Masai in seeing and photographing a giraffe any more than you can interest a New Yorker in a taxicab. Similarly, the restrictions on grazing and farming in an African park or preserve are as perplexing to the natives as a law that prevents a New Yorker from living in and using ten square blocks of midtown Manhattan would be.
>
> (1982, p. 344)

The international interest for wilderness also prompted formation of international organizations concerned with parks and protected areas. International interest in protection of the natural environment advanced considerably after World War II, with the formation of the

Plate 7.1 Lake Manyara National Park in Tanzania, Africa.

234

International Union for the Conservation of Nature and Natural Resources (IUCN) in 1956 (Nash, 1982). The IUCN (or The World Conservation Union) is comprised of individual nations, governmental agencies, and non-governmental organizations who work with nations and other international agencies involved with the natural environment (Hendee et al., 1990). Membership in the IUCN started with 18 government agencies, seven international and 107 national organizations. Today there are over 1,000 member organizations (IUCN, The World Conservation Union, 2007).

Within the myriad of important functions undertaken by the IUCN, the World Commission on Protected Areas (WCPA) has been charged with the task of developing common nomenclature for park classification (Dearden & Rollins, 2002). Impetus for a common classification system came from the United Nation's mandate to keep records of all national parks in the world (Eagles & McCool, 2002). The IUCN classification system is provided in Table 7.3. Eagles and McCool (2002) suggest that the system clearly has an ecological basis and is of limited utility for recognizing visitor impacts and parks of a historical nature.

Keeping track of all parks and protected areas throughout the world is a daunting task. From this global perspective, considerable growth is evident over the past 90 years. As illustrated in Figure 7.2, both the size and number of parks and protected areas increased significantly. Prior to 1900, parks were virtually non-existent throughout the world. In 1990 there were over 10,000 world parks (Eagles & McCool, 2002). There are roughly an additional 100,000 protected areas worldwide, which translates to roughly 12% of the earth's surface or 18.8 million sq. km (Chape, Blyth, Fish, Fox & Spalding, 2003).

The IUCN is only one of many international initiatives oriented towards the protection of the natural environment and the preservation of wilderness characteristics. The oldest international convention regarding the natural environment is the Ramsar Convention on Wetlands of International Importance held in 1971, which prompts nations to recognize the importance of wetlands for waterfowl (Hendee et al., 1990). The United Nations

Table 7.3 IUCN's Category System for National Parks and Protected Areas

Category I	Strict Nature Reserve/Wilderness Area: protected area managed mainly for science or wilderness protection
Category IA	Strict Nature Reserve: protected area managed mainly for science
Category IB	Wilderness Area: protected area managed mainly for wilderness protection
Category II	National Park: protected area managed mainly for ecosystem protection and recreation
Category III	Natural Monument: protected area managed mainly for conservation of specific natural features
Category IV	Habitat/Species Management Area: protected area managed mainly for conservation through management intervention
Category V	Protected Landscape/Seascape: protected area managed mainly for landscape/seascape conservation and recreation
Category VI	Managed Resource Protected Area: protected area managed mainly for the sustainable use of natural ecosystems

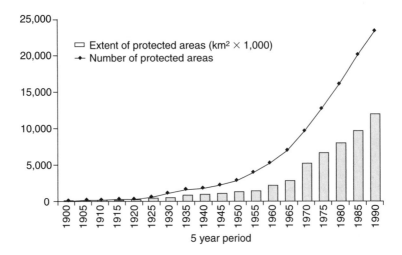

Legend:
□ Extent of protected areas (km² × 1,000)
→ Number of protected areas

5 year period

Figure 7.2 Growth of Parks and Protected Areas Worldwide.

Educational, Scientific and Cultural Organization (UNESCO) also initiated the Man and Biosphere (MAB) program in 1971. At the heart of this program, as launched in 1979, is the concept of the biosphere reserve that:

> provides one useful model and starting point for bioregional management. In the model reserve, a protected "core area" is surrounded by a "buffer zone" and then a "transition area". Use of the buffer zone is limited to activities compatible with the protection of the core area, such as certain research, education, training, recreation and tourism, while development activities are permitted in the transition area.
>
> (WRI et al., 1992, p. 100)

Currently the MAB program consists of research initiatives and natural resource training programs in over 100 countries (UNESCO, n.d., online). These committees and programs serve to implement environmental conventions, namely Agenda 21 and the Convention on Biological Diversity. A second international initiative undertaken by UNESCO in 1972 was development of World Heritage Sites which encompass areas of both cultural and natural significance. For a particular site to be considered for inclusion it must fulfill one of the following criteria:

1. be an outstanding example representing the major stages of the earth's evolutionary history;
2. be an outstanding example representing significant ongoing geological processes, biological evolution, and man's interaction with his natural environment;
3. contain superlative natural phenomena, formations or features, or areas of exceptional natural beauty;
4. contain the foremost natural habitats where threatened species of animals or plants of outstanding universal value can survive (Hendee et al., 1990, p. 55).

There are currently 830 properties designated by UNESCO as World Heritage Sites—644 of these are cultural sites, 162 are natural sites, and 24 are a combination of both natural and cultural elements (United Nations Educational, Scientific and Cultural Organization, 2007). Gough and Inaccessible Islands in the United Kingdom is an example of a world heritage site. Although prestige is associated with receiving such a designation, obligations for protection and management remain with the nation in which the site is located (Hendee et al., 1990).

THE FUTURE OF PARKS AND PROTECTED AREAS

Parks and protected areas have become an increasing issue of worldwide interest. The World Commission on Environment and Development (WCED) called for action on a global scale and set the target of 12% of natural areas to be set aside (WCED, 1987). However, it is crucial to go beyond protecting a set proportion of land. Representation of natural ecosystems is of equal importance as made clear in Canadian experience with the Endangered Spaces Campaign (McNamee, 2002b). The cultural context related to wilderness and associated import–export phenomena, combined in the current era of globalization, provide a situation within which the international perspective for protection is to become increasingly important. Within this situation, those interested in the future of parks and protected areas throughout the world must come to terms with the following emerging issues.

Parks are a reflection of societal values that have changed over time (Dearden & Rollins, 2002; Eagles & McCool, 2002). Figure 7.3 illustrates this changing emphasis within parks over time and depicts the changing role or focus of parks from one of recreation to one of ecology. It shows that over time threats to parks have moved from activities initially permitted within park boundaries (e.g., forestry, mining, grazing) to those originating from the external environment (e.g., atmospheric pollution, deforestation). Within this shift an

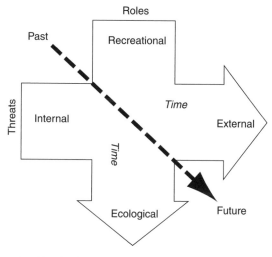

Figure 7.3 Changing Emphasis in Parks Over Time.

237

ecosystem-based approach to management has become paramount because it reflects the interconnected nature of parks as well as their linkages. Protecting "islands" without sufficient linkages presents considerable challenges and few parks in the world have focused on large-scale initiatives that embrace both the size and complexities required at an ecosystem scale (Dearden & Rollins, 2002). Increasing loss of known flora and fauna species, as well as loss of potential species yet to be discovered, largely advanced under the banner of biodiversity, is an issue of utmost concern (WRI et al., 1992).

Although parks are a visible manifestation of societal values, what happens when the concept of a park is inconsistent with the culture of the people who live and/or own the land/water where the park is to be designated? Expropriation is clearly not an acceptable avenue. The role and rights of aboriginal persons related to parks and protected areas are of emerging importance (Berg, Fenge & Dearden, 1993; Peepre & Dearden, 2002). The historical record of early park formation and Aboriginal persons in North America has been negative as the formation of Yellowstone was part of a crusade to subdue plains Indians who were subsequently forced out of the park area and onto reserves and similar experiences were had by the Siksika and Nakoda tribes with Banff National Park in Canada (Peepre & Dearden, 2002). Unfortunately, such examples are abundant throughout the world including Australia, New Zealand, and most developing countries where importers have exerted considerable influence on such populations (Booth & Simmons, 2000; Boyd & Butler, 2000; Hall, 2000b). Hall writes that "until recently, the creation of national parks was marked by the exclusion of Aboriginal populations as undesirable elements in the 'natural' landscape" (2000b, p. 57). Assessing this approach leads Berg et al. to conclude that:

> establishing protected areas without regard for the needs of Aboriginal people has created problems both for Aboriginal societies and conservation initiatives. Displacement of Aboriginal people, for example, often disrupts traditional social and economic systems and results in catastrophic social problems such as malnutrition and loss of cultural identity.
>
> (1993, pp. 225–226)

More recent approaches offer both hope and caution. Land claims and subsequent agreements in Canada, such as the Inuit Land Claim and the Nunavut Agreement, have provided a basis for negotiations between two equal nations (First Nations with Land Claims and the Government of Canada) of which parks often form an important component and a mechanism for cooperative management (Peepre & Dearden, 2002). Such examples of active involvement should be viewed cautiously, both within Canada and in the international context. Hall, for example, identifies that:

> Aboriginal rights are a highly controversial political topic in Australia. A number of High Court decisions have led to the overturning of the previous legal doctrine of *terra nullius*—the notion that Australia was unoccupied when the British claimed the continent—and has upheld Aboriginal claims to ownership of public land to which they have demonstrated ongoing traditional relationships.
>
> (2000a, p. 62)

Tourism was a significant factor in the inception of both the Canadian and American park systems and continues to be an enduring force. According to Rollins and Robinson "although there is some debate about appropriate recreation and tourism use in parks and protected areas, there is a consensus that some forms of visitor use are acceptable or desirable" (2002, p. 117). Beyond semantic differences between recreation and tourism, the number of individuals interested in parks and protected areas has been increasing rapidly (Buckley, 2000). This sector of the tourism industry has a considerable economic impact of $220 billion per year in the United States, while a majority of tourism in other countries may exclusively be based on this sector (Buckley, 2000). Concern about the relationship between tourism and parks has been recognized as a void in the tourism literature (Boyd & Butler, 2000; Eagles & McCool, 2002). The desire to visit unique features (e.g., ecological, wildlife, natural landforms, historical, cultural) has increased at such a rate that "ecotourism is considered to be the fastest growing of all tourism submarkets with tremendous potential for increasing visitation in parks' protected natural landscapes" (Eagles & McCool, 2002, p. 44). These travelers are particularly motivated to visit areas that are different (e.g., polar regions), have ecologically outstanding characteristics (e.g., Galapagos Islands), and afford particular opportunities for outdoor recreation (e.g., Nepal for climbing) (Marsh, 2000; Nepal, 2000; Weaver, 2002).

While tourism and parks are often advanced as a beneficial development tool throughout the world, "there is still a significant gap between rhetoric and reality.... Even where limited success has been achieved, new problems have surfaced such as gender discrimination, and social inequity and injustice" (Nepal, 2000, p. 74). Increasing numbers of tourists impact the social experience of others (Rollins & Robinson, 2002) as well as the natural environment. Recognition of the latter is particularly important as parks are often formed because of sensitive or vulnerable environments (Weaver, 2002). The tension between protected areas and their use (tourism/recreation) leads to paradoxical situations as pressures for financial self-sufficiency may work against the protection mandate, instances of conflict are intensifying despite greater sense of cooperation, and increasing emphasis is being placed on a scientific approach combined with greater public input and involvement (Swinnerton, 1999).

So what can parks and protected areas expect in the future? Soulé is unequivocal and straightforward in writing that "the pressure on wildlands, on national parks, and on other kinds of protected areas can only increase" (1989, p. 297). The issue of scarcity and increasing demand has long been recognizable in the American system as well as worldwide due to increases associated with tourism development (Eagles & McCool, 2002). Within North America a paradoxical situation has emerged in which parks enjoy a high degree of public support, but have experienced widespread environmental degradation and budgetary restrictions (Dearden & Rollins, 2002). Dearden and Rollins observe that:

> on a global scale, species extinction continue, global warming is a reality, ozone depletion continues, and attempts to improve air quality through international negotiations such as the Kyoto Summit have not translated into significant actions internationally. These global-scale changes and the ensuing ecological dislocations that occur will be a challenge to protected area managers all over the world. Parks and protected areas play

239

a role in addressing these major environmental issues, but it is apparent that steward-ship outside of parks is equally significant.

(2002, p. 406)

SUMMARY

This chapter broadly addressed geographical areas that have received varying degrees of pro-tection and/or are recognized for their special characteristics. It started by discussing the basis for parks and how their emphasis has generally shifted towards ecological integrity. The development of national parks in Canada and the United States were presented as they have had an enduring influence on park systems elsewhere in the world. Park planning and management were systematically examined in terms of guiding legislation, approaches to planning, and managerial considerations. The subsequent discussion broadened from parks and protected areas to focus specifically on understanding wilderness and its scope in North America. The final portion of the chapter focused on the international context, addressing the influence of the North American experience in other parts of the world, tensions between regions and nations for resource protection, and international initiatives. Contem-plating the future of parks and protected areas revealed substantial challenges as well as hope.

KEY CONCEPTS

Conservation biology

Export–import phenomenon

Island biogeography

IUCN

Man and biosphere

Management plans

Methods of allocating park use

Parks

Park services

Systems approach

Wilderness

Wilderness values

Zoning

SUGGESTED KEY SOURCES FOR MORE INFORMATION

Butler, W. & Boyd, S. W. (Eds.). (2000). *Tourism and national parks: Issues and implications.* New York: John Wiley & Sons.

Dearden, P. & Rollins, R. (Eds.). (2002). *Parks and protected areas in Canada: Planning and management* (2nd ed.). Don Mills, ON: Oxford University Press.

Hendee, J. C., Stankey, G. H. & Lucas, R. C. (1990). *Wilderness management.* Golden, CO: North American Press.

Hultsman, J., Cottrell, R. L. & Hultsman, W. Z. (1998). *Planning parks for people* (2nd ed.). State College, PA: Venture.

International Journal of Wilderness http://ijw.wilderness.net

IUCN—The World Conservation Union http://www.iucn.org

Muir, J. (1991). *Our national parks.* San Francisco: Sierra Club Books. (Original work published 1901.)

Nash, R. (1982). *Wildnerness and the American mind* (3rd ed.). Binghamton, NY: Yale University Press.

National Parks Service http://www.nps.gov
Parks Canada http://www.pc.gc.ca
The Wilderness Society http://www.wilderness.org
United Nations Educational, Scientific and Cultural Organization www.unesco.org

REVIEW QUESTIONS

1. What is a park?
2. Identify and describe three values associated with parks. Explain how the emphasis of parks has changed over time.
3. Why are parks and protected areas that focus on large areas of the landscape important?
4. Describe the relationship between legislation, park systems, and management plans.
5. Identify and describe two types of tools used by park administrators to manage visitors.
6. What is wilderness?
7. Compare and contrast the situation of wilderness between Canada and the United States.
8. Explain how the park movement in North America has influenced the development of park systems in other countries.
9. How do international organizations contribute to parks and protected areas?
10. What issues are parks and protected areas currently confronting that will shape their future?

Chapter 8

Outdoor Education and Interpretation

OBJECTIVES

This chapter will:

■ answer the question, what is outdoor education?
■ explore the philosophy of outdoor education;
■ examine theories that explain how learning occurs;
■ introduce the subject of interpretation and develop an understanding of its basis;
■ discuss how interpretation is practiced;
■ present potential benefits from outdoor education and interpretation.

INTRODUCTION

Outdoor education and interpretation are paramount to developing awareness about the natural environment, ourselves, and our relationship with the world. This chapter is initiated with a broad discussion of outdoor education in terms of its history, definition, and philosophy. Conceptual depth is added by discussing theories that have offered explanations of how learning occurs. Benefits associated with outdoor education are subsequently discussed. Communication and learning theories connect outdoor education and interpretation. Focus shifts in the second half of the chapter to interpretation, which is distinguished from outdoor education. A brief background to interpretation is given, a definition of interpretation is offered, and attention is given to the process by which interpretation occurs. Benefits of interpretation are reflected upon in the conclusion.

OUTDOOR EDUCATION

Outdoor education cannot, and should not, be distinguished from understanding the more general development of education (Hammerman & Hammerman, 1973). Sharpe and Partridge explain that:

the idea of learning in the out-of-doors is not new. Indeed, learning by direct experience accompanied by personal instruction was the customary method of passing on human culture long before there were classrooms, libraries, texts, or professional teachers. And this early type of education must have been effective, because it worked. The culture it carried was passed on from one generation to another, and the priceless gems of human knowledge that grew into our science, art, and industry remained sufficiently intact to be passed on and added to through the centuries.

(1973, p. 57)

As educational institutions developed and flourished in eighteenth-century Europe concentration was primarily directed to studies of classical linguistic and religion (Spielvogel, 1991). Despite the popularization of this type of education, a clear counter-movement persisted. Sharpe and Partridge write:

Perhaps every generation has had its vocal advocates of more realism in education. It is almost as if it were following the lines of least resistance to become more verbose. The study of books, the delivering of lectures, the assignment of rote learning all takes less imagination and effort on the part of the teacher than to organize experiences around actual life situations. All through human history, education without constant vigilance has fallen into this pattern. Pestalozzi rebelled against it and set up his own unique method of learning by living. Rousseau rebelled against it, too, on a philosophical level. Others saw in his writings a battle cry to carry youngsters away from artificial, meaningless routines into the fresh air of realism.

(1973, pp. 57–58)

The open-air school movement is an excellent example of this counter movement. Open-air schools started in Germany around 1900 and spread to England to counter industrial environments by enhancing physical activity (Hughes, 2004).

The spirit of active challenge and the immense appeal of realism firmly took hold in North America and grew from individual resistance to an entrenched approach. In America "the protest against shallow verbalism and rote learning has been more than an individual manner. It has taken the form of an organized movement which grew out of our natural heritage of outdoor living into a basic philosophy that has assumed extensive proportions" (Sharpe & Partridge, 1973, p. 58). The development of this considerable movement in North America is best understood by examining the three distinct periods of inception, experimentation, and standardization (Hammerman & Hammerman, 1973). In this text, a fourth modern period of outdoor education is added to capture the contemporary context.

Early "outing trips" during summer programs in California at the turn of the century and in Atlantic public schools in the 1920s provide some of the earliest examples of outdoor education. These trips came about as schools broadened their scope and attempted to educate the "whole child" (Hammerman & Hammerman, 1973). Camping in particular became an important part of educating the "whole person" and the popularization of this movement was expressed in *Red Book Magazine* by Dr. Dudley Sargent in 1923 when he wrote:

Our boys and girls take to camp life as naturally as ducks take to water, and in the opinion of many, this kind of life, for a part of the year, has become almost a biological necessity. For untold generations sunlight and fresh air, woods, fields, lakes and mountains, have served as nature's background for development to make man, through contact with these natural agents, all that he is today.

(as cited in Gibson, 1973, p. 69)

The growth of camping education and concerted interest in incorporating it into traditional education characterizes the experimental stage of outdoor education during the 1940s and early 1950s (Hammerman & Hammerman, 1973; Smith, 1973a). During this time period the number of residential outdoor schools began to grow. The term outdoor education was increasingly accepted and utilized as advancements in curriculum developed (Smith, 1973a). Consequently, some states (e.g., Michigan, California, Texas, Ohio, New York, Washington) attempted to integrate outdoor education into their curriculum, passed enabling legislation, and provided teacher training and instruction (Elliott & Smith, 1973; Smith, 1973a).

The third stage of outdoor education (standardization) involved a fundamental "transition from extracurricular, summertime activity, to a fully accepted function of the ongoing instructional program of the schools" (Hammerman & Hammerman, 1973, p. 56). A steady increase in interest and application of outdoor education (particularly organized camping) throughout the 1950s reached a high point at the end of the 1960s (Donaldson & Donaldson, 1973; Smith, 1973b). Expansion was bolstered by sweeping interests in the natural environment and public interest in outdoor recreation, as demonstrated through the ORRRC. Outdoor education during this period enjoyed "wide acceptance as a development in education—with many new patterns unfolding, gains in the number of land areas and facilities, and the emergence of many new leaders" (Smith, 1973a, p. 51). In addition to the popularity of incorporating outdoor education into the curriculum, the availability of in-service and pre-service instruction to educators was bolstered through college and university offerings, including graduate programs at such institutions as Indiana, Pennsylvania State, and Northern Colorado at Greeley (Smith, 1973a). The American Association for Health, Physical Education, and Recreation (AAHPER) also responded to the desire for outdoor education by establishing the Outdoor Education Project (Smith, 1973b). As a result of this and other initiatives, many teachers and other leaders received training, outdoor education was incorporated into many school curriculums (some 1,000 school districts in 1965), publications and conferences on the subject became available, and 2.5 million students (at all levels) received some form of outdoor education (Smith, 1973b).

So what developments have occurred in the decades since the 1970s? Outdoor education now occurs at all levels of education including preschool, elementary and secondary schools, colleges and universities, and graduate programs (Ibrahim & Cordes, 2002). The extent to which outdoor education is incorporated into the school experience varies considerably from occasional field trips to more complete curricular integration. Friends of the Earth in the United Kingdom is an example of the latter as they connect aspects of the outdoors (e.g., environment, citizenship, sustainable development) with existing curriculums on a national scale (Friends of the Earth, n.d.). Non-school organizations continued to play a critical role in the provision of outdoor education. Organizations such as the Boy Scouts

245

and Girl Guides facilitate learning about the natural environment. Increases are also evident in the number of professional organizations (e.g., Ontario Camping Association (OCA), North American Association for Environmental Education (NAAEE)), means of information dissemination, and the number of educators with an interest in the outdoors.

Outdoor education has also faced many recent challenges. Budget reductions from the provincial governments are an enduring challenge. Priest and Gass observe that post-secondary programs in the United States seem to focus heavily on theory and lack under-standing as to the usefulness of adventure. They further comment that "these concerns, coupled with growing financial cutbacks and course reductions in the tertiary education sector, may mean that the preparation of outdoor leaders is short lived in universities and colleges" (Priest & Gass, 1999, p. 478).

What is Outdoor Education?

Outdoor education presents a complex terminological quagmire to students. While the term has broad intuitive appeal, clear definition becomes increasingly difficult as it is often interchanged with other concepts (Ibrahim & Cordes, 2002). In 1958 Donaldson and Don-aldson wrote that "outdoor education is education *in*, *about*, and *for* the outdoors" (1958, p. 17). This remains the most widely cited and commonly recognized definition of outdoor education (Henderson, 1987; Ibrahim & Cordes, 2002). Each of the key phrases contained in the definition illuminate an important aspect. The fact that outdoor education should take place outdoors may appear obvious. However, many subjects about the outdoors can be taught indoors through classroom instruction. Consequently, outdoor and indoor instruc-tion can be complementary vehicles for learning, but knowledge is enhanced and under-standing is further developed by actually being outdoors. Donaldson and Donaldson assert that "for" is the most important word in their definition because it limits the field and "implies positive and moral approach. It strongly suggests that both the learner and the out-doors are better because of the experience" (1958, p. 17).

Recent efforts have attempted to capture the essence of outdoor education and reflect its holistic nature. Drengson views the outdoors as an environment conducive to the process of education. He writes that:

> the aim of education in a free society must be the growth and development of well integrated, confident, whole persons. . . . Education is a process in which the educator is a Socratic midwife whose aim is to aid the development of the capacity to engage in intelligent action and inquiry.
>
> (1980, p. 112)

Henderson (1987) builds upon this notion and makes the case that outdoor education needs to go beyond just activities and focus more holistically on educational elements. Ibrahim and Cordes nicely bring together components from many of the aforementioned perspectives and offer that: "Outdoor education, then, represents a holistic approach to the study of the inter-relationships of nature, humans, attitudes, for caring about the environment, and skill devel-opment in using natural resources for survival as well as leisure pursuits" (2002, p. 332).

Philosophy of Outdoor Education

While the definitions above describe outdoor education in general terms, knowledge of the philosophy underpinning it greatly enhances this understanding. The definition of outdoor education advanced by Donaldson and Donaldson (1958) has endured because it simply and effectively communicates the intent of outdoor education. Each of the key words emphasized in their definition (*in*, *about*, *for*) not only illuminate an aspect of outdoor education, but provide an entry point to explore the underlying philosophy.

The term "in" has referred to curriculum-enrichment factors in which students depart from the classroom and venture outdoors (Henderson, 1987). The philosophy of experiential education embraces these unique benefits to learning through actually encountering the outdoors. The precise meaning and background of an experiential philosophy is difficult to articulate and frequently unclear, although many outdoor educators subscribe to it.

Chapman, McPhee and Proudman (1992) have explored the ambiguities surrounding experiential education. From their perspectives, three somewhat divergent responses emerge to what experiential education involves. Chapman writes that experiential education is "an approach which has students actively engaged in exploring questions they find relevant and meaningful, and has them trusting that feeling as well as thinking, can lead to knowledge" (1992, p. 18). According to Proudman (1992), experiential education is at a crossroads between being a learning process and emphasizing associated activities. He argues that experiential education can best be understood as both a series of relationships (e.g., learner to self) as well as a methodology consisting of working principles that highlight a mixture of content and processes, de-emphasis of teacher direction, purposeful engagement, emotional attachment and the fostering of reflection. McPhee (1992) takes a very different position and reasons that the very act of defining experiential education is counterproductive to its spirit and that inherent value is in the experience of asking the question.

Common to each of these approaches is the view experience is critical to learning. Drengson (1995) recognizes the conceptual importance of experience to the philosophy of Hume who viewed experience as the origin of all knowledge, emphasizing sensory impressions through which principles of associations are formed. Drengson (1995) builds upon Hume's philosophy of inductive knowledge acquisition and Kant's systematic ordering by using Spinoza's four ways of knowing (vague experience, signs, concepts, and intuitive understanding). In this way, Drengson stresses that without the experience we have, at best, a partial understanding and that "life flourishes (this is Spinoza's claim); it reaches its greatest authenticity and touches reality most completely, when we know in the fourth way, by being in them" (1995, p. 92). Donaldson and Vinson also recognize contributions of William James as they write that:

> pragmatic philosophy is so central to the theoretical framework of experience-based education and group work, regardless of the widely diverse terminology currently used to designate such education (experiential education, out-of-school education, outdoor education, risk education, community-based education, etc.) that a book written eighty years ago remains "must reading" for anyone who believes in and seeks to practice what

247

folk wisdom has called "the school of hard knocks". If there is substance to the age-old wisdom that "experience is the best teacher," then William James is a major prophet in the experiential school.

(1995, p. 95)

Although James did not coin the term pragmatism himself, he is recognized to have greatly advanced it in America where he lectured extensively on the topic (Donaldson & Vinson, 1995).

The second portion of our working definition of outdoor education highlights the word "about." Part of the underlying philosophy of outdoor education is that certain subjects and lessons are best learned in natural environments. Wheeler and Hammerman offer the following list of subjects, which is still relevant today:

- appreciations and insights relating to a better understanding of one's physical environment;
- acquiring outdoor recreational skills which lead to the more fruitful use of one's leisure;
- pursuing healthful, physical activity in natural settings;
- coming to grips firsthand with some of the basic concepts underlying the biological and physical sciences;
- extending the classroom to the natural environment, from time to time, can provide a methodological pipeline for enriching "in school" curriculum contents with "outdoor school" concrete experience (1973, p. 12).

The natural environment clearly has the potential to be conducive to subjects of physical activity and skill; these topics are not pursued further here as they are addressed in Chapter 9. In addition to augmenting school curriculum about the natural environment, learning about the outdoors is also critical for subjects that are process oriented as understanding is enhanced by direct immersion in the subject matter rather than verbal communication based on cognitive abstraction (Donaldson & Donaldson, 1958). Learning about the outdoors promotes integration and holism. The potential for outdoor education to foster this perspective is important as "if we are to bring urbanized man to a fuller understanding of his environment, our schools must embark on a comprehensive environmental education program" (Stapp, 1973, p. 312).

Outdoor education is purposefully for the out-of-doors. The philosophy of outdoor education is explicit in its intent of fostering positive behaviors and attitudes about the natural environment. This component of outdoor education philosophy largely coincided with the upsurge in environmental concerns and interest of the 1970s as well as advanced the notion of environmental education. Illustrative of the excitement for environmental education during this time, Hammerman writes:

the aim of most environmental education programs is to produce a citizenry that is knowledgeable concerning our biophysical environment and its associated problems, aware of how to help solve these problems, and motivated to work towards their solution.... The schools of tomorrow must impart more than a body of skills and knowledge. There is a growing appreciation that it is not enough to give people tools without defining the context in which they will be used.

(1973, pp. 301–304)

The sentiments of appreciation and respect remain central to the philosophy of outdoor education (Ibrahim & Cordes, 2002). The notion that schools are the major purveyors of these values still holds merit. The task of sharing information and fostering respect about the environment has also broadened considerably and is not the exclusive domain of outdoor education. One of the central goals of interpretation is to foster positive environmental values. Interpretation occurs in a diverse array of natural environments (e.g., parks) and addresses a variety of audiences. Stewardship also encourages individuals and organizations to be considerate of the natural environment (Dempsey, Dearden & Nelson, 2002). It has emerged as another avenue prompting ecologically positive values broadly, largely in response to the limitations of public agencies.

The Process of Learning

The philosophical elements underpinning outdoor education make clear the commitment to the experience of being in nature, the subject of the environment, and the purpose of appreciation and respect. Outdoor education also soundly resonates with the aspirations of education. Smith is explicit about this connection as she writes that:

outdoor education thus is anchored in the basic principles of learning and the best curriculum practices. The reaches of outdoor education are encompassed in the basic objectives of education and are made possible through direct and concrete experiences which fall in the cognitive, affective and motor performance domains of education. Outdoor education may well make its unique contribution to the affective domain—behavioral change.

(1973, p. 53)

Learning is defined as "an enduring change in behavior, or in the capacity to behave in a given fashion, which results from practice or other forms of experience" (Schunk, 2004, p. 2). From this definition, learning may be understood to involve:

1. behavioral change where it is possible to demonstrate an ability that was previously not possible (e.g., skill of starting a fire);
2. the change is enduring in that it must be demonstrated over a period of time to exclude sources of temporary change; and,
3. the change happens as a result of practice or experience as opposed to developmental processes (e.g., attending a lecture) (Schunk, 2004).

Within this broad definition, three specific domains contribute to the process of learning. The cognitive domain encompasses information processing and "intellectual" elements as facilitated through concepts; the affective dimension involves the emotional response or

249

feelings elicited through engagement such as discussions or art; and the kinesthetic domain involves the development of motor skills (Knudson, Cable & Beck, 2003).

While considerable attention has been directed at the critical issues of how learning occurs, emphasis in this chapter is placed on three approaches with instructional commonalties to inform both outdoor education and interpretation. In this manner most learning theories agree that: individuals progress through various stages or phases; various factors are emphasized by teachers in the facilitation of behavior change; regimented practice is critical to performance and development; and motivational factors of the learners are an important consideration (Schunk, 2004). A fourth approach is subsequently presented to clarify the uniqueness of experiential learning, which is both a substantive strategy in outdoor education and synonymous with interpretation.

Cognitive development is one theoretical approach utilized to explain how people learn. Piaget is recognized in this regard for his contributions regarding cognitive development in children (Pulaski, 1980). Klausmeier explains that "the Piagetian system is child centered and purports to explain why development occurs the way it does and to describe the sequence of development" (1979, p. 3). Although not immediately recognized when first published, it is now considered one of the major theories of human development (Schunk, 2004).

Inhelder and Piaget (1958) advanced a four-stage model of cognitive development that relates age to development abilities. According to Inhelder and Piaget (1958) individuals are ready for various types of learning at each of four specific stages, as summarized in Table 8.1. At the sensorimotor stage development is focused on learning that occurs through the senses and experiences with movement. As people age their developmental abilities increase and they enter the preoperational stage where words and symbols are acquired. In the final two stages (concrete and formal operations) individuals are able to generalize from their experiences, deal with abstractions, and formulate solutions to potential challenges. Applying this theory and model to education makes clear the need to: understand the progression

Table 8.1 Piaget's Stages of Cognitive Development

Age	Stage	Development abilities
0–2 years	Sensorimotor	Develops organized patterns of behavior and thought (schemes). Uses sensory and motor activities, primarily.
2–7 years	Preoperational	Masters symbols (words). Centers attention on one characteristic at a time. Cannot mentally reverse actions.
7–11 years	Concrete operations	Generalizes from concrete experiences. Unable to mentally manipulate conditions not yet experienced.
>11 years	Formal operations	Able to form hypotheses. Deals with abstractions. Solves problems systematically. Engages in mental manipulations.

Source: adapted from Pomerantz, 1990.

of cognitive development when assessing abilities; tailor the amount and role of active engagement in learning environments; facilitate incongruity or present challenges and appropriately introduce social interactions as a source for such development (Schunk, 2004).

A second approach to learning that has been extensively utilized is Bloom's taxonomy. Bloom arranged levels of thought into a hierarchy. The most basic type of thought occurred when the individual focused on learning specific facts. Over time an individual progressed from knowledge to the subsequent levels of comprehension, application, analysis, synthesis and evaluation (Bloom, 1987; Chung, 1994; Knudson et al., 2003). At the highest level of learning, evaluation, the individual has a superior command of the material and is able to effectively combine each of the previous levels of knowledge. Bloom writes that "in our original consideration of the project we conceived of it as a method of improving the exchange of ideas and materials among test workers, as well as other persons concerned with educational research and curriculum development" (1987, p. 10).

Application of Bloom's taxonomy to outdoor education provides an opportunity for individuals to gain information at each of the levels of thought. The holistic nature of outdoor education makes it particularly well suited to facilitate comprehension, application, analysis, and synthesis. Bloom's taxonomy can also enhance the learning experience afforded by both outdoor educators and interpreters. Knudson et al. (2003) suggest that the status of the learner or client should be recognized as each level requires a corresponding change for the role of the interpreter. In the initial levels of thought the interpreter has a more central role as purveyor of knowledge and translator of the natural environment to visitors. The role of the interpreter changes significantly in the higher levels of thought to a more peripheral task of facilitator who provides resources and discusses ideas.

A third theory utilized to both explain the process of how individuals learn and to guide outdoor educators is based on psychological processing. Winzer explains that "psychological processing (more often called *learning styles* today) refers to how an individual processes sensory information and puts it to meaningful intellectual use" (2002, p. 95). The potential difference in the manner in which information is processed has been an enduring interest in the field of education for 40 years (Winzer, 2002). The concept that different people learn differently is both intuitively appealing as well as conceptually grounded. Building upon earlier works that identified particular temperament qualities of individuals, Golay (1982) developed the Learning Pattern Assessment. This assessment tool assists educators in determining the natural style of learning of a student by making assessments on a battery of questions. As a result of this assessment, Golay (1982) contends that students may be identified as having one of the following four primary learning patterns. The first pattern consists of actual-spontaneous learners (approximately 38% of students). These students have little interest in knowledge acquisition as an end in itself and exhibit strong preferences to gain experience through action. Actual-routine learners, also constituting about 38% of students, are highly structured in their actions and prefer clearly articulated expectations. These types of learners respond well to lectures or classroom settings in which instructors set forth materials in a conventional manner and become distressed if asked to invent their own procedures. A third type of learning pattern is conceptual-specific. The approximately 12% of students classified as this type find routine and structure boring. They tend to take a

251

problem-solving orientation (often facilitated by the research process) in seeking explanation and greater understanding of situations. Predication and understanding principles make research and knowledge acquisition particularly appealing. The final learning pattern identified is conceptual-global. These learners have "more of an interest in conceptualizations than actualizations, in what could be than in what was or is" (Golay, 1982, p. 39). This learning type, consisting of approximately 12% of students, focuses on the meaning inherent in the experience and the potential to apply this to their personal life. They are generally motivated achievers who also seek companionship.

Outdoor educators are often afforded the creative latitude to meet the needs of diverse learning styles. The power of outdoor education is perhaps best illustrated in the example of a student who is largely unresponsive to traditional classroom instruction but who becomes actively engaged in the outdoor environment through direct experience (Knudson et al., 2003). With the possible exception of individuals who learn best through traditional modes of instruction, direct experience and associated opportunities with outdoor education may enhance each of the other types of learning.

While the patterns above typify the manner in which individuals learn best, they do not explicitly acknowledge the possibility of self-directed or discovery learning. Learners obtaining knowledge by themselves is at the heart of discovery learning (Schunk, 2004). Schunk explains that "discovery is important for cognitive learning—especially of complex forms—because it involves formulating and testing hypotheses rather than simply reading or listening to teacher presentations. Discovery is a type of inductive reasoning, because students move from studying specific examples to formulating general rules, concepts, and principles" (2004, p. 242). Instructors in the context of discovery learning take on the role of a facilitator who prompts and encourages inherent curiosities and wonder (Schunk, 2004). While not a replacement for traditionally classroom activities, discovery learning is an appropriate way to emphasize process elements, problem-solving situations, and to motivate the learners to acquire associated skills (Schunk, 2004). The potential of discovery learning is that it can combine the different learning patterns identified above and provide a framework for exploration by individuals. Blackwood best captures the merits of this approach in writing that:

> the great value of the discovery approach, then, is that pupils have real experience in using the methods of scientists. The ideas gained about their environment will have more meaning when pupils have learned them through direct observations based on investigations of their own. But equally important, the ability to use the methods of discovery will remain as a powerful tool for further learning long after specific facts have been forgotten.
>
> (1973, p. 118)

Outdoor education may facilitate specific experiences that are conducive to a variety of primary learning patterns and discovery learning. These opportunities are possible because of the unique information process associated with experiential learning, as distinguished from traditional modes of instruction (classroom learning) by Wurdinger and Priest (1999). As illustrated in Figure 8.1, traditional classroom instruction starts with students receiving

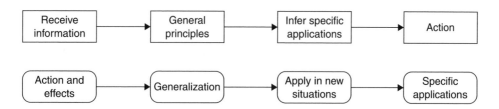

Figure 8.1 The Distinction Between Information Assimilation and Experiential Learning.
Source: Priest & Gass, 1998.

information. This information may come in various forms including written materials, verbal instruction such as a lecture, and/or other mediums. After receiving the information it is amalgamated and from it general principles are formed. It is from these general principles that application is inferred to a specific situation and which cognitive dimensions are required or stressed (Wurdinger & Priest, 1999). The final step in the process of information assimilation is where the individual acts upon the information received.

Experiential learning takes an opposite view in which action forms the first step of gaining knowledge. From this initial action an individual is able to make observations that permit generalizations about the particular experience and subsequently apply them to other situations. The final step in the experiential learning process would see the individual make specific applications about the phenomena. The example of building a fire makes clear the differences between the two types of learning. Following the first example of information assimilation, students may be in a classroom and be instructed as how to build a fire as well as read about the various techniques of fire construction. From this information they may glean some general ideas about how fires work (air, draft, wood) and be able to take these principles to specific applications (e.g., making a fire in the rain). Testing inferences made by actually making a fire under different conditions would be the final step in the process. The same subject of fire-building may be facilitated through experiential learning. Individuals would start by building an actual fire and from this action develop generalizations about fire construction that they could apply in other situations. Distinguishing between learning from the experience and experiential learning is important as the former is inherent in all education, including information assimilation (Wurdinger & Priest, 1999). Wurdinger and Priest (1999) argue that experiential education is critical because it provides, and indeed stresses, the importance of information application that is the hallmark of knowledge acquisition.

It is the interplay between theory and application that is central to proactive experiential learning, as illustrated in Figure 8.2. Wurdinger and Priest (1999) explain that this model of experiential learning is initiated with a problem (a perplexing situation that is engaging) for which an individual must formulate a theory (used here as a tentative plan towards solution). Application occurs as the plan is implemented and a solution is explored by the individual that is both personally meaningful as well as outcome-oriented. Conceptual development of proactive experiential learning was initiated to overcome previous models that were uni-directional, involved considerable gaps between theory and practice, and

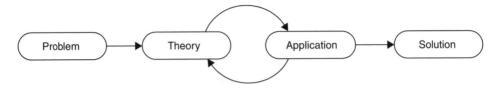

Figure 8.2 Proactive Experiential Learning.

lacked problem solving (Wurdinger & Priest, 1999). In addition to overcoming concerns with previous models, proactive experiential learning clearly accounts for the four primary learning patterns and provides a means to structure the concept of discovery learning.

Benefits

Implicit throughout the first part of this chapter is the acknowledgment of benefits from outdoor education. In the *Taft Campus Outdoor Education Award* lecture, Julian Smith identified that outcomes from outdoor education included:

■ better self-concept (self-realization);
■ awareness of and respect for the natural environment;
■ adventure in learning;
■ communications;
■ behavioral changes (social; teacher–student and student to students; care and protection and improvement of the physical environment);
■ lifelong interests and skills for the constructive use of time;
■ creativity;
■ development of the inner man (spiritual) (Smith, 1973a, p. 53).

These outcomes of outdoor education are equally relevant today as when they were initially offered in the 1970s. Some 20 years later Cooper (1994) offers an almost identical list of nine factors developed through education in the article "The role of outdoor education in education for the 21st century." He emphasizes the additional dimension of community that students require, but are not receiving from traditional schools (Cooper, 1994).

Outdoor education carries the prospect of experiential engagement. Experience is critical to meaningfully engage diverse learners and enrich opportunities for understanding and knowledge acquisition (Chapman et al., 1992; Donaldson & Vinson, 1995; Drengson, 1995). The natural environment also provides a forum that is particularly well suited to some types of learning which are not accommodated through traditional means of instruction. Education may particularly use the outdoors as a medium for discovery learning.

Outdoor education also provides considerable societal benefits. Concerns about the future of the natural environment initially prompted the immense interest in outdoor education. Outdoor education intends to make positive change in the human–nature relationship. Environmental responsibility, stewardship and respect are all concepts inherent in outdoor education (Dempsey et al., 2002; Ibrahim & Cordes, 2002). These societal benefits from outdoor education are best captured by Hammerman when explaining the excitement about environmental education in the 1970s. He wrote:

> whether we can rely on education to bail us out of our present impasse is something that now looks doubtful, but not impossible. What is important is that we view the environmental education in a context which is broader than that of the birdwatcher, the salesman of air filters, the anti-litter crusader, or any one of the other fragmented advocates, each of whom may be honest, bold, high-minded but also must have the vision to see the environment as a whole. That, if we hope to survive, is what environmental education should be all about.
>
> (1973, p. 309)

INTERPRETATION

The practice of interpreting natural, cultural, and historic features has a shared history with individuals who promoted scenic features. While certainly distinct from the modern interpretation, Hyde (1971) documents the manner by which modern appreciation of mountains in Europe developed. Interpretation is also closely connected with the formation of parks. Catlin and Lanford were members of the expedition that led to the formation of Yellowstone National Park and emphasized the need for understanding of the natural environment as a prerequisite for appreciation (Butler & Hvenegaard, 2002). John Muir led many nature walks in what became Yosemite National Park to both gain income and accompany notable individuals (e.g., Emerson and Roosevelt) (Nash, 1982). Muir first used the term interpretation when he wrote "I'll interpret the rocks, learn the language of flood, storm and avalanche. I'll acquaint myself with the glaciers and wild gardens, and get as near the heart of the world as I can" (as cited in Butler & Hvenegaard, 2002, p. 180).

These early ideas regarding "interpretation" quickly spread. In Canada, it was James Harkin's admiration for Muir that prompted him to use both similar language and sentiment in writing early policy documents that explicitly referred to parks as "outdoor museums" (Butler & Hvenegaard, 2002). The National Park Service in the United States recognized the importance of education in their 1916 policy statements. The practice of interpretation in national parks was precipitated by efforts at Fallen Leaf Lodge at Lake Tahoe (Butler & Hvenegaard, 2002). The lodge was implementing an experimental initiative where professors (Harold C. Bryant and Loye H. Miller) from the University of California made presentations to guests about the natural environment, based on the European concept of guides. Upon investigating and viewing the success of this initiative, Stephen Mather initiated transfer of the program into the national park system where interpreters were given the title of naturalists. While it is important to acknowledge that interpretation may occur anywhere, attention is primarily given to the context of parks because their purposes (e.g., wilderness, nature, historical) reflect the diversity of settings applicable to interpretation. Connections are also made to Chapter 7 as interpretation is often a key feature for visitors and a key tool for managers.

The history of interpretation in North American parks is given in Box 8.1. Three phases have occurred within park interpretation (Butler & Hvenegaard, 2002). At the inception of interpretive services in park systems, focus was directed to acquainting visitors with the most outstanding natural features of the specific park. The second phase of park interpretation coincided with the greater societal awareness of the environment. Attention in this phase focused on ecology (linkages and interconnections) within the park landscape. Butler and Hvenegaard write that

> phase three was defined by an expansion of park interpretation to foster a broader environmental consciousness among park visitors and the public at large. This involved a shift from an internal, within-the-frame viewpoint to a greater external awareness of the ecosystems surrounding the park.
>
> (2002, p. 184)

This shift coincides with the theme of ecology as well as the ecosystem and landscape approaches being advanced under the representative mandate of park systems and concerns about fragmentation.

Although the emphasis of interpretation in parks has changed with time, many of the ideas

BOX 8.1 HISTORY OF PARK INTERPRETATION IN NORTH AMERICA

1784	First natural history museum to utilize interpretive techniques opens in Philadelphia, with Charles Wilson Peale exhibiting wildlife collections from the American west.
1869	First park interpretive book, *The Yosemite Guidebook*, is published by California State Geologist, J. D. Whitney.
1870s	John Muir leads groups on interpretive hikes into Yosemite backcountry.
1887	Scottish caretaker and guide, David Galletly, conducts visitors through the lower Hot Spring cave, Banff. These are the first formal interpretive walks conducted by an interpreter in a Canadian national park.
1889	Enos Mills, the father of nature guiding, formalizes and teaches principles of nature guiding in Rocky Mountain National Park, Colorado. He later wrote *Adventures of a nature guide and essays in interpretation*.
1895	First park interpretive museum, and first museum in any national park, is established at Banff.
1904	First park interpretive trail is established at Yosemite; Lt. Pipes of the Army Medical Corps establishes a trail with labeled trees and other plants.
1905	C. H. Deutschman, who discovered Nakimu Caves in Glacier National Park, British Columbia, begins to conduct visitors through the cave system.
1911	Evening campfire programs and tours of park features are well established in several Canadian and US national parks, but all are conducted by concessions.
1914	First Canadian National Park interpretive publications appear in Banff.
1915	Esther Burnell Estes becomes first licensed woman interpreter in the US.
1918	US establishes its first park museum in Mesa Verde, Colorado, with exhibits and lectures given; the next museum opens in 1921, in Yosemite.
1919	Nature guiding becomes popular in Rocky Mountain resorts in US. Steven

	Mather, Director of US Parks Service, institutionalizes interpretation in the US national parks system.
1920	First US Park Service interpretive programs begin with government-employed interpreters in Yosemite and Yellowstone.
1929	First seasonal interpretive programs begin in the Rocky Mountain National Parks of Canada, with the appointment of J. Hamilton Laing.
1931	Grey Owl employed as interpreter by Parks Canada at Riding Mountain, Manitoba; later transferred to Prince Albert, Saskatchewan.
1944	Early interpretive events conducted in Banff; wildlife warden, Hubert Green, feeds aspen cuttings to beavers of Vermilion Lakes before 25–30 tourists nightly while discussing beaver life history.
1954	Interpretive programs begin in provincial parks of Ontario.
1958	First coordinated interpretive service established in Ottawa for Canada's national park system.
1964	First permanent naturalists located in Canadian Rocky Mountain national parks.
1969	First Canadian wildlife interpretation center opens at Wye Marsh, near Midland, Ontario.
1983	Hector Ceballos-Lescuráin, a naturalist tour operator in Mexico, coins "ecotourism" (ecology-based tourism promoting positive environmental ethics). This preferred form of tourism for parks and nature reserves will soon grow to be the fastest-rising sector of the tourism industry. There will soon be more employment opportunities for interpreters in the private sector of the tourism industry than in the public sector of parks, forests, and urban nature centers (the former principal employment source).
1985	A national Canadian assembly on national parks and protected areas, formed to mark the Centennial of Canada's national parks, encourages the development of more interpretive programs.
1988–1994	Governmental downsizing efforts result in drastic budget cuts for interpretive staff and services in Canada's national parks.
1990s	Scattered attempts to "privatize" interpretive services, particularly in provincial parks. Quality of services and professionalism decline. Important "windows of opportunity" are lost or diminished to reach thousands of visitors who support protected area initiatives.
1991	The Canadian Environmental Advisory Council (1991) advises Parks Canada to dedicate more resources to support interpretation and education programs that increase public awareness of the intrinsic values of protected areas.
2000	Panel on the Ecological Integrity of Canada's National Parks recommends that interpretation have ecological integrity as its core purpose and that interpretive funding in national parks be doubled.

central to both the philosophy and practice of interpretation have endured. Three specific individuals should be recognized for popularizing interpretation and significantly influencing the subject. Enos Mills (1870–1922) was born in Kansas and exerted considerable influence on nature guiding from his resort in Colorado. Mills escorted approximately 250 parties up Long's Peak (elevation of 14,225 feet) and while on these trips he explained various elements of the natural environment to clients and supplemented these forays with "fireside lectures" to increase both their comfort and awareness of their surroundings (Beck & Cable, 2002; Knudson et al., 2003). The success of this approach propelled Mills to: train others as nature guides; lecture nationally on his approach; lobby extensively for national parks, including presidents; and write a book (*The Adventures of a Nature Guide,* 1920) in which he explained principles for guiding (Beck & Cable, 2002; Knudson et al., 2003).

Freeman Tilden is synonymous with the art of interpretation and is often referred to as "the father of interpretation" (National Parks, 2000). Tilden was born in Massachusetts and was originally a writer (fiction and plays) before focusing on conservation and cultural symbolism of the natural environment (Beck & Cable, 2002). He was able to successfully transfer his talents to produce three very influential books (*Interpreting our Heritage* (1957), *The National Parks* (1986), *The Fifth Essence* (n.d.)) and acted as a consultant to the National Parks Service (Beck & Cable, 2002). In *The Fifth Essence* Tilden makes clear the inextricable connection between interpretation and parks. He writes that:

> Vital to any administrative program that envisages the fullest and finest use of Parks— whether areas of solacing wilderness or historic shrines—is the work of creating understanding. It is true that each preserved monument "speaks for itself." But unfortunately it speaks partly in a language that the average visitor cannot comprehend. Beauty and the majesty of natural forces need no interlocutor. They constitute a personal spiritual experience. But when the question is "why?" or "what?" or "how did this come to be?" people must have the answers. And this requires both patient research and the development of a program fitted to a great variety of needs.
>
> (as cited in Beck & Cable, 2002, pp. 1–2)

While Mills and Tilden greatly contributed to developing the foundations of interpretation, the story of Grey Owl has, relatively recently, brought the practice of interpretation into the mainstream media. The movie *Grey Owl* chronicles the life of Archibald Stansfeld Belaney, an Englishman who took on the identity of an indigenous person. It documents his dedication to protecting wilderness through writing, lecturing and interpreting. In addition to conveying the importance and power of interpretation of natural and cultural features, it also raises questions about the natural environment and authenticity.

What is Interpretation?

Freeman Tilden is acknowledged as the first to formally define the term interpretation and his writings are universally recognized and frequently quoted by those writing about interpretation (Beck & Cable, 2002; Ham, 1992; Jubenville & Twight, 1993; Knudson et al., 2003). According to Tilden interpretation is:

An educational activity which aims to reveal meanings and relationships through the use of original objects, by firsthand experience, and by illustrative media, rather than simply to communicate factual information.... Interpretation is the revelation of a larger truth that lies behind any statement of fact. [The interpreter] goes beyond the apparent to the real, beyond a part to the whole, beyond a truth to a more important truth.

(1977, p. 8)

In the above passage, Tilden eloquently informs readers of the very essence of interpretation. The enduring popularity of this definition stems from its applicability throughout the various shifts that have occurred within interpretation. Most notably, the notion that interpretation ought to go beyond what is physically present (phase one), to parts of the whole (phase two), and ultimately advance understanding of the natural environment (phase three).

While Tilden's definition conveys the depth of the term interpretation, other definitions highlight its breadth and functional aspects. Knudson et al. write that:

simply described, interpretation translates or brings meaning to people about natural and cultural environment. Interpreters help their clients to better understand and enjoy museums, camps, landscapes, cities, industries, historical, archeological resource areas, and thus to better understand their home environments.

(2003, p. 3)

Professional organizations have also sought to operationally define the term interpretation. In the United States development and certification of interpreters as well as advancement of the profession occurs through the National Association for Interpretation (NAI). They assert that "interpretation is a communication process that forges emotional and intellectual connections between the interests of the audience and the inherent meanings in the resources" (National Association for Interpretation, 2007, online).

While the above definitions reflect similar elements of communication, revelation and understanding, the meaning of interpretation is frequently misunderstood. This is "because interpretation encompasses so many possibilities in so many different places, the public is often confused about what interpretation is or what interpreters do" (Beck & Cable, 2002, p. 5). Tilden similarly recognized and attempted to address this very issue. He wrote:

Because of the fear of misconception arising from conflicting definitions of the word, and also because some have thought it a pretentious way of describing what they believe to be a simple, activity, there has been objection to the use of the word "interpretation" even among those engaged in this newer device of education. For myself I merely say that I do not share this objection. I have never been able to find a word more aptly descriptive of what we ... are attempting to do.

(1977, p. 4)

Beck and Cable (2002) suggest that prefixing the term interpretation with the matter being interpreted as well as employing consistent titles will assist in avoiding such misconceptions.

259

Toward an Understanding of Interpretation

As identified at the outset of the chapter, outdoor education and interpretation share many similar attributes and much of a common theoretical basis. The process of communication is presented in this section as it provides the most direct basis for interpretation. Comparisons and connections to other key concepts (education, recreation, learning approaches, outdoor recreation management) are subsequently offered.

Communication provides the basis of all types of interpretation. The basic process of communication is illustrated in Figure 8.3 and is explained using a situation in which two individuals are birding. The process of communication is initiated when an individual (encoder) has a concept that he or she wants to express to someone else. In our example Norm is very excited because he has just seen what he believes to be a rare duck. The first step in the communication process involves the individual taking the image that he saw (a rare duck) and encoding it. Encoding involves the individual affixing some type of label to the concept. This may occur in any number of forms: a lengthy description, a series of hand gestures, and/or a specific name. Once the individual has encoded the concept he or she projects the message. In our birding example, Norm tries to be very quiet so as to not disrupt any of the incoming waterfowl. He whispers the word "Bufflehead" and points to the location of the bird in question. His experienced birding companion (Brett) receives the message and decodes it. In decoding the message, the recipient attempts to make sense of the intended idea. In our example, the diction with which the duck's name was said and accompanying hand gesture lead Brett to decipher that Norm was making a query regarding the nature of the duck in question. Brett takes a quick look at the duck and shakes his head from side to side with a smile. He whispers the word "Fulvous" back to Norm with a big smile on his face thereby providing feedback.

The importance of communication to interpretation warrants a few additional comments

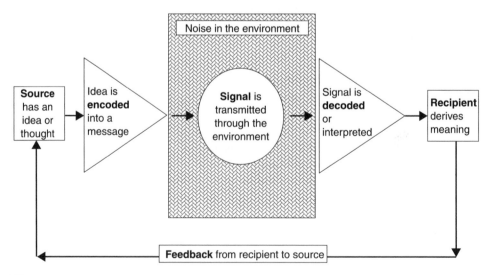

Figure 8.3 *The Communication Process.*

Source: adapted from Allen, 1998.

beyond these basic elements. As illustrated in the exchange between our two avid birders, more than just words are frequently employed in communication. Non-verbal communication greatly enhances the message being communicated. Non-verbal communication is "the way in which people communicate, intentionally, without words; nonverbal cues include facial expressions, tones of voice, gestures, body position and movement, the use of touch and eye gaze" (Aronson et al., 2001, p. 104). While these non-verbal expressions are also encoded and decoded, primary facial expressions are done so universally (Aronson et al., 2001). In the above example our two birders also used gestures that they both clearly understood. An action such as nodding your head from side to side is an example of an emblem. Emblems are "nonverbal gestures that have well-understood definitions within a given culture; they usually have direct verbal translations" (Aronson et al., 2001, p. 110). A final point to highlight is the potential for the message to get lost or altered. All types of settings in which communication takes place have such potential. In our birding example, the wind limits the distance at which voices can be heard.

Communication plays a critical role in both interpretation and education; yet the two are different enterprises. Knudson et al. support this assertion as they write "educators have published many articles arguing the distinctions between the terms environmental education and interpretation. Although these have some academic interest, it seems that the differences relate more to audience characteristics than to purpose" (2003, p. 8). Ham (1992) asserts that captive audiences are associated with education while non-captive audiences are associated with interpretation. Table 8.2 expands upon this notion to make clear the difference between education and interpretation.

Table 8.2 Differences Between Captive and Non-Captive Audiences

Captive audiences	Non-captive audiences

• Involuntary audience
• Time commitment is fixed
• External rewards important
• Must pay attention
• Will accept a formal, academic approach
• Will make an effort to pay attention, even if bored
• Examples of motivations:
  • grades
  • diplomas
  • certificates
  • licenses
  • jobs/employment
  • money
  • advancement
  • success
• Typical settings:
  • classrooms
  • job training courses
  • professional seminars
  • courses required for a license (e.g., driving)
	• Voluntary audience
	• Have no time commitment
	• External rewards not important
	• Do not have to pay attention
	• Expect an informal atmosphere and a non-academic approach
	• Will switch attention if bored
	• Examples of motivations:
	  • interest
	  • fun
	  • entertainment
	  • self-enrichment
	  • self-improvement
	  • a better life
	  • passing time (nothing better to do)
	• Typical settings:
	  • parks, museums, reserves, etc.
	  • extension programs
	  • at home watching television,
	  • listening to radio, reading a magazine

In educational settings (e.g., lecture halls, classrooms, professional development courses) participation is mandatory and there is a tremendous level of tolerance for a formal or academic approach, often involving one-way communication from the professor to students with the assistance of visual aids. In these settings students are typically extrinsically motivated by grades and future employment opportunities. In contrast, individuals voluntarily choosing to participate in interpretation are intrinsically motivated by interest and curiosity. The reduced importance of external rewards also means that if interest is not maintained individuals will switch to another activity or leave the program. Ham writes that "the only reward noncaptive audiences seek is internal. As long as the information they're receiving continues to be more interesting and entertaining than other things around them, noncaptive audiences will pay attention to it" (1992, p. 6). Appreciating these distinctions is particularly important for those making the transition from the role of educator to the role of interpreter, as most people have direct experience with the former but limited familiarity with the latter.

Interpretation bridges education and recreation. Knudson et al. explain that "interpretation lifts recreation beyond mundane fun to intelligent use of leisure time. It takes people from passive appreciation to exciting understanding of the cultural and natural environments" (2003, p. 13). Although in reality such distinctions often become blurred, education tends to emphasize learning, recreation tends to emphasize fun and entertainment, and interpretation endeavors to combine the two in a meaningful way. This connection is also crucial because it explicitly acknowledges that the difference between education and interpretation extends beyond the characteristics of the audience to its purpose.

Despite these distinctions, interpretation draws upon the learning theories introduced earlier in this chapter. Interpretation may be informed by and respond to each of the four stages of cognitive development. Knudson et al. explain that "interpreters apply Piaget's theory by (a) offering information consistent with how the children in the audience can process it, and (b) using different interpretive techniques that fit the different levels of cognitive development represented in the audience" (2003, p. 133). Primary patterns of learning may mediate the effectiveness with which interpretive messages are understood by participants and should prompt interpreters to employ diverse structural elements in their programs (Knudson et al., 2003). Discovery learning is the conceptual basis for many interpretive techniques that incorporate problems, puzzles, and/or situations in which the visitor starts with experience.

Interpretation is also a means of conveying the value of something (e.g., the natural environment, art, culture, an organization or agency) to others in a holistic manner (Beck & Cable, 2002; Ham, 1992; Knudson et al., 2003). In this way, interpretation is connected to the experience of participants and the realm of outdoor recreation management. The following three objectives of interpretation capture these important aspects.

The first priority or primary objective of interpretation is to assist the visitor in developing a keener awareness, appreciation, and understanding of the area he or she is visiting. Interpretation should help to make the visit a rich and enjoyable experience.

The second objective of interpretation is to accomplish management goals. It can be done in two ways. First, interpretation can encourage thoughtful use of the recreation resources on the part of the visitor, helping to reinforce the idea that parks are special places requiring special behavior. Second, interpretation can be used to minimize human impact on the resource by guiding people away from fragile or overused areas into areas that can withstand heavier use.

The third objective of interpretation is to promote public understanding of an agency and its programs (Sharpe, 1982, p. 4). Interpretation therefore may also be understood as a communication vehicle to enrich the experiences of visitors, share information about specific features, and indirectly manage their actions.

The Practice of Interpretation

Knudson et al. assert that "interpretation, properly carried out, serves as an indispensable tool to achieve successful, intelligent cultural and natural resource stewardship" (2003, p. 13). This section focuses on the practice of interpretation. It starts with a brief overview of who conducts interpretation and locates where it occurs. Both traditional and modern principles adhered to by interpreters are detailed and specific techniques commonly employed by those practicing interpretation are presented. Modes of delivery for interpretation are reviewed and applied considerations are highlighted.

The Provision of Interpretation

Interpretation services are provided by a diverse array of organizations and agencies. Government agencies entrusted with the protection of natural and cultural features often use interpretation to foster stewardship and to fulfill their educational mandates. Knudson et al. (2003) observe that interpretation is also undertaken by the private sector including industry, commercial firms, non-profit organizations, and individuals and groups. Specific examples of agencies that provide interpretation within both of these sectors are given in Table 8.3.

Interpretation occurs in a wide variety of settings, as conveyed by many of the locations/systems/events described in Table 8.3. Although the major properties where interpretation occurs are separated to make this point, it is important to recognize that in reality they may occur together within a single geographic area. Given the focus of this text on outdoor recreation, attention is predominately given to interpretation of the natural environment. Parks remain one of the most common settings for interpretation and an important tool for managers to address visitor use.

Titles given to individuals practicing interpretation include: park naturalist, art gallery director, ecotourism operator, program director, and researcher (Knudson et al., 2003). Organizations and agencies that provide interpretive services have developed these specific titles to reflect associated employment responsibilities. The proliferation of titles presents considerable confusion and contributes to the lack of public recognition of the profession (Beck & Cable, 2002). Knudson et al. (2003) argue that despite these many titles, individuals in these positions view themselves first and foremost as interpreters who convey the meaning of landscapes and heritage features (natural, cultural and built).

Table 8.3 Organizations Providing Interpretive Services in North America

Sector/agency	Major properties
Federal	
National Park Service/Parks Canada	National parks, historic sites, trails, scenic rivers, national recreation areas
USDA Forest Service/Environment Canada	National forests, trails
US Fish and Wildlife Service	National wildlife refuges
US Bureau of Land Management	National resource areas
US Army Corps of Engineers	Reservoir recreation areas
National Museums	Museums, zoos
Tribal/First Nation	
Tribal and Intertribal Councils	Centers, parks, museums
State/Province	
State/Provincial Parks Agencies	State/provincial parks
Special Districts	Parks, conservation areas
State/Provincial Wildlife Agencies	Wildlife, bird areas
State/Provincial Forestry Agencies	State forests/crown lands
State/Provincial Historical Agencies	State/provincial museums
State Outdoor Recreation Agencies	Scenic rivers and trails
County/Township	
County Park/Conservation Districts	County parks, nature centers, trails
Multicounty Park Districts	Parks, reserves, trails
County Historical Boards/County	Museums, historic sites
City/Town/Municipality	
City Park Districts/Departments	Park systems
Private Sector	
Industry	Company plant tours, industry museums, forest parks, mass media
Commercial firms	Tourism/ecotourism package firms, resorts, caves, ships, trains, buses, museums and exhibitions, guiding services, flightseeing
Individuals and groups	Freelance guides, speakers, writers, performing and graphic artists
Consulting firms	Design and fabrication of exhibits, interpretive planning, training, coaching
Non-profit organizations	Art societies, friends of museums, zoos, botanical gardens, arboreta, historical societies, nature center associations, sponsoring associations, camps, conservation organizations, educational foundation centers and forests, risk adventure and survival organizations, youth groups

Practicing Nature Interpretation

While the first person to explicitly use the term interpretation remains a point of debate, as the principles advanced by Mills and Tilden are strikingly similar (see Beck & Cable, 2002), it has been Tilden's six principles of interpretation that have inspired and directed individuals in the practice of interpretation over the past 40 years (Knudson et al., 2003). In his seminal work, *Interpreting our heritage*, Tilden observed that:

1. Any interpretation that does not somehow relate what is being displayed or described to something within the personality or experience of the visitor will be sterile.
2. Information, as such, is not interpretation. Interpretation is revelation based on information. Interpretation is revelation based on information, but they are entirely different things. However, all interpretation includes information.
3. Interpretation is an art which combines many arts, where the material is scientific, historical or architectural. Art is in some degree teachable.
4. The chief aim of interpretation is not instruction but provocation.
5. Interpretation should aim to present a whole rather than a part, and must address itself to the whole, rather than any phase.
6. Interpretation to children should not be a dilution of the presentation to adults, but should allow a fundamentally different approach. To be at its best, it will require a separate program

(1977, p. 9).

It is difficult to convey the impact of Tilden's six principles on the individuals engaging in interpretation. Tim Merriman, the Executive Director of the National Association for Interpretation, wrote that:

> when I was a park interpreter, I experimented with my work with naivete, foolish courage, and passion. I remember first reading Tilden's book and feeling like I had discovered the Holy Grail. It gave this young interpreter with limited experience six general guidelines that helped me to improve.
>
> (as cited in Beck and Cable, 2002, p. x)

Although these principles still offer considerable guidance, Tilden himself encouraged others to add to them (Beck & Cable, 2002). It is in this spirit of continued refinement and relevancy that Beck and Cable (2002) have recast Tilden's six principles, and added nine of their own. These 15 principles of interpretation are detailed in Table 8.4. Their effort both reflects the contributions of earlier works (i.e., Tilden) as well as provide guidance to assist individuals attempting interpretation in the contemporary information age.

The Interpretive Approach

The above principles of interpretation greatly enhance the communication of information, but how does interpretation actually occur? Ham (1992), in his straightforward guide to the practice of environmental interpretation distinguishes the interpretative approach as having four qualities. A first quality of interpretation is that it is pleasurable. This quality reflects the earlier discussion of interpretation as a bridge between education and recreation. A second quality is that it is relevant. Interpreters strive to connect information to something that their audience is previously aware of as well as something that their audience cares about; in this way interpretation should be both personal and meaningful. Ham (1992) suggests that self-referencing (encouraging people to think about their own experiences) and labeling (directing attention to things that people can or would like to associate with) are

Table 8.4 Principles of Interpretation

1. To spark an interest, interpreters must relate the subject to the lives of the people in their audience.
2. The purpose of interpretation goes beyond providing information to reveal deeper meaning and truth.
3. The interpretive presentation—as a work of art—should be designed as a story that informs, entertains, and enlightens.
4. The purpose of the interpretive story is to inspire and to provoke people to broaden their horizons.
5. Interpretation should present a complete theme or thesis and address the whole person.
6. Interpretation for children, teenagers, and seniors—when these comprise uniform groups— should follow fundamentally different approaches.
7. Every place has a history. Interpreters can bring the past alive to make the present more enjoyable and the future more meaningful.
8. Technology can reveal the world in exciting new ways. However, incorporating this technology into the interpretive program must be done with foresight and thoughtful care.
9. Interpreters must concern themselves with the quantity and quality (selection and accuracy) of information presented. Focused, well-researched interpretation will be more powerful than a longer discourse.
10. Before applying the arts in interpretation, the interpreter must be familiar with basic communication techniques. Quality interpretation depends on the interpreter's knowledge and skills, which must be continually developed over time.
11. Interpretive writing should address what readers would like to know, with the authority of wisdom and its accompanying humility and care.
12. The overall interpretive program must be capable of attracting support—financial, volunteer, political, administrative—whatever support is needed for the program to flourish.
13. Interpretation should instil in people the ability, and the desire, to sense the beauty in their surroundings—to provide spiritual uplift and to encourage resource preservation.
14. Interpreters can promote optimal experiences through intentional and thoughtful program and facility design.
15. Passion is the essential ingredient for powerful and effective interpretation—passion for the resource and for those people who come to be inspired by it.

two useful techniques to gain the attention of participants. Interpretation is also organized. This quality further reflects the likelihood that a non-captive audience will exert relatively little effort and time to understand the interpretive session. This quality also relates the amount of ideas and information conveyed. Ham asserts that as a general guide the number of ideas should be 7 ± 2 and adds the requirements that: "(1) the audience can easily distinguish between the main points and the subordinate information you attach to them, and (2) the number of main points you present doesn't, in fact, exceed five" (1992, p. 21). The final quality of an interpretative approach is that interpretation should have a theme. A theme ultimately responds to the "so what" question.

The need for interpreters to develop themes is broadly recognized (Beck & Cable, 2002; Ham, 1992; Knudson et al., 2003). Beck and Cable (2002) assert that a theme is the hallmark of holistic interpretation and that pragmatic aspects of thematic interpretation have been significantly advanced by Ham (1992). The basis of thematic interpretation is clearly communicating the intended message to the audience. Although in common exchanges the terms topic and theme are frequently used interchangeably, they should be clearly distinguished as "the topic of a presentation (whether written or oral) is simply its *subject* matter, whereas the theme of the presentation is the specific message about the subject we want to communicate to the audience" (Ham, 1992, p. 34). Thematic interpretation has distinct advantages to the interpreter and the audience; a theme focuses the interpreter on what information is required and clarifies the process of developing his/her program; it also makes the main message clearly comprehensible and increases interest from the audience (Ham, 1992). Ham (1992) contends that anyone can write a theme. Figure 8.4 describes his simple three-step process by which interpreters can organize their work by themes. After gaining experience interpreters naturally undertake a similar process.

Modes of Interpretation

While employing a thematic approach is critical for effective interpretation, there are many different factors that can influence the message being communicated. Knudson et al. observe that "people's responses to and understanding of interpretive messages depend on their reactions to (a) the person who interprets, (b) the location, and (c) their own physical

---

In three steps, anybody can write a theme

Sometimes interpreters have difficulty writing good themes simply because they aren't yet used to thinking thematically. Expressing a theme is easy, however, if you remember the difference between the topic (subject matter) of the presentation and the theme (the principal message you want to communicate to your audience about the topic). As a communicator, your task is to relate *themes* to your audience, not just information about the topic.

Steps in theme writing—an example

1. Select your general topic (for example, 'our soil') and use it to complete the following sentence:

    "Generally, my presentation (talk, exhibit, etc.) is about
    <u>   our soil."   </u>
    (put your general topic here)

2. State your topic in more specific terms and complete the following sentence:

    "Specifically, I want to tell my audience about
    <u>the importance of conserving our soil."</u>
    (put your specific topic here)

3. Now, express your theme by completing the following sentence:

    "After hearing my presentation (or reading my exhibit, etc.), I want my audience to understand that it's necessary to conserve our soil in order to increase our crops and to protect the quality of our water."
    (put your theme here)

Figure 8.4 Steps to Writing a Theme.

or emotional conditions, prejudices, and experiences" (2003, p. 112). Similar to other professionals, interpreters are perceived as knowledgeable persons and authority figures (Knudson et al., 2003). Interpreters are responsible for ensuring that: the information they convey is accurate and credible; they are well presented and polite; and that they are well versed in the "technical" aspects of interpretation, even if they have limited actual experience (Beck & Cable, 2002).

All interpreters can aim to achieve the following three goals:

1. reach every visitor on the property and the non-visitors that support the facility;
2. make the interpretive offerings so productive and compelling that they become the central feature of the visit;
3. promote the power of perception among all clientele so they see the world in a more meaningful way (Knudson et al., 2003, p. 113).

Interpreters have various modes of communication at their disposal to achieve these goals. By making available a range of potential interpretive services, visitors are able to select the one that is both accessible and of interest. Modes of delivering interpretation, for the purposes of this discussion, can be classified as activities that are either directly or indirectly delivered by interpreters. Ham (1992) makes a similar distinction by utilizing the terminology conducted (oral) versus non-conducted (written and graphic) activities.

In the first category the interpreter directly delivers the content to visitors. In his description of conducted activities, Ham observes that "what makes them different from most other kinds of presentations is that the interpreter controls the order in which the audience receives ideas and information" (1992, p. 41). The personal element is important in interpretation as it conveys a sense of service orientation on behalf of the organization and "has the most value where flexibility is necessary, when many different questions have to be answered, and where the individual's personality or character is an essential ingredient" (Knudson et al., 2003, p. 277). Examples of directly delivered interpretation include: talks, guided walks or tours, living history demonstrations, roving interpretation, storytelling, dance, activities and programs (Ham, 1992; Knudson et al., 2003).

The linear nature of the presentation is critical to this mode of interpretation because the interpreter may reveal the theme at the start and revisit it at the end (Ham, 1992). In one of the best practical guidelines for developing programs and talks, Ham (1992) recognizes that preparing a thematic talk requires a logical three-part structure. It should have a clear introduction that garners interest or engages visitors in the topic, shares the theme of the presentation with the visitors, and indicates the main points of the presentation. The body of the presentation contains information which develops or builds the theme of the presentation. The final part of the presentation (conclusion) demonstrates the connections between the various portions of the presentation and reinforces the theme.

Interpreters conduct a diversity of activities. Readers may be most familiar with the interpretive talks offered by naturalists at parks and other outdoor facilities including: orientation talks, site talks, exhibit talks, skill demonstration and campfire talks (Ham, 1992). Interpreters also communicate with individuals while guiding them through both natural and cultural features. Many forms of guided tours are offered by interpreters including:

guided walks, extended hikes, building tours, site tours, and various forms of transportation tours (e.g., bus) (Ham, 1992). Despite many similarities between talks and tours they should be distinguished as tours move, place extra emphasis on visual stimulation, and require more time and energy from visitors (Ham, 1992).

Interpreters conduct many other activities. They design, plan, and implement living history demonstrations. Beck and Cable recognize the close connection between interpretation of history, natural, and culture themes in writing that:

> the fundamental principles and techniques of effective interpretation do not change with the subject. Heritage interpretation and natural resource interpretation take place in similar settings. Both occur in museums and visitor centers; along trails and roadsides; and at public parks and private tourist centers. Every natural area has a history to interpret and every historical site is linked to a natural resource base that can be fruitfully interpreted.
>
> (2002, p. 69)

Puppet shows, information stations, performances, storytelling, and music are a few additional examples of activities conducted by interpreters (Ham, 1992; Knudson et al., 2003).

While it is difficult to argue with the impact of well-conducted activities that offer personal interaction with an interpreter, such an approach does present some limitations. Knudson et al. (1999) observe that interpreters have a limited amount of time that they can

Plate 8.1 Interpreter at Kings Canyon, Watarrka National Park, Australia.

Plate 8.2 Traditional Forms of Non-Personal Interpretation

be on duty, may not present the same message throughout the day, are limited as to the number of sites and potential times they can offer activities, and are relatively expensive.

Limitations associated with direct delivery of interpretation prompted attention to a second category of delivering interpretation in which interpreters are indirectly involved. Tilden himself offered the following comparison of direct and indirect forms of interpretation:

> A good device is far better than no contact at all, but poor interpretation by a gadget may be worse than none.
>
> A good result by device is better than a poor performance by an individual. On the other hand, a poor interpretation by mechanical means is worse than a poor interpretation by personal contact.

(1977, p. 96)

Indirect or non-personal interpretation are available at all times, don't require personal salaries to implement, may be fairly inexpensive, and permit people to enjoy them when and how they want (Ham, 1992; Knudson et al., 2003). There characteristics provide intriguing possibilities to overcome some of the constraints associated with personal or direct interpretation.

Non-personal or indirect interpretive mediums can be classified into two forms—traditional and technology based. Although the distinction is somewhat arbitrary as some forms of technology may be used to generate traditional mediums, the term technology based is used to recognize those forms that rely entirely on technology. Traditional forms of non-personal interpretation typically incorporate written and/or photographic material. An important distinction should be made between this form of interpretation and conducted activities as in the former it is the audience who dictates the order of which information is received (Ham, 1992). Traditional non-personal forms of interpretation are non-linear because no fixed sequence exists that visitors must view the information.

A diverse range of non-personal or indirect methods of interpretation exist. The term exhibits is used to encompass indoor displays, outdoor signs and exhibits, portable expositions, bulletin boards, markers and regulatory signs (Ham, 1992). When using exhibits, the interpreter has a very limited window of opportunity to communicate his/her main message to the audience. Jubenville and Twight are direct about the importance of interpretation requiring minimal effort on the participants in writing that "let's face it, imperatives are rare for people enjoying their leisure in a park or recreation area" (1993, p. 232).

Although both conceptual and artistic design is important, no research has demonstrated a significant relationship between the cost of an exhibit and the effectiveness with which it communicates its message (Ham, 1992). Good exhibits should be:

1. attractive, using principles of design and aesthetic appeal to bring attention to objects;
2. brief, simple, and straightforward conveying in few words the main message of the exhibit so little effort is required by the audience to gain information; and,
3. clear, so the main intent or message of the exhibit can be gained in a few seconds (Ham, 1992).

The self-guided tour is another common non-personal interpretive technique which incorporates exhibits with other visitor management features. Self-guided tours may again take numerous forms including: trails, buildings, towns, facilities, sites, and travel routes by automobile, boats, and airplanes (Ham, 1992). These tend to use a variety of means to communicate with visitors. Exhibits, such as signs, are often located at features of particular interest and are sometimes supplemented by brochures and audio commentary. Although many studies have been conducted in an attempt to ascertain which means of communication is the best, no conclusions have been made that any single self-guided medium has a particular advantage (Ham, 1992). Managerial concerns, however, should be taken into consideration. In this regard signs may be obtrusive in the natural environment and pose difficult situations requiring multiple languages, while brochures add maintenance problems and are limited as to the amount of people who can gain information at a single time (Ham, 1992).

Emerging technological innovations offer many novel ways to conduct interpretation. The debate regarding technology in the practice of interpretation is not entirely new and has been ongoing with proponents on both sides advocating associated benefits and potential pitfalls (Beck & Cable, 2002; Knudson et al., 2003). Technology poses a conundrum for interpreters as:

On the one hand, technology-based interpretation can be expensive, impersonal, complex, and therefore counterproductive. High-tech exhibits that threaten the audience with their complexity or sophistication result in a technological arrogance. Many people, especially older adults, are still intimidated by computers and other technological devices. Without friendly interpreters to personally encourage, assist, and guide visitors, the technologically timid will be driven away by the machines.

On the other hand, modern technology can allow visitors to view objects that previously could not be seen, experience environments that could not be experienced, and manipulate and respond to stimuli that previously could not be perceived. These

271

advances expand, rather than stifle, interpretive opportunities. Fresh and exciting visual and audio information resulting from new technology can bridge diverse learning styles. We can open new worlds of revealing and meaningful experiences to our visitors.

(Beck & Cable, 2002, p. 82)

Despite this tension, it appears as though the role of technology is becoming increasingly accepted as a tool for interpretation as information technology and electronic mediums are important additions in the most recent interpretation resources (see Beck & Cable, 2002; Knudson et al., 2003).

The manner in which technology is applied appears to be central to this issue. Beck and Cable (2002) argue that high technology is properly applied when it is engaging and provides opportunity for enjoyable education, dependable and cost effective in terms of both acquisition and maintenance, and reveals information that was previously inaccessible. Just as there are a diversity of means of delivering interpretation using other techniques, technology also provides interpreters with an array of options including: animatronics (robots with moving parts that speak), holograms, videos, remote sensing/geographic information systems, interactive computer exhibits, electronic storage devices (e.g., compact discs), digital cameras, and the Internet. From all of the technologies available, it is the Internet that has prompted the most change. The Internet provides a means to greatly extend the reach of the interpreter from people visiting their particular location to people throughout the world. Web-based interpretation is beneficial because it is: relatively inexpensive; conducive to facilitating discussion and exchanges between interpreters and those who are interested; available at all times; and allows a means to conduct research by interpreters and a way to work with both formal education systems through curriculum and non-formal organization (Beck & Cable, 2002). As interpretation continues to incorporate technology it moves from a format intended for a small group of visitors who are at a site (e.g., Mills at Fallen Leaf Lodge) to a means of communicating to thousands of people. In this way interpretation is a form of mass communication as media is utilized to reach large audiences (Knudson et al., 2003).

A MODEL OF INTERPRETATION

Thus far interpretation has been discussed along conceptual and applied dimensions. In this section Jubenville and Twight's (1993) model of interpretation is explored, as shown in Figure 8.5. This model sets interpretation within the larger context of outdoor recreation and highlights linkages between the conceptual and applied dimensions covered thus far.

Central to the interpretive model is the outdoor recreation site at which interpretation occurs. Interpretation may occur at parks, conservation areas, museums, historical sites, gardens, parkways, and on private properties. The arrows pointing in a clockwise direction illustrate the practice of interpretation. Appreciation and understanding, initially of the particular site, is fostered by interpreters who utilize the principles presented in this section to effectively communicate their messages to visitors. Interpreters have a number of means by which they are able to apply these principles. The applications discussed above included conducted and non-conducted activities. Most commonly, interpreters employ a thematic approach to develop and implement programs with the intended outcome of fostering appreciation about the outdoor recreation site. Arrows from each component of the interpretive model, pointing toward the outdoor recreation site, signal the contributions made by interpretation towards achieving managerial goals and assisting with visitor management.

The arrows emanating outward from the outdoor recreation site at the center of Figure 8.5 illustrate or reflect the philosophical basis for interpretation. It is through better appreciation and enhanced understanding that visitors are able to take information learned from the particular experience and transfer it back to other elements of their life. Fostering this process is a delicate balance for an interpreter as:

> we all tend to glorify idealism to want to have some impact on the world beyond our park, it is awfully naïve to think of our efforts as saving or even having a meaningful impact on that world. Rather than dwelling on the grandiosity of the interpretive model, then, it is better to go back to the basics of history/natural interpretation.
>
> (Jubenville & Twight, 1993, p. 225)

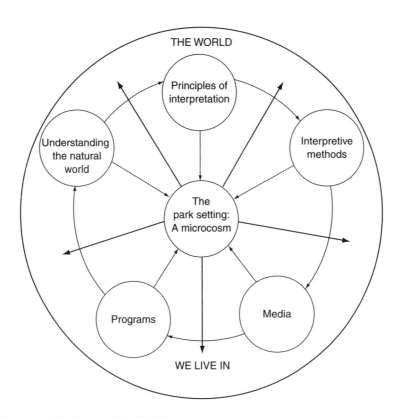

Figure 8.5 The Interpretive Model.

Jubenville and Twight (1993) remind those practicing interpretation that such fundamental change occurs in small increments through stages of appreciation, understanding, and knowledge.

The arrows pointing outwards from the site also signify the changing reach of interpretation. As noted in the indirect methods of interpretation, the Internet is greatly enhancing the capability of interpreters to reach more people throughout the world. Changes in communication may both bring attention and interest to the particular site, resulting in more visitors as well as developing shared values. In their discussion of modern interpretation methods, Beck and Cable observe that "the possibilities for human enrichment through Internet travel are endless. The Internet can be both a source of information for interpreters and a means for interpreters to interpret their site to the world" (2002, p. 91).

BENEFITS

Interpretation offers benefits to individuals who participates in outdoor recreation, society as a whole, and management/resource agencies and organizations. The effects of interpretation at a personal level can be profound. Knudson et al. eloquently capture this benefit of interpretation in the following passage:

> interpretation aims to affect people positively. It excites and equips people for observing and studying the beauty and legacy around them. It gives them basic information and direction. It provokes them to better interpret for themselves. It lifts them to a higher, more satisfying level of living and recreating.
>
> (2002, p. 46)

At an individual level, interpretation is inextricably linked to the process of learning and education. This philosophical connection is evident from Tilden's principles as well as the move towards the incorporation of formalized school curriculums (Knudson et al., 2003). Education alone, however, is only a portion of the benefits afforded to individuals. Interpretation aims to be enjoyable and enhance the recreation experience of individuals while also evoking an emotional response, which may further reinforce individual motivation for participation (Knudson et al., 2003).

Environmental education and stewardship were recognized as two goals of outdoor recreation in Chapter 1. Education via interpretation contributes to societal betterment as it reinforces values associated with recreation in general. Knudson et al. recognize that "interpretation contributes several specific values in the civic operation of society. They include (a) information for democratic decision making, (b) identity with our land and culture, and (c) an ethical sense of our place in history and our role in the world" (2003, p. 57). These societal benefits, shared by both interpretation and education, may initially appear lofty. However, knowledge and information is central to the civics perspective as well as good governance. The history of outdoor recreation illustrates the centrality of the connection between resources and identity, especially in the United States. History also demonstrates how understanding and advocacy may prompt conservation and preservation efforts.

Considerable benefits from providing interpretation are derived from resource manage-ment agencies and a variety of organizations. Both agencies and organizations have long recognized the benefits of interpretation and employed it as a management strategy (Butler & Hvenegaard, 2002; Knudson et al., 2003; Pigram & Jenkins, 1999). The Interpretation Australia Association (IAA), for example, states that "we believe that interpretation makes an essential contribution to the conservation of Australia's natural, social and cultural her-itage by raising public awareness and creating opportunities for understanding, appreciation and enjoyment" (Interpretation Australia Association, 2007, online). Pigram and Jenkins (1999) believe that interpretation is to assist in achieving management objectives. In this regard interpretation frequently contributes by fostering appreciation of the natural environment and the agencies mission, developing public support for the organization, dis-persing information about both resource protection, management policies and public safety, and shaping the behaviors of visitors while at the site (Knudson et al., 2003; Pigram & Jenkins, 1999).

As a powerful management tool, questions also arise about the misuses of interpretation. Knudson et al. (2003) recognize that changing attitudes held by visitors are a frequently cited goal of interpreters and environmental educators. They suggest that ethical concerns surround this as a central focus of interpretation. They also note the challenges associated with alteration/embellishment of information to assist in the achievement of managerial goals. While interpretation offers considerable benefits, interpreters need to exercise sound judgment concerning these ethical issues.

SUMMARY

This chapter focused on learning about the natural environment through outdoor education and interpretation. The historical context documented clearly established that education in the out-doors has been a dominant means of transferring knowledge about all aspects of life. Although not as pronounced as other approaches in "modern" education, an enduring counter force has emphasized the value of experience and the philosophical basis of outdoor education. Explana-tions for how learning occurs were pursued by discussing cognitive development theory, Bloom's taxonomy, psychological processing/learning styles, and discovery inquiry. Differ-ences between in-class instruction and outdoor (experiential) education were highlighted. Benefits accrued to both individual participants as well as to wider society were documented.

Outdoor education and interpretation are complementary areas within outdoor recre-ation that share a similar conceptual basis in learning and communication theories. Although the two enterprises are integrally connected, distinctions were made in the chapter between formal instruction and interpretation. Historical development, guiding principles, and key consideration in the professional practice of interpretation were documented. A model of interpretation was utilized as a means to synthesize conceptual and pragmatic information about interpretation. The chapter closed with a discussion of benefits (individual, societal, resource agency) from interpretation.

275

KEY CONCEPTS

Benefits of interpretation

Benefits of outdoor education

Bloom's taxonomy

Cognitive development theory

Difference between captive and
  non-captive audiences

Direct or conducted delivery

Experiential learning

Indirect or non-conducted delivery

Nature interpretation

Outdoor education

Philosophy of outdoor education

Psychological processing (learning styles)

The communication process

The interpretive model

Tilden's six principles of interpretation

SUGGESTED KEY SOURCES FOR MORE INFORMATION

Beck, L. & Cable, T. (2002). *Interpretation for the 21st century. Fifteen guiding principles for interpreting nature and culture* (2nd ed.). Champaign, IL: Sagamore.

Ham, S. H. (1992). *Environmental interpretation: A practical guide for people with big ideas and small budgets.* Golden, CO: North American Press.

Hammerman, D. R. & Hammerman, W. M. (Eds.). (1973). *Outdoor education: A book of readings.* Minneapolis: Burgess.

Institute for Outdoor Learning http://www.outdoor-learning.org/index.htm

Journal of Experiential Education http://jee.lakeheadu.ca

Knudson, D. M., Cable, T. T. & Beck, L. (2003). *Interpretation of cultural and natural resources* (2nd ed). State College, PA: Venture.

Tilden, F. (1977). *Interpreting our heritage* (3rd ed.). Chapel Hill, NC: The University of North Carolina Press.

National Association for Interpretation http://www.interpnet.com

REVIEW QUESTIONS

1. When did the practice of outdoor education become popular? How would you explain why it became so popular?

2. Donaldson and Donaldson observed that "outdoor education is education *in*, *about*, and *for* the outdoors" (1958, p. 17). How do each of the terms in italics relate to the underlying philosophy of outdoor education?

3. How would you know if learning has occurred during outdoor education?

4. Identify and describe three theories of learning that inform outdoor education.

5. Compare and contrast traditional instruction with experiential learning.

6. What is progressive experiential education?

7. Identify two key people in the early development of interpretation. Describe their contributions.

8. Illustrate and explain the process of communication. Why is understanding communication important to the practice of interpretation?

9. What values does interpretation seek to communicate?

10. Explain the process of thematic interpretation. Apply the process to an example of your choice.

Chapter 9

Adventure Recreation

OBJECTIVES

This chapter will:

- discuss the human fascination with adventure;
- investigate the conceptual basis of adventure;
- explore how adventure has been applied to the therapeutic and educational contexts;
- examine how adventure education may influence group development, decision-making and leadership;
- document how transference occurs from the adventure context to everyday life;
- critically assess the "reality" of risk.

INTRODUCTION

Adventure pursuits are often iconic images to convey the excitement inherent in some forms of outdoor recreation. This chapter starts by tracing the human fascination with adventure from ancient times through to today. After setting the context, attention shifts from adventure in popular culture to develop a scholarly understanding. Definitions of the term adventure are pursued, the associated idea of risk is presented, and conceptual explanations are explored. Just as adventure has a long history as enhancing the experience of individuals during their leisure time, adventure has also been recognized and employed with specific intent. Specific applications of adventure to therapy and education are presented. The manner in which adventure is a medium to enable change (e.g., group development, leadership, decision-making) and can be transferred to everyday life is subsequently discussed. The chapter closes with a critical assessment of the "reality" of risk associated with adventure pursuits and how it may be negotiated.

HUMAN FASCINATION WITH ADVENTURE

Early records of exciting escapades come from pictographs that depict adventurous experiences (Conway, 1993). Stories of adventures and adventurers have also been passed down through generations in almost every culture through the spoken word. As language and writing became increasingly formalized, chronicling adventures became a popular subject for some of the earliest works of literature. Among these early efforts Homer's *Odyssey* stands out. The *Odyssey* is the story of Odysseus who leaves his family and homeland to travel alone to distant parts of the earth, farther than any other man had ever gone (West, 1997). These early accounts of adventure demonstrate the human fascination with excitement as well as the human aptitude/willingness to enter into these situations.

The appeal of adventure goes well beyond intrigue and may actually contribute to our success as a species. Csikszentmihalyi and Csikszentmihalyi (1990) identify the ability for exploration and delight in confronting the unexpected as advantageous and relatively unknown survival mechanisms. Quinn supports this contention and notes the work of Ardrey, who offers that:

> The magnet of our nature commanded that we investigate certain blue Ethiopian hills, and what lay beyond. And so in the vast concourse of time we moved past the veto of desert, into the chill of winters that our equatorial existence had never anticipated. But we did not go back. And that is what is so interesting. . . . There has to be ancient winds within us, old primate curiosities, newer predator demand for exploration. These were not so much the biological consequences of cultural advance, but very old biological demands—that inhabit us still, to become a dominant quality in the life of our species.
>
> (1976, pp. 135–136)

In the above quotation, from *The Hunting Hypothesis*, Ardrey (1976) makes explicit the connection between human development throughout the world and our innate sense of adventure.

The conjecture that adventure is part of the human condition is intriguing because it positions adventure as a necessary condition or desirable experience that humans seek. Csikszentmihalyi and Csikszentmihalyi observe that:

> Someday we shall be able to document exactly the physiological benefit that "adrenaline rushes" provide rock climbers or sky divers, or the release of endorphins that a "runner's high" brings to the nervous system of athletes. In the meantime, even though we lack an understanding of the biological mechanisms, it is quite clear that facing challenge of the unknown is generally pleasurable to most people. The "spirit of adventure" is not dead, and it must have been strong and healthy through the endless stretches of nameless centuries in which our ancestors struggled to gain a foothold on the earth.
>
> (1990, p. 149)

As proposed in the above quotation, the spirit for adventure by humans appears to be insatiable. Exploration has extended to all regions of this planet as well as other planets.

During the twentieth century the "spirit of adventure" changed. Prior to this time unknown dangers were vigorously pursued for "God, glory, and gold" as well as a concerted effort to expand empires (Spielvogel, 1991, p. 484). While these factors may certainly still exert some influence on adventurers, the contemporary circumstances under which pursuits occur are characterized by personal challenge and often occur during leisure time. The first successful ascent of Mount Everest by Sir Edmund Hillary in 1953 provides an illustrative example. Hillary, a beekeeper from Auckland, New Zealand, had climbed all over the world before summiting Everest. The first successful ascent of Everest proved it was possible for mountaineers to reach the top of the highest peak in the world. There are many examples of individuals today who pursue adventure although they are already very successful. Perhaps the best example of this is Sir Richard Branson, the billionaire businessman and leader of the Virgin Group who vigorously pursues adventure records in both sailing and ballooning. The continued pursuit of adventure beyond the twentieth century confirms its establishment as an ingrained part of human psyche. Even in the absence of monetary rewards, pressure for national expansion, and religious zeal, humans still choose to undertake dangerous activities.

Although everyone may not personally want to pursue dangerous or exciting situations, the human fascination with stories of adventures endures. Literature accounts of dangerous journeys remain popular. For example, *Into Thin Air* (1997) by Jon Krakauer documented the tragic events of a Mount Everest expedition and became a bestseller. Making stories of outdoor adventures into feature-length motion pictures further demonstrates the popularity and interest in such pursuits. Climbing has been an activity incorporated by Columbia Pictures in many releases, including: *Cliffhanger*, with Sylvester Stallone as a mountain guide in 1993; *Vertical Limit*, with Chris O'Donnell leading the rescue of a group that attempt assent of K2 in 2000; and *Into Thin Air*, based on the best-selling book, which documented the tragic ending to the ascent of Mount Everest in 1997. Most recently, the prospect of watching adventures unfold has been used to capture the interests of millions of television viewers. Mark Burnett, the executive producer of unscripted or "reality" television programs, has employed dangerous and exciting situations in both his eco-challenge and survivor series.

WHAT IS ADVENTURE?

A number of terms have been employed in the initial section of this chapter to communicate the subject matter of adventure including dangerous, exciting and unknown. This section moves from discussing the place of adventure in human heritage and popular culture to its definition and key characteristics.

Adventure and its many surrogates (experiential education, outdoor recreation, outdoor pursuits) have been plagued with terminological challenges. Ewert defines adventure recreation as "activities utilizing a close interaction with the natural environment, that contain elements of real or perceived risk and danger" (Ewert, 1989, as cited in Ewert, Galloway & Estes, 2001, p. 27). In his discussion of semantics, Priest (1990) reconciles the above terms in a different way. He asserts that adventure is a subset of leisure and, therefore, it must both be undertaken voluntarily and be intrinsically motivating for the individual. Adventure, he contends, is therefore distinguishable from other leisure activities because it involves uncertainty and can only be experienced while at leisure. Galloway (2006) observes that adventure permeates all domains of leisure and contends that it is a type of deviant leisure which may be both constructive and deconstructive.

In exploring the semantics associated with adventure, Priest (1990) stresses the importance of understanding the concepts of uncertainty, risk, danger, peril and hazard. He offers the following:

> The outcome of an adventure is uncertain when information (critical to the completion of a task or the solution of a problem) is missing, vague, or unknown.

> Risk is the potential to lose something of value. The loss may lead to physical (broken bones), mental (psychological fear), social (peer embarrassment), or financial harm (lost or damaged equipment).

> Danger gives rise to risk. The two are not the same. Dangers are present in both people and their surroundings.

> Perils are the sources of the loss.

> Hazards are the conditions that influence the probability or likelihood of a loss occurring.

> (1990, p. 115)

Understanding the term adventure is furthered by realizing the relationship among the above concepts. Priest (1990) explains that uncertainty in an adventure comes from a situation where the potential for loss is present (risk). The idea of perceived risk is common in all definitions of adventure recreation and is the amount of risk or danger a person believes is inherent in a given situation. Perceived risk is subjective and varies from person to person. Ewert et al. (2001) suggest that perceived risk has physical, psychological, financial, functional, time and social dimensions. Risk (real and perceived) is precipitated by either human and/or environmental dangers, which may be further classified as perils (sources of loss) and hazards (the likelihood of realizing loss) to account for factors that lead to loss (Priest, 1990).

While Priest (1990) provides a useful guide to negotiate terminology associated with the concept of adventure, others have attempted to capture its spirit. In describing the essence of adventure Quinn writes: "Adventure speaks of beginning, boldness, and power. Adventure connotes participation and active involvement in life. An adventure, a quest, begins because of a human desire, a drive to experience that which is hidden and unknown" (1999, p. 149).

The above quotation considers attributes humans derive from the experience of adventure. Quinn's (1999) philosophical musings offer insightful glimpses into the essence of adventure as an element that people desire that is currently missing in their life. The process of adventure affords the occasion to rely on skills and abilities to overcome tenuous situations, the greater duration of which the outcome is unknown the more profound the

280

adventure experience (Quinn, 1999). Henderson deepens understanding of the adventure experience by suggesting that it ought to include a "stretching out of the imagination" that encompasses the boundaries of both space and time; "part of each of us desires to be grounded in a heritage, to see ourselves as reflections on the past, yet evolving!" (Henderson, 1999, p. 144). Perhaps the most vexing account of adventure was provided by Leroy (1983) who suggests that it does not have purpose. He offers, respectfully, the following quotation by G. K. Chesterton and his interpretation:

> I think the immense act has something about it human and excusable; and when I endeavor to analyze the reason for this feeling I find it to lie, not in the fact that the thing was big or bold or successful; but in the fact that the thing was perfectly useless to everybody, including the person who did it.
>
> Because some answer does lie within this paradox. The immense act is useless in one sense: useless in terms of most characteristics that our culture places value upon; useless in a materialistic sense. Adventure is not a materialistic experience it is a spiritual or perhaps a humanistic experience. Is there any use in our civilization for materially useless, spiritually rich experiences? The question, I am sure, need only be asked rhetorically, particularly when the audience is a crowd of mountaineers.
>
> (1983, pp. 230–231)

While the meaning of adventure will be a source of continued dialogue, it is important to maintain a consistent "working" definition. In this book "adventurous experiences are activities within uncertain outcomes (due to the presence of situational risks) which necessitate people applying their personal competence to meet the challenge and resolve the uncertainty" (Priest, 1999a, p. xiii). Despite the multiple meaning of the term adventure, all adventurous experiences contain:

1. some degree of difficulty associated with the enterprise regardless of its form;
2. elements of danger, both real and perceived, that "are filled with growth potential and are actually what we seek";
3. commitment to persist (both cognitively and to the unknown) to the eventual outcome; and,
4. subjugation to understandable stress which we require correct responses to alleviate perilous situations (Leroy, 1983, p. 230).

THE CONCEPT OF ADVENTURE

The various meanings of adventure were explored in the preceding section. Scholars working in the social sciences have gone beyond the definition of adventure and have sought to explain how it functions. In this section the conceptual basis of adventure is pursued through the idea of flow and the adventure experience paradigm. Connections are also made to the social-psychology topics of satisfaction, recreation choice, and self-concept (Chapter 4).

281

Adventure and the Concept of Flow

Csikszentmihalyi found that intrinsic rewards and transcendence experiences were striking common motives in his investigation of individuals participating in diverse activities (including adventure pursuits) (Mitchell, 1983). To communicate this finding he employed the term flow and suggested that:

> flow refers to the holistic sensation present when we act with total involvement. It is a kind of feeling after which one nostalgically says: "that was fun," or "that was enjoyable." It is the state in which action follows upon action according to an internal logic which seems to need no conscious intervention on our part. We experience it as a unified flowing from one moment to the next in which we are in control of our actions, and in which there is little distinction between self and environment; between stimulus and response; or between past, present, and future.
>
> (Csikszentmihalyi, 1975, p. 58)

While the development of flow was described in Chapter 4, focus here is given to its utilization in the specific context of adventure. In this regard, Mitchell (1983) sought to develop a theoretical model of enjoyment associated with mountaineering based on three key propositions associated with flow. These propositions include freedom of choice, limiting the stimulus field (emphasizing engagement in uncertainty), and merging of action and awareness. In reflecting upon these propositions and bringing them together he offers that:

> The key to maintaining this selfless concentration lies in the simplicity of flow-producing activities. In climbing, reality places easily understood, noncontradictory demands for action on the participants and provides prompt and immediate feedback— find a safe anchor, get out of the storm, dodge the falling rock; if one foot slips, the other foot and the hands must not.... For the climber the urgency of the immediate situation clearly distinguishes good from bad. Safe is good, unsafe is bad. Goals and means are logically ordered. People are not expected to do incompatible things on the mountain as they are in real life. They know, or believe they know, what the results of various possible outcomes will be.
>
> (Mitchell, 1983, p. 168)

As Mitchell (1983) illustrates, the concept of flow may clearly be applied and utilized to explain the experience sought in mountaineering. Csikszentmihalyi & Csikszentmihalyi have further addressed the connection between flow and adventure, and assert that "certainly it [adventure] responds to the human desire for novelty, discovery, uncertainty, and problem solving" (1990, 1999, p. 156).

In probing the core of this connection between flow and adventure, it is the high autotelic factor that causes individuals to derive enjoyment from these experiences (Csikszentmihalyi & Csikszentmihalyi, 1999). In this context "autotelic means that the purpose of an activity lies in the activity itself" (Mannell & Kleiber, 1997, p. 174). More specifically, individuals pursuing adventurous types of activities rank high on the first of the following

282

eight autotelic factors, as they are actively seeking experiences not available in everyday activities:

1. the enjoyment of the experience and the use of skills;
2. the activity itself: the pattern, the action, the world it provides;
3. friendship, companionship;
4. development of personal skills;
5. measuring self against own ideals;
6. emotional release;
7. competition, measuring self against others; and,
8. prestige, regard, glamour (Csikszentmihalyi & Csikszentmihalyi, 1999, p. 157).

The concept of flow also directs attention to congruency between the adequacy of skills and challenges posed by the environment. In summarizing the applicability of the flow concept to adventure in the leisure domain:

> the dependence of enjoyment on a balancing of challenges and skills suggests the importance of a capacity to continuously adjust this balance by using anxiety and boredom as information, and identifying new challenges as skills grow. Being able to tolerate the anxiety-provoking interactions that test one's skills also appears to be important. Finally, other attributes are likely to have an effect outside of the particular interaction; among these would be the ability to delay gratification, which is necessary for the eventual enjoyment of the activities that require a significant investment of energy before they start providing intrinsic rewards. Clearly all of these are important in leisure activities.
>
> (Csikszentmihalyi & Csikszentmihalyi, 1999, p. 157)

The Adventure Experience Paradigm

At the outset of his most recent work developing the adventure experience paradigm, Priest instructs that "paradigms are merely conceptual models and theories designed to view and explain phenomena in life" (1999b, p. 159). In this spirit, the adventure experience paradigm endeavors to capture the reality of adventure with explicit heritage to the concept of flow (Martin & Priest, 1986; Priest, 1990, 1999b; Priest & Baillie, 1987). The adventure experience paradigm is illustrated in Figure 9.1. Priest (1999b) emphasizes the need for semantic differentiation between the terms risk (potential loss), competency (combination of technical and human skills), and challenge (the relationship between risk and competence). This is shown in Figure 9.1 as the term risk is used to denote the vertical axis and the term competence is used on the horizontal axis—challenge is represented by the black line that connects risk and competence. Challenge, the balance or interplay between risk and competence, may result in five expected situations or outcomes of exploration and experimentation, adventure, peak adventure, misadventure, and devastation and disaster (Priest, 1999b). Challenge involved in each of the aforementioned conditions varies considerably. At one end of the continuum (exploration and experimentation) there is low risk

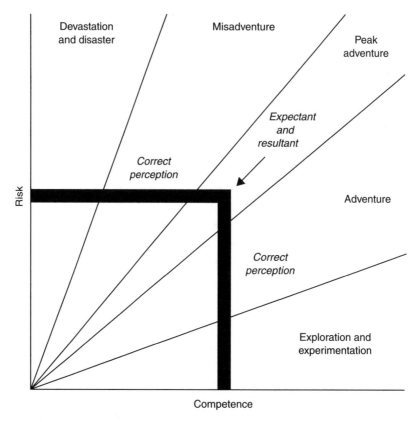

Figure 9.1 The Adventure Experience Paradigm.
Source: Martin & Priest, 1986.

while competence is considerable. Learning to boulder in an indoor setting illustrates such a situation. At the other end of the continuum (devastation and disaster) risks exceed competence. An attempt to climb Mount Everest that ends tragically provides an example in which loss is realized. It is the middle condition of peak adventure where risk and competence are in roughly equal proportions that individuals may feel challenged and experience flow.

The importance of individual perception to adventure is made clear by Mitchell (1983) and reinforced by Priest (1990, 1999b) in the adventure experience paradigm. In addition to five potential outcomes of the experience, Priest observes:

> adventures are personally specific (based on personal competence) and situationally specific (based on situational risks). In other words, an adventure for one person, in a particular place, at a given time, may not be adventure for another, or for the same person in a different place or time.... The state of mind concept dictates human behavior and, in turn, is driven by human perceptions of reality. Hence, both the risk and competence (the two axes of the model) may be thought of as having two possible values: real and perceived.

(1999b, p. 160)

284

Plate 9.1 Are These Adventurers Experiencing Flow?

As highlighted in Figure 9.1 by the terms "expectant and resultant," peak adventure occurs not only when risk and competence are in balance, but also when they are perceived correctly by the participant. Priest (1990) distinguished between two common situations for those beginning outdoor pursuits—people who are timid or scared and people who are arrogant and fearless. Priest (1990) uses the adventure experience paradigm to illustrate the profile of the timid or fearful individual, as shown in Figure 9.2. Individuals starting to undertake adventurous activities who are timid and fearful tend to perceive there to be a greater amount of risk, while also perceiving themselves to be less than competent. In the case of skiing, for example, an individual with a fear of falling may believe that a relatively small hill poses a considerable challenge that is well beyond his or her skill level. For the purpose of the example it can be assumed that he or she has successfully completed many lessons and has reached a basic level of proficiency. Although his or her perception of risk and competence is aimed at peak adventure, as indicated by the darker shading in Figure 9.2, the outcome or result from the actual experience, as illustrated by the lighter shading, is exploration and experimentation. As a result, it is unlikely that he or she will be stimulated by the experience and, in turn, may fail to realize the many benefits of adventure challenges (Priest, 1999b).

A second common profile is the arrogant or fearless individual (Priest, 1990). The adventure experience paradigm again illustrates this situation, as shown in Figure 9.3. Priest (1990) explains that arrogant or fearless people fail to appreciate, or underappreciate, the amount of risk while simultaneously overestimating their ability regarding the pursuit. While perception is again aimed at achieving peak adventure, the outcome is far from it. This situation results in the realization of risk (loss) in terms devastation and disaster, as illustrated in Figure 9.3. Staying with the earlier example of skiing, consider a novice skier who has taken a single lesson. Unlike our earlier individual, this person has supreme confidence in his or her ability or competence. Perhaps he or she made it down the starting hill a few times without falling. In addition to perceiving him or herself to be a competent skier, he or she believes that skiing poses little risk. After all, skiing appears to be very easy on television and after trying it a few times it seems very easy. Based on these perceptions the most difficult hill is selected. Differences between his or her perceptions and the reality of

285

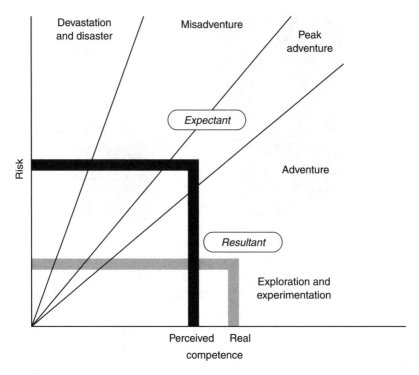

Figure 9.2 Profile of the Timid Individual.

Source: Priest, 1990.

the situation become immediately apparent as the feedback he or she received confirms that he or she is ill-equipped to handle the selected route and consequently an injury occurs.

In addition to illustrating the experience of novice adventurers, the paradigm also provides a means to explain the approach of more experienced adventurers. In response to the previously identified perceptual obstacles, "these kinds of shortcomings are often avoided by experienced adventurers. Through repeated application of their competence, these people have become astute: accurate in their perceptions" (Priest, 1999b, p. 161). A seasoned skier, to complete the example, would develop an appreciation of his/her competencies as well as a through understanding of the potential for loss posed by a situation. In an attempt to experience peak adventure, he/she would select a ski hill that poses challenges commensurate with his/her skills. As skills continue to develop and change, so must the amount of risk posed by the environment, for the skier to experience peak adventure.

ADVENTURE AND THE SOCIAL-PSYCHOLOGY TRADITION

The relationship between flow and adventure foreshadows the close connection between the social-psychology tradition in leisure studies and adventure. This section builds upon key concepts introduced in Chapter 4 (motivation, self-concept, satisfaction) and examines their specific application to adventure.

The concept of motivation was given a central place in Chapter 4 as it explains why

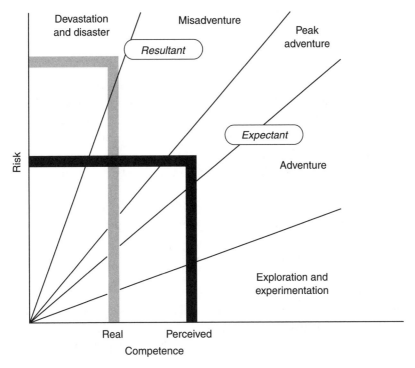

Figure 9.3 Profile of the Arrogant Individual.

Source: Priest, 1990.

people choose to pursue outdoor recreation activities. Consider the example of sky-diving. Many people find it difficult to fathom why an individual is motivated to jump out of an air-craft and willingly undertake, what some may perceive as, considerable risk. Theories of motivation can help understand why people want to participate in adventure.

The idea of self and intrinsic motivation is common or central to the three general theo-ries of motivation presented in Chapter 4. Self-actualization is placed at the top of Maslow's hierarchy of needs (1970), intrinsic rewards through challenge of self is the highest level of leisure needs identified by Iso-Ahola (1980), and moving towards (seeking and escaping) optimal and intrinsic challenge is identified by Iso-Ahola (1989). The importance of both intrinsic motivation as well as self-actualization in motivation has been a dominant theme in the adventure recreation literature, as it specifically relates to the concept of flow (see Mitchell, 1983; Priest, 1990, 1999b). As described above in the adventure experience para-digm, the result of appropriate challenge is optimal experience. Over time challenge must shift to correspond to changes in ability to realize the rewards from flow.

Self-concept also has relevance as it relates to motivation and as a separate idea in social psychology. Blumer identifies the contributions of George Herbert Mead in this regard, and writes that:

> in asserting that the human being has a self, Mead simply meant that the human being is an object to himself. The human being may perceive himself, have conceptions of

himself, communicate with himself, and act toward himself—addressing himself, communicate with himself, and act toward himself.

(1970, p. 282)

In applying this notion of self to the adventure context, "self-control should be seen as the process by which attention is shifted to oneself, either inwardly or to oneself as a component of an environmental transaction, as a result of transactions in which there is little scope for external control" (Scherl, 1989, p. 125). Self-actualization may be facilitated via adventure as control over externalities (e.g., weather) is not possible, which causes an inward focus and presents opportunities that require self-control and provide for personal growth (Scherl, 1989).

Klint (1999) acknowledges the numerous theories of self-concept and synthesizes the state of current knowledge by offering the following five principles:

1. self-concept is a function of social interactions;
2. self-concept is multi-dimensional;
3. affect is associated with the development of self-concept;
4. the degree to which success and failures influence self-concept is a function of the importance one attributes to the activity;
5. self-concept levels influence motivation levels (Klint, 1999, p. 164).

At an intuitive level, the above principles of self-concept resonate with adventure as they frequently occur with others, provide a space for activities that are multi-dimensional, give opportunities to exert an affect on the outcome through competency, and afford chances for the pursuit of autotelic activities. It is the final principle, the influence of self-concept to influence motivation, where specific motivation theories have been both extended and directly applied to account for the experience of adventure.

Klint (1999) introduces the potential application of motivation theories to adventure by combining Bandura's (1977) concept of self-efficacy and Harter's (1981) theory of competence. Self-efficacy, as employed by Klint (1999), refers to the belief by an individual that he/she is able to achieve a specific task. These beliefs relate to elements of magnitude (perceived difficulty of the task), generality (transferability of abilities to different situations), and strength (the amount of time an individual will maintain belief in light of feedback). It is also important to recognize Bandura's (1977) assertion that feedback, or information regarding efficacy, may come from either the individual (internal) or the outside environment (external). Klint (1999) applies this general notion of self-efficacy to adventurous situations by using Harter's (1981) theory of competence, as illustrated in Figure 9.4.

The manner in which competence motivation applies to adventure activities is best explained by working through an example. To illustrate this concept, consider a group of four friends who are undertaking a kayaking trip with many difficult rapids. After the individual in the lead boat successfully negotiates a series of rapids he signals for the next boat. In an attempt to master the rapid the next person starts down the river. If she successfully negotiates the rapid she experiences success (left side of Figure 9.4) which may, depending on her competence and the difficulty of the environment, achieve an optimal experience and

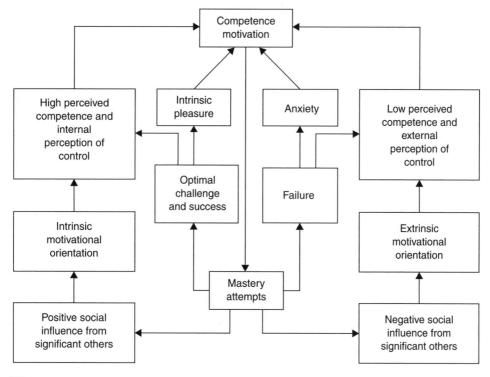

Figure 9.4 Harter's Theory of Competence Motivation.
Source: Weiss, 1987.

derive considerable intrinsic satisfaction from the experience. In addition to the internal feelings of accomplishment, she may experience external rewards and reinforcement from her friends who are waiting up and down stream. Klint (1999) asserts that positive reinforcement also causes an intrinsic motivation orientation in which the individual selects activities that produce continued self-satisfaction, achieves individually set standards, and increases individual perception of competence. Consequently, the positive motivation received (both internal and external) by the individual in our situation will likely lead to an increased motivation to undertake similar activities, as indicated by the circuitous feedback loop in Figure 9.4.

If the same individual was to be unsuccessful in negotiating the rapids (repeatedly overturned her kayak and ultimately had to pull into an eddy to be assisted by her friends) a very different experience would occur, as illustrated in the right side of Figure 9.4. As shown in the inner track, she would initially experience failure as she was unable to master the attempt of running the rapids. She may search for reasons as to why she failed to negotiate the rapids (e.g., leaning the wrong way in the kayak, insufficient bracing) and with the encouragement of her friends may try again. While she may experience some anxiety from the initial attempt, repeated failed mastery attempts may eventually lead her to question her paddling competency as well as her perceived control over the conditions (Klint, 1999). These factors may cause the individual to offer various explanations to account for her lack

289

of success, either attributing it to internal factors (e.g., not being able to execute a high brace) and/or external factors which she perceives to have little control over (e.g., weather, luck). She may also receive feedback from her paddling partners. Perhaps these friends are supportive during the first few mastery attempts, but eventually grow impatient and make suggestions to try again another day. The individual may, in light of the search for peer acceptance, start to place increasing importance on the performance standards set by other people, which tend to decrease effectance motivation (Klint, 1999). Single application of the theory of competence motivation (regardless of the result) does not necessarily alter motivation, but contributes to self-perception in a cumulative fashion (Klint, 1999).

Adventure is also informed by social-psychology theories which explain satisfaction. Satisfaction was introduced in Chapter 4 as the degree of congruency between expectations and the actual experience (Mannell & Kleiber, 1997; Manning, 1999). Congruency between anticipated and actual outcome from an experience is central to expectancy theory (Fishbein & Ajzen, 1975). Accurate perception of both competencies and challenges importantly influences the adventure experience (Priest, 1990, 1999b). Drawing upon the profile of a timid individual who perceives the amount of risk to be substantial and his/her competencies or skills to be lacking, incongruence occurs between the expected (peak experience) and actual outcome (experimentation and exploration). Diminished satisfaction is an associated result, as illustrated by the outcome resulting outside of the flow channel. Despite the potential for sub-optimal experiences, adventurous experiences are recognized as being favorable to achieve flow (Csikszentmihalyi & Csikszentmihalyi, 1999; Mitchell, 1983).

The tradition of social-psychology also helps to understand the complex array of factors that influence if an adventure is satisfying. In Chapter 4 the work of Whisman and Hollenhorst (1998) was recognized because it emphasizes the individual nature of overall satisfaction based on situational variables and subjective evaluations. Within subjective evaluations, variables of experience, attitudes, and preferences and norms are particularly relevant to the adventure domain as they underscore the importance of individual perception. The amount of challenge being sought through a particular activity, the influence of motivation (illustrated above using the competence motivation), and the behavior of other participants all affect the overall satisfaction derived from the experience.

The behavioral approach employed by Manning (1999) brings together motivation and satisfaction elements and allows specification of why adventure experiences are demanded. Activities and settings constituted the first and second levels of Manning's (1999) hierarchies of demand. Henderson, writing in the context of physical education, observes that:

> it is generally agreed that the benefits and arguments for justification of outdoor pursuits are: improved physical skills, i.e. canoeing, enhanced fitness, improved social interaction between peers and between teacher/student, and much needed adventure/challenge in a novel, universally enjoyable, aesthetic setting—Nature.
>
> (1987, p. 9)

The third level of motivations is clearly connected to adventure as Manning (1999) himself uses elements of risk-taking and challenges as illustrative examples. Higher order benefits are the final level established and adventure may: enhance self-concept or esteem (personal benefits); foster family or peer solidarity (social benefits); enhance corporate functioning and development (economic benefits); and foster awareness of the natural environment (environmental benefits).

APPLICATIONS OF ADVENTURE

Adventure is the main focus of this chapter and thus far it has been discussed as a leisure pursuit. Contemporary society also uses adventure for therapeutic and educational purposes (Ewert et al., 2001). The following two sections explore the topics of adventure therapy and adventure education. Although the focus in these sections shifts to the application of adventure, these subjects remain largely the purview of leisure studies as a body of knowledge on these topics has been developed by leisure scholars and practice has been shaped by recreation professionals.

Adventure Therapy

The utilization of recreation and adventure in the domain of therapy is well established (Ewert et al., 2001; Gillis & Ringer, 1999). Therapeutic recreation is broadly defined as "a purposeful intervention directed at the individual and his environment that aims to enhance health and impact functioning in many critical life domains" (Bullock, Mahon & Selz, 1997; as cited in Searle & Brayley, 2000). This notion of combining adventure and therapy is a point of confluence between those interested in these two aspects of recreation and has been referred to as wilderness adventure therapy, adventure-based counseling, and outdoor adventure pursuits (Gillis & Ringer, 1999; Searle & Brayley, 2000; Sheldon & Arthur, 2001). The term adventure therapy is used in this book to refer to the "deliberate, strategic combination of adventure activities with therapeutic change processes with the goal of making lasting changes in the lives of participants" (Gillis & Ringer, 1999, p. 29). Adventure therapy is distinct from other applications of adventure because:

1. potential clients are assessed and screened prior to their being accepted into a program;
2. persons of psychological significance to the clients, such as relatives, friends and mentors are often involved in the program;
3. programs incorporate "treatment" plans to suit the development of each *group* of clients;
4. multidisciplined staff teams are usually deployed because the combination of outdoor activity skills and therapeutic skills required is usually beyond the capacity of any one leader;
5. interventions are constantly "fine tuned" because the complexity of human systems suggests that progress is not predictable for any part of the system;
6. program design and implementation includes follow-up, clear termination with each client, closure of each group, and referral of clients to other agencies where applicable (Gillis & Ringer, 1999, p. 31).

Specific types of programs falling within the classification of "adventure therapy" can be classified into categories of adventure-based therapy, wilderness therapy, and long-term residential camping (Gillis & Ringer, 1999). Adventure-based therapy (the most frequently employed form in North America) tends to be group-oriented, problem-solving in orientation, and occurs in relative proximity to facilities (Gillis & Ringer, 1999). Outward Bound's programs for troubled teens and Survivors of Violence Recovery Programs for adult women are examples (Sheldon & Arthur, 2001). Wilderness therapy incorporates short- and long-term expeditions into the out-of-doors with a focus on skill development, therapeutic goals and transference. The Hope Center Wilderness Camp is a good example of this type of program as 85% of their campers do not recidivate within six months of completion (Clagett, 1990). Long-term residential camping programs involve clients staying for extended periods of time. Easter Seals Camps which offer camp experiences to children with disabilities during the summer months are an excellent example of this type of program.

One of greatest challenges to individuals attempting to assert positive change is that their solutions tend to be reinforcing rather than transformative (Nadler, 1999). Adventure offers hope in this regard as random events and unexpected solutions have been shown to prompt spontaneous change (Nadler, 1999). Yet, the simple event of venturing into wilderness does not automatically have therapeutic value and therefore attention must be directed to how adventure therapy programs are designed and implemented (Wichman, 1991). While "the unknown" is an important aspect for the client, facilitators require an acute awareness of adventure therapy to maximize the likelihood of transference from the experience. Nadler's (1999) model of adventure therapy is helpful in this regard, as illustrated in Figure 9.5. This model begins with the client and establishes that he/she will bring preconceived notions of what the experience may involve to the therapy. This internal state changes either prior to or upon initiation of the experience. The client becomes acutely aware that his/her existing ways of processing information do not work as clients are placed into novel settings outside their comfort zone, which usually produces some amount of anxiety (Nadler, 1999). In creating a cooperative environment (by using an "appropriate" amount of structure) inter- and intrapersonal development may occur, innovative solutions to problems may be explored, and accomplishments may be realized. In processing, clients are encouraged to make sense of their experiences and are assisted in understanding the potential to transfer these lessons to future situations.

Variations of the adventure therapy model presented above have been advanced for specific client groups. Although not exclusive to adventure therapy, adolescents are often one of the most frequent client groups (Clagett, 1990; Davis-Berman & Berman, 1999; Wichman, 1991). Davis-Berman and Berman (1999) describe adolescence as a time of significant change (psychological stress and conflicts as well as physical developments) that coincide with identity formation, often accompanied by experimentation. They further assert that societal factors further stress this segment of the population which results, in some cases, in delinquency and/or asocial behaviors. Although adventure therapy was initially criticized for lacking a theoretical basis and empirical results, Wichman (1991) has established that such programs are effective at both increasing self-esteem as well as reducing asocial behavior. Davis-Berman and Berman (1999) observe that adventure-based programs for adolescents are successful because they provide the least restrictive environment for clients, encourage development of active solutions, and place them outside of their comfort zone.

292

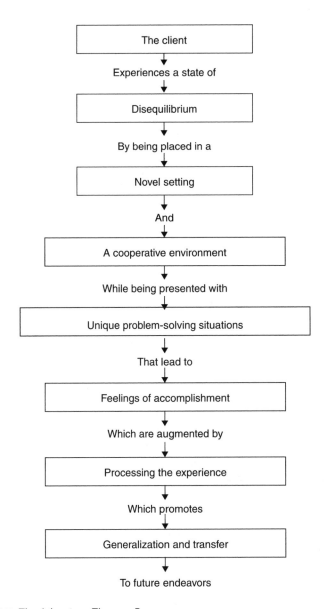

Figure 9.5 The Adventure Therapy Process.

While it is beyond the scope of this book to explore the numerous and diverse client groups that may benefit from adventure therapy, a cornerstone of adventure therapy is the idea that innovative solutions will stem from the clients themselves as they explore a new or novel environment. This concept is presented by Nadler (1999) as a comfort zone that an individual must break through in order to pursue new possibilities, as illustrated in Figure 9.6. Equally important as exploring these edges of comfort, is facilitated "retreat" to prompt transference and generalization to other experiences (Nadler, 1999). In this way adventure therapy strives to make lasting change.

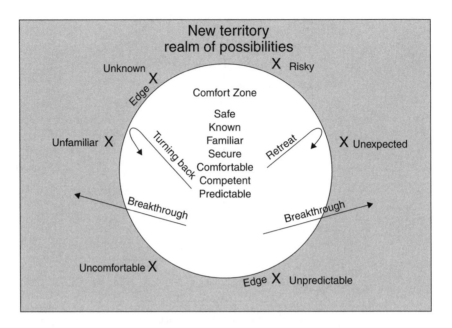

Figure 9.6 *Breaking Through Limits to New Growth.*

Adventure Education

The lineage of adventure education is outdoor education. Priest (1990) contends that environmental education and adventure education branches exist within outdoor education and explains that the former stresses ecosystemic (ecological and biological processes) and ekistic (societal and natural resources) relationships and the latter emphasizes intrapersonal (within the individual) and interpersonal relationships (between people).

This section begins by focusing on the character of adventure education and how it relates to traditional modes of instruction. Objectives associated with adventure education (group development, decision-making, leadership) are subsequently examined.

Priest (1990) clearly and succinctly articulates the premise upon which adventure education is founded, the intent of the approach, its process qualities, and its anticipated outcomes.

> The premise of adventure education is that CHANGE may take place in groups and individuals from direct and purposeful exposure to: Challenge, *H*igh *A*dventure, and *N*ew *G*rowth *E*xperiences. This is not to say that adventure education causes change; just that it highlights a need to change and supports any personal decision to make change.
>
> The purpose of adventure education is to bring about an awareness for these positive changes. A sub-purpose is to enhance the self-concept and improve social interactions.
>
> The process of adventure education involves the use of adventurous activities such as recreational pursuits in the outdoors or the so-called artificial environs (ropes courses and group initiatives). These activities are used to provide a group or individual with tasks to accomplish. These tasks often involve problem-solving and challenge. The problem-solving requires decision-making, judgment, cooperation, communication, and trust.

294

The product of adventure education is personal growth and development. By responding to seemingly insurmountable tasks, groups and individuals learn to overcome almost any self-imposed perceptions of their capacity to succeed. They are able to turn limitations into abilities; and, as a result, they learn a great deal about themselves and how they relate to others.

(Priest, 1990, p. 114)

The above quotation sets forth a strong basis to understanding why adventure education is employed as strategy for learning and what outcomes may be anticipated from the process. Recent evidence from an examination of program offerings by NOLS confirms the influence of specific change mechanisms on many aspects of development including communication, leadership, small group development, judgment, skills, and awareness of the environment (Sibthorp, Paisley & Gookin, 2007).

Despite the clear purpose of adventure education, it is often perceived to conflict with "traditional" notions of classroom learning because of its experiential basis (Horwood, 1999; Jernstedt, 1995; Shuttenberg & Poppenhagen, 1995). Shuttenberg and Poppenhagen observe that:

the value of experiential learning has been one of the main tenets of adult education theory and practice for decades. In the more academic sectors of post-secondary education, however, especially in colleges and universities, experiential learning has been traditionally viewed as necessary, perhaps, for some aspects of "professional training," but definitely inferior to cognitive study.

(1995, p. 141)

Jernstedt (1995) challenges this perception and contends that testing which involves life experiences is an integral component for individuals. Advances in learning theory by Kolb (1976) reinforce the need to actively engage individuals in the learning process to affect both cognitive and affective dimensions (Shuttenberg & Poppenhagen, 1995).

Fundamental synergies exist between education and adventure. Evidence from research

Plate 9.2 Example of a Ropes Course.

295

reveal that effective education (either traditional or adventure models) share five common characteristics of: "(1) small learning group size; (2) cooperative learning environment; (3) communication of high expectations for students; (4) building on student success; and (5) creating an identifiable classroom culture reflecting positive, supportive values" (Riggins, 1986, p. 1). Horwood (1999) utilizes a descriptive narrative to probe the connection between adventure and schooling. He starts by examining criteria for an activity to be adventurous (uncertainty, risk, inescapable consequences, energetic action and willingness participation) and provides examples as to how each may be found in the school environment. In describing examples of modifying each variable it becomes clear as to how the concept of adventure becomes equally applicable in the classroom environment as the concept of education is applicable to adventure in outdoor settings. Regardless of incorporating adventure into the classroom or extending the classroom into outdoor environments, "what is essential is the wholehearted, wide-eyed spirit of adventure in both teachers and students who, together, seek to do their utmost with hands, heads and hearts" (Horwood, 1999, p. 12).

Group Development

In observing young British sailors, Sir Lawrence Holt commented on the lack of connection between them and their fellow sailors. As indicated by the mission of Outward Bound, cohesiveness transcends the mariner environment to all aspects of an individual's life. Interpersonal relationships are emphasized within adventure education (Priest, 1990) and group development is an important consideration for adventure programming (Priest, 1999c).

A group consists of multiple individuals. The characteristics of individuals are reflective of the group process (Schutz, 1971). In conveying what happens in the development of groups, a participant in such a process offered that:

> well, first you're concerned about the problem about where you fit in the group; then you're wondering about what you'll accomplish. Finally, after a while you learn that people mean something. Your primary concern becomes how people feel about you and each other.
>
> (Schutz, 1971, p. 3)

Literature examining the processes of small groups is extensive as there have been well over 100 articles written on the topic (Mitten, 1999). Classical investigations by Tuckman (1965), Schutz (1971), and Weber (1982) have documented steps through which a group progresses from inception to maturity, as shown in Table 9.1. The classical approaches are presented in this text (Table 9.1) because they remain pertinent and are foundational to more recent literature.

Weber's (1982) model is explored in depth due to its multi-dimensional nature and popularity. Weber (1982) conceptualizes group development to consist of three stages, which each have unique interpersonal issues, group behavioral patterns, group tasks and leadership issues. These stages are visualized as a series of concentric circles through which a group progresses, as illustrated in Figure 9.7. In the first stage (forming), individuals tend to have superficial or "safe" interactions which emphasize inclusion and rely extensively on the leader for direction, which may lead to various outcomes (pleasant or frustrating) depending

Table 9.1 Stages of Group Development

Stage of group development	Classical theories of group development		The Group Lifecycle (Weber, 1983, pp. 68–71)
	Developmental Sequence in Small Groups (Tuckman, 1965, pp. 384–399)	Developmental Stages of Group Inclusion (Schutz, 1971).	
Stage One	Testing and orientation—dependence exhibited on external roles as members attempt to determine inclusion and map boundaries related to the task at hand.	Inclusion—period of time at the start of group formation in which people determine their fit characterized by energy and determining boundaries.	Infancy or forming—initial formation of group is characterized by superficial interactions aimed at inclusion in the group. It is dependent upon leadership.
Stage Two	Hostility—characterized by conflict over individual rights, issues of control and leadership struggles.	Control—often accompanying the process of decision-making power and responsibilities become issues as the group strives for functionality.	Adolescence or storming—differences among members becomes evident, leadership is questioned, and decision-making processes are established.
Stage Three	Group cohesion—identity forms as the group increases functionality. Opinions are exchanged as evaluation occurs where emotions become evident.	Affection—follows resolution of the above phase in which feelings among members become evident.	Adulthood or norming and performing—group comes together and functions as a cohesive unit. Affection develops among group members.
Stage Four	Functional role-relatedness—internalized structure as the group becomes task oriented and interdependent.		

Sources: Schutz, 1971; Tuckman, 1965; Weber, 1982.

on those involved. As the group begins to challenge differences (e.g., power, decision-making), it moves into the storming stage. Weber (1982) observes that it is frequently under task demands that people respond in an attempt to regain their sense of individualism and react negatively to either the formal group leader or those individuals demonstrating leadership qualities. This stage is similar to adolescence in human development which is typically unpleasant but essential to develop skills necessary for the future, as without persevering through this stage the collective can go no further (Weber, 1982). As the group negotiates roles and clarifies tasks they move to the third stage of norming and performing, where functional relationships and inter-dependence from the leader is established. In performing the group exhibits an affinity for each other and functions cohesively to deal with tasks efficiently and effectively. It is within this final stage that the group achieves synergy, or a feeling of uniqueness, as illustrated as the central feature of Figure 9.7.

Each group will progress through the above stages at different speeds and with varying degrees of torment. If a group completes all stages they will cycle through each again and

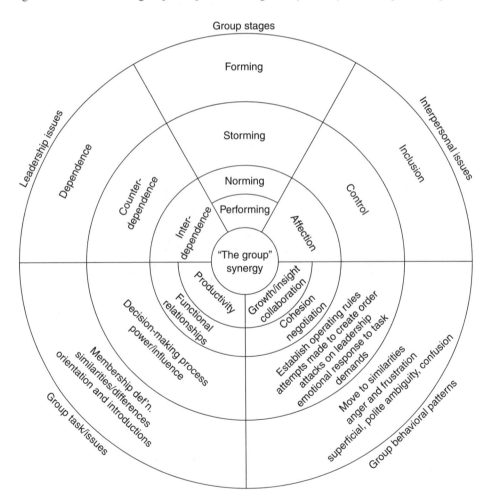

Figure 9.7 Life Cycle of Groups.

re-confront the challenge with insights gained from their past experiences (Weber, 1982). Weber (1982) identifies a fourth transformative stage that occurs when a group has either achieved a goal and/or after limitations of time have been realized. At this point the group needs to either redefine itself around another goal or disband. Adventure educators and outdoor leaders need to be cognizant of these stages of group development that are likely to occur, anticipate the potential pitfalls associated with each of the stages, and allow the group to experience the process that ultimately will result in the identity of the group.

The potential to enhance the development of small groups has placed increasing demand on adventure programming. Priest explains that "developmental adventure programs change the way people behave: their primary purpose is to improve functional actions. If I conduct group initiatives to help people become a high-performing team or to communicate better, then my adventure program is developmental" (1999, p. xiv). As many businesses and corporations are moving away from traditional management models and towards new, team-based workplace structures, adventure training models are offering skill-building experiences which meet the mandates of the "new corporate culture" (Kay & Laberge, 2002, p. 23).

Adventure-based training (also experience-based training and development or EBTD) can help corporations and businesses achieve a wide variety of goals and has become a lucrative industry. The two most typical types of corporate goals are "group focused objectives" (communication, working as a team, leadership) and "personal growth objectives" (self-esteem, stress management) (Petrini, 1990, p. 25). Miner observes that:

> EBTD goes by many names (corporate adventure training, outdoor management development, outdoor training), but whatever it is called it is without question a form of adventure education; in fact, it is one of the newest and most vibrant forms of adventure education being practiced.
>
> (1999, p. 395)

Participation in EBTD in the 1990s was substantive as approximately 200,000 clients participated in North America, one out of six Fortune 500 companies in the United States employed such methods, and the industry generated more than $200 million in sales (Miner, 1999).

Decision-Making

Individuals and groups must make reasoned choices among competing alternatives each day. The consequences of these decisions may be relatively minor (e.g., which book to read) or major (e.g., selecting the wrong route and getting lost). In the adventure context the immediacy and magnitude of choices are amplified due to the unrelenting consequences of the natural environment (Horwood, 1999). Decision-making is understood as a cognitive process signaled by action or inaction (Sung, 2004, p. 346).

Many factors influence the decision-making process, ranging from socioeconomic status of the individual to the level of perceived adventure or risk (in some cases people may choose an activity based on a higher perceived level of risk, in other cases people may do the

299

opposite). For example, a study on adventure travelers found that the specific type of activity and the experience afforded were the two strongest factors which influenced travelers' decision-making (Sung, 2004). The process of making choices becomes increasingly complicated when multiple parties are involved, as alluded to in the group development process. The ability of a decision to be made that satisfies the needs of all individuals is doubtful. Therefore, the process by which group decisions are made is critical to functioning of the group and should be discussed in advance. Some of the many different decision-making techniques are subsequently discussed along with their associated benefits and challenges.

The work of Johnson and Johnson (1982) illustrates the range of potential decision-making processes that may be employed in small groups. They identify and describe seven potential forms of decision-making that may be more or less appropriate depending on the situational circumstances as each also has particular consequences to the group in the future. The seven modes of decision-making offered by Johnson and Johnson (1982, pp. 100–109) are summarized below:

1. Decision by authority without group discussion. In this first method of decision-making the leader, either designated or self-proclaimed, makes decisions for the group without discussion to other group members.
2. Decision by expert. In this second method the decision-making power is given to the individual in the group with demonstrated expertise in the particular decision-making domain.
3. Decision by averaging individuals' opinions. In this third method the leader queries all legitimate group members for their input regarding a particular situation. The decision is subsequently based on the choice that is most popular, although the choice may represent less than 50% of the group.
4. Decision by authority after group discussion. In this fourth method of decision-making the group leader, holder of legitimate power, makes the judgment after speaking to members of the groups.
5. Decision by minority. There are a variety of circumstances in which it may be appropriate for a subsection of the larger group to make a decision for the entire group. A few group members may act as an executive and make routine choices on behalf of the group or be charged as a task force to consider a particular issue and make recommendations back to the group. Illegitimate forms of decision-making by minority are also possible including proposing a quick course of action and "railroading" other group members or making recommendations forcibly.
6. Decision by majority vote. This frequently employed method of decision-making has all group members engage in discussion until more than 51% of the group is committed to a single course of action. This method resembles the election process and is routinely applied differently in groups. Decision-making by majority in groups is undertaken dichotomously and highlighting winners and losers, often negating further support for the decision.
7. Decision by consensus. Achieving consensus involves everyone in the group agreeing as to the decision that should be made. This manner of making a decision is also referred to as arriving at a collective opinion. Consensus ought not to be confused with unanimity as degrees of consensus exist; all group members involved understand and support the decision to some extent.

Each of the seven methods of making decisions presented above has distinct advantages and disadvantages, as summarized in Table 9.2. The consensus method is the most likely approach to yield innovations that are well supported, utilizes resources of all group members and ultimately enhances group capacity (Johnson & Johnson, 1982). Despite the benefits inherent in the consensus model, each method of decision-making has utility in different situations. Time is an important consideration as it directly increases with the number of people involved in making the decision, although once a broadly supported decision is reached implementation may occur in an expedited manner (Johnson & Johnson, 1982). There are many instances in the adventure context where speed is of the essence and other forms of decision-making should be employed. In climbing, for example, dangerous situations may present themselves abruptly (e.g., changes in weather) that require an immediate decision. In such cases expertise and leadership are required to promptly devise a course of action. Decision by consensus, under such circumstances, would take too long and in the process of determining a course of action agreed upon by all the entire group may suffer.

From the above discussion on the various modes of decision-making two principles are offered to those in adventure contexts. First, the correct method of decision-making is the one that is most appropriate under the circumstances confronting the individual or group. Second, in group situations, discussion of how decisions will be made should occur in advance of actually being required to make them. Knowing how decisions will be made and why those modes of decision-making will be utilized reduces potential interpersonal conflicts.

Leadership

Leadership is important to a broad range of endeavors (e.g., business, sports, communities) (Polglase, 2003), and especially pertinent to outdoor recreation. Priest observes that "leadership is a critical element in any field of activity, but especially so in one like adventure programming where the safety of participants is of central concern" (1999c, p. 235). Leadership emerges as an issue in the previous two sections on group processes and decision-making as well as an explicit goal of many adventure-based organizations. The National Outdoor Leadership School is an example of such an organization that specifically focuses on leadership development.

In tracing the development of the term leadership three discernible shifts are apparent from early definitions which focused on group process and activity, those which directed attention to the art of influencing others to comply, and a more recent emphasis on power, role differences and initiating structure (Thomson, 1992). Jordan expands upon these ideas and defines leadership as:

> a dynamic process of interactions between two or more members of a group which involves recognition and acceptance of leader-follower roles by group members within a certain situation. It also involves activities on the part of the leader and followers which aid the group in moving toward its goals.
>
> (1996, p. 5)

301

Table 9.2 Advantages and Disadvantages of Decision-Making Methods

Method of decision-making	Advantages	Disadvantages
1. Decision by authority without discussion	Applies more to administrative needs; useful for simple, routine decisions; should be used when very little time is available to make the decision, when group members expect the designated leader to make the decision, and when group members lack the skills and information to make the decision any other way.	One person is not a good resource for every decision; advantages of group interaction are lost; no commitment to implementing the decision is developed among other group members; resentment and disagreement may result in sabotage and deterioration of group effectiveness; resources of other members are not used.
2. Expert member	Useful when the expertise of one person is so far superior to that of all other group members that little is to be gained by discussion; should be used when the need for membership action in implementing the decision is slight.	It is difficult to determine who the expert is; no commitment to implement the decision is built; advantages of group interaction are lost; resentment and disagreement may result in sabotage and deterioration of group effectiveness; resources of other members are not used.
3. Average of members' opinions	Useful when it is difficult to get group members together to talk, when the decision is so urgent that there is no time for group discussion, when member commitment is not necessary for implementing the decision, and when group members lack the skills and information to make the decision any other way; applicable to simple, routine decisions.	There is not enough interaction among group members for them to gain from each other's resources and from the benefits of group discussion; no commitment to implement the decision is built; unresolved conflict and controversy may damage group effectiveness in the future.
4. Decision by authority after discussion	Uses the resources of the group members more than previous methods; gains some of the benefits of group discussion.	Does not develop commitment to implement the decision; does not resolve the controversies and conflicts among group members; tends to create situations in which group members either compete to impress the designated leader or tell the leader what they think he or she wants to hear.

5. Majority control	Can be used when sufficient time is lacking for decision by consensus or when the decision is not so important that consensus needs to be used, and when complete member commitment is not necessary for implementing the decision; closes discussion on issues that are not highly important for the group.	Usually leaves an alienated minority, which damages future group effectiveness; relevant resources of many group members may be lost; full commitment to implement the decision is absent; full benefit of group interaction is not obtained.
6. Minority control	Can be used when everyone cannot meet to make a decision, when the group is under such time pressure that it must delegate responsibility to a committee, when only a few members have any relevant resources, and when broad member commitment is not needed to implement the decision; useful for simple, routine decisions.	Does not utilize the resources of many group members; does not establish widespread commitment to implement the decision; unresolved conflict and controversy may damage future group effectiveness; not much benefit from group interaction.
7. Consensus	Produces an innovative, creative, and high-quality decision; elicits commitment by all members to implement the decision; uses the resources of all members; the future decision-making ability of the group is enhanced; useful in making serious, important, and complex decisions to which all members are to be committed.	Takes a great deal of time and psychological energy and a high level of member skill; time pressure must be minimal, and there must be no emergency in progress.

This definition incorporates the structure of a group and signals the range of influence the leader exerts on the dynamics of the group.

While delving into leadership theory is beyond the scope of this text, appreciating the range of perspectives applied to the topic enhances understanding. Thomson's leadership theory triangle (Figure 9.8) categorizes these associated theories as to their individual, group or environmental basis. The individual category directs attention to the leader as a pivotal person with particular attributes and abilities. Group process theories focus on the interpersonal interactions between group members and the leader and highlight structural and functional elements. The environment category emphasizes the particular conditions (situational theories) and interactions between leadership and groups in specific situations. Bi-directional arrows along each side of the triangle illustrate the connections between each of these categories, as shown in Figure 9.8. Thomson explains that "placing leadership training, experience, and skill in the centre of the triangle reflects the notion that leaders are chosen, are appointed or emerge, because of one or more of a combination of these factors" (1992, p. 24). Rather than being an inherent quality, these factors can be learned, nurtured and developed.

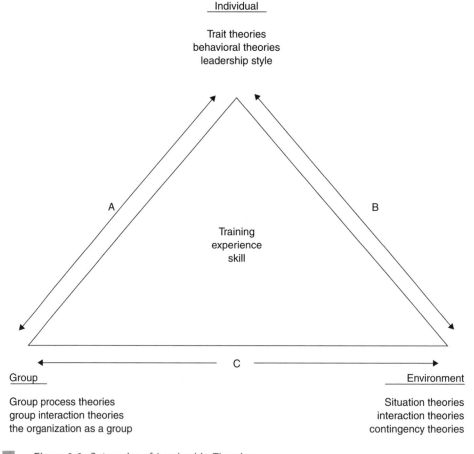

Figure 9.8 Categories of Leadership Theories.

Leadership is relevant to adventure recreation as it is important to providing a safe and satisfying experience. Adventure, with the goal of education, provides a vehicle to develop and refine the leadership factors identified above. Priest describes an outdoor leader as:

> someone who is designated, by the agency sponsoring the adventure, to be in charge of the adventure. Being in charge simply means holding legal and moral responsibility for the organization, instruction, and supervision of the group, and for the safety, protection, and enjoyment of the individuals in the environment.
>
> (1990, p. 211)

Specific types of skills are required by leaders of outdoor activities. Although various terms have been used as labels, skills related to outdoor leadership are typically grouped into three categories (Green, 1990; Phipps & Swiderski, 1990; Priest, 1990, 1999). The terms "hard" or "technical" are typically used to describe the first set of skills which an individual requires before leading others. Hard skills refer to a demonstrated competency or mastery of precise skill related to a specific outdoor pursuit (Green, 1990; Priest, 1999c). Demonstrating the herringbone technique to climb a hill is an example of a technical skill associated with the pursuit of cross-country skiing. Technical skills may be regionally specific and leaders must insure proficiency in a geographic area prior to leading (Green, 1990). The term "soft" has been almost universally used to refer to skills which focus on the people or social component within outdoor recreation groups (Green, 1990; Phipps & Swiderski, 1990; Priest, 1999c; Rosol, 2000). Soft skills are crucial as "it is no longer acceptable to be solely technically competent in hard skills such as navigation, use of equipment, trip logistics, etc." (Phipps & Swiderski, 1990, p. 223). Soft skills can be divided into subsections of social (e.g., group processes and wellness), psychological (e.g., relating to behavior and mindset of participants), and communication (e.g., information exchanges) (Phipps & Swiderski, 1990). The ability to understand and facilitate the process of group development is an example of a soft skill. The final group is meta skills which involve problem-solving, decision-making, and judgment (Green, 1990; Priest, 1999c; Priest & Gass, 1997). Green observes that "in a given day a leader might have to make 10 to 100 good decisions, and many of those decisions will involve problem-solving and good judgment" (1990, p. 219). The importance of experience, particularly in the adventure domain, is emphasized as with this skill-set leaders are required to make decisions with incomplete information (Priest, 1999c). Ethics and communication are additional examples of leadership skills often placed in the category of meta skills (Priest & Gass, 1997).

Skills emerging from the adventure leadership literature have recently been synthesized by Priest (1999c) in the brick wall model of outdoor leadership, as shown in Figure 9.9. It illustrates specific skills associated with each category (hard, soft and meta) and recognizes the relationship between them. At the basis of the brick wall model are the theories from related disciplines that inform outdoor recreation and upon which leadership is predicated. The "bricks" in the wall consist of hard (e.g., activity, safety, and environmental) and soft (e.g., instructional, organizational, facilitation) skills. These hard and soft skills are held together by meta skills, understood to be higher order abilities (e.g., problem-solving, flexible leadership style) to integrate all other skills and apply them in a meaningful way (Priest, 1999c).

305

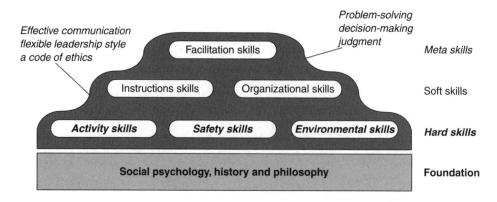

Effective communication
flexible leadership style
a code of ethics

Problem-solving
decision-making
judgment

Facilitation skills

Meta skills

Instructions skills   Organizational skills

Soft skills

Activity skills   Safety skills   Environmental skills

Hard skills

Social psychology, history and philosophy

Foundation

Figure 9.9 Brick Wall Model of Outdoor Leadership.

While the brick wall model provides a comprehensive picture of the skills outdoor leaders require, it provides little direction for how leadership must change throughout the group process. Phipps and Swiderski (1990) make an important contribution in this regard as they integrate the stages of group development, situational leadership, and experiential leadership education. Situational leadership (Figure 9.10) illustrates the need to employ different leadership styles depending on the task and relationship of the group as it moves through stages from formation (immature) to completion (mature). Early in the process the group is highly dependent upon the leader for task specific information, hence the high task and low relationship. In this stage it is appropriate for a leader to use a "telling" style that orientates the group and give only specific necessary information. As the group masters some of the basic tasks and continues to mature they enter the conflict stage. Leadership, under these conditions, is faced with maintaining both high task and high relationship, where the leader must provide a safe space for the group to work through the conflict stage while still being direct about what must occur. As the group matures the style of leadership moves along the situational curve to a participating style. At this stage the group is well versed in the required tasks and the leader focuses on group relationships as leaders within the group begin to emerge and decisions begin to be made by the group. At the highest level of group maturity, illustrated as having both low relationship and low task, the leader takes a "step back" and delegates decision-making and other functions to members of the group, while still being ready to interject if required. Similar to the potential for groups to cycle back through the stages of group development, leaders must constantly adjust their leadership style to that of the group.

Just as leadership is central to a safe and satisfying experience in the adventure domain, adventure also provides a vehicle for individuals to both learn and practice leadership. The increasing popularity of outdoor leadership is not just the sole purview of specialized service providers and corporate training consultants as the number of colleges and universities are increasing such program offerings (141% increase from 1987 to 1997) (Raiola & Sugerman, 1999). It is at the post-secondary level that aspects of training and knowledge are mutually reinforced. Raiola and Sugerman (1999) capture this idea in the outdoor leadership development cycle, as illustrated in Figure 9.11. A student in a university course, for example,

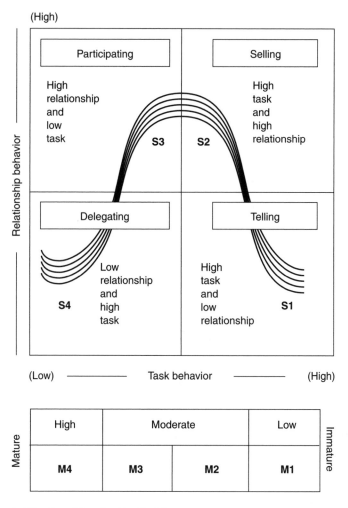

(High)

Relationship behavior

| Participating | Selling |

High
relationship
and
low
task

High
task
and
high
relationship

S3   S2

| Delegating | Telling |

Low
relationship
and
high
task

High
task
and
low
relationship

S4   S1

(Low) ———————— Task behavior ———————— (High)

Mature	High	Moderate	Low	Immature
	M4	M3	M2	M1

Figure 9.10 Situational Leadership Model.

starts as an unconscious incompetent, as prior to learning about outdoor leadership the individual is not aware of what leadership skills ought to be exhibited and is further unable to demonstrate such abilities. Through participating in a course the student first becomes aware of leadership skills and starts to understand his/her abilities in relation to these practices. Experiences designed to foster leadership development and facilitate these practices prompts the student to become conscious of the particular leadership practice as well as able to demonstrate competency of that particular skill. When the student unconsciously displays competency of the leadership practice and is able to facilitate the group process without thinking about the specific stages of group development he/she has reached the final stage.

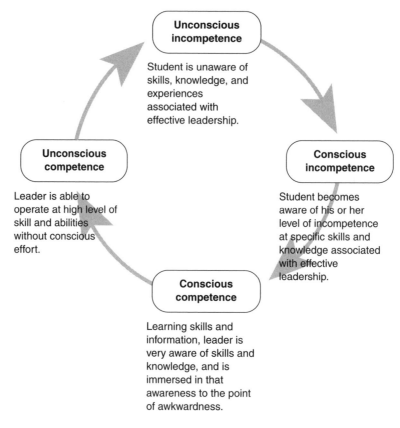

Figure 9.11 Outdoor Leadership Development Cycle.
Source: Raiola, 1990.

TRANSFERRING THE EXPERIENCE

Adventure is distinguished from everyday experience. Adventure therapy and adventure education use adventure as a vehicle for learning, with the premise that information and skills gained through participation will be transferred to the participants' "regular" life. Similar logic also provides the basis for corporate training and development (Miner, 1999; Priest, 1999).

The importance and challenge of transfer is captured by Gass, who observes that:

> transfer is critical to the field of adventure education, probably no other concept is so often misunderstood. Much of the confusion plaguing the transfer of learning has resulted from two main factors. First is the concern that the initial learning usually takes place in an environment (e.g., mountains) quite different from the environment where the student's future learning will occur. Second is the lack of knowledge concerning the variety of methods available to promote transfer.

(1999a, p. 227)

Transfer is simply the effect that a given experience exerts on a learning experience in the future (Gass, 1999a). Skills and experiences gained from an adventure activity can be learned from and used in decision-making and experiences in the future. In the context of corporate training, many companies believe that adventure will facilitate learning by their employees that will in turn help them with workplace decisions in the future (Kay & Laberge, 2002). Transfer may apply to individuals in many different circumstances. Nicholson (1986) recounts a case in which a woman who was having trouble in her married life embarked on an adventure experience program. The woman initially had trouble rappelling, afraid to face her fears. Once she was able to work through those fears and accomplished the task, she was able to confront issues in her own life and resolve them.

Gass (1999a) identifies three specific theories of learning that explain how transfer works in adventure education. The first two theories utilized come from Brunner's work in the 1960s. Brunner observed:

> There are two ways in which learning serves the future. One is through its specific applicability to tasks that are highly similar to those we originally learned to perform. Psychologists refer to this specific phenomenon as specific transfer of training: perhaps it should be called the extension of habits or associations. Its utility appears to be limited in the main to what we speak of as skills. A second way in which earlier learning renders later performances more efficient is through what is conventionally called non-specific transfer, or, more accurately, the transfer of principles and attitudes. In essence, it consists of learning, initially, not a skill but a general idea which can then be used as a basis of recognizing subsequent problems as special cases of the idea originally mastered.
>
> (1960, p. 17; as cited in Gass, 1999a, p. 228)

Gass (1999a) adds a third theory of metaphoric transfer in which students generalize principles from one experience to a future experience. The principles in this form of transfer are similar or analogous and therefore stress the "likeness" between two seemingly different experiences. An illustrative example (Figure 9.12) clarifies the manner in which each of the above theories applies in the adventure context. Gass (1999a) utilizes the three examples to highlight the applicability of transfer. The first graphic (1A) depicts an individual belaying his friend while top-roping. Belaying involves the utilization of a device to produce friction which prevents the climber from falling. In the second graphic (1B) the individual has successfully taken the habits and associations (e.g., hand movements associated with belaying) and applied to the task of rappelling, which requires the same hand skills. In the second method of transfer, a group of individuals are participating in a trust initiative (2A). In non-specific transfer, the individual generalizes common principles from an experience and applies them to subsequent experiences. Reciprocity may be a common principle from a trust initiative (Gass, 1999a). This principle is then transferred into a different setting, such as a classroom environment (2B) where it is equally applicable. The example for metaphoric transfer (3A) depicts two individuals canoeing. While canoeing, the two individuals realize that synchronizing their paddling efforts reduces the total effort required. These same two

309

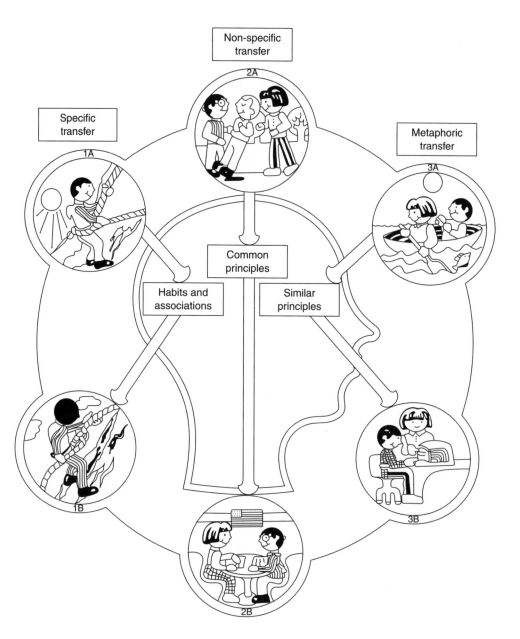

Figure 9.12 Three Theories of Transfer in Adventure Education.
Source: Gass, 1990, p. 202.

individuals realize that paddling the canoe is analogous to or like effective communication in the work environment. Metaphoric transfer has occurred when similar principles are conveyed.

Facilitating the learning process is a prime function of teachers in traditional classroom settings. Increasing attention has been directed as to how facilitators of adventure experiences promote or foster both making sense of the experience as well as promoting transference to other non-adventure environments. Priest and Gass write that "since reflection is the key to deeper learning that leads to more lasting change in adventure programming, anything that a 'facilitator' does to enhance reflection before, during, or after an experience is called facilitation" (1999, p. 215). Essentially, it is this "guidance" which further differentiates adventure recreation from its applications with specific outcomes (e.g., therapy, education) (Priest & Gass, 1999). There are many factors (awareness of transfer theories, activities employed, and facilitation techniques utilized) that facilitators may manipulate to increase achievement of the desired outcomes as well as raise the odds for the transference (Gass, 1999a).

In reviewing the history of facilitation in adventure education, Priest and Gass (1999a) identify six generations of facilitation skills that have occurred since the 1940s, when an experience was generally left to "speak for itself." In the contemporary context a host of debriefing techniques are employed such as speaking for the experience, discover learning after the experience, communicating prior to the experience, and indirectly telling participants about the experience prior to it (Priest & Gass, 1999). Knapp (1999) utilizes the term processing in a similar manner to refer to internalization of meaning from the experience. He asserts that "traditionally, this event occurs in a group gathered together to verbalize about personal feelings, thoughts, and human interactions under the guidance of an adventure educator" (Knapp, 1999, p. 219). While the facilitator may take a leadership role in formulating closure on an adventurous experience to facilitate transference, many other techniques permit individuals and/or groups to make sense of their experience including introspection, special places, solos, guided fantasy, journal writing and small group discussions (Knapp, 1999).

NEGOTIATING ELEMENTS ASSOCIATED WITH RISK

Over 20 years ago Meier (1978) recognized that leisure activities involving challenge and risk were increasing in popularity as people searched for adventure. Both the popularity of these types of pursuits and the number of programs that provide such services continue to increase (Attarian, 2001). In some cases the potential to lose something (risk) has been realized. Brown (1999) observes that such activities have a high profile and, in turn, attract "sensational media attention." Instances, such as the Lake Timiskaming tragedy (see Box 9.1) and 1996 Mount Everest Expedition serve as haunting examples.

The number of lawsuits relating to adventure education in particular have also increased as a function of more participants, an apparent lack of understanding of risks by participants, and increased opportunities for litigation (Attarian, 2001; Ewert, 1987). This observation is not restricted to just adventure recreation, nor does it convey the severity of the issue. Kozlowski asserts that:

BOX 9.1 THE TIMISKAMING TRAGEDY

DEATH ON THE WATER: THE MASTERS KNEW NOT WHAT THEY WERE DOING

The St. John's School of Ontario, along with its sister schools in Manitoba and Alberta, staked its reputation on taking troubled boys and molding them into responsible young men. It sought to achieve this through strict discipline, a classical education, prayerful devotion and the rigorous challenges of outdoor adventure. In theory, it was a noble mission; in practice, it culminated in one of the most horrific of tragedies.

On a sunny June morning in 1978, 27 boys and four leaders embarked on a canoeing expedition that was to take them from the south shores of Lake Timiskaming to James Bay. It was to be a three-week trek. It seemed unthinkable that less than eight hours after setting out all four canoes would be capsized, and that by the following morning 13 lives would be lost to the icy waters of the big lake. For the 15 boys and three adult leaders who survived, the event marked them for life.

Deep Waters is Ontario author and canoeing expert James Raffan's meticulous investigation into the Timiskaming affair. Unlike the initial inquest, Raffan sets out to answer not so much the question of how such a terrible thing happened, but why.

For Raffan, the chain of events leading to that horrible day were not only inevitable, but were put into motion long before the boys set out on their trip. He draws the line back to Ted Byfield, co-founder of the original St. John's School in Manitoba, and the mentality upon which the institution was built. "We found," says Byfield, "that the only possible teacher–student relationship was not one of partnership, not the let's-learn-together of the modern classroom. It was a relationship of master and servant. And the master does not need the servant."

Byfield, a newspaper reporter, and Frank Wiens, a schoolteacher, set about establishing the first St. John's School in Selkirk, Man., with its atmosphere of servility, in direct response to the progressive ideas taking hold in the public school system. St. John's was staffed by members of the Company of the Cross, a lay order created by Byfield and Wiens in association with the Anglican Church, who were paid one dollar a day. They were given room and board, and the opportunity "to be involved for the good of society."

Again, a noble gesture, but not one, you might think, destined to attract the most qualified of applicants. Still, the St. John's School at Selkirk, as well as those to follow, found an audience with parents such as Joan and Oz Mansfield of Angus, Ont., whose son Michael had become increasingly difficult to deal with at home and at school. In a similar situation were Leslie and Barry Nelson of Markham, who thought "more discipline and adventure in his school life would be a godsend" to their son, Barry.

Raffan builds his case against the school with the precision of a veteran barrister. First he looks to the lake itself. Timiskaming had long been known by locals as an unpredictable and unforgiving body of water. There was also the question of the poor St. John's track record on adventure outings, namely the death in 1970 of 15-year-old Markus Jannasch, who succumbed to "cerebral edema and hypoxia" during the annual 35-mile inter-school snowshoe race. Then there were the canoeing accidents, the dumpings, which occurred with such frequency that it seems positively inevitable something terrible was in the offing. A main culprit here is the canoes themselves, which had been altered in such a way, Raffan explains, as to make them dangerously tippy.

These things alone, however, were not enough to seal the fate of the boys. Rather than being contemplative, the masters of St. John's were incompetent: an incompetence born of hubris.

From the very early days of the first school, Byfield and Wiens eschewed any formal training for the masters in favour of a "learn by experience" ethos. That, and the belief that what they couldn't do themselves, God would look after. Referring to earlier non-fatal, though no less dangerous canoeing mishaps, Byfield said: "I think ... we had an awful lot of luck—more likely it was the grace of God."

Mike Mansfield, who survived the Timiskaming debacle, though his two best friends did not, saw things quite differently. "Basically," Mansfield said some years later, "these guys were playing God with people's lives and they didn't do a very good job. They might have given the impression that St. John's was a well-oiled machine, but it wasn't that at all. God didn't provide."

It is very difficult not to be affected by *Deep Waters*. It is at once infuriating, heart-breaking and terribly frustrating. While Raffan has succeeded masterfully in answering the question of why, in the end, his success feels somewhat hollow. The consignment of blame does little to lessen the crime.

Stephen Finear, *Toronto Star*, June 30, 2002, P.D 15.

this, however, only represents the tip of the iceberg. There is no way of telling the number of lawsuits filed, many of which are settled or disposed of at the trial level, and never considered in an appellate court decision. These appellate court decisions, however, are the best indication of the applicable rules of law, which will be applied in this type of case.

(as cited in Attarian, 2001, p. 146)

Publicity of tragedies and the proliferation of liability have had far-ranging and unfortunate consequences. A study by Dunn and Gulbis (1976), for example, concluded that public recreation should not provide risky activities. Meier explains the ramifications from such conclusions: "because of potential danger and possible accidents, many public recreation and leisure service agencies (including schools) question the validity of offering such activities as a regular part of their programs. This hesitancy is usually cloaked in fear that inevitable accidents could result in litigation" (1987, p. 23). This move towards only "safe" offerings has lead to the continued loss of programs as well as opportunities for benefits associated with risk today (Brown, 1999). This section discusses the nature and frequency of accidents, some basic legal considerations to outdoor recreation, and approaches to manage risk.

An accident, according to the *Oxford English Dictionary*, is an event that is either unexpected and/or unintended that results in damage or injury. The term accident is therefore similar to the realization of risk. A "public dimension" also tends to magnify risk (Brown,

1999). Brown formalizes this idea in the following equation: Risk = (Probability × Magnitude) + Public Outrage.

So how frequent are accidents in outdoor recreation? The movement towards a comprehensive database (e.g., International Safety Network Injury Information Database) of incidents (including close calls) is now being recognized (Attarian, 2001; Brown, 1999). Both Ewert (1987) and Brown (1999) urge outdoor recreation leaders to not just document accidents that occur in loss, but rather, account for all incidents that occur. Brown (1999) utilizes the accident ratio triangle to highlight the important relationship between "close calls" and serious injuries, as shown in Figure 9.13. From incident data collected the chance of serious accidents is very low, injury rates are less than many sports, and human factors and adverse weather represent the most common causes of accidents (Brown, 1999).

North America is litigious. Yet, differentiation is required between outdoor recreation activities themselves and the people who are liable. According to van der Smissen "this fear of liability is based in ignorance regarding legal concepts of liability and responsibilities for safety. It is not the activity that brings liability, but the leaders, participants, and the manner of conducting the activity" (1998, p. 12; van der Smissen & Gregg, 1999). The following is not an exhaustive examination of the law; rather, it is a succinct overview of some of the most relevant concepts. Torts (negligence, strict liability, nuisance, intentional) are the area of law that governs relationships among people and other entities in society (e.g., organizations, governments) (Peterson & Hronek, 1992). Negligence, one of the four main types of torts, appears most applicable to outdoor recreation (Fennell, 2006; Frakt, 1987; van der Smissen, 1987, 1998). van der Smissen explains that:

> negligence is an unintentional tort, an act or wrong by one person against another, whereby a person is injured. The one injured usually brings the lawsuit against not only the person who was the tortfeasor or wrongdoer, but also the corporate entity, that is the agency, institution, association, or private enterprise sponsoring the activity, the provider of the service, program or opportunity. There are four components of negligence, all of which must occur (or be proven) for an injured party to recover compensation for the injury. These components are:

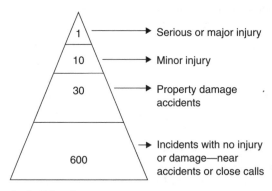

Figure 9.13 Accident Ratio Triangle.

Source: adapted from Bird & Germaine, 1987.

1. a duty is owed to protect the injured from unreasonable risk of harm;
2. the act breaches the standard of care required to protect the participants;
3. this breach is the proximate cause of the injury; and,
4. damage does, in fact, occur.

(1998, p. 12)

Attention is generally directed at the second component of negligence; standards of care that are both situational and determined by professional practices for the environment, the activity, and the type of participants (Fennell, 2006; van der Smissen, 1998). Standard of care, in essence, means that the entity must be familiar with the environment he/she is taking others into, competent in the activity being pursued, understand the participants or clients and, perhaps most importantly, have an appreciation of the relationship among these three factors. Standards of care are considered in light of the "best and latest" professional practices as they are situational and inherently complex (van der Smissen, 1998).

Negligence was identified as one of the most applicable torts utilized in lawsuits in outdoor recreation. Equally important as understanding the legal background of negligence is grasping appropriate defenses—immunity, contract and elements of negligence (van der Smissen, 1998). Again note that this is not a definitive statement of the law per se as considerable variations exist by jurisdiction, it is a general discussion of principles. The first defense to negligence relevant to outdoor recreation as well as managers of recreation resources is that of immunity in which entities are protected from claims of negligence. van der Smissen (1998) directs attention to statutes related to volunteers, specific activities, and the government. Volunteers, for example, are afforded protection from being liable (with the exception of gross negligence) under specific statutes or Good Samaritan laws. Statutes are also aimed at specific activities (e.g., skiing) that make individuals responsible for knowledge and skills pertaining to the activity and abiding to those parameters. Recently, Recreational User Statutes have been enacted in which the duty of care to recreationists is equivalent to trespassers—warning of ultra-hazardous conditions (van der Smissen, 1998). Government is a final area which, in some jurisdictions, has immunity. The legality of government immunity captured public attention when government agencies were sued for animal attacks (Kozlowski, 1999). In such cases, it would appear that immunity from liability has been retained due to the exercise of discretion (Kozlowski, 1999). A second defense to negligence is by way of contract. van der Smissen (1998) notes that independent contractors, lease agreements and participant waivers are particularly useful. The last of these, the participant waiver, is especially important when dealing with adult participants and clients as they routinely hold up against regular, as opposed to gross, negligence if they:

1. use language that is explicit and clear; and,
2. the format is easily readable in exculpatory (clearing from guilt) language (van der Smissen, 1998).

The other important defense is challenging the actual elements of negligence which includes: the foreseeability of risk (could the risk have been anticipated); primary assumption of risk (voluntary consent and understanding of inherent risks in the activity that are

315

either implied or expressed); and, secondary assumption of risk (contribution of or conduct by the participant) (Rankin, 1987; van der Smissen, 1998).

In the introductory remarks to his chapter on legal liability, Frakt writes that "one would search long and unsuccessfully for any instances in which injuries arising out of properly organized adventure programs have resulted in liability on the part of the program or its leaders, instructors, or supervisors" (1987, p. 422). The key word in this statement is "properly" and considerable attention has been thus directed under the heading of risk management. Risk management is a "a systematic approach to the development of a plan aimed at controlling the range and impact of potential losses associated with adventure activities" (Brown, 1999, p. 273). It cannot be overemphasized that the management of risk is a shared responsibility and that risk management extends as an imperative well beyond the adventure context (van der Smissen & Gregg, 1999). From his considerable work in this area Ewert (1987) presents a general item-decision model upon which, he contends, most risk management plans are derived. As illustrated in Figure 9.14, there are a series of decision-points for consideration before, during, and after an outdoor recreation activity; at any of these decision-points continuing, modifying, and/or ceasing the activity may be required. Central to this decision-making process is the ability to accurately assess risk, in this regard the risk assessment (Ewert, 1987) or risk analysis matrix (van der Smissen & Gregg, 1999) is frequently employed in which the frequency and severity of risk are assessed.

As attention on liability in outdoor recreation has increased so has consideration of risk management. While the information discussed in this section highlights some of the main concepts, it is by no means exhaustive. Emerging from the larger compendium of liability and risk management literature is the realization that "one should not fear liability, but be confident in the quality of one's operational practices and move forward positively and with enthusiasm" (van der Smissen & Gregg, 1999, p. 297). It is particularly unfortunate when the fear of liability restricts opportunities for outdoor experiences.

SUMMARY

Human fascination with adventure was used as an entry point for this chapter. The centrality of adventure was established as the human ability to enjoy the unknown was recognized as an important evolutionary feature (Csikszentmihalyi & Csikszentmihalyi, 1990). Despite widespread use of the term adventure, precise semantics of associated terminology was probed from both technical and experiential perspectives. The concept of adventure was explored in the second section of the chapter. The idea of flow was recognized for its particular connection to adventure and the adventure experience paradigm and linkages to the social-psychology tradition in leisure studies were discussed. Application of adventure to therapy and education was subsequently explored. Within the realm of adventure education three specific areas were discussed—group development, decision-making, and leadership. Regardless of the application of adventure, making sense or processing the experience is a paramount concern. It is through well-crafted and effectively facilitated applications of adventure that participants are able to learn and transfer these lessons to other aspects of their lives. The chapter closed with a critical discussion of how elements of risk can be negotiated.

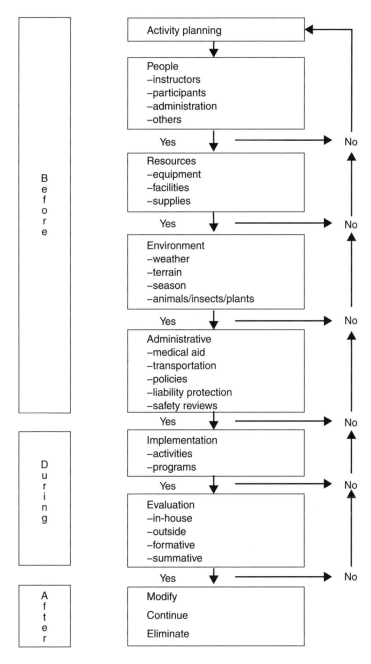

Figure 9.14 Model of Risk-Management Planning.

KEY CONCEPTS

Accident ratio triangle

Adventure and social-psychology

Adventure education

Adventure therapy process

Brick wall model of outdoor leadership

Competence motivation

Danger

Group life cycle

Hazards

Heritage of adventure

Leadership

Meaning of adventure

Modes of decision-making

Outdoor leadership development cycle

Perils

Risk

Risk-management planning

Self-efficacy

Situational leadership theory

Stages of group development

The adventure experience paradigm

Transfer from experience

SUGGESTED KEY SOURCES FOR MORE INFORMATION

Dougherty, N. J. (Ed.). (1998). *Outdoor recreation safety*. Champaign, IL: The School and Community Safety Society of America.

Journal of Adventure Education and Outdoor Learning http://www.outdoor-learning.org

Meier, J. F., Morash, T. W. & Welton, G. E. (Eds.). (1987). *High-adventure outdoor pursuits: Organization and leadership*. Columbus, OH: Publishing Horizons.

Miles, J. C. & Priest, S. (Eds.). (1990). *Adventure education*. State College, PA: Venture.

Miles, J. & Priest, S. (Eds.). (1999). *Adventure programming*. State College, PA: Venture.

REVIEW QUESTIONS

1. Identify three of the main elements involved with the concept of adventure and describe their relationship.

2. The adventure experience paradigm explains the relationship between competence (real and perceived) and risk. Apply the adventure experience paradigm to an individual who is arrogant and fearless.

3. Identify the stages of the adventure therapy process. Illustrate how this model could be applied.

4. Identify and describe the stages a group progresses on an adventure experience from start to finish.

5. What method of decision-making would you use in an emergency situation? Explain the method you select and provide rationale for your choice.

6. Why is leadership important in adventure education?

7. Outdoor leaders are required to effectively exhibit hard, soft and meta skills. Describe each of these skill types and provide an example.

8. How is competence motivation influenced by unsuccessful mastery attempts?
9. Transferring lessons learned from adventure to "everyday" life is critical for adventure to be successful. If you were leading a group of elementary school students, how would you facilitate this process?
10. How can risks associated with adventure be managed?

Chapter 10

Issues in Outdoor Recreation

OBJECTIVES

This chapter will:

■   consider the need for outdoor recreation opportunities by all segments of society;

■   discuss the advantages and disadvantages of professional recognition and certification;

■   critically assess the implications of technology for outdoor recreation;

■   probe the nature and implications of ecotourism;

■   explore philosophical and ethical considerations associated with outdoor recreation;

■   apply an interdisciplinary perspective to a particular case study.

INTRODUCTION

This chapter is markedly different from the preceding chapters. It focuses on issues emerging in the contemporary context of outdoor recreation. The term issue is purposefully located at the beginning of the chapter title to connote the importance of establishing constructive dialogue on each topic. Topics selected for inclusion cut across or transcend the dimensions and subjects discussed. They also have been selected because they represent critical junctures for outdoor recreation as both a leisure pursuit and as an area of study. The manner in which individuals and the profession respond will, to some extent, provide the basis for decisive changes and mark a new course. While the inclusion of issues is ultimately somewhat subjective, the pressing nature of each is well supported in the literature. Issues confronting outdoor recreation to be discussed include: integration and accessibility, professional certification, technology, ecotourism, philosophy and ethics, and an interdisciplinary outlook. Each issue is succinctly described. The most pressing aspects to the study and/or practice of outdoor recreation are subsequently identified. Case Studies highlight pragmatic considerations.

OUTDOOR RECREATION FOR ALL?

Recreation as a "public" good has been an enduring theme throughout its development, as chronicled in Chapter 2. However, subsegments of society and individuals experience specific barriers to participation in outdoor recreation (Anderson & Kress, 2003; Kelly & Freysinger, 2000). Concern and attention to this important issue has resulted in an emphasis on inclusion in recreation as well as attention to using recreation as therapy. The background to each approach is briefly described, implications for outdoor recreation are examined, and practical examples are considered.

Demographic considerations and barriers to participation by specific subsectors within society are notable and considered within most leisure studies texts (e.g., Godbey, 1999; Searle & Brayley, 2000). These considerations are highlighted through the inclusive approach. According to Hutchison:

> inclusive recreation refers to the full participation of citizens who have been devalued in community life. Regular homes, schools, workplaces, recreation services, and community settings provide the context for experiencing valued roles, developing social relationships, and accessing a full range of recreation opportunities.
>
> (personal communication, July 7, 2001)

Integration is therefore central to recreation as all people have an inherent right to full participation. Hutchison and McGill (1998) views the target of inclusive recreation to include all devalued persons due to disability, age, gender, sexual preference, or ethnicity.

Studies specific to outdoor recreation have implicitly recognized the importance of inclusion by identifying differences in rates of participation as well as examining some of the barriers experienced by subsegments of society. The biological, sociological and psychological aspects of aging in the context of adventure programming has been observed and "this population has been seriously neglected and that there is a need to develop programs for them that revive their former skills and interests and teaches new ones" (Sugerman, 1999, p. 388). Gender differences relating to outdoor recreation have also received increasing attention, largely through the critical feminist lens (e.g., Pohl, Borrie & Patterson, 2000; Warren, 1999). Warren (1999) has exerted considerable effort to dispelling particular myths (accessibility, egalitarianism, square one, superwoman, heroic quest) which act as barriers for women and contribute to unresponsiveness in adventure programs. Gender meanings of particular outdoor recreation activities have included recreational fishing (Toth & Brown, 1997), wilderness recreation (Pohl et al., 2000) and environmental preferences (Virden & Walker, 1999). This research has been fruitful as wilderness recreation can positively influence elements in the everyday lives of women (Pohl et al., 2000).

Ethnicity and culture have also emerged in outdoor recreation as issues receiving considerable attention due to the increasing diversity of users (Gobster, 2002; Manning, 1999; Virden & Walker, 1999). As noted in Chapter 4, the term ethnicity refers to "groups of people who share distinguishing characteristics such as religion, language, customs, and ancestry" (Manning, 1999, p. 36). The initial generation of research on the role of ethnicity in outdoor recreation concentrated on similarities and differences in participation among

322

ethnic groups in outdoor recreation activities or settings (e.g., Washburne, 1978; West, 1993). This approach has been criticized as being simplistic and inadequately capturing the complexity of the variable (e.g., Carr & Williams, 1993; Virden & Walker, 1999; Walker, Deng & Dieser, 2001). Attention in "second generation" research has focused on understanding the experience and/or meaning of outdoor recreation and parks utilizing more refined intra-group measures (Carr & Williams, 1993; Gobster, 2002; Gomez, 2002; Thapa, Graefe & Absher, 2001; Virden & Walker, 1999; Walker et al., 2001). Additional attention has been specifically focused on the role of culture, which Taylor (1971) understood as "that most complex whole which includes knowledge, belief, art, morals, law, custom, and many other capabilities and habits acquired by individuals within a society" (as cited in Sasidharan, 2002, p. 3). Although its complexity makes the concept challenging to operationalize, it has been employed to examine competing claims to recreational resources such as Devils Tower National Monument (Dustin, Schneider, McAvoy & Frakt, 2002). Studies on differences in participation, inquiries on the meanings of outdoor experiences and investigations have found clear differences. Sasidharan (2002) cautions that research must also consider the similarities, "thus alleviating some of the agony facing recreation resources managers and policy makers" (2002, p. 8)

Attention has also been directed to persons with disabilities. The right to outdoor recreation for all is legally entrenched in North America. In the United States the passing of the Americans with Disabilities Act (ADA) mandates that persons with disabilities have similar opportunities to society as a whole and has focused attention on service provision (McAvoy & Lais, 1999; Sugerman, 2001). In Canada, these rights are set forth in the Charter of Rights and Freedoms (1982) as well as more specific provincial legislation such as the Ontario Disabilities Act (ODA). The language in the ADA is particularly interesting as it emphasizes that the provision of such services should be inclusive in nature.

Leisure preferences among people with disabilities are just as diverse as the population at large and their participation in outdoor and adventure recreation activities has been increasing (McAvoy & Lais, 1999; Sugerman, 2001). McAvoy and Lais (1999) argue that persons with disabilities experience the full range of benefits from outdoor activities and it is the place at which they start and the societal barriers they encounter which emphasizes the magnitude of these benefits. Positive effects from therapeutic recreation extend beyond participants with disabilities to participants without disabilities when outdoor recreation activities occur in an integrated setting (McAvoy & Lais, 1999). Particularly troubling, given the above findings, has been the fact that:

persons with disabilities have had limited opportunities to experience adventure programs in the past because of the stereotypic attitudes of service providers that limited opportunities, overprotectiveness of well-meaning family and caregivers, lack of role models, and a lack of appropriate equipment.

(McAvoy & Lais, 1999, p. 405)

This is, thankfully, changing.

As people with disabilities are increasingly pursuing outdoor recreation activities both the quality and quantity of information to guide facilitators has developed. The personal attitudes of facilitators need to be addressed as approaches employed have generally been either

323

from a compensation perspective (the professional must compensate for the loss through the provision of human or technological aids) or from a transcendence perspective (people with a disability can achieve independence by managing their own aids if resources are provided by the professional) (Sugerman, 1999). Regardless of the perspective taken, facilitation of outdoor recreation activities for persons with disabilities should:

1. use person first language and avoid stereotypes;
2. be respectful of personal dignity;
3. seek input from the person with a disability;
4. keep adaptations to a minimum, stress functionality of the adaptation, involve the person in the adaptation; focus on action, group challenges and emphasize choice; and,
5. emphasize all types of contributions and recognize success (Kennedy, Austin & Smith, 1987; McAvoy & Lais, 1999; Sugerman, 1999).

Camping has been an outdoor recreation activity with an established tradition of including people with disabilities. Kennedy (1987) documents this tradition back to the 1880s. Despite the similarities between residential camping and wilderness components for persons with and without disabilities, he observes that "less than one tenth of people with disabilities in the United States have had the opportunity to participate in organized camping and wilderness programs" (Kennedy, 1987, p. 205). Despite this recognized shortcoming, there are some outstanding organizations dedicated to the provision of such opportunities. The example of the Easter Seals Society is documented in Box 10.1.

BOX 10.1 EASTER SEALS CAMP MERRYWOOD

An Overview of Camp Merrywood

KAREN NATHO

Easter Seals camps provide a special recreational experience for children and youth who have a physical disability and their families. Developing and promoting independence and skills are the focus of all activities. Campers are encouraged to be independent, supported and encouraged by staff. Every camper is challenged to the best of his/her ability. Special adaptations have been made to ensure campers are getting the most out of each activity.

Easter Seals Camp Merrywood (opened 1948) is situated on a peninsula that stretches out into Big Rideau Lake near Perth, Ontario. Campers are exhilarated by the adventurous activities on land, on the lake and off-site on canoe, rafting and overnight trips. Merrywood is one of three summer residential camps for children and youth with physical disabilities in Ontario, Canada. Campers from all over the province come to Merrywood for a ten-day individual camp or five-day Family Camp experience. The most common disabilities at camp are Cerebral Palsy, Spina Bifida and Muscular Dystrophy. All Easter Seals Camps provide a variety of programs, such as swimming, campfires, arts and crafts, sports, and leadership development training. Easter Seals Camp Merrywood also has a full waterfront program including sailing, canoeing, overnight tenting, four-day canoe trips, whitewater rafting and kayaking

Merrywood's main mission is to provide campers with an outdoor recreational experience focusing on individual choice, personal challenges and life skills development. The camp also strives to:

- Provide a camping experience to Easter Seals children/youth that is fun and safe;
- Promote the development of life skills that enhance future independence;
- Build self-esteem through activities that challenge each child's individual abilities;
- Provide opportunities for social interaction, building friendships and the development of healthy interpersonal behaviors.

THE IMPORTANCE OF CAMPER CHOICE

An important focus of the Easter Seals camping program is to allow campers to make choices about the activities in which they participate. At the beginning of the session campers have the opportunity to try each programming area. On the third day until the end of the session, campers choose their activities on a daily basis. One of the choices is the overnight canoe trip and four-day canoe trip. Packing campers' equipment (wheelchairs, braces and canes) and their healthcare supplies (attends, medications) are things that must be taken into consideration.

The Easter Seals camp experience is a unique one for both campers and staff. Merrywood is able to provide a high-quality camping program for children and youth with physical disabilities. Merrywood creates opportunities for campers to develop independence, build self-esteem through achievement and help campers learn new skills and develop friendships. Working together as a team in all programming areas, campers have a fun, productive and rewarding summer.

Outdoor recreation for all was the subtitle used to initiate discussion of inclusive and therapeutic recreation. Legislative developments such as the ADA in the United States brought increased attention to providing outdoor experiences for persons with disabilities and doing so in an inclusive way. Pragmatic considerations related to such provision remain a challenge to service providers. How accessible should wilderness be? An equally important dilemma being faced by managers is how to prioritize the multiplicity of values and preferences for outdoor spaces being expressed by increasingly diverse resource users.

OUTDOOR RECREATION AS A PROFESSION—QUESTIONS OF CERTIFICATION?

Recreation largely emerged as a social movement out of the Industrial Revolution. As the provision of recreation services gained attention they became recognized as a public good and governments became involved in their provision. Accompanying these developments have been substantive accumulations of knowledge, supportive institutions, and industry-based organizations. The professionalization of recreation has been a contested issue, especially since therapeutic and outdoor areas of concentration have moved towards certification. The major qualities of a profession are described below and lead to a specific discussion of certification issues in outdoor recreation. Although much of the certification issue has been driven by those working in the adventure domain, it is important to recognize that the issue is inherently broader as both foresters and planners, many who frequently focus on aspects of outdoor recreation, have moved forward and gained professional status.

The "profession" question has been addressed in general recreation texts (e.g., Edginton, Hanson, Edginton & Hudson, 1998; Searle & Brayley, 2000) and has emerged as a "special theme" in the *Journal of Experiential Education* (Guthrie, 2001). Professions have existed for considerable periods of time (e.g., medicine, law, teaching) and are characterized by:

- mechanisms of self-regulation (certification) that are sanctioned by the government (licensing) which requires demonstrated competencies (theory, skills, values) and adherence to standards of practice;
- shared norms and values of conduct;
- specialized knowledge, skills, and abilities which are often communicated through a technical vocabulary. These are typically written in professional literature, transmitted by post-secondary institutions, and developed by ongoing research in both theory and practice; and,
- organizations or association that control their affairs (control entry into the profession), assist/support members (conferences, publications, workshops), and levy sanctions/penalties for violators (Guthrie, 2001; Searle & Brayley, 2000).

Within therapeutic recreation there has certainly been a movement towards professional establishment. Certified Therapeutic Recreation Specialist is a title given to members of the National Council for Therapeutic Recreation Certification, an agency that establishes standards and certification for professionals within the therapeutic recreation field (National Council for Therapeutic Recreation Certification, in press, online). Members must meet the Council's standards in order to gain certification and be able to practice therapeutic recreation. Is outdoor recreation moving in a similar direction?

Outdoor recreation as an area of both study and practice certainly exhibits some of the characteristics of a profession. Professional associations (e.g., Association for Experiential Education, Wilderness Education Association), supporting conferences (e.g., National Recreation and Parks Association Annual Conference, Northeastern Recreation Resource Symposium) and literature (e.g., *Leisure Studies*, *Society and Natural Resources*) are evident. Common standards and competencies are also shared by organizations such as Outward Bound, the National Outdoor Leadership School, and the Wilderness Education Society (Guthrie, 2001). Notwithstanding these characteristics, Guthrie observes that "in comparison to related fields such as education or psychology, we have a very small body of literature specific to the profession, relatively little on-going research, and we are not *generally* valued, recognized or supported by the public" (2001, p. 133). He continues to identify a host of interrelated issues to support his assertion. These include: open entry into employment that is often accompanied by only on-site training and failure to share "professional" values; few, if any, sanctioned standards; lack of common curriculum standards in institutions of post-secondary education; and lack of research and/or evaluation (Guthrie, 2001, p. 132).

More specific than the professionalization debate within outdoor recreation has been the issue of certification and accreditation (Attarian, 2001; Fennell, 2003; Gass, 1999b; Guthrie, 2001; Plaut, 2001). Certification has been an ongoing debate since the 1970s and is "a process whereby certain minimum standards of competency have been met or exceeded by a professional as evaluated by a certifying agency" (Attarian, 2001, p. 145). While numerous examples of certification exist for many outdoor recreation activities (e.g., climbing, kayaking, canoeing, etc.), some have gained worldwide acceptance. The international certification for diving (PADI) is an example with wide international acceptance (PADI, n.d.). Despite efforts in the 1970s to certify individual instructors, certification of outdoor leaders has not materialized and a formal certification program does not currently exist in North America (Attarian, 2001). Numerous reasons have been identified to explain the failure of certification. These tend to focus on the: difficulty in assessing soft and meta skills; cost and amount of time required; exclusion of uncertified, but highly experienced persons; and inability to examine all forms of outdoor programming in a systematic way (geographically, different programs, environmental factors) (Attarian, 2001; Gass, 1999b). The most "critical" flaw in the certification concept was the assumption that certification was related to safety as even the most capable leader who is certified is susceptible to accidents due to other circumstances (e.g., old equipment, poor weather) (Attarian, 2001; Gass, 1999b).

A second approach to professional assessment in outdoor recreation has been accreditation. Accreditation focuses on all aspects of a program or service providers' operation. Gass observes that:

> accreditation retains the strengths of individual certification without being bound by some of its weaknesses. For example, accreditation (1) provides adventure programs with the ability to achieve standards without losing the flexibility to decide and design how these standards are met; (2) takes a "systemic view" of the process of adventure programming rather than dividing it into individualized categories; (3) encourages improvement through internal and external review; (4) assures clients, agencies, and the custodians of the lands that a program has clearly defined and appropriate objectives, and (5) maintains conditions under which their achievement can be reasonably met.
>
> (1999b, p. 249)

Accreditation in the specific field of adventure was initiated in the 1990s by the Association for Experiential Education. The potential applicability of accreditation is broad as it has been extended into: common curriculum in leadership programs (Raiola & Sugerman, 1999); degree-granting institutions which encompass "adventure education," outdoor recreation, experiential education and environmental education (Plaut, 2001); and ecotourism (Fennell, 2003).

Accreditation and auditing associated with adventure outdoor activities is extending beyond the United States to New Zealand, and is also being considered in Australia and the United Kingdom (Chisholm & Shaw, 2004). Despite the perceived benefit of increased transparency around safety by instructors and organizations, Chisholm and Shaw (2004)

327

raise critical questions about underlying power relationships, trust (both too little in experience and too much in measures), and decreased quality.

The issues of professionalization, certification and accreditation continue to be points of dialogue in outdoor recreation. As outdoor recreation continues to develop as both an area of study as well as an area of practice, it may well move towards gaining professional status. This move may be lauded by some due to enhanced status, financial rewards, greater protection, and increased accountability; while others may resent it due to increased professional control and over-dependence, increased specialization, and greater prescribed standards (Fennell, 2003; Searle & Brayley, 2000). Although Ewert's (1987) assertion that certification of instructors would increase by 2000 has not occurred, increased certification in specific program areas (e.g., rock climbing) are anticipated to rise with regulation and in conjunction with accreditation (Attarian, 2001). While outdoor recreation has largely not moved in the direction of certification, save perhaps for that of swimming and first aid, the option of no or minimum standards are unrealistic. Opportunity exists here to learn from ecotourism, which is seemingly attempting to advance the certification and accreditation issue through recent discussions at the World Ecotourism Summit in 2002 (Fennell, 2003).

TECHNOLOGY

"Technology noun 1 the scientific study of mechanical arts and applied sciences (e.g., engineering). 2 these subjects, their practical application in the industry etc." (Pollard, 1994, p. 824).

Technology has profoundly changed outdoor recreation. This is clearly illustrated in the following scenario:

On May 29, 1953, Edmund Hillary and Tenzing Norgay were the first people to stand on the summit of Mt. Everest. During their two-month climb, they used Swiss reindeer

Plate 10.1 *Fishing can be Simple and Involve a Limited Amount of Technology.*

Plate 10.2 Some Forms of Fishing have been Heavily Influenced by Technology.

boots, woolen underclothes and eiderdown jackets (Sufrin, 1966). By 1996 over 600 people had made it to the summit of Mt. Everest. While most of these 600 climbers still wore eiderdown jackets, this is where the resemblance stops. The modern-day climber now practices the trade of mountaineering accompanied by a host of techno-logical advances such as plastic boots, synthetic clothing, titanium ice screws, hand-held GPS (global positioning systems) units, and communications devices that can provide instant connection with park or rescue organizations.

(Ewert & Shultis, 1999, p. 3)

The above passage recognizes just some of the many implications of technology to outdoor recreation. Four of the most prominent considerations under the issue of technology are discussed below.

Immediately apparent has been the application of technology to both outdoor clothing and gear (Ryan, 2002). There has been a "virtual explosion" of technology relevant to back-country recreation (Ewert & Shultis, 1999). This pervasive application of technology has been received with encouraging applause and expressed concern. In their critical assessment of this issue, Ewert and Shultis (1999) assert that technology affects backcountry recreation in the five specific areas of access and transportation, comfort, safety, communication, and information. Table 10.1 summarizes their critical assessment by identifying examples, docu-menting effects, and gauging potential implications for each of the above categories. Their assessment leads them to propose a model of technological impacts on outdoor recreation, illustrated in Figure 10.1. This model usefully recognizes the pervasiveness of technological influences in outdoor recreation (five categories), accounts for various factors that have led

Table 10.1 Categories of Technological Effects and Implications for Backcountry Recreation

Category	Examples	Effects	Major implications/issues
Access and transportation	Automobile, airplane, ATV, parapentes, snowmobile, RTV, mountain bike, helicopter	Increased use, willingness to participate, recreation conflicts, more human–natural environment interactions (e.g., with wildlife)	Management need for more attention on carrying-capacity, user conflicts, environmental impacts, infrastructure development, and a more diverse set of recreationists (e.g., experience levels)
Comfort	Synthetic fabrics, plastic, internal frame pack, light-weight tents	Longer visits, increased use, expanded use (e.g., families, less fit, elderly), increased desire for facilities	Increased attention to carrying-capacity, environmental impacts, search and rescue, visitor demands for amenities (e.g., showers, etc.)
Safety	Synthetic fabrics, stronger materials, more effective means of protection (e.g., climbing aids, non-collapsible kayaks)	Longer and more remote visitation, recreation during the "shoulder periods" (e.g., winter), a general "pushing back" of the perceived margin of safety, more risk-taking activities	Search and rescue, increasing lack of congruency between the type of situation (i.e., level of danger) and the skills and experience of the individual, expectation that "experiences" will be without risk
Communication	Radio, cellular and digital phones, GPS, datalink watches	More rapid linkages to other groups, expectation that remote backcountry tripping can stay "connected" to outside world	Increased safety and planning capability, expectations that information and ability to "connect in" will be available (e.g., park radio frequencies, avalanche warnings at the site, etc.)
Information	Television, satellite TV, Internet	Increased awareness, use and appreciation, more informed public, increased options and opportunities	Managers will be expected to provide more information and in a variety of formats, greater level of accuracy in expectations of the backcountry site and experience

to an increase in backcountry recreation, and explores salient impacts. Ryan's (2002) examination of discourse accompanying technological advances in both clothing and equipment adds an interesting viewpoint. In reviewing advertisements by popular outdoor clothiers he concludes that

> the message is clear: human beings are not good enough; they need technology to be outdoors. More than a mere luxury, the discourse around new clothing materials promotes the technological innovations to such an extent that to be outdoors in inclement weather without them is seen as risky, bordering on foolhardy.
>
> (2002, p. 270)

Technology has also prompted the creation of new outdoor activities as well as the ability to bring the natural environment indoors. One example of technology that has resulted in both new pursuits as well as being management opportunities is the global positioning system (GPS). Originally designed for military applications, handheld GPS units have been adapted for recreational pursuits and combination with the Internet to result in the new pursuit of geocaching (Clemens, 2004; Wright, 2003). The activity of geocaching is described in Box 10.2. GPS technology has also been identified for having extensive management implications including interactive mapping, interpretive displays, and visitor management (McElravy, 1999). Such communication devices also have been identified for increasing safety and information efficiencies (Ewert & Shultis, 1999). The United States

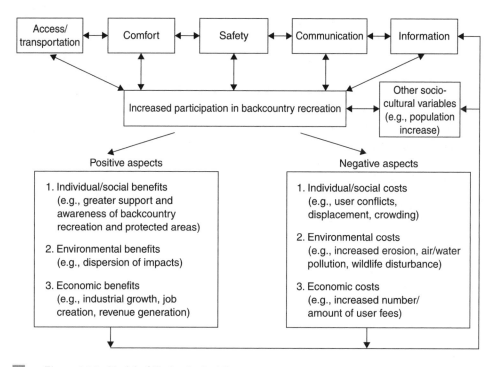

Figure 10.1 Model of Technological Impacts.

331

Forest Service, for example, has implemented an eTRACS program in which a mobile recorder is used to inventory and assess conditions and provide management with timely information (USDA Forest Service, n.d.). In addition to such examples of taking technology into the out-of-doors, technology has also been utilized to bring activities that have largely occurred outdoors inside. These activities are typically prefixed with the term simulated indicating that they are like real pursuits. Simulated activities include golf, climbing, surfing, whitewater kayaking/canoeing, archery, and target shooting.

BOX 10.2 GEOCACHING (pronounced "gee-oh-cash-ing")

COLLEEN BEARD

Geocaching is a relatively new recreational activity, but growing tremendously in popularity. Some refer to it as an outdoor "high-tech treasure hunt," a "hide-and-seek" pursuit, or a "nature walk" with a purpose! Whatever the term, it certainly has its recreational and academic merits. There are now several geocaching organizations and websites; it is also becoming popular as a teambuilding activity in the corporate sector. Geocaching is similar to the sport of orienteering, except that rather than the location being identified by a visible marker, it involves uncovering a hidden object.

The "Geo" refers to "geography" and the "cache" means "treasure" or a hiding place for goods. Geocaches are hidden all over the world by anyone, and consist of a container with various trinkets, memorabilia, jewelry, etc., and a logbook to record your visit. They are identified by a geographical coordinate and posted to a geocache database on the web, usually with additional clues to its location. As of November 2007, there were 487,758 active caches worldwide listed on the Official Global GPS Cache Hunt Site (www.geocaching.com). Using a Global Positioning System (GPS), or a map and compass, one can take to the outdoors and locate the geocache by setting the GPS to the coordinates. However, the GPS will only take you to within a certain range of the geocache, perhaps a few meters at best. The challenge is to locate the cache using the other clues provided since the cache itself will not be visible. Once the cache is found, the rule is to sign the logbook and take an item from the cache replacing it with an item of equal value. But beware! There have been stories of valuable coins, jewelry, and money found in some caches. An optional rule, that geocachers usually follow, is posting their experience on the website, also referred to as a "cache log." Geocaches can also be themed for trading certain objects: sports cards, books, or recipes. There are even underwater geocaches. There have been accounts of toys (such as Mr. Potato Head) that have traveled the world from geocaching activity.

Apart from the health and fitness benefits, geocaching may lead participants into scenic and unexplored territory, and can be done as a free time activity with family, friends or solo. Geocaches that are posted on a website database often include a level of difficulty, either as an "easy find" or involving difficult terrain and requiring much physical activity. Several locations may also be specified in multi-cache cases. These assessments are useful when planning an activity involving different audiences, such as children, older adults, or the experienced outdoors person seeking a challenge. Geocaching has also evolved into a serious competitive sport.

Geocaching is also educational. Because it involves the use of several elements—GPS functionality; coordinate systems (latitude and longitude); map and compass reading (a GPS is not necessary to partake in geocaching)—it can be included in curriculums at any education level in a multitude of disciplines. The functions of a GPS unit, such as tracking a route using waypoints, can even lead to enhanced computer mapping activities in the classroom.

The one criticism of geocaching is that it compels geocachers to encroach on areas that could have a negative impact on the natural environment. However, the rules for hiding a geocache are well established. For example, a geocache is not to be placed in environmentally sensitive areas, national parks, or sites where human activity may place wildlife (or yourself) in danger. It is also encouraged that geocachers carry an empty bag for collecting trash along their route.

There are several resources available for getting started with geocaching: from searching a database for geocaches in your local area; using a GPS unit; map-reading skills; to creating your own geocache—all of which make this activity very appealing, just for the fun of it!

SUGGESTED READING

McNamara, J. (2004). *Geocaching for dummies*. New Jersey: Wiley.
Cooke, D. (2005). *Fun with GPS*. Redlands, CA: ESRI Press.

INTERNET SITE

www.geocaching.com (The Official Global GPS Cache Hunt Site)

Critical attention has also been directed at the many applications of technology in the outdoors. Ladd cautions that:

> because a radically new technology makes certain moral practices (and inhibitions) out of date, that is, non-functional or even dysfunctional, we find ourselves presented with a sort of moral vacuum, as traditional norms, principles and institutions lose their force and become "irrelevant" and new norms, principles and institutions to meet new conditions, opportunities and powers have not yet been developed.
>
> (1997, p. 9)

This caution resonates with those concerned with the integrity or "meaning" of backcountry/wilderness experiences as well as managers (Baltic, 1999; Ewert & Shultis, 1999; Ryan, 2002). Ryan (2002), from a critical postmodern viewpoint, employs cybernetic theory (cyborgs are part human, part technology and part animal) to question traditional categorical barriers associated with wilderness. He concludes that:

> to ask what kind of ecological selves we could create without the image of the spaceship earth is not just an academic exercise. Re-configuring how technology affects our self-perception (or embracing its effects on us already) will have profound effects on your discourses about who we are, what wilderness is, the place of technology in the wilderness, and especially the stability of such categories in the first place.
>
> (2002, p. 279)

So what do people who believe technology detracts from the wilderness suggest? One proposal is that at least some backcountry zones should be technology and/or rescue free (Ewert & Shultis, 1999). Proponents of rescue-free wilderness areas suggest that these areas are required to counteract: responsibilities by management agencies for visitors in wilderness which is an inherent oxymoron; utilization of high-technology and associated rescue equipment; and the contemporary licentious mentality (McAvoy, 1999). The benefits and drawbacks to such areas are discussed by Harwell (1987) and Peterson (1987). Harwell (1987) clearly advocates for no-rescue wilderness, by offering the following benefits: lack of restraint and opportunity for true choice and freedom, responsibility for one's actions, and increased satisfaction with the experience (being able to do it on one's own). Peterson (1987) argues that no-rescue policies are discriminatory (he cites the example of a pregnant woman hiking, would agencies not rescue her?), immoral, and devalue life.

ECOTOURISM

In Chapter 1 the term outdoor recreation was defined and conceptualized. Considerable attention was directed at differentiating it from related concepts within leisure studies. Mieczkowski's (1981) model was used to assist readers in visualizing areas of overlap and distinction. Boundaries between outdoor recreation and tourism were further identified as being a matter of perceptual debate and therefore "soft." This distinction becomes even less pronounced when considering outdoor recreation and forms of tourism that focus on the natural environment. Boyd and Butler (2000) assert that it is impossible to differentiate between outdoor recreation and tourism when considering those visiting parks, a trend that will continue into the future. Buckley captures the essence of this trend in writing "that there is now substantial coalescence, in markets, operators and concepts, between nature-based, ecotourism, adventure travel and outdoor recreation; and this coalescence is sufficient to recognize a distinct nature, eco- and adventure tourism (NEAT)" (2000, p. 438). Ecotourism, a specific type of travel, is presented here as an issue requiring consideration for outdoor recreation due to its burgeoning popularity, associated impacts, and related opportunities.

The study of tourism has progressed through four phases or platforms of mass tourism, advocacy, cautionary, and adaptancy (Jafari, 1989). It is in the most recent phase that various types of tourism have been posited that are "alternatives" to mass tourism and its associated negative connotations (Weaver, 2001). Even within the alternative tourism paradigm, hybridization is pervasive and categories are rarely mutually exclusive (Weaver,

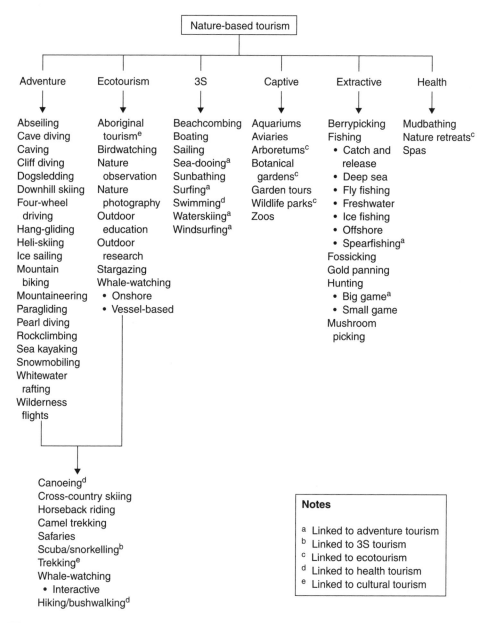

Figure 10.2 *Dichotomy of Nature-Based Tourism.*

Source: adapted from Weaver, Faulkner & Lawson, 1999.

2001). Weaver (2001) illustrates the dichotomy even within nature-based tourism by providing specific examples of activities, as shown in Figure 10.2. A scan of these activities reveals extensive similarities with those classified as "outdoor recreation." Within this array of tourism forms, ecotourism is exclusively addressed below due to its increasing popularity, critical questions of intentions and impacts, and notable academic attention.

335

Ecotourism and ecodevelopment have a "convergent evolution" as evidence suggests the concept was being broadly applied in various contexts as far back as the 1960s and 1970s (Fennell, 2003). It is broadly accepted that there are numerous ways to define the term ecotourism (Cater, 1994; Fennell, 2003; Page & Dowling, 2002; Stem et al., 2003; Weaver, 2001, 2002). Cater evocatively asks:

> is it a form of "alternative tourism" (furthermore, what is "alternative tourism"?)? Is it responsible (defined in terms of environmental, socio-cultural, moral or practical in terms)? Is it sustainable (however defined)? The list is endless and, it is feared, much of the debate counter-productive.
>
> (1994, p. 3)

In heeding the caution expressed by Cater above, a debate on terminology is avoided here. Based on his observations of the ecotourism semantic debate, Weaver (2002) gleans three "core" criteria: nature is the primary attraction; the tourist–attraction interaction is learning focused; and it should have the appearance of being environmentally and socio-culturally sustainable. In bringing these three elements together in a concerted fashion, ecotourism is:

> a sustainable form of natural resource-based tourism that focuses primarily on experiencing and learning about nature, and which is ethically managed to be low-impact, non-consumptive, and locally oriented (control, benefits, and scale). It typically occurs in natural areas, and should contribute to the conservation or preservation of such areas.
>
> (Fennell, 2003, p. 25)

As noted at the beginning of this section, ecotourism has developed into an area of academic concentration and the product of this has been a growing volume of literature. This section provides a succinct overview and makes familiar some of the emerging issues. Cater (1994) observes that interest in ecotourism is diverse, but can be usefully grouped into four main areas of tourist guests, tourist organizations, host populations, and the environment. Each of these areas of interest is subsequently discussed, with host populations and the environments being subsumed into a more general discussion of impacts.

Who is an ecotourist? More specific attention is needed than is typically employed in tourism marketing segmentation (grouping of tourists with similar traits) to answer this question (Page & Dowling, 2002). The formulation of typologies that classify ecotourists with similar characteristics is a common approach and has utilized both empirical and non-empirical data (see Fennell, 2003; Page & Dowling, 2002; Weaver, 2001). One of the most useful typologies is the ecotourism continuum, first suggested by Laarman and Durst (1987). Weaver's (2002) generalized presentation of the ecotourism spectrum is illustrated in Figure 10.3. At opposite ends of the continuum are ideal or extreme types. Hard ecotourists are very committed to the natural environment (biocentric), desire deep interactions with the natural environment, and are active in all aspects of the ecotourism experience. Shallow ecotourists are more passive towards their experience, tend to be anthropocentric or "human centered" in stressing comfort and convenience, and are "superficially" committed to the environment. The term "ideal types" is employed to signal that in reality individuals contain various combinations of these attributes. More traditional socio-demographic variables (e.g., gender, age, education) have also been employed to characterize ecotourists. Ecotourists are (compared to tourists in general) disproportionately male (but feminization is evident since the mid-1990s), slightly older, and have higher levels of education and income (most tend to have professional occupations) (Fennell, 2003; Page & Dowling, 2002; Weaver, 2002). A final point of interest here is the type of experience desired by the ecotourist. Page and Dowling observe that "the tourist experience is a complex combination of factors which shape the feelings and attitudes of the tourist towards their visit" (2002, p. 97). What this means is that the experience itself, including geographic dimensions of source of origin and destination, are becoming increasingly important to understanding the ecotourist (Fennell, 2003; Page & Dowling, 2002; Weaver, 2002).

While persistent challenges make it difficult to precisely determine the extent of the ecotourism sector, the ecotourism industry has been expanding quickly since the 1990s (The Ecotourism Society, 2005). Despite this, relatively few systematic investigations have occurred regarding the "global dimensions of the nature tourism industry or the way in which this emerging business structure is shaping the identity, organization, and impacts of ecotourism" (Eagles & Higgins, 1998, p. 11). Attention has been subsequently directed to the ecotourism industry in an effort to achieve a more complete understanding of it. In one of the initial works in this regard, Wood (1998) identified the basic structure of the ecotourism industry to involve travel agents/retailers, outbound tour operators, inbound/ground operators, ecolodge/accommodations and local vendors. This work has been furthered by Page and Dowling (2002) who conceptualize the above elements as a transaction chain in which a range of mediating entities may exist. Given the often substantive role that governments play related to tourism, due consideration within ecotourism has also been directed to the influence of policy and direction setting by governments (see Fennell, 2003; Fennell & Dowling, 2003; Page & Dowling, 2002).

Hard (active, deep)	**Soft** (passive, shallow)
The ecotourism spectrum	
Strong environmental commitment	Moderate or superficial environmental commitment
Enhancive sustainability	Steady state sustainability
Specialized trips	Multi-purpose trips
Long trips	Short trips
Small groups	Larger groups
Physically active	Physically passive
Physical challenge	Physical comfort
No services expected	Services expected
Deep interaction with nature	Shallow interaction with nature
Emphasis on personal experience	Emphasis on mediation
Make own travel arrangements	Rely on travel agents and tour operators

Figure 10.3 The Ecotourism Spectrum.

Source: Weaver & Lawton, 2001.

Observed increases in ecotourism travel and corresponding industry expansion are unlikely to recede:

> The world, clearly, is not going to stop taking holidays—but equally clearly we can no longer afford to ignore the consequences. And if one of the major culprits has been the industrialialisation of travel, a genuine post-industrial tourism, with the emphasis on people and places rather than products and profits, could turn out to be significantly more planet-friendly.
>
> (Nicholson-Lord, 1997; as cited in Page & Dowling, 1998, p. 148)

As indicated in the above quotation and the definition of ecotourism earlier, ecotourism purports to be a more sensitive form of travel. Commentary on the impacts from ecotourism has thus been aimed at establishing if such claims are reality or rhetoric. An initial distinction must be made between those activities and service providers committed to ecotourism principles and those who, sometimes knowingly, misrepresent and/or mislabel their services as ecotourism to attract clients, as the latter exhibits impacts relatively similar to mass tourism and has led to abuse of the term ecotourism (Weaver, 2002). Impacts (positive and negative) are generally discussed in categories of economy, cultural/local community and environment (Fennell, 2003; Page & Dowling, 2002; Weaver, 2002). These categories reflect those used to discuss positive and negative impacts from tourism on local communities in Table 5.5. Weaver (2002) further highlights the indirect nature of impacts: such costs from ecotourism may occur in terms of the environment (e.g., commoditization of nature), the economy (e.g., uncertainty of revenue) and socio-cultural sustainability (e.g., resentment). The international context of tourism further confounds the "realities" of ecotourism. Fennell (2003) utilizes development theory to examine relationships that exist between rich and poor countries in regards to control of development and beneficiaries of ecotourism. Weaver (2002) asserts that the manner in which positive impacts are realized and negative ones are addressed will serve as the litmus test for ecotourism.

At the start of this section it was suggested that the boundaries between outdoor recreation and ecotourism should be considered "soft." As a growing industry, ecotourism has many direct implications to outdoor recreation. Outdoor recreation and ecotourism: both depend on natural resources; may stress adventure, education, activity and stewardship; incorporate interpretation and program planning; and positively and negatively impact the natural environment. The line between outdoor recreation and ecotourism may, at times, become almost indistinguishable. Ecotourism is an important consideration for outdoor recreation because of the spatial emphasis—substantial numbers of people are being encouraged, and actively traveling to, ecologically sensitive environments. Despite the attention directed at how this is occurring:

> one of the unfortunate realities of ecotourism is that despite its altruistic intentions, to date there is little evidence that it is less intrusive than other types of tourism development. It is indeed frustrating that we continue to talk of appropriate means by which to control development, yet have very few successes to report on.
>
> (Fennell, 2003, p. 175)

Perhaps the most profitable nexus between outdoor recreation and ecotourism is in the areas of management, policy development and ethics—evidence suggests that a shared literature is emerging based on synergies between these areas (see Fennell, 2003; Hall & Page, 1999).

PHILOSOPHICAL AND ETHICAL CONSIDERATIONS IN OUTDOOR RECREATION

The issues discussed thus far in this chapter reflect the range of challenges associated with outdoor recreation confronting participants, students, and resource professionals. Beyond the relevant pragmatic and conceptual considerations that have been discussed lie questions of a more philosophical nature. Philosophy is "rationally critically thinking, of a more or less systematic kind about the general nature of the world (metaphysics or theory of existence), the justification of belief (epistemology or theory of knowledge), and the conduct of life (ethics or the theory of value)" (Honderich, 1995, p. 666). It is the third area of philosophy, theory of value, which has perhaps greatest relevance to outdoor recreation. Three key elements are associated with theories of values—morality, ethics and values. Morality, derived from Latin origins, is social in both its origins and functions and provides guidance to individuals and groups for actions (Frankena, 1963). In this manner morality is understood to refer to both patterns of conduct as well as rules of action and poses the question, "what is acceptable" (Fennell, 2006)? Ethics, Greek for *ethos* or habitual mode of conduct, has been a topic of dialogue for some 2,500 years in an effort to answer "what should one do in order to be good" (Fennell, 2006). Although some have suggested that morality and ethics ought to be used synonymously (Guy, 1990), a distinction here is made between morality, which concerns the rightness of conduct, and ethics, which concerns rules for good actions. Values also hold importance and are understood as "that which one acts to gain and/or keep" (Rand, 1964, p. 15). Values therefore may be either instrumental and linked to a cost–benefit calculation or intrinsic that are coveted for inherent reasons (Fennell, 2006). As evidenced in the discussion on environmental ethics (Chapter 3) both instrumental and intrinsic values have been articulated. The manner in which the "theory of values" is fundamental to outdoor recreation is illustrated below using each of the three key elements.

As presented in the preceding paragraph, morality is concerned with patterns of "right" conduct. So are outdoor recreation activities moral? This question has been increasingly posed to individuals participating in outdoor recreation activities that are consumptive, such as hunting. As humans evolved the importance placed on hunting declined; at present it is predominately undertaken as an outdoor recreation activity in North America. According to the United States Fish and Wildlife Service, approximately 13 million people in the United States hunted in 2001 (United States Fish and Wildlife Service, n.d.). The morality of this activity, particularly when undertaken for sport, is the source of considerable debate. Arguments about hunting, both for and against, typically take opposite positions on issues including: human instinct (biology) and social construction; the ability of animals to feel emotions; utilitarianism; human rights; ecological and ecosystem health; and human culture (Mouser, 2003; Swan, 1995). Although much attention has been directed at these arguments, questions of mortality are really fundamental. Causey indicates that "anti-hunters believe, instinctively, that it is morally wrong to kill for pleasure. Period" (1989, p. 336). Loftin

339

takes an alternative view by summarizing Aldo Leopold's position that "there is nothing intrinsically wrong with hunting, so long as it does not endanger species or degrade biotic communities the moral value or disvalue of hunting depends on how one goes about it" (1984, p. 243). The purpose here is not to resolve, or even tackle the morality of hunting, rather it is to illustrate the relevance of the question.

So what of outdoor recreation activities that utilize resources but do not consume them; are questions of morality still relevant? Consider the activity of catch-and-release fishing where anglers use human constructed materials to imitate natural food sources to trick fish into striking for the benefit of "fighting" them and upon completion release the fish. The morality of using other species has received much attention as of late, even from the most "spiritual" forms of angling. In his article, "A theology of fly fishing" Olmstead asks:

> Why fly fish? Is it "right" to treat a living creature as a plaything for amusement? Is that what I am doing? Is my fishing an act of reverence and respect? Or egocentric curiosity? To want to be in touch with and actually feel and see the beauty of these animals and share in their dimension of existence? In our drastically shrinking world can I justify this pastime? Or, is it for the very reason that our entire ecosystem, not to mention the tiny fraction of which is made up of trout streams, is being grossly ravaged for commercial purposes that our attempts at preservation are so obviously justified? Or, is all of this a cheap insincere rationalization of a "blood sport" in a day and age that prefers these con-fined to movies, video arcades, "true crime" television shows, and the overseas news?
>
> (2001, p. 4)

Such vexing questions have permeated all types of angling and various levels of discourse. In the popular literature writers such as Meredith (2000) have suggested that angling itself may be at a crossroads. In the academic literature, controversy has surrounded the promotion of bill-fishing as ecotourism. Holland, Ditton and Graefe (1998) initiated this debate in their examination of bill-fish fisheries from an ecotourism perspective. Fennell's (2000) commen-tary on the issue challenges this view that such an activity ought to be considered ecotourism, or at best be conceptualized as being located at one end of the ecotourism continuum. He pas-sionately argues that:

> what is disturbing is that although ecotourism is founded upon respect for plants and animals, somewhere along the way they have been forgotten in our attempts to define the concept. In the process, pseudo ecocultures and pseudo ecoproducts have materialized that pay only lip service to matters of the environment.
>
> (2000, p. 345)

Holland, Ditton and Graefe (2000) responded further to express concern about such increas-ingly narrow definitions of activities that are considered ecotourism.

While the activities of hunting and fishing have drawn considerable attention regarding morality, ethical questions are perhaps more broadly applicable or at least less contested in outdoor recreation. Box 10.3 tackles the question "is outdoor recreation anti-environmental?" Despite the traditional view that outdoor recreation was regarded as a relatively benign

BOX 10.3 DEBATE: IS OUTDOOR RECREATION ANTI-ENVIRONMENTAL?

YES

- Some recreation is appreciation rather than exploitation. So much recreation, however, requires altering the environment that, on balance, recreation is destructive of natural environments. Ski runs strip mountainsides, pollute streams, and require roads, airports, and other massive development. Power boats pollute water. Visitors litter everywhere. Even appreciation can turn a valley floor into virtual concrete.

- Developing recreation technologies destroy and pollute nature. Snowmobiles and off-road vehicles tear up the terrain and invade protected areas. Helicopters invade the formerly secluded mountaintops and backcountry terrain to bring sightseers and skiers. Commercial recreation providers constantly find new ways to invade natural areas with their technologies.

- Even public land is developed with long-term leases on prime locations: marinas, ski and fishing resorts, bike and horse rentals, and concessions at viewpoints. Business investment requires long-term commitments on the part of public managers. Development, once installed, can never be restored.

- The purpose of recreation investment is to maximize profits. That means using the resource to attract the largest sustainable number of users at the maximum market price. The natural resource then, becomes a means to a greater end. It is not surprising that recreation interests increasingly form coalitions with those who have other commercial purposes for public land and water against conservation restrictions. The value order becomes use first and conservation second.

- Recreation is invasive, even when regulated. Even small groups in the wilderness leave their signs of invasion. Wildlife habitats are disrupted even by photographers. Fires may get out of control. Rescue operations are massive and mechanized. Recovery in some especially fragile areas is slow. Tire tracks in the desert may last a century.

- Even "leave no trace" users leave some impacts, especially when employing the latest backpacking gear and organized by commercial "experience-providing" businesses that return to the same trails and sites over and over.

- Management becomes more political than scientific. Those with the most influence, however purchased, in legislative and administrative bodies tend to get their way. Where is the old-growth forest, the unpolluted stream, or the undeveloped beach? The assumption in the United States that there is always more land is no longer tenable. Conservation requires saying "no" to some recreation.

NO

- Those who know and use natural resources for recreation are often the strongest supporters of preservation. Environmental organizations have hikers, campers, and other appreciative recreationists as a major source of membership and funding. Recreational use helps build support for conservation of wildlands.

■ Recreation can be located in places where the activity is appropriate to the resource. Such location is a matter of planning and management that takes the environment into account. Unique environments can be protected. Cars can be banned from the Yosemite valley and the Grand Canyon rim. Development can be placed at a safe distance from water. It is not recreation but bad planning that is poorly enforced that is the problem.

■ There are millions of acres of land available. There is space for a variety of recreational uses and for preservation.

■ Many recreation uses are educational. For example, family camping and hiking will help children become adults who care about the natural environment and may be willing to support political action.

■ Recreation provides a variety of ways to experience natural environments. There is at least some appreciation even in intensive uses such as skiing or extractive uses such as hunting and fishing.

■ Land and water use can be regulated through licensing and access restrictions. It is better to regulate than to close off so many resources that many will break the law and use the resources in destructive ways. Regulated use also permits education for conservation.

■ Recreation is often the best alternative to other activity such as tree-cutting, mining, grazing, and other extraction. Recreation also provides an alternative economic basis for communities being turned away from extraction.

■ Intelligent recreation planning will not destroy the resource that attracts business. Major investments have a time frame for recovery and profit that support unpolluted water and attractive scenery.

form of resource use, it is now well established that all outdoor recreation activities have some form of impact on the natural environment (Hall & Page, 1999; Hammitt & Cole, 1998). The forms and extent of these impacts were presented earlier. It is important to critically question the relationship between outdoor recreation and the natural environment.

Ethical considerations have accompanied acknowledgment of these impacts and raise critical questions as to how individuals ought to conduct themselves when in the out-of-doors. As suggested in the initial examination of the term ethics, these often manifest themselves in guides or rules for behavior. Codes of ethics are "a set of guiding principles which govern the behaviour of the target group in pursuing their activity of interest" (The British Columbia Ministry of Development, Industry, and Trade, 1991; as cited in Fennell, 1999). Fennell (1999) has provided extensive commentary on these in the realm of ecotourism. Codes of ethics are also evident in outdoor recreation. Perhaps the best known of these are the Leave No Trace (LNT) guidelines (see Box 10.4) which specify how one ought to act during outdoor recreation activities. While the LNT code of ethics is broadly applicable to a number of activities (e.g., camping, hiking, mountain-biking), codes of ethics have also been advanced for particular activities and locations.

BOX 10.4 LEAVE NO TRACE PRINCIPLES

The Leave No Trace Principles of outdoor ethics form the framework of Leave No Trace's message:

1. Plan Ahead and Prepare
2. Travel and Camp on Durable Surfaces
3. Dispose of Waste Properly
4. Leave What You Find
5. Minimize Campfire Impacts
6. Respect Wildlife
7. Be Considerate of Other Visitors

1. Plan Ahead and Prepare
   - Know the regulations and special concerns for the area you'll visit.
   - Prepare for extreme weather, hazards, and emergencies.
   - Schedule your trip to avoid times of high use.
   - Visit in small groups. Split larger parties into groups of 4–6.
   - Repackage food to minimize waste.
   - Use a map and compass to eliminate the use of marking paint, rock cairns or flagging.

2. Travel and Camp on Durable Surfaces
   - Durable surfaces include established trails and campsites, rock, gravel, dry grasses or snow.
   - Protect riparian areas by camping at least 200 feet from lakes and streams.
   - Good campsites are found, not made. Altering a site is not necessary.
   - In popular areas:
       - Concentrate use on existing trails and campsites.
       - Walk single file in the middle of the trail, even when wet or muddy.
       - Keep campsites small. Focus activity in areas where vegetation is absent.
   - In pristine areas:
       - Disperse use to prevent the creation of campsites and trails.
       - Avoid places where impacts are just beginning.

3. Dispose of Waste Properly
   - Pack it in, pack it out. Inspect your campsite and rest areas for trash or spilled foods. Pack out all trash, leftover food, and litter.
   - Deposit solid human waste in catholes dug 6 to 8 inches deep at least 200 feet from water, camp, and trails. Cover and disguise the cathole when finished.
   - Pack out toilet paper and hygiene products.
   - To wash yourself or your dishes, carry water 200 feet away from streams or lakes and use small amounts of biodegradable soap. Scatter strained dishwater.

4. Leave What You Find
   ■ Preserve the past: examine, but do not touch, cultural or historic structures and artifacts.
   ■ Leave rocks, plants and other natural objects as you find them.
   ■ Avoid introducing or transporting non-native species.
   ■ Do not build structures, furniture, or dig trenches.

5. Minimize Campfire Impacts
   ■ Campfires can cause lasting impacts to the backcountry. Use a lightweight stove for cooking and enjoy a candle lantern for light.
   ■ Where fires are permitted, use established fire rings, fire pans, or mound fires.
   ■ Keep fires small. Only use sticks from the ground that can be broken by hand.
   ■ Burn all wood and coals to ash, put out campfires completely, then scatter cool ashes.

6. Respect Wildlife
   ■ Observe wildlife from a distance. Do not follow or approach them.
   ■ Never feed animals. Feeding wildlife damages their health, alters natural behaviors, and exposes them to predators and other dangers.
   ■ Protect wildlife and your food by storing rations and trash securely.
   ■ Control pets at all times, or leave them at home.
   ■ Avoid wildlife during sensitive times: mating, nesting, raising young, or winter.

7. Be Considerate of Other Visitors
   ■ Respect other visitors and protect the quality of their experience.
   ■ Be courteous. Yield to other users on the trail.
   ■ Step to the downhill side of the trail when encountering pack stock.
   ■ Take breaks and camp away from trails and other visitors.
   ■ Let nature's sounds prevail. Avoid loud voices and noises.

Ultimately morals (what is acceptable) and ethics (what is good conduct) express values (what one covets). Outdoor recreation and environmental thought are also critical here. Some of the salient paradigms that probe the human relationship with the environment were presented in Chapter 3. This too is a matter of some debate as statements of environmental values (also called environmental ethics) include instrumental arguments (e.g., sustainable development), intrinsic arguments (e.g., deep ecology), and critical perspectives on the very question (see Vogel, 2002). This proliferation of discourse has prompted Hargrove (2003) to argue that environmental ethics is overly complex and trivial. Light and Katz support this perspective as they observe:

As environmental ethics approaches its third decade it is faced with a curious problem. On the one hand, the discipline has made significant progress in the analysis of the moral relationship between humanity and the non-human world. The field has produced a wide variety of positions and theories in an attempt to derive morally justifiable and adequate environmental policies. On the other hand, it is difficult to see what practical effect the field of environmental ethics has had on the formation of environmental polity. The intramural debates of environmental philosophers, although interesting, provocative and complex, seem to have no real impact on the deliberations of environmental scientists, activists and policy-makers. The ideas within environmental ethics are, apparently, inert—like Hume's Treatise, they fall deadborn from the press.

(1996, p. 1)

Despite the above challenges, individuals passionate about the out-of-doors and its associated meanings are committed to continued enunciation of its values. One of the most recent efforts in this regard is the edited volume, *Nature and the Human Spirit: Towards an Expanded Land Management Ethic*, which extensively and eloquently articulates many of the inherent values associated with the natural environment (Driver, Dustin, Baltic, Elsner & Peterson, 1999). List and Brown urge us all to continue such explorations:

Although wolf dogs may unravel some of what we have done, we, and others, will keep returning to weave again. Ours has been but a first step in what promises to be a most interesting spiritual journey toward a deeper understanding of relationship with the Earth that sustains us.

(1999, p. 455)

EMPLOYING AN INTERDISCIPLINARY PERSPECTIVE

Outdoor recreation is a phenomenon that is "best understood by those willing to transgress the artificial barriers constructed by those who wish to segment knowledge into academic departments" (Wall, 1989, p. 4). A host of possibilities and pitfalls accompany the employment of an interdisciplinary perspective to outdoor recreation as a subject area. An interdisciplinary approach: takes a problem orientation that is well suited to the subject of outdoor recreation; realizes synergies by drawing upon multiple sources of knowledge; and offers a holistic approach commensurate with the scale and complexity of inquiry (Brewer, 1999; Manning, 1999; Savory, 1988). Students and researchers working in an interdisciplinary domain are required to negotiate institutional constraints and boundaries and reconcile disparate terminology, methods, and approaches (Brewer, 1999; Savory, 1988). They are also simultaneously faced with the challenge of understanding the breadth and depth of information (e.g., key concepts, theories, research traditions) associated with the subject as well as having an understanding of interdisciplinary inquiry (Mitchell, 1989).

This text communicates the breadth of information available related to the subject of outdoor recreation. It also conveys the potential depth of research investigations conducted on various aspects of the subject. An interdisciplinary perspective was developed in the introduction as a logical and timely approach to the subject of outdoor recreation. A framework (Figure I.2) was provided to assist readers in conceptualizing the phenomenon and to illustrate important connections in pursuing the problem domain of outdoor recreation. This higher order concept serves as a common purpose to coordinate knowledge areas from which the phenomenon has been addressed, applied areas of study and practice, and contemporary issues.

One of the greatest challenges to employing an interdisciplinary perspective to outdoor recreation is the ability to focus on the problem domain and combine understanding across levels of the framework in a meaningful way. Opportunities for innovation and insights reside at the interface among one or more areas of focus (Atkins, 2004; Mitchell, 1989). The holistic vantage offered by an interdisciplinary perspective comes from integrating and synthesizing knowledge (Brewer, 1995; Savory, 1998). Combing areas of focus and transcending levels in the conceptual framework are important steps to more fully appreciate outdoor recreation. The following case is described using the interdisciplinary perspective to demonstrate how an enriched understanding of outdoor recreation may be gained.

The Grand River watershed encompasses 6,800 sq. km of southern Ontario, Canada. Despite the mainly rural (93%) character of this region, considerable development pressures are evident as the population (800,000) is expected to increase by 30% in the next 20 years (Nelson, 2004; Veale, 2004). The Grand River itself is 300 km in length and was designated as a Canadian Heritage River for its exceptional cultural and recreational attributes (Nelson, 2004). As a reflection of the shared jurisdiction for management of natural resources and land use in Canada, all levels of government (federal, provincial, municipal) have varying degrees of responsibility for resources within the watershed. In the province of Ontario watersheds are utilized as an additional unit of management as established under the Conservation Authorities Act. The Grand River Conservation Authority (GRCA) was formed in 1966. The mission of the GRCA is to "develop and implement programs, directly or with our partners, to improve water quality, reduce flood damages, maintain a reliable water supply, facilitate watershed planning, protect natural areas and biodiversity, and provide environmental education" (2007, online). The Grand Strategy is the major strategic planning mechanism of the GRCA and involves ongoing collaboration between the GRCA and its many partners (Veale, 2004). A land claim by Six Nations of the Grand River and their land holdings in the watershed are important contextual issues.

Within this watershed setting, the case study focuses on the approximately 20 km portion of the Grand River from the Shand Dam to the Elora Gorge. The desire to control river flow and alleviate frequent flooding and low-water conditions throughout the Grand River precipitated the construction of the Shand Dam, which was completed in 1941 and was the first multiple-purpose dam and reservoir in Canada (Mitchell & Shrubsole, 1992). Numerous outdoor recreational opportunities have resulted as a consequence of this substantial alteration of the environment. Mitchell and Shrubsole document that "although it had not been originally considered that the reservoir might provide recreational facilities, several people requested permission to establish summer camps" (1992, p. 55). This initial request has grown exponentially as today the Belwood Reservoir is a resource for cottages (land leases), boating, fishing, day-use activities (e.g., picnics, family gatherings), and windsurfing. As the dam regulates flow rates, the Grand River has become immensely popular for water-based activities including swimming, fishing, and canoeing. Characteristics of the natural environment combine with fluctuations in water flows to afford opportunities for kayaking and tubing in the Elora Gorge. The Elora Gorge campground operated by the GRCA additionally offers trails, playing fields, and overnight camping.

One of the most specialized opportunities for outdoor recreation offered in this portion of the river is fly-fishing for brown trout. In 1987 a consortium of government and angling organizations recognized the potential to create a "tailwater" fishery because of the cold water released by the Shand Dam. As a consequence of an ambitious stocking program and implementation of special angling regulations, considerable notoriety was gained in a short time as a "world-class" fishery (Bastian, 1995). Attention is specifically focused on this activity because of the attention it has gained and the research that has been conducted on it.

A series of surveys conducted from 1996 to 2006 have illuminated some of the many social and economic dimensions of this tailwater fishery (see Plummer, Kulczycki, FitzGibbon & Smith, under review, for a full summary). Since the level of use was unknown prior to 1995, a systematic stratified random sampling technique was employed in 1996. This survey revealed that approximately 6,312 individuals angled in the tailwater fishery per year. Although catching and keeping fish may influence the motivation for some anglers, findings consistently revealed that if anglers were given a choice they would release all fish. Such findings have interesting parallels to Bryan's (1977) work concerning recreation specialization and the development of angling preferences. Results also consistently indicated a high level of satisfaction with the tailwater angling experience. In 1996 and 2006 economic impact analyses were conducted in which anglers were surveyed as to their direct expenditures and the Municipal Recreation Economic Impact Model (FitzGibbon & Reid, 1987) was used to generate indirect economic impacts of the fishery. Modeling the economic impact of the tailwater fishery to the regional economy revealed contributions of \$1,052,538.48 (CDN) in 1996 and \$603,925,24 (CDN) in 2006. Feedback from a local angling store owner and guide suggested this decline was at least partially due to fewer American anglers following the events of 9/11 and SARS (Ken Collins, personal communications).

The tailwater fishery also highlights the importance of outdoor recreation management as this recreational resource was essentially created by a consortium of government agencies and volunteers from angling groups through stocking efforts and application of special angling regulations. Success came quickly as the fishery garnered attention from outdoor recreation writers. Bastian, for example, observed that "the Grand River offers world-class brown-trout fishing comparable to the best in North America, and the river is still improving" (1995, p. 32). As the popularity of the resource increased, managers and resource users were confronted with environmental degradation, vandalism and littering; lack of locations to park safely and access the river; conflicts between anglers and some owners of property adjacent to the river; and communication of user information and education about etiquette. Enforcement of the special angling regulations and concerns about liability were additional concerns.

Responding to these issues has been an ongoing and innovative process. Fisheries management is an important part of the Grand Strategy and in that spirit it was undertaken in a collaborative and participatory fashion with leadership being shared from the province of Ontario and GRCA (Cherry, 2003). Two rounds of "townhall" meetings were held to gain input from the public and receive feedback on the proposed plan, an implementation committee was struck, and many of the specific initiatives identified have since been undertaken. A more refined plan for the specific tailwater area is currently underway. The Friends of the Grand River organization has simultaneously emerged as a civic response to some of these issues. The Friends of the Grand River exist to "develop, promote and implement Projects which will preserve, conserve and enhance the ecology of the Grand River watershed" (Friends of the Grand River, 2007, online). Over the last years the group has diligently undertaken stewardship projects, stocked fish, improved access points along the reach of river, and enhanced awareness and communication through brochures and interpretive signs. The collaborative relationship between the "formal" managing agencies and "informal" organizations have been the source of innovative "enforcement" and monitoring programs by citizen volunteers and shared undertaking of major events such as the Canadian Fly Fishing Championships in 2007. Such efforts appear to be paying dividends as 90% of anglers surveyed over the last ten years believe managing agencies are doing a "good job" (Plummer et al., under review).

Extensible benefits are realized from the tailwater fishery. The activity of fly-fishing and natural setting afford a recreational opportunity from which many individuals derive satisfaction. Quantitative measures of satisfaction above were confirmed by qualitative responses. A respondent in the 2006 survey shared that "I love this area! [It is an] undiscovered treasure" (Plummer et al., under review). Many forms of benefits (economic impact, fulfillment of management mandates, civic pride, opportunities for fulfillment) are realized by the surrounding communities and management agencies. Moreover, the environmental quality of this portion of the river has improved considerably (GRCA, 2001). Many of the activities directly or indirectly related to the tailwater fishery contribute to a sense of environmental stewardship and/or appreciation of the resource.

Applying an interdisciplinary lens to consider this case is useful because it prompts recognition of many of the core elements conveyed throughout each of the levels in Figure I.2. It also highlights the importance of interconnections among the elements within a level. For example, the human-modified environmental conditions associated with building of the Shand Dam had a cascading affect and created recreational opportunities. The specific activity of fly-fishing and setting attributes led to considerable satisfaction from particular individuals as well as resulted in considerable economic impacts. Equally important are interconnections among the different levels. In the above case, management both shaped the provision of opportunities as well as responding extensively to the needs of the resource users and adjacent communities. The application of technology that permits volunteers to communicate with conservation officers is a positive example of an emerging issue. Most importantly, the interdisciplinary perspective conveys a holistic picture of the situation. Integrative synergies were realized in the above case as resource users worked with anglers and citizens to realize recreational opportunities afforded by the environmental conditions. Consistent with a holistic view, the above case is "more than the sum of its parts." Failure to consider any of the specific elements (e.g., environment, economics, interpretive signs) as well as interconnections among them (e.g., collaborative planning, contributions by citizen organizations) considerably reduces understanding of the system functioning and associated benefits. The above case purposefully focused on a small scale and on one primary activity. Adding multiple activities, accounting for competing resource uses, and considering other scales adds magnitudes of complexity. Although an interdisciplinary perspective may appear to be a daunting task it offers considerable opportunities and insights.

SUMMARY

This chapter raised some of the salient emerging issues in outdoor recreation today. These included integration and accessibility, professional certification, technology, ecotourism, philosophy and ethics, and an interdisciplinary outlook. Each issue was initially described with a relatively broad scope and specific considerations were explored in terms of both study and practice.

A few additional observations are warranted from the discussion of outdoor recreation issues. Outdoor recreation is a function of human behavior and therefore should always be considered in the context of human society. This means that issues facing outdoor recreation are inextricably linked to more pervasive issues confronting society. Issues addressed throughout this text (e.g., environmental change, governance, education, liability) and in this chapter (e.g., integration, technology, ethics, knowledge development) are equally relevant to many aspects of the contemporary society. These issues are often interrelated and inherently complex. It is also important to recognize that these issues are a result of human action and/or inaction. Solace is gained here from the issues of professional conduct, philosophy and ethics. Ultimately, humans must address their conduct in order to address more fundamental change towards the natural environment and other participants in outdoor recreation.

KEY CONCEPTS

An interdisciplinary approach
Consumptive recreation
Ecotourism
Environmental ethics
Ethics
Inclusive recreation
Leave No Trace Principles
Morality

Rescue-free wilderness
Technological impacts (positive and negative)
Technology
The ecotourism continuum
Therapeutic recreation
Types of nature-based tourism
Values

SUGGESTED KEY SOURCES FOR MORE INFORMATION

Driver, B. L., Dustin, D., Baltic, T., Elsner, G. & Peterson, G. (Eds.). (1999). *Nature and the human spirit: Toward an expanded land management ethic.* State College, PA: Venture.
Fennell, D. A. (2003). *Ecotourism* (2nd ed.). New York: Routledge.
Fennell, D. A. (2006). *Tourism ethics.* Clevedon: Channel View.
Kelly, J. R. & Freysinger, V. J. (2000). *21st century leisure current issues.* Needham Heights, MA: Allyn & Bacon.
McKibben, B. (1999). *The end of nature.* New York: Anchor Books.
National Parks and Recreation Association http://www.nrpa.org
Ryan, S. (2002). Cyborgs in the woods. *Leisure Sciences, 21,* 265–284.
The International Ecotourism Society www.ecotourism.org
The Journal of Ecotourism http://www.multilingual-matters.com

349

REVIEW QUESTIONS

1. Explain some important considerations when conducting outdoor recreation programs as therapy.
2. Professional status within recreation has been a point of debate in leisure studies, with therapeutic recreation moving towards this approach. Take a position on the debate and explain either why outdoor recreation should or should not become a profession.
3. Differentiate accreditation from certification.
4. Identify and describe four implications of technology for outdoor recreation.
5. The use of technology in the wilderness is rapidly increasing. Does the use of technology change the meaning of the wilderness experience?
6. How are "hard" ecotourists different from "soft" ecotourists?
7. Morality and ethics is usually the domain of philosophers. Why are morality and ethics of interest to those studying outdoor recreation?
8. Leave No Trace guidelines have been advanced as a way for people to act while participating in outdoor recreation activities. Identify and describe these seven guidelines.
9. What can be gained from employing an interdisciplinary perspective?
10. Select a geographic place in which outdoor recreation activities are evident. Explain how you would employ an interdisciplinary perspective.

Conclusion

OBJECTIVES

This chapter will:

- reflect upon the main message of this book;
- consider potential future avenues that may appeal to the reader.

Most people are intuitively familiar with the concept of outdoor recreation and may actively participate in outdoor pursuits or be employed in a related field. Thinking about outdoor recreation in a formal or systematic manner is a central premise of this text. The progressive development of knowledge and practice regarding outdoor recreation has lead to realization of its interdisciplinary nature (Manning, 1999; Wall, 1989).

The interdisciplinary framework developed throughout this book provides a structure to logically consider the phenomenon of outdoor recreation. It raises the specter of innovative possibilities because it focuses on solving problems, adds value by combining knowledge from multiple disciplines, and offers an appropriate scale for holistic considerations (Brewer, 1995, 1999; Savory, 1988). A pressing issue for those involved in outdoor recreation is to understand the whole (which is greater than the sum of the parts) and the linkages among the various parts.

THE JOURNEY AHEAD

Three future paths emerge from exploring outdoor recreation from an interdisciplinary perspective—further education and research, "professional" practice, and personal enjoyment. Each has been a recurring theme throughout this text. And, thankfully for those who wish to pursue more than one, the paths are not mutually exclusive. They can be explored together and enrich the experience of the pursuant.

You may be reading this book in association with a formal course of study at a college or university or as a self-directed investigation to gain knowledge about outdoor recreation. If we accept that the goal of education is to "free students to explore, for a lifetime, the possibilities and limits of the human intellect" (Jernstedt, 1995, p. 109), then learning about outdoor recreation is a valid and necessary part of education. The need to acquire such knowledge is emphasized by its role in human development and the pervasiveness of participation in outdoor activities. History demonstrates that outdoor recreation activities have become an engrained part of our human heritage and that our sense of adventure may partially account for the success of our species (Csikszentmihalyi & Csikszentmihalyi, 1990). Recent statistics reveal that 94.5% of people in the United States participate in some form of outdoor recreation activity at least once a year (Cordell et al., 1999).

This book conveys a fraction of the existing knowledge regarding outdoor recreation. It aims to familiarize readers with salient concepts, introduce the scope of the subject area, and give insight into the manner in which research has advanced knowledge. Recognizing the limitations of this text are important because they acknowledge there is much more to learn. Readers are encouraged to pursue aspects of interest.

Complementing the acquisition of knowledge is the process of inquiry that generates it. Specialized research undertaken during advanced study and reported in scholarly journals was presented throughout this text to both support assertions and give insight where appropriate. In his recent work, *Studies in Outdoor Recreation*, Manning observes that:

> research in outdoor recreation has, then, evolved in the classic manner of most emerging fields of study. Most early studies were descriptive and exploratory, substituting data for theory, and were disciplinary-based. An expanding database allowed more conceptual and analytical developments, and ultimately a more multidisciplinary and interdisciplinary approach.
>
> (1999, p. 8)

The above quotation makes clear the analytical advancement of outdoor recreation research and the appropriateness of the interdisciplinary approach taken in this book. Both are signs of a maturing area of study. But much work remains as outdoor recreation research is a relatively "young" field of study. Energy, enthusiasm and optimism are inherent virtues of youth that propel forward outdoor recreation research in new and exciting ways. Young scholars initiating research are encouraged to embrace the benefits and challenges that come with conducting interdisciplinary investigations.

A second evident path is that of "professional" practice. The term professional is distinguished to convey that although outdoor recreation does not currently have professional status evidence suggests that it may be moving in such a direction. Individuals come to be gainfully employed in jobs related to outdoor recreation through both chance and design. An individual may follow the typical progression from camper, to leader in training, and subsequent camp counselor, with little thought that a career path is developing. Conversely, another individual may purposefully pursue an undergraduate degree in outdoor recreation and a master's degree in planning to complement his/her employment experience with a land-management agency and in so doing work towards his/her goal of being a professional planner. Manning (1999) observes that the inherent diversity in outdoor recreation is one of its most distinctive characteristics. This is especially apparent in the array of employment opportunities related to outdoor recreation. A multitude of positions are directly associated with each of the applied areas described in this book including: outdoor recreation management, parks, outdoor education, interpretation, and adventure. Knowledge, skills and experience gained pertaining to outdoor recreation, however, do not limit one to pursue a career in the above domains. The skill set developed through most college and university programs is highly transferable and provides a basis to pursue related endeavors. These may include environmental planning, traditional forms of education, business, resource management, consulting, and research. Given the increasing demand for outdoor recreation opportunities, rising pressures being asserted on natural areas, and the breadth of the sectors charged with meeting demand and protecting the environment (government, private, non-government/voluntary) the outlook for postings is good. Financial incentives commensurate with levels of education and experience complement the personal rewards associated with working in outdoor recreation.

The final path that emerges is one of active participation in outdoor recreation activities during an individual's leisure. This is an appropriate place to conclude as the path is littered with potential pitfalls and rewards. Although once considered relatively benign, the potential for outdoor recreation to negatively impact both the experiences of other people as well as the integrity of the natural environment is now established (Pigram & Jenkins, 1999). In venturing into nature without due respect for such ecosystems outdoor recreation may be viewed as part of human domination of the natural world. In his draconian but fair account, appropriately titled *The End of Nature*, McKibben writes:

> The important thing to remember is that the end of nature is not an impersonal event, like an earthquake. It is something we humans have brought about through a series of conscious and unconscious choices: *we* ended the natural atmosphere, and hence the natural climate, and hence the natural boundaries of the forests, and so on. In so doing we exhibit a kind of power thought in the past to be divine (much as we do by genetically altering life).
>
> (1999, p. 78)

Such perspectives challenge us to consider the moral and ethical implications of outdoor recreation. However, outdoor recreation also provides a means to re-connect and think about the human relationship with the natural environment. An explicit goal of outdoor recreation is to foster a sense of stewardship. Outdoor education and interpretation play a particularly important role in this regard as they aim to develop understanding, reveal underlying meaning, foster appreciation, and ultimately instil a sense of responsibility toward the natural environment.

Outdoor recreation activities are often undertaken with family and friends and serve to strengthen social bonds. Interest in a particular outdoor pursuit may also give opportunity to meet others who share your passion. Numerous organizations and clubs exist with an outdoor recreation focus that transcends traditional societal barriers such as age, race and gender. While reducing such constraints requires constant vigilance, outdoor recreation activities may be inclusive and undertaken throughout the life course.

Immense personal benefits come from participating in outdoor recreation activities. The experience desired and potential benefits received have been explained in different ways throughout the text. In some instances an adventurous experience may be desired in which

353

personal abilities are matched to demands of the environment. In other situations quiet contemplation is pursued for personal introspection and spiritual enlightenment. Across these enterprises, it is evident that participation in outdoor recreation is often intrinsically motivated and provides a platform to realize flow. It is this magical feeling that attracts people to the outdoors.

Bibliography

Absolon, M. (1995). Paul tells his story. *The Leader*. Retrieved April 17, 2007, from http://www.nols.edu/alumni/leader/95fall/paultellshisstory.shtml

Ajzen, I. (1985). From intentions to actions: A theory of planned behaviour. In J. Kuhl & J. Beckmann (Eds.), *Action-control: From cognition to behaviour* (pp. 11–39). Heidelberg, Germany: Springer.

Ajzen, I. & Fishbein, M. (1980). *Understanding attitudes and predicting social behaviour*. Englewood Cliffs, NJ: Prentice Hall.

Allen, G. (1998). Modern management supervision. Available online: http://ollie.dcccd.edu/mgmt1374/look_contents/3organizing/commun/communic.htm

Anderson, H. A. (1986). *The chief*. College Station, TX: Texas A & M Press.

Anderson, L. & Kress, C. B. (2003). *Inclusion: Including people with disabilities in parks and recreation opportunities*. State College, PA: Venture.

Anderson, M. A., Stewart, M. H., Yates, M. V. & Gerba, C. P. (1998). Modeling the impact of body-contact recreation on pathogen concentrations in a source drinking water reservoir. *Water Research, 32*(11), 3293–3306.

Anderson, S. T. & West, S. E. (2006). Open space, residential property values, and spatial context. *Regional Science and Urban Economics, 36*(6), 773–789.

Arai, S. M. (2000). Typology of volunteers for a changing sociopolitical context: The impact on social capital, citizenship and civil society. *Society and Leisure, 23*(2), 327–352.

Archer, B. (1982). The value of multipliers and their policy implications. *Tourism Management, 3*(3), 236–241.

Ardrey, R. (1976). *The hunting hypothesis: A personal conclusion concerning the evolutionary nature of man*. New York: Atheneum.

Arms, K. (1990). *Environmental science*. Philadelphia: Saunders College Publishing.

Aronson, E., Wilson, T. D., Akert, R. M. & Fehr, B. (2001). *Social psychology* (2nd Canadian ed.). Toronto: Prentice Hall.

Atkins, P. (2004). Interdisciplinarity and personality. *Interdisciplinary Science Reviews, 29*(1), 2–5.

Atlas of Canada (2007). Retrieved April 21, 2007, from http://atlas.nrcan.gc.ca

Attarian, A. (2001). Trends in outdoor adventure education. *The Journal of Experiential Education, 24*(3), 141–149.

Australian Bureau of Statistics. (2002). *ABS culture, sport, and recreation statistics: Current activities and future strategy*. Sydney, Australia: Australian Bureau of Statistics.

Australian Bureau of Statistics. (2007). *Participation in sports and physical recreation, Australia, 2005–2006* (Report No. 4177.0). Sydney, Australia: Australian Bureau of Statistics.

Australian Government Department of Family and Community Services. (2005). *Giving Australia: Research on philanthropy in Australia*. Canberra, ACT: Author.

Backman, K. F., Wicks, B. & Silverberg, K. E. (1997). Coproduction of recreation services. *Journal of Parks and Recreation Administration, 15*(3), 58–75.

Baltic, T. (1999). Technology and the evolution of land ethics. In B. L. Driver, D. Dustin, T. Baltic, G. Elsner & G. Peterson (Eds.), *Nature and the human spirit: Toward an expanded land management ethic* (pp. 263–276). State College, PA: Venture.

Bammel, G. & Burrus-Bammel, L. L. (1990). Outdoor/environmental education. *Journal of Physical Education, Recreation and Dance, 61*(4), 49–54.

Bandura, A. (1977). *Social learning theory.* Englewood Cliffs, N.J: Prentice Hall.

Bandura, A. (1998). *Social foundations of thought and action: A social cognitive theory.* Englewood Cliffs, NJ: Prentice Hall.

Baron, R. A., Earhard, B. & Ozier, M. (1998). *Psychology* (2nd Canadian ed.). Scarborough, ON: Prentice Hall.

Bastian, D. (1995). Ontario's grand river. *Fly Fisherman, 26*(6), 33–35; 73–77.

Baumert, K. A. & Kete, N. (2002). Introduction: An architecture for climate protection. In K. A. Baumert, O. Blanchard, S. Llosa & J. F. Perkins (Eds.), *Building on the Kyoto Protocol: Options for protecting the climate.* [no place listed]: The World Resources Institute.

Baym, N. (1995) (Ed.). *The Norton anthology American literature.* New York: W. W. Norton & Company.

Beck, L. & Cable, T. (2002). *Interpretation for the 21st century: Fifteen guiding principles for interpreting nature and culture* (2nd ed.). Champaign, IL: Sagamore.

Beeler, C. S. (1999). Recreation and park agencies. In H. K. Cordell (Ed.), *Outdoor recreation in American life: A National assessment of demand and supply trends* (pp. 124–130). Champaign, IL: Sagamore.

Bell, S. (1997). *Design for outdoor recreation.* London: Spon Press.

Belshaw, C. (2001). *Environmental philosophy: Reason, nature and human concern.* Montreal: McGill-Queen's University Press.

Berg, L., Fenge, T. & Dearden, P. (1993). The role of aboriginal people in national park designation, planning, and management in Canada. In P. Dearden & R. Rollins (Eds.), *Parks and protected areas in Canada: Planning and management* (pp. 225–255). Toronto: Oxford University Press.

Berkes, F. & Farvar, M. T. (1989). Introduction and overview. In F. Berkes (Ed.), *Common property resources: Ecology and community-based sustainable development* (pp. 1–17). London: Belhaven Press.

Berkes, F. & Folke, C. (1998). Linking social and ecological systems for resilience and sustainability. In F. Berkes & C. Folke (Eds.), *Linking social and ecological systems: management practices and social mechanisms for building resilience* (pp. 1–27). New York: Cambridge University Press.

Betz, C. J., English, D. B. K. & Cordell, H. K. (1999). Outdoor recreation resources. In H. K. Cordell, B. L. McDonald, R. J. Teasley, J. C. Bergstrom, J. Martin, J. Bason & V. R. Leeworthy (Eds.), *Outdoor recreation in American life: A national assessment of demand and supply trends* (pp. 39–182). Champaign, IL: Sagamore.

Bigg, G. (2003). *The oceans and climate* (2nd ed.). Cambridge: Cambridge University Press.

Bird, F. E. & Germaine, G. R. (1987). *Practical loss control leadership: The conservation of people, property, process and profits.* Loganville, GA: Institute Publishing.

Bixler, R. & Morris, B. (1998). *The role of outdoor capital in the socialization of wildland recreationists.* Proceedings of the 1997 Northeastern Recreation Research Symposium. USDA Forest Service General Technical Report NE-241, 237–242.

Blackwood, P. E. (1973). Outdoor education and the discovery approach to learning. In D. R. Hammerman & W. M. Hammerman (Eds.), *Outdoor education a book of readings* (pp. 114–118). Minneapolis, MN: Burgess.

Bloom, B. S. (Ed.). (1987). *Taxonomy of educational objectives: Book 1 cognitive domain.* New York: Longman.

Blumer, H. (1970). Sociological implications of the thought of George Herbert Mead. In G. P. Stone & H. A. Farberman (Eds.), *Social psychology through symbolic interactionism* (pp. 282–293). Toronto: Xerox College Publishing.

Boeker, E. (1995). *Environmental physics.* West Sussex, England: John Wiley & Sons.

Bolitzer, B. & Netusil, N. R. (2000). The impact of open spaces on property values in Portland, Oregon. *Journal of Environmental Management, 59*(3), 185–193.

Booth, K. L. & Simmons, D. G. (2000). Tourism and the establishment of national parks in New Zealand. In R. W. Butler & S. W. Boyd (Eds.), *Tourism and national parks: Issues and implications* (pp. 39–49). New York: John Wiley & Sons.

Boren, C. (1977). *Roman society.* Lexington, MA: D. C. Health and Company.

Botkin, D. B. & Keller, E. A. (1995). *Environmental science: Earth as a living planet.* New York: John Wiley & Sons.

Bowker, J. M., Cordell, H. K. & Johnson, C. Y. (1999a). User fees for recreation services on public lands: A national assessment. *Journal of Parks and Recreation Administration, 7*(1), 1–14.

356

Bowker, J. M., English, D. B. K. & Cordell, H. K. (1999B). Projections of outdoor recreation participation to 2050. In H. K. Cordell, B. L. McDonald, R. J. Teasley, J. C. Bergstrom, J. Martin, J. Bason & V. R. Lee-worthy (Eds.), *Outdoor recreation in American life: A national assessment of demand and supply trends* (pp. 223–350). Champaign, IL: Sagamore.

Boy Scouts of America. (2007). *Boy Scouts of America*. Retrieved April 17, 2007, from http://www.scouting.org

Boyd, D. R. (2002). *Wild by law: A report card on laws governing Canada's parks and protected areas, and a blueprint for making these laws more effective*. Victoria, BC: The Polis Project on Ecological Governance, University of Victoria.

Boyd, S. W. & Butler, R. W. (1996). Managing ecotourism: An opportunity spectrum approach. *Tourism Management, 17*(8), 557–566.

Boyd, S. W. & Butler, R. W. (2000). Tourism and national parks: The origin of the concept. In R. W. Butler & S. W. Boyd (Eds.), *Tourism and national parks: Issues and implications* (pp. 13–27). New York: John Wiley & Sons.

Braithwaite, R. (1998). Conservation biology: a fool's errand or an inadequate paradigm. In N. W. P. Munro & J. H. M. Willison (Eds.), *Linking protected areas with working landscapes conserving biodiversity* (pp. 36–50). Wolfville, NS: Science and Management of Protected Areas Association.

Brennan, S. & Miles, J. C. (2003). National parks, wilderness, and protected areas in the United States. In. J. G. Nelson, J. C. Day & L. Sportza (Eds.), *Protected areas and the regional planning imperative in North America* (pp. 45–60). Calgary, AB: University of Calgary Press.

Brewer, G. D. (1995). Environmental challenges: Interdisciplinary opportunities and new ways of doing business. The 1995 MISTRS Lecture. Stockholm: MISTRA.

Brewer, G. D. (1999). The challenges of interdisciplinarity. *Policy Sciences, 32*, 327–337.

Brewer, G. D. (1988). *The science of ecology*. Philadelphia: Saunders College.

Bricker, K. S. & Kerstetter, D. L. (2002). An interpretation of special place meanings whitewater recreationists attach to the South Fork of the American River. *Tourism Geographies, 4*(4), 396–426.

Brockman, C. F. & Merriam Jr., L. C. (1979). *Recreational use of wild lands* (3rd ed.). New York: McGraw-Hill.

Brotherton, D. (1973). The concept of carrying of countryside recreation areas. *Recreation News Supplement, 9*, 6–11.

Brown, P. (1981). Psychological benefits of outdoor recreation. In J. Kelly (Ed.), *Social benefits of outdoor recreation*. Champaign, IL: University of Illinois Press.

Brown, T. J. (1999). Adventure risk management. In J. C. Miles & S. Priest (Eds.), *Adventure programming* (pp. 273–284). State College, PA: Venture.

Brunson, M. & Shelby, B. (1993). Recreation substitutability: A research agenda. *Leisure Sciences, 15*, 67–74.

Bryan, H. (1977). Leisure value systems and recreation specialization: The case of trout fishermen. *Journal of Leisure Research, 9*(3), 174–187.

Bryan, H. (1979). *Conflict in the great outdoors: Toward understanding and managing for diverse sportsmen preferences*. Birmingham, AL: Bureau of Public Administration, University of Alabama.

Bryan, R. (1972). *Much is taken, much remains*. Scitate, MA: Duxbary Press.

Buckley, R. (2000). Neat trends: Current issues in nature, eco- and adventure tourism. *International Journal of Tourism Research, 2*, 437–444.

Budwig, L. (1997). *Breaking nature's silence: Pennsylvania's Rachel Carson*. Retrieved April 17, 2007, from http://www.depweb.state.pa.us/heritage/cwp/view.asp?a=3&Q=442627

Bultena, G. & Taves, M. (1961). Changing wilderness images and forest policy. *Journal of Forestry, 59*(3), 167–171.

Burch Jr., E. S. (2004). The caribou Inuit. In R. B. Morrison & C. R. Wilson (Eds.), *Native peoples: The Canadian experience* (pp. 74–96). Toronto: Oxford University Press.

Burch Jr., W. (1964). Two concepts for guiding recreation decisions. *Journal of Forestry, 62*, 707–712.

Burdge, R. & Field, D. (1972). Methodological perspectives for the study of outdoor recreation. *Journal of Leisure Research, 4*(1), 63–72.

Butler, R. W. (2000). Tourism and national parks in the twenty-first century. In R. W. Butler & S. W. Boyd (Eds.), *Tourism and national parks: Issues and implications* (pp. 323–335). New York: John Wiley & Sons.

Butler, J. R. & Hvenegaard, G. T. (2002). Interpretation and environmental education. In P. Dearden &

R. Rollins (Eds.), *Parks and protected areas in Canada: Planning and management* (2nd ed.) (pp. 178–203). Don Mills, ON: Oxford University Press.

Campbell, R. & Hunter, B. (2000). *Moral epistemology naturalized.* Calgary, AB: University of Calgary Press.

Canada Land Inventory. (2000). *Canada Land Inventory (CLI).* Retrieved May 14, 2007, from http://geogratis.cgdi.gc.ca/CLI/frames.html

Canadian Parks and Wilderness Society. (2005, Spring). *Canadian wilderness.* Ottawa, ON: Canadian Parks and Wilderness Society.

Carr, D. S. & Williams, D. R. (1993). Understanding the role of ethnicity in outdoor recreation experiences. *Journal of Leisure Research, 25*(1), 22–38.

Carson, R. (1962). *Silent spring.* Boston: Houghton Mifflin.

Castro, A. P. & Nielsen, E. (2001). Indigenous people and co-management: Implications for conflict management. *Environmental Science and Policy, 4*, 229–239.

Catano, V. M., Pond, M. & Kelloway, E. K. (2001). Exploring commitment and leadership in volunteer organizations. *Leadership & Organization, 22*(6), 256–263.

Cater, E. (1994). Introduction. In E. Cater & G. Lowman (Eds.), *Ecotourism: A sustainable option?* (pp. 3–17). Milton, Queensland: John Wiley & Sons.

Cater, E. (2003). Between the devil and the deep blue sea: Dilemmas for marine ecotourism. In B. Garrod & J. C Wilson. (2003), *Marine ecotourism: Issues and experiences* (pp. 37–47). Clevedon, England: Channel View.

Caughley, G. & Sinclair, A. R. E. (1994). *Wildlife ecology and management.* Cambridge, MA: Blackwell Science.

Causey, A. S. (1989). On the morality of hunting. *Environmental Ethics, 11*, 327–343.

Certo, S. C., Appelbaum, S. H. & Shapiro, B. (1993). *Modern management in Canada: Quality, ethics and the global environment.* Scarborough, ON: Prentice Hall.

Chape, S., Blyth, S., Fish, L., Fox, P. & Spalding, M. (2003). United Nations list of protected areas. Cambridge: UNEP–WCMC.

Chapman, S. (1992). What is the question? *The Journal of Experiential Education, 15*(2), 16–18.

Chapman, S., McPhee, P. & Proudman, B. (1992). What is experiential education? *The Journal of Experiential Education, 15*(2), 16–23.

Charron, L. (1999). An analysis of planning processes of Parks Canada. Prepared for the Panel for the Ecological Integrity of Canada's National Parks.

Cherry, D. (2003). *Process manual for the preparation of the Grand River fisheries management plan.* Cambridge, ON: Grand River Conservation Authority.

Chisholm, H. & Shaw, S. (2004). Prove it! The "tyranny" of audit and accreditation in the New Zealand outdoors industry. *Leisure Sciences, 23*(4), 317–327.

Chubb, M. & Chubb, H. R. (1981). *One third of our time? An introduction to recreation behavior and resources.* New York: John Wiley & Sons.

Chung, B. M. (1994). The taxonomy in the republic of Korea. In L. W. Anderson & L. A. Sosniak (Eds.), *Bloom's taxonomy: A forty-year retrospective* (pp. 164–173). Chicago: The University of Chicago Press.

Cicchetti, C. J. (1972). A multivariate statistical analysis of wilderness users in the United States. In J. V. Krutilla (Ed.), *Natural environments: Studies in theoretical and applied analysis* (pp. 142–170). Baltimore: The Johns Hopkins University Press.

City of Fredericton. (2004). *Recreation.* Retrieved June 4, 2004, from http://www.city.fredericton.nb.ca/eb2.asp?581

City of Fredericton. (2007). *Fredericton.* Retrieved April 19, 2007, from http://www.fredericton.ca

Clagett, A. F. (1990). Effective therapeutic wilderness camp programs for rehabilitating emotionally-disturbed, problem teenagers and delinquents. *Journal of Offender Counseling, Services and Rehabilitation, 14*(1), 79–93.

Clark, R. & Stankey, G. (1979). Control of vandalism in recreation areas—fact, fiction or folklore? *USDA Forest Service General Technical Report PSW-17*, Oregon: USDA Forest Service.

Clawson, M. (1959). The crisis in outdoor recreation. *American Forests, 65*(3), 22–31.

Clawson, M. & Knetsch, J. L. (1966). *Economics of outdoor recreation.* Baltimore: The Johns Hopkins University Press.

Clawson, M., Held, R. B. & Stoddard, C. H. (1960). *Land for the future.* Baltimore: Resources for the Future by the Johns Hopkins Press.

Clemens, M. (2004). A walk in the woods. *Scientific American, 290*(2), 92–94.

Cohen, M. P. (1988). *The history of the Sierra Club, 1892–1970*. San Francisco: Sierra Club Books.

Cole, D. N. & Monz, C. A. (2004). Spatial patterns of recreation impact on experiential campsites. *Journal of Environmental Management, 70*(1), 73–84.

Collins, J. P. & Storfer, A. (2003). Global amphibian declines: sorting the hypotheses. *Diversity and Distribution, 9*, 89–98.

Conrad, M., Finkel, A. & Jaenen, C. (1993). *History of the Canadian Peoples*. Mississauga, ON: Copp Clark Pitman.

Conway, T. (1993). *Painted dreams: Native American rock art*. Minocqua, WI: North Wood Press.

Cooper, G. (1994). The role of outdoor education in education for the 21st century. *Journal of Adventure Education and Outdoor Leadership, 11*(2), 9–12.

Cordell, H. K. (1999). Framework for the assessment. In H. K. Cordell, B. L. McDonald, R. J. Teasley, J. C. Bergstrom, J. Martin, J. Bason & V. R. Leeworth (Eds.), *Outdoor recreation in American life: A national assessment of demand and supply trends* (pp. 31–38). Champaign, IL: Sagamore.

Cordell, H. K. & Betz, C. J. (2000). Trends in outdoor recreation supply on public and private lands in the US. In W. C. Gartner & D. W. Lime (Eds.), *Trends in outdoor recreation, leisure and tourism* (pp. 75–90). Wallingford, UK: CABI Publishing.

Cordell, H. K. & Super, G. R. (2000). Trends in Americans' outdoor recreation. In W. C. Gartner & D. W. Lime (Eds.), *Trends in outdoor recreation, leisure and tourism* (pp. 133–144). Wallingford, UK: CABI Publishing.

Cordell, H. K., Betz, C. J. & Green, G. T. (2002). Recreation and environment as cultural dimensions in contemporary American society. *Leisure Sciences, 24*, 13–41.

Cordell H. K., Green, G. T. & Betz, C. J. (2002). Recreation and the environment as cultural dimensions in contemporary American society. *Leisure Sciences, 24*(1), 13–42.

Cordell, H. K., Lewis, B. & McDonald, B. L. (1995). Long-term outdoor recreation participation trends. Proceedings of *The Fourth International Outdoor Recreation and Tourism Trends Symposium and the 1995 National Recreation Resource Planning Conference*. Minneapolis: University of Minnesota, 35–38.

Cordell, H. K., McDonald, B. L., Teasley, R. J., Bergstrom, J. C., Martin, J., Bason, J. & Leeworthy, V. R. (1999). Outdoor recreation participation trends. In H. K. Cordell, B. L. McDonald, R. J. Teasley, J. C. Bergstrom, J. Martin, J. Bason & V. R. Leeworth (Eds.), *Outdoor recreation in American life: A national assessment of demand and supply trends* (pp. 219–322). Champaign, IL: Sagamore.

Costanza, R. & Folke, C. (1996). The structure and fintin of ecological systems in relation to property-right regimes. In S. S. Hanna, C. Folke & K. Mather (Eds.), *Rights to nature* (pp. 13–34). Washington, DC: Island Press.

Coward, H. (1997). Hindu spirituality and the environment. *Ecotheology, 3*, 50–60.

Coward, H., Sindu, T. & Singer, P. A. (2000). Bioethics for clinicians: 19. Hinduism and Sikhism. *Canadian Medical Journal Association, 163*(9), 1167–1171.

Craik, H. (1977). Multiple scientific paradigms in environmental psychology. *International Journal of Psychology, 12*(2), 147–158.

Crandall, R. & Lewko, J. (1976). Leisure research, present and future: Who, what, where. *Journal of Leisure Research, 8*(3), 150–159.

Crawford, D. & Godbey, G. (1987). Reconceptualizing barriers to family recreation. *Leisure Sciences, 9*(3), 119–127.

Csikszentmihalyi, M. (1975). *Beyond boredom and anxiety*. San Francisco: Jossey-Bass.

Csikszentmihalyi, M. (1988). The flow experience and its significance for human psychology. In M. Csikszentmihalyi & I. S. Csikszentmihalyi (Eds.), *Optimal experience: Studies of flow in consciousness* (pp. 15–35). Cambridge: Cambridge University Press.

Csikszentmihalyi, M. (1990). *Flow: The psychology of optimal experience*. New York: Harper & Row.

Csikszentmihalyi, M. & Csikszentmihalyi, I. S. (1990). Adventure and the flow experience. In J. C. Miles & S. Priest (Eds.), *Adventure education* (pp. 149–157). State College, PA: Venture.

Csikszentmihalyi, M. & Csikszentmihalyi, I. S. (1999). Adventure and the flow experience. In J. C. Miles & S. Priest (Eds.), *Adventure programming* (pp. 153–157). State College, PA: Venture.

Curry, N. (1994). *Countryside recreation, access and land use planning*. London: E. & F. N. Spon.

Curry, N. (2004). The divergence and coalescence of public outdoor recreation values in New Zealand and England: An interplay between rights and markets. *Leisure Studies, 23*(3), 205–223.

Curtis, J. E. (1979). *Recreation: Theory and practice*. London: C. V. Mosby Company.

Daigle, J. J., Hrubes, D. & Ajzen, I. (2002). A comparative study of beliefs, attitudes, and values among hunters, wildlife viewers, and other outdoor recreationists. *Human Dimensions of Wildlife, 7*(1), 1–20.

Davis, G. W. (1995). Playing God in endangered spaces: Perspectives of a donor. In M. Hummel (Ed.), *Protecting Canada's endangered spaces* (pp. 181–189). Toronto: Key Porter Books.

Davis-Berman, J. & Berman, D. (1999). The use of adventure-based programs with at-risk youth. In J. C. Miles & S. Priest (Eds.), *Adventure programming* (pp. 365–370). State College, PA: Venture.

Davis-Berman, J. & Berman, D. S. (1994). *Wilderness therapy: Foundations, theory and research*. Dubuque, IA: Kendall/Hunt.

DeAngelis, D. L. (1992). *Dynamics of nutrient cycling and food webs*. London: Chapman & Hall.

Dearden, P. & Rollins, R. (2002). The time they are still a changin'. In P. Dearden & R. Rollins (Eds.), *Parks and protected areas in Canada: Planning and management* (2nd ed.) (pp. 3–21). Don Mills, ON: Oxford University Press.

deGroot, R. S. (1992). *Functions of nature*. Amsterdam: Wolters-Noordhoff.

Dempsey, J., Dearden, P. & Nelson, J. G. (2002). Stewardship: Expanding ecosystem protection. In P. Dearden & R. Rollins (Eds.), *Parks and protected areas in Canada: Planning and management* (2nd ed.) (pp. 379–400). Don Mills, ON: Oxford University Press.

Dennis, S. & Zube, E. H. (1987). Voluntary association membership of outdoor recreationists: An exploratory study. *Leisure Sciences, 10*, 229–245.

DesJardins, J. R. (1993). *Environmental ethics: An introduction to environmental philosophy*. Belmont, CA: Wadsworth.

Devall, B. & Sessions, G. (1985). *Deep ecology. Living as if nature mattered*. Salt Lake City, UT: Peregrine Smith Books.

Diamond, J. (2000). Blitzkrieg against the Moas. *Science, 287*(5461), 2170–2172.

Ditton, R. B., Loomis, D. K. & Choi, S. (1992). Recreation specialization: Re-conceptualization for a social worlds perspective. *Journal of Leisure Research, 24*(1), 33–51.

Donaldson, G. W. & Donaldson, A. L. (1973). Outdoor education: Promising future. In D. R. Hammerman & W. M. Hammerman (Eds.), *Outdoor education: A book of readings* (2nd ed.) (pp. 126–135). Minneapolis: Burgess Publishing Company.

Donaldson, G. W. & Donaldson, L. E. (1958). Outdoor education: A definition. *Journal of Health, Physical Education and Recreation, 29*(17), 17–63.

Donaldson, G. W. & Vinson, R. (1995). William James, philosophical father of experience based education. In R. Kraft & M. Sakofs (Eds.), *The theory of experiential education, association for experiential education* (2nd ed.) (pp. 94–96). Boulder, CO: Association for Experiential Education.

Donnelly, M. P., Vaske, J. & Graefe, A. (1986). Degree and range of recreation specialization: Toward a typology of boating related activities. *Journal of Leisure Research, 18*(2), 81–95.

Dooling, P. J. (1985). Heritage landscapes: Rethinking the Canadian experience. *The Forestry Chronicle, 61*, 319–322.

Douglass, R. W. (1982). *Forest recreation* (3rd ed.). New York: Pergamon Press.

Downes, S. M. (2001). Some recent developments in evolutionary approaches to the study of human cognition and behavior. *Biology and Philosophy, 16*, 575–595.

Drengson, A. R. (1980). Wilderness travel as an art and as a paradigm for outdoor education. *Quest, 3*(1), 110–120.

Drengson, A. R. (1995). What means this experience? In R. Kraft & M. Sakofs (Eds.), *The theory of experiential education, Association for experiential education* (2nd ed.) (pp. 87–93). Boulder, CO: Association for Experiential Education.

Driver, B. & Brown, P. (1978). *A social-physiological definition of recreation demand, with implications for recreation resource planning*. Appendix A of Assessing demand for outdoor recreation. Washington, DC: US Bureau of Outdoor Recreation.

Driver, B. & Brown, P. (1984). Contributions of behavioural scientists to recreation resource management. In I. Altman & J. F. Wolhwill (Eds.), *Behaviour and the natural environment* (pp. 307–339). New York: Plenum Press.

Driver, B. L. & Brown, P. J. (1983). Contributions of behavioral scientists to recreation resource management. In I. Altman & J. F. Wohlwill (Eds.), *Human behavior and the environment* (pp. 307–339). New York: Plenum Publishing.

Driver, B. L. & Tocher, S. R. (1970). Towards a behavioural interpretation of recreational engagements, with implications for planning. In B. L. Driver (Ed.), *Elements of outdoor recreation planning* (pp. 9–32). Ann Arbor, MI: The University of Michigan Press.

Driver, B. L. (1972). Potential contributions of psychology to recreation resource management. In J. F. Wohlwill & D. H. Carson (Eds.), *Environment and the social sciences: Perspectives and applications* (pp. 233–249). Washington, DC: American Psychological Association.

Driver, B., Brown, P., Stankey, G. & Gregorie, T. (1987). The ROS planning system: Evolution, basic concepts and research needed. *Leisure Sciences, 9*, 201–212.

Driver, B. L., Dustin, D., Baltic, T., Elsner, G. & Peterson, G. (Eds.). (1999). *Nature and the human spirit: Toward an expanded land management ethic.* State College, PA: Venture.

Dumazedier, J. (1967). *Toward a society of leisure.* New York: The Free Press.

Dunn, D. R. & Gulbis, J. M. (1976). The risk revolution. *Parks and Recreation, 16*.

Dustin, D. L., McAvoy, L. H. & Schultz, J. H. (1996). *Stewards of access, custodians of choice: A philosophical foundation for the park and recreation profession.* Champaign, IL: Sagamore.

Dustin, D. L., Schneider, I. E., McAvoy, L. H. & Frakt, A. N. (2002). Cross-cultural claims on devils tower national monument: A case study. *Leisure Sciences, 24*, 79–88.

Eagles, P. F. J. (1993). Parks legislation in Canada. In P. Dearden & R. Rollins (Eds.), *Parks and protected areas in Canada: Planning and management* (pp. 57–74). Don Mills, ON: Oxford University Press.

Eagles, P. F. J. (2002). Environmental management. In P. Dearden & R. Rollins (Eds.), *Parks and protected areas in Canada: Planning and management* (2nd ed.) (pp. 265–294). Don Mills, ON: Oxford University Press.

Eagles, P. F. J. & Higgins, B. R. (1998). Ecotourism market and industry structure. In J. Johnson (Ed.), *Ecotourism: A guide for planners and managers* (Vol. 2) (pp. 11–44). North Bennington, VT: The Ecotourism Society.

Eagles, P. F. J. & McCool, S. F. (2002). *Tourism in national parks and protected areas planning and management.* New York: CABI Publishing.

Edginton, C. R., Hanson, C. J., Edginton, S. R. & Hudson, S. D. (1998). *Leisure programming: A service centered and benefits approach* (3rd ed.). Boston: McGraw-Hill.

Edginton, C. R., Jordan, D. J., DeGraaf, D. G. & Edginton, S. R. (1995). *Leisure and life satisfaction: Foundational perspectives.* Madison: Brown & Benchmark.

Elliott, E. B. & Smith, J. W. (1973). The Michigan program in action. In D. R. Hammerman & W. M. Hammerman (Eds.), *Outdoor education: A book of readings* (pp. 84–98). Minneapolis: Burgess.

Ellis, M. J. (1973). *Why people play.* Englewood Cliffs, NJ: Prentice Hall.

Elton, G. R. (Ed.). (1968). *Renaissance and reformation 1300–1648* (2nd ed.). London: Macmillan.

Emerson, R. W. (1969). Nature. In M. M. Seaton, Jr. & A. R. Ferguson (Eds.), *Emerson's Nature: Origin, growth and meaning* (pp. 7–38). New York: Dodd, Mead & Company.

Enger, E. D. & Smith, B. F. (1995). *Environmental science: A study of interrelationships.* Dubuque, IA: Wm. C. Brown.

Environment Canada. (1999). *The importance of nature to Canadians: Survey highlights* (Cat. No En 47–311/199E). Ottawa: Minister of Public Works and Government Services Canada.

Environment Canada. (2003). *Freshwater website quickfacts.* Retrieved May 27, 2004, from http://www.ec.gc.ca/water/en/e_quickfacts.htm

Environment Canada. (2007). *Technical supplements.* Retrieved April 21, 2007, from http://www.ec.gc.ca

Evernden, L. L. N. (1993). *The natural alien: Humankind and the environment.* Toronto: University of Toronto Press.

Ewert, A. (1987). The risk management plan: Promises and pitfalls. In J. F. Meir, T. W. Morash & G. E. Welton (Eds.), *High adventure outdoor pursuits: Organization and leadership* (pp. 412–421). Columbus, OH: Publishing Horizons.

361

Ewert, A. & Shultis, J. (1999). Technology and backcountry recreation. *The Journal of Physical Education, Recreation and Dance, 70*(8), 23–30.

Ewert, A. W., Dieser, R. B. & Voight, A. (1999). Conflict and the recreational experience. In E. L. Jackon & T. L. Burton (Eds.), *Leisure studies: Prospects for the 21st century* (pp. 335–343). State College, PA: Venture.

Ewert, A., Galloway, S. & Estes, C. A. (2001). Adventure recreation: What's new for resource managers, public policy analysts, and recreation providers. *Parks and Recreation, 36*(2), 26–34.

Ewert, A., Place, G. & Sibthorp, J. (2005). Early-life outdoor experiences and an individual's environmental attitudes. *Leisure Sciences, 27*, 225–239.

Feher, T. (2005, Spring). The idea of wilderness. *Canadian Wilderness, 2–5.*

Fennell, D. A. (1999). *Ecotourism: An introduction.* New York: Routledge.

Fennell, D. A. (2000). Comment: Ecotourism on trial—the case of billfish angling as ecotourism. *Journal of Sustainable Tourism, 8*(4), 341–345.

Fennell, D. A. (2002). *Ecotourism programme planning.* New York: CABI Publishing.

Fennell, D. A. (2003). *Ecotourism* (2nd ed.). New York: Routledge.

Fennell, D. A. (2006). *Tourism ethics.* Clevedon: Channel View.

Fennell, D. A. & Dowling, R. K. (Eds.). (2003). *Ecotourism policy and planning.* Cambridge, MA: CABI Publishing.

Finucan, S. (2002, June 30). Death on the water. *Toronto Star,* D 15.

Fishbein, M. & Ajzen, I. (1975). *Belief, attitude, intention and behaviour: An introduction to theory and research.* Reading, MA: Addison-Wesley.

FitzGibbon, J. & Reid D. (1987). An economic approach to the evaluation of municipal recreation expenditures. *Recreation Research Review, 13*(3), 22–27.

Floyd, M. F. & Johnson, C. Y. (2002). Coming to terms with environmental justice in outdoor recreation: A conceptual discussion with research implications. *Leisure Sciences, 24*(1), 59–77.

Foot, D. K. (1996). *Boom, bust & echo: how to profit from the coming demographic shift.* Toronto: MacFarland Walter & Ross.

Ford, P. & Blanchard, J. (1993). *Leadership and administration of outdoor pursuits* (2nd ed.). State College, PA: Venture.

Frakt, A. N. (1987). Adventure programming and legal liability. In J. F. Meier., T. W. Morash & G. E. Welton (Eds.), *High-adventure outdoor pursuits: Organization and leadership* (pp. 422–426). Columbus, OH: Publishing Horizons.

Frankena, W. K. (1963). *Ethics.* Englewood Cliffs, NJ: Prentice Hall.

Fridgen, J. (1991). *Dimensions of tourism.* East Lansing, MI: Educational Institute, American Hotel & Motel Association.

Friends of Algonquin Provincial Park. (n.d.). *Who are the friends of Algonquin Provincial Park?* Retrieved June 4, 2004, from http://www.algonquinpark.on.ca/friends.html

Friends of Algonquin Provincial Park. (2007). *Algonquin Provincial Park.* Retrieved April 28, 2008, from http://www.algonquinpark.on.ca/friends/index.html

Friends of the Earth. (n.d.). *Resource: Free national curriculum-based teaching resources.* Retrieved May 1, 2007, from http://www.foe.co.uk/learning/educators/resource/index.html

Friends of the Grand River. (2007). *About us.* Retrieved April 12, 2007, from www.friendsofthegrandriver.com/about.htm

Gailus, J. (2001). Yellowstone to Yukon. *Alternatives, 27*(4), 36–29.

Galloway, S. (2006). Adventure recreation reconceived: Positive forms of deviant leisure. *Leisure/Loisir, 30*(1), 219–232.

Garst, B., Schneider, I. E. & Baker, D. (2001). Outdoor adventure program participation impacts on adolescent self-perception. *Journal of Experiential Education, 24*(1), 41–49.

Gass, M. A. (1990). Transfer of Learning in adventure education. In J. C. Miles & S. Priest (Eds.), *Adventure programming* (pp. 199–208). State College, PA: Venture.

Gass, M. A. (1999a). Transfer of Learning in adventure programming. In J. C. Miles & S. Priest (Eds.), *Adventure programming* (pp. 227–233). State College, PA: Venture.

Gass, M. A. (1999b). Accreditation and certification: Questions for an advancing profession. In J. C. Miles & S. Priest (Eds.), *Adventure programming* (pp. 247–251). State College, PA: Venture.

Getz, D. (1977). The impact of tourism on host communities: A research approach. In B. S. Duffield (Ed.), *Tourism: A tool for regional development* (pp. 9.1–9.13). Edinburgh: Tourism and Recreation Research Unit, University of Edinburgh.

Gibson, H. W. (1973). The history of organized camping: establishment of institutional camps. In D. R. Hammerman & W. M. Hammerman (Eds.), *Outdoor education a book of readings* (pp. 69–76). Minneapolis: Burgess.

Gillis, H. L. & Ringer, T. M. (1999). Adventure as therapy. In J. C. Miles & S. Priest (Eds.), *Adventure programming* (pp. 29–35). State College, PA: Venture.

Gleitman, H. (1992). *Basic psychology* (3rd ed.). New York: Norton.

Gobster, P. H. (2002). Managing urban parks for a racially and ethnically diverse clientele. *Leisure Sciences, 24*, 143–159.

Godbey, G. (1999). *Leisure in your life* (5th ed.). State College, PA: Venture.

Golay, K. (1982). *Learning patters and temperament styles*. Newport Beach, CA: Manas-Systems.

Goldman, M. (1998). Inventing the commons: Theories and practices of the common's professional. In M. Goldman (Ed.), *Privatizing nature* (pp. 20–54). Piscataway, NJ: Rutgers University Press.

Goldstein, E. B. (1994). *Psychology*. Pacific Grove, CA: Brooks/Cole.

Gomez, E. (2002). The ethnicity and public recreation participation model. *Leisure Sciences, 24*, 123–142.

Gössling, S. (2002). Global environmental consequences of tourism. *Global Environmental Change, 12*, 282–302.

Gothein, M. L. (1928). *A history of garden art*. Toronto: J. M. Dent & Sons Limited.

Government of Canada. (1990). *Canada's green plan* (ISBN 0–662–18291-X). Ottawa: Minister of Supplies and Services.

Graefe, A. R. (1990). Visitor impact management. In R. Graham & R. Lawrence (Eds.), *Towards serving visitors and managing our resources* (pp. 213–234). Waterloo, ON: Tourism Research and Education Centre, University of Waterloo and Canadian Parks Service, Environment Canada.

Graham, R. (1990). Visitor management and Canada's National Parks. In R. Graham & R. Lawrence (Eds.), *Towards serving visitors and managing our resources* (pp. 271–296). Waterloo, ON: Tourism Research and Education Centre, University of Waterloo and Canadian Parks Service, Environment Canada.

Grand River Conservation Authority. (2001). *Conserving our future*. Retrieved July 19, 2005, from www.grandriver.ca

Grand River Conservation Authority. (2007). *Our vision and mission*. Retrieved April 12, 2007, from /www.grandriver.ca

Gray, G. G. (1993). *Wildlife and people: The human dimensions of wildlife ecology*. Urbana, IL: University of Illinois Press.

Gray, P. G., Duwors, E., Villeneuve, M., Boyd, S. & Legg, D. (2003). The socioeconomic significance of nature-based recreation in Canada. *Environmental Monitoring and Assessment, 86*, 129–147.

Great Barrier Reef Marine Park Authority (2007). *What tourism experiences are on offer*. Retrieved May 10, 2007, from http://www.gbrmpa.gov.au/corp_site/key_issues/tourism/tourism_on_gbr

Green, P. (1990). Outdoor leadership preparation. In J. C. Miles & S. Priest (Eds.), *Adventure education* (pp. 217–221). State College, PA: Venture.

Grumbine, E. (1994). What is ecosystem management? *Conservation Biology, 8*, 27–38.

Guest, G. (2003). Fishing behavior and decision-making in an Ecuadorian community: A scaled approach. *Human Ecology, 31*(4), 611–644.

Guthrie, S. P. (2001). The profession of adventure education leadership. *The Journal of Experiential Education, 24*(3), 132–135.

Guy, M. E. (1990). *Ethical decision making in everyday work situations*. Westport, CT: Greenwood Press.

Hahn, K. (1960, July). *Outward bound, address by Dr. Kurt Hahn at the annual conference meeting of the Outward Bound Trust on 20th July, 1960*. Retrieved June 20, 2004 from http://www.KurtHahn.org

Hahn, K. (1936, March). Education and peace: The foundations of modern society. *The Inverness Courier*.

Hales, D. (1989). Changing concepts of national parks. In D. Western & M. Pearl (Eds.), *Conservation for the twenty-first century* (pp. 139–145). New York: Oxford University Press.

Hall, C. M. (1992). *Wasteland to world heritage: Preserving Australia's wilderness*. Carlton: Melbourne University Press.

Hall, C. M. (2000a). Tourism and the establishment of national parks in Australia. In R. W. Butler & S. W. Boyd (Eds.), *Tourism and national parks: Issues and implications* (pp. 29–38). New York: John Wiley & Sons.

Hall, C. M. (2000b). Tourism, national parks and Aboriginal Peoples. In R. W. Butler & S. W. Boyd (Eds.), *Tourism and national parks: Issues and implications* (pp. 57–73). New York: John Wiley & Sons.

Hall, C. M. & Page, S. J. (1999). *The geography of tourism and recreation.* London: Routledge.

Hall, L. (1995). *Olmsted's America.* Boston: Little, Brown and Company.

Hall, M., McKeowan, L. & Roberts, K. (2001). *Caring Canadians, involved Canadians: Highlights from the 2000 national survey of giving, volunteering, and participating.* Ottawa: Ministry of Industry.

Halverson, W. H. (1972). *A concise introduction to philosophy.* New York: Random House.

Ham, S. H. (1992). *Environmental interpretation: A practical guide for people with big ideas and small budgets.* Golden, CO: North American Press.

Hamblin, W. K. (1989). *The earth's dynamic systems* (5th ed.). New York: Macmillan.

Hammerman, D. R. & Hammerman, W. M. (1973). Chapter two historical perspective: Introduction. In D. R. Hammerman & W. M. Hammerman (Eds.), *Outdoor education: A book of readings* (2nd ed.) (pp. 55–57). Minneapolis: Burgess.

Hammerman, W. M. (1973). Why the excitement about environmental education? In D. R. Hammerman & W. M. Hammerman (Eds.), *Outdoor education: A book of readings* (pp. 301–304). Minneapolis: Burgess.

Hammitt, W. E. (1990). Wildland recreation and resource impacts. A pleasure-policy dilemma. In J. D. Hutcheson, F. P. Noe & R. E. Snow (Eds.), *Outdoor recreation policy: Pleasure and preservation* (pp. 17–30). New York: Greenwood Press.

Hammitt, W. E. & Cole, D. N. (1998). *Wildland recreation: Ecology and management* (2nd ed.). New York: John Wiley and Sons.

Hammitt, W. E. & Schneider, I. E. (2000). Recreation conflict management. In W. C. Gartner & D. W. Lime (Eds.), *Trends in outdoor recreation, leisure and tourism* (pp. 347–356). Wallingford, UK: CABI Publishing.

Hanley, N. & Wright, R. E. (2003). Valuing recreational resources using choice experiments: Mountaineering in Scotland. In N. Hanley, W. D. Shaw & R. E. Wright (Eds.), *The new economics of outdoor recreation* (pp. 40–59). Cheltenham, UK: Edward Elgar.

Hanley, N., Shaw, W. D. & Wright, R. E. (2003). Introduction. In N. Hanley, W. D. Shaw & R. E. Wright (Eds.), *The new economics of outdoor recreation* (pp. 1–20). Cheltenham, UK: Edward Elgar.

Hanna, G. (1995). Wilderness related environmental outcomes of adventure and ecology education programming. *Journal of Environmental Education, 27*(1), 21–33.

Hardin, G. (1968). The tragedy of the commons. *Science, 162,* 1243–1248.

Hargrove, E. (2003). What's wrong? Who's to blame? *Environmental Ethics, 25,* 3–4.

Hargrove, E. C. (1989). *Foundations of environmental ethics.* Englewood Cliffs, NJ: Prentice Hall.

Harter, S. (1981). A new self-report scale of intrinsic versus extrinsic orientation in the classroom: Motivational and informational components. *Developmental Psychology, 17,* 300–312.

Harwell, R. (1987, June). A "no rescue" wilderness experience. *Parks and Recreation,* 34–37.

Heintzman, P. (2003). The wilderness experience and spirituality. *The Journal of Physical Education, Recreation and Dance, 74*(6), 27–32.

Hendee, J. & Burdge, R. (1974). The substitutability concept: Implications for recreation management and research. *Journal of Leisure Research, 6*(2), 157–162.

Hendee, J. C., Stankey, G. H. & Lucas, R. C. (1990). *Wilderness management* (2nd ed.). Golden, CO: North American Press.

Henderson, B. (1987). Looking beyond the activity of outdoor pursuits. *CAPHER, 53*(2), 9–13.

Henderson, K. A. (1986). *A leisure of one's own: A feminist perspective on women's leisure.* State College, PA: Venture.

Henderson, K. A. (1994). Perspectives on analyzing gender, women, and leisure. *Journal of Leisure Research, 26*(2), 119–137.

Henderson, K. A., Bialeschki, M. D., Shaw, S. M. & Freysinger, V. J. (1996). *Both gains and gaps: Feminist perspectives on women's leisure.* State College, PA: Venture.

Henderson, R. (1999). Every trail has a story: The heritage context as adventure. In J. C. Miles & S. Priest (Eds.), *Adventure programming* (pp. 141–145). State College, PA: Venture.

Hendricks, J. & Burdge, R. (1972). The nature of leisure research: A reflection and comment. *Journal of Leisure Research, 4*, 215–217.

Herbert, G. J. (1999). *Canada's oceans dimensions: A factbook (NIOBE papers, volume 11)*. Halifax, NS: Maritime Affairs.

Heywood, J. L. (2002). The cognitive and emotional components of social norms in outdoor recreation. *Leisure Sciences, 24*(3/4), 271–282.

Heywood, J. L. & Aas, O. (1999). Social norms and encounter preferences for cross-country skiing with dogs in Norway. *Leisure Sciences, 21*(2), 133–145.

Heywood, J. L., Manning, R. E. & Vaske, J. J. (2002). Normative research in outdoor recreation: Progress and prospects for continued development and applications. *Leisure Sciences, 24*, 251–253.

Hinch, T. D. & Higham, J. E. S. (2001). Sport tourism: A framework for research. *International Journal of Tourism Research, 3*, 45–58.

Hjelmar, U. (1996). *The political practice of environmental organizations*. Avebury, VT: Brookfield.

Hogan, J. M. (1968). *Impelled into experiences: The story of the Outward Bound Schools*. Wakefield, UK: Educational Productions.

Holgen, P., Mattsson, L. & Li, C. Z. (2000). Recreation values of boreal forest stand types and landscapes resulting from different silvicultural systems: An economic analysis. *Journal of Environmental Management, 60*(2), 173–180.

Holland, S. M., Ditton, R. B. & Graefe, A. R. (1998). An ecotourism perspective on billfish fisheries. *Journal of Sustainable Tourism, 6*(2), 97–116.

Holland, S. M., Ditton, R. B. & Graefe, A. R. (2000). A response to "Ecotourism on trial—the case of billfish angling as ecotourism." *Journal of Sustainable Tourism, 8*(4), 346–351.

Honderich, T. (Ed.). (1995). *The Oxford companion to philosophy*. Oxford: Oxford University Press.

Horna, J. (1994). *The study of leisure*. Toronto: Oxford University Press.

Horwood, B. (1999). Education adventure and schooling. In J. C. Miles & S. Priest (Eds.), *Adventure programming* (pp. 9–13). State College, PA: Venture.

Howard, D. R. & Crompton, J. L. (1980). *Financing, managing and marketing recreation & park resources*. Dubuque, IA: Wm. C. Brown Company.

Hrubes, D., Ajzen, I. & Daigle, J. J. (2001). Predicting hunting intentions and behavior: An application of the theory of planned behavior. *Leisure Sciences, 23*(3), 165–178.

Hughes, D. (2004). Just a breath of fresh air in an industrial landscape? The Preston Open Air School 1926: A school medical service insight. *Social History of Medicine, 17*(3), 443–461.

Huhtala, A. (2004). What price recreation in Finland? A contingent valuation study of non-market benefits of public outdoor recreation areas. *Journal of Leisure Research, 36*(1), 23–44.

Huizinga, J. (1950). *Homo ludens: A study of the play-element in culture*. Boston: Beacon Press.

Hultsman, J., Cottrell, R. L. & Hultsman, W. Z. (1998). *Planning parks for people* (2nd ed.). State College, PA: Venture.

Hummel, M. & Hackman, A. (1995). Introduction. In M. Hummel (Ed.), *Protecting Canada's endangered spaces* (pp. xi–xix). Toronto: Key Porter Books.

Hutchison, P. & McGill, J. (1998). *Leisure, integration, and community* (2nd ed.). Toronto: Leisureability Publications.

Hvenegaard, G. T. (2002). Birder specialization differences in conservation involvement, demographics and motivations. *Human Dimensions of Wildlife, 7*(1), 21–37.

Hyde, W. W. (1971). The development of the appreciation of mountain scenery in modern times. *Geographical Review, 3*(2), 107–118.

Ibrahim, H. (1991). *Leisure and society*. Boston: WCB McGraw-Hill.

Ibrahim, H. & Cordes, K. A. (1993). *Outdoor recreation*. Boston: WCB McGraw-Hill.

Ibrahim, H. & Cordes, K. A. (2002). *Outdoor recreation enrichment for a lifetime* (2nd ed.). Champaign, IL: Sagamore.

Inhelder, B. & Piaget, J. (1958). *The growth of logical thinking from childhood to adolescence*. New York: Basic Books.

Institute for Volunteering Research. (1997). 1997 national survey of volunteering in the UK. Retrieved May 1, 2007 from http://www.ivr.org.uk/nationalsurvey.htm

International Olympic Committee. (2007). *Olympic movement*. Retrieved April 15, 2007 from http://www. olympic.org/uk/organisation/movement/index_uk.asp

Interpretation Australia Association. (2007). *Who are we?* Retrieved May 1, 2007, from http://www.interpreta-tionaustralia.asn.au/index.htm

IPCC. (2001). *Climate change 2001: Synthesis report summary for policy makers*. United Kingdom: IPCC.

IPCC. (2007). *IPCC fourth assessment report*. Available from http://www.ipcc.ch/ipccreports/ar4-syr.html

Irland, L. C., Adams, D., Alig, R., Betz, C. J., Chen, C., Hutchins, M., McCarl, B. A., Skog, K. & Sohngen, B. L. (2001). Assessing socioeconomic impacts of climate change on US forests, wood-product markets, and forest recreation. *Bioscience, 51*(9), 753–766.

Iso-Ahola, S. E. (1980). *The social psychology of leisure and recreation*. Dubuque, IA: W. C. Brown Co. Publishers.

Iso-Ahola, S. E. (1989). Motivation for leisure. In T. Burton & E. Jackson (Eds.), *Understanding leisure and recreation: Mapping the past, charting the future* (pp. 247–279). State College, PA: Venture.

Iso-Ahola, S. E. (1999). Motivational Foundations of leisure. In E. L. Jackson & T. L. Burton (Eds.), *Leisure studies: Prospects for the twenty-first century* (pp. 35–49). State College, PA: Venture.

IUCN. (2003). *What is IUCN?* Retrieved August 8, 2004, from http://wwwiucn.org/about/index.htm

IUCN. (2006). *Mountains*. Retrieved May 2, 2007, from http://www.iucn.org/themes/cem/ ecosystems/ mountains/index.html

IUCN, The World Conservation Union. (2007). *IUCN governance*. Retrieved May 1, 2007, from http://www. iucn.org/en/about/governance.htm

Jackson, E. (1989). Perceptions and decisions. In G. Wall (Ed.), *Outdoor recreation in Canada* (pp. 75–133). Toronto: John Wiley & Sons.

Jacobi, C. & Manning, R. (1999). Crowding and conflict on the carriage road of Acadian national park: An application of the visitor experience and resource protection framework. *Park Science, 19*(2), 1–13.

Jafari, J. (1989). An English language literature review. In J. Bystrzanowski (Ed.), *Tourism as a factor of change: A sociocultural study* (pp. 17–60). Vienna: Centre for Research and Documentation in Social Sciences.

Jantsch, E. (1972). *Technological planning and social futures*. New York: Halsted Press.

Jensen, C. R. (1995). *Outdoor recreation in America* (5th ed.). Champaign, IL: Human Kinetics.

Jernstedt, G. C. (1995). Experiential components in academic courses. In K. Warren, M. Sakofs & J. S. Hunt Jr. (Eds.), *The theory of experiential education* (2nd ed.) (pp. 109–117). Boulder, CO: Association for Experiential Education.

Johnson, D. W. & Johnson, F. P. (1982). *Joining together: Group theory and group skills*. Englewood Cliffs, NJ: Prentice Hall.

Johnson, R. L. & Moore, E. (1993). Tourism impact estimation. *Annals of Tourism Research, 20*, 279–288.

Jones, J. J. & Hinton, J. L. (2007). Study of self-efficacy in a freshman wilderness experience program: Measuring general versus specific gains. *Journal of Experiential Education, 23*(3), 382–385.

Jordan, D. J. (1996). Leadership: The state of the research. *Parks and Recreation, 33*(10), 32–40.

Jorgensen, B. S., Syme, G. J., Smith, L. M. & Bishop, B. J. (2004). Random error in willingness to pay measurement: A multiple indicators, latent variable approach to the reliability of contingent values. *Journal of Economic Psychology, 25*(1), 41–59.

Jubenville, A. & Twight, B. W. (1993). *Outdoor recreation management: Theory and application* (3rd ed.). State College, PA: Venture.

Kaplan, R. & Kaplan, S. (1989). *The experience of nature: A psychological perspective*. Cambridge: Cambridge University Press.

Kappelle, M., Van Vuuren, M. M. I. & Baas, P. (1999). Effects of climate change on biodiversity: A review and identification of key research issues. *Biodiversity and Conservation, 8*, 1383–1397.

Karlis, G. (2006). The future of leisure, recreation and sport in Canada: A SWOT for small sized enterprises. *The Sport Journal, 9*(2). Retrieved May 3, 2007, from http://www.thesportjournal.org/2006Journal/Vol9-No2/Karlis.asp

Karoly, D. J., Braganza, K., Stott, P. A., Arblaster, J. M., Meehl, G. A., Broccoli, A. J. & Dixon, K. W. (2003). Detection of a human influence on north American climate. *Science, 302*, 1200–1203.

Kaufman, D. A. & Cloutier, N. R. (2006). The impact of small brownfields and greenspaces on residential property values. *Journal of Real Estate Finance and Economics, 33*(1), 19–30.

Kay, J. & Laberge, S. (2002). The new corporate habitus in adventure racing. *International Review for the Sociology of Sport, 37*(1), 17–37.

Keller, B. (1984). *Black wolf: The life of Ernest Thompson Seton*. Vancouver: Douglas and McIntyre.

Kelly, J. R. (1980). Outdoor recreation participation: a comparative analysis. *Leisure Sciences, 3*, 121–132.

Kelly, J. R. (1982). *Leisure*. Englewood Cliffs, NJ: Prentice Hall.

Kelly, J. R. (1990). *Leisure* (2nd ed.). Englewood Cliffs, NJ: Prentice Hall.

Kelly, J. R. (1996). *Leisure* (3rd ed.). Boston: Allyn & Bacon.

Kelly, J. R. & Freysinger, V. J. (2000). *21st century leisure current issues*. Needham Heights, MA: Allyn & Bacon.

Kennedy, D. W. (1987). *Special recreation: Opportunities for persons with disabilities*. New York: CBS College Publishing.

Kennedy, D., Austin, D. & Smith, R. (1987). *Special recreation: Opportunities for persons with disabilities*. Philadelphia: Saunders.

Kim, S. S. & Crompton, J. L. (2001). The effects of different types of information messages on perceptions of price and stated willingness-to-pay. *Journal of Leisure Research, 33*(3), 299–318.

Klausmeier, H. J. (1979). Introduction. In H. J. Klausmeier & Associates (Eds.), *Cognitive learning and development: Information-processing and Piagetian perspectives*. Cambridge, MA: Ballinger.

Klint, K. A. (1999). New directions for inquiry into self-concept and adventure experiences. In J. C. Miles & S. Priest (Eds.), *Adventure programming* (pp. 163–168). State College, PA: Venture.

Kluckhohn, C., Hill, W. W. & Kluckhohn, L. W. (1971). *Navaho material culture*. Cambridge, MA: The Belknap Press of Harvard University.

Knapp, C. E. (1999). Processing the adventure experience. In J. C. Miles & S. Priest (Eds.), *Adventure programming* (pp. 219–224). State College, PA: Venture.

Knight, R. L. & Gutzwiller, K. J. (Eds.). (1995). *Wildlife and recreationists: Coexistence through management and research*. Covelo, CA: Island Press.

Knopf, R. C. (1990). The limits of acceptable change (LAC) planning process: Potentials and limitations. In R. Graham & R. Lawrence (Eds.), *Towards serving visitors and managing our resources* (pp. 201–213). Waterloo, ON: Tourism Research and Education Centre, University of Waterloo.

Knudson, D. M. (1984). *Outdoor recreation* (revised ed.). New York: Macmillan.

Knudson, D. M., Cable, T. T. & Beck, L. (1999). *Interpretation of cultural and natural resources*. State College, PA: Venture.

Knudson, D. M., Cable, T. T. & Beck, L. (2003). *Interpretation of cultural and natural resources* (2nd ed.). State College, PA: Venture.

Kolb, D. A. (1976). *The learning style inventory: Technical manual*. Boston: McBer.

Kooiman, J. (1993). *Modern government, new government, social interaction*. London: Sage.

Kouzes, J. M. & Posner, B. Z. (2003). *The leadership challenge* (3rd ed.) (pp. 3–15). Indianapolis, IN: Jossey-Bass.

Kozlowski, J. C. (1999). When animals attack: Governmental immunity and liability. *Parks and Recreation, 34*(3), 48–55.

Kraus, R. G. (2001). *Recreation and leisure in modern society* (6th ed.). Sudbury, MA: Jones and Bartlett.

Kreutzwiser, R. (1989). Supply. In G. Wall (Ed.), *Outdoor recreation in Canada* (pp. 21–41). Toronto: John Wiley & Sons.

Krutilla, J. V. & Knetsch, J. L. (1974). Outdoor recreation economics. In D.W. Fischer, J. E. Lewis & G. B. Priddle (Eds.), *Land and leisure: Concepts and methods in outdoor recreation* (pp. 167–174). Chicago: Maaroufa Press.

Laarman, J. & Durst, P. (1987). Nature travel in the tropics. *Journal of Forestry, 5*, 43–46.

Ladd, J. (1997, September). Ethics and the computer world: A new challenge for philosophers. *Computers and Society*, 8–13.

LaPage, W. F. (2000). Partnerships and the changing world of park management. In W. C. Gartner & D. W. Lime (Eds.), *Trends in outdoor recreation, leisure and tourism* (pp. 365–772). Wallingford, UK: CABI Publishing.

Lazarus, R. & Folkman, S. (1984). *Stress, appraisal and coping*. New York: Springer.

Lear, L. (1998). *Rachel Louise Carson*. Retrieved April 17, 2007, from http://www.rachelcarson.org

367

Leave No Trace. (2004). *Leave no trace principles.* Retrieved June 21, 2004, from http://www.lnt.org/teach-ingLNT/LNTEnglish.php

Lee, J. H., Scott, D. & Floyd, M. F. (2001). Structural inequalities in outdoor recreation participation: A multiple hierarchy stratification perspective. *Journal of Leisure Research, 33*(4), 427–450.

Leitner, M. J. & Leitner, S. F. (1996). *Leisure enhancement* (2nd ed.). New York: The Haworth Press.

Leopold, A. (1921). The wilderness and its place in forest recreational policy. *American Forests*, 718–721.

Leopold, A. (1966). *A sand county almanac.* New York: Ballantine Books. (Original work published 1949.)

Leopold, A. S. & Darling, F. F. (1953). *Wildlife in Alaska: An ecological reconnaissance.* New York: The Ronald Press Company.

Leroy, E. (1983). Adventure and education. *Journal of Experiential Education, 6*(1), 18–23.

Liddle, M. (1991). Recreation ecology. Effects of trampling on plants and corals. *Trends in Ecology and Evolution, 6*(1), 1–17.

Liddle, M. (1997). *Recreation ecology.* London: Chapman and Hall.

Liddle, M. & Greig-Smith, P. J. (1973). A survey of tracks and paths in a sand dune ecosystem. *Journal of Applied Ecology, 12*, 893–908.

Light, A. & Katz, E. (1996). *Environmental pragmatism.* New York: Routledge.

Lindenberg, K., McCool, S. & Stankey, G. (1997). Rethinking carrying capacity. *Annals of Tourism Research, 24*, 461–464.

Linkages. (2006). *Twelfth session of the Conference of the Parties to the Climate Change Convention and second meeting of the Parties to the Kyoto Protocol.* Retrieved May 2, 2007, from http://www.iisd.ca/climate/cop12

List, P. & Brown, P. (1999). Moving towards an expanded land management ethic. In B. L. Driver, D. Dustin, T. Baltic, G. Elsner & G. Peterson (Eds.), *Nature and the human spirit: Toward an expanded land management ethic* (pp. 457–465). State College, PA: Venture.

Loehle, C. (2004). Climate change: Detection and attribution of trends from long-term geologic data. *Ecological Modeling, 171*(4), 433–450.

Loftin, R. W. (1984). The morality of hunting. *Environmental Ethics, 7*, 231–239.

Loomis, J. (1990). Comparative reliability of the dichotomous choice and open-ended contingent valuation techniques. *Journal of Environmental Economics and Management, 18*(1), 78–85.

Loomis, J. (2005). Updated outdoor recreation use values on national forests and other public lands (Gen. Tech. Rep. PNW-GTR-658). Portland, OR: U.S. Department of Agriculture, Forest Service, Pacific Northwest Research Station.

Loomis, J. & Crespi, J. (1999). Estimated effects of climate change on selected outdoor recreation activities in the United States. In R. Mendelsonn and J. E. Newman (Eds.), *The impact of climate change in the United States economy* (pp. 289–314). Cambridge: Cambridge University Press.

Loomis, J., Rameker, V. & Seidl, A. (2004). A hedonic model of public market transactions for open space protection. *Journal of Environmental Planning and Management, 47*(1), 83–96.

Lucas, R. (1964). *The recreational capacity of the Quetico-Superior area.* USDA Forest Service Research Paper, LS-15.

Luttik, J. (2000). The value of trees, water and open space as reflected by house prices in the Netherlands. *Landscape and Urban Planning, 48*(3–4), 161–167.

McAvoy, L. (1999). Rescue-free wilderness areas. In J. C. Miles & S. Priest (Eds.), *Adventure programming* (pp. 325–329). State College, PA: Venture.

McAvoy, L. & Lais, G. (1999). Programs that include persons with disabilities. In J. C. Miles & S. Priest (Eds.), *Adventure programming* (pp. 403–414). State College, PA: Venture.

McCloskey, M. (1966). The wilderness act: Its background and meaning. *Oregon Law Review, 45*(4), 288–321.

McCool, S. F. & Patterson, M. E. (1999). Trends in recreation, tourism and protected area planning. In W. C. Gartner & D. W. Lime (Eds.), *Trends in outdoor recreation, leisure and tourism* (pp. 111–120). Wallingford, UK: CABI Publishing.

McDonald, C. D. (1996). Normative perspectives on outdoor recreation behavior: Introductory comments. *Leisure Sciences, 18*(1), 1–5.

Mace, B. L., Bell, P. A. & Loomis, R. J. (2004). Visibility and quiet in national parks and wilderness areas. *Environment and Behaviour, 36*(1), 5–33.

MacEachern, A. (2001). *Natural selections: National parks in Atlantic Canada, 1935–1970*. Montreal: McGill-Queen's University Press.

McElravy, G. (1999). GIS technology will make outdoor recreation a walk in the park. *Computing Canada, 25*(42), 29–32.

McFarland, E. M. (1970). *The development of public recreation in Canada*. Vanier, ON: Canadian Parks–Recreation Association.

McIntosh, R. W., Goeldner, C. R. & Ritchie, J. R. (1995). *Tourism principles, practices, philosophies* (7th ed.). New York: John Wiley & Sons.

McIntyre, N. & Pigram, J. (1992). Recreation specialization reexamined: The case of vehicle based campers. *Leisure Sciences, 9*, 251–257.

McKibben, B. (1999). *The end of nature*. New York: Anchor Books.

McLaughlin, A. (1995). The heart of deep ecology. In G. Sessions (Ed.), *Deep ecology for the 21st century: Readings on the philosophical and practice of the new environmentalism* (pp. 85–95). Boston: Shambhala.

McNamee, K. (1993). From wild places to endangered spaces: A history of Canada's national parks. In P. Dearden & R. Rollins (Eds.), *Parks and protected areas in Canada: Planning and management* (pp. 17–44). Don Mills, ON: Oxford University Press.

McNamee, K. (2002a). From wild places to endangered spaces. In P. Dearden & R. Rollins (Eds.), *Parks and protected areas in Canada: Planning and management* (2nd ed.) (pp. 21–50). Don Mills, ON: Oxford University Press.

McNamee, K. (2002b). Protected areas in Canada: The endangered spaces campaign. In P. Dearden & R. Rollins (Eds.), *Parks and protected areas in Canada: Planning and management* (2nd ed.) (pp. 51–68). Don Mills, ON: Oxford University Press.

McPhee, P. (1992). Asking the question. *The Journal of Experiential Education, 15*(2), 19.

Manfredo, M. J., Driver, B. L. & Tarrant, M. A. (1996). Measuring leisure motivation: A meta-analysis of the recreation experience preference scales. *Journal of Leisure Research, 28*(3), 188–213.

Mannell, R. C. & Kleiber, D. A. (1997). *The social psychology of leisure*. State College, PA: Venture.

Manning, R. (2001). Visitor experience and resource protection: A framework for managing the carrying capacity of national parks. *Journal of Park and Recreation Administration, 19*(3), 93–108.

Manning, R. E. (1999). *Studies in outdoor recreation* (2nd ed.). Corvallis, OR: Oregon State Press.

Manning, R. E. (2000). Coming of age: History and trends in outdoor recreation research. In W. C. Gartner & D. W. Lime (Eds.), *Trends in outdoor recreation, leisure and tourism* (pp. 121–131). New York: CABI Publishing.

Manning, R. E., Newman, P., Valliere, W. A., Wang, B. & Lawson, S. R. (2001). Respondent self-assessment of research on crowding norms in outdoor recreation. *Journal of Leisure Research, 33*(3), 251–271.

Marchetti, C., Meyer, P. S. & Ausubel, J. H. (1996). Human population dynamics revisited with the logistical model: How much can be modeled and predicted? *Technological Forecasting and Social Change, 52*, 1–30.

Marsh, J. (2000). Tourism and national parks in polar regions. In R. W. Butler & S. W. Boyd (Eds.), *Tourism and national parks: Issues and implications* (pp. 123–136). New York: John Wiley & Sons.

Marsh, J. & Wall, G. (1982). Themes in the investigation of the evolution of outdoor recreation. In G. Wall & J. Marsh (Eds.), *Recreational land use: Perspectives on its evolution in Canada* (pp. 1–14). Ottawa: Carleton University Press.

Marsh, W. M. & Grossa, J., Jr. (2002). *Environmental geography: Science, land use, and earth systems* (2nd ed.). New York: John Wiley and Sons Limited.

Martin, D. C. (2004). Apartheid in the great outdoors: American advertising and the reproduction of a racialized outdoor identity. *Journal of Leisure Research, 36*(4), 513–535.

Martin, P. & Priest, S. (1986). Understanding the adventure experience. *Journal of Adventure Education, 3*, 18–21.

Maslow, A. (1970). *Motivation and personality* (2nd ed.). New York: Harper & Row.

Mathieson, A. & Wall, G. (1982). *Tourism: Economic, physical and social impacts*. London: Longman.

Matthews, M. M. (1986). The influence of gender on the environmental cognition of young boys and girls. *Journal of Genetic Psychology, 147*(3), 295–303.

Matthiessen, P. (1987). *Wildlife in America*. New York: Viking Penguin.

369

Meadowcroft, J. (1998). Co-operative management regimes: a way forward? In P. Glasbergen (Ed.), *Co-operative environmental governance* (pp. 21–42). Dordrecht: Kluwer.

Meier J. F. (1978). Is the risk worth taking? *Journal of Physical Education and Recreation, 49*, 31–33.

Meier J. F. (1987). Is risk worth taking? In J. F. Meier., T. W. Morash & G. E. Welton (Eds.), *High adventure outdoor pursuits: Organization and leadership* (pp. 442–455). Columbus, OH: Publishing Horizons.

Melbourne Victoria Australia. (n.d.). *The Great Ocean Road.* Retrieved May 10, 2007, from http://www.visitvictoria.com/displayObject.cfm/ObjectID.1283A740–17E0–4AB2-B12FDDBA419F5318/vvt.vhtml

Meredith, D. H. (2000). Is angling at a crossroads. *Alberta Outdoorsman (June/July).* Retrieved June 14, 2004, from http://www.donmeredith.ca/outdoorsmen/AnglingCross5.html

Michaels, G., O'Neal, K., Humphrey, J., Bell, K., Camacho, R. & Funk, R. (1995). *Ecological impacts from climate change: An economic analysis of freshwater recreational fishing.* Washington, DC: US Environmental Protection Agency, Office of Policy, Planning, and Evaluation.

Mieczkowski, Z. T. (1981). Some notes on the geography of tourism: A comment. *Canadian Geographer, 25*, 186–191.

Miller, E. D. (1984). *Questions that matter: An invitation to philosophy.* New York: McGraw-Hill.

Miller, G. T., Jr. (1996). *Living in the environment: Principles, connections and solutions* (9th ed.). Belmont: Wadsworth.

Miller, L. J. (1993). Culture and socialization. In P. S. Li & B. S. Bolaria (Eds.), *Contemporary sociology* (pp. 4–24). Toronto: Copp Clark Pitman.

Miner, T. (1999). Adventure in the workplace. In J. C. Miles & S. Priest (Eds.), *Adventure programming* (pp. 395–400). State College, PA: Venture.

Miner, J. & Boldt, J. (2001). *Outward Bound USA.* Seattle: Mountaineers Books.

Minnegal, M. (1996). A necessary unity: The articulation of ecological and social explanations of behaviour. *Journal of the Royal Anthropological Institute, 2*, 141–158.

Mitchell, A. (1983). *The nine American lifestyles: Who we are and where we're going.* New York: Macmillan.

Mitchell, B. (1989). *Geography and resource analysis* (2nd ed.). Essex: Longman.

Mitchell, B. & Shrubsole, D. (1992). *Ontario conservation authorities: Myth and reality.* Waterloo, ON: Canadian Water Resources Association.

Mitten, D. (1999). Leadership for community building. In J. Miles & S. Priest (Eds.), *Adventure programming* (pp. 253–261). State College, PA: Venture.

Moncrief, L. W. (1970). Trends in outdoor recreation research. *Journal of Leisure Research, 2*, 127–130.

More, T. & Stevens, T. (2000). Do your user fees exclude low-income people from resource based recreation? *Journal of Leisure Research, 32*(3), 341–358.

Mouser, C. (2003). Wounding in nature. *Gatherings ... Seeking Ecopsychology, 8*, http://www.ecopsychology.org

Mozumder, P., Starbuck, C. M., Berrens, R. P. & Alexander, S. (2007). Lease and fee hunting on private lands in the US: A review of the economic and legal issues. *Human Dimensions of Wildlife, 12*(1), 1–14.

Muir, J. (1991). *Our national parks.* San Francisco: Sierra Club Books. (Original work published in 1901.)

Murphy, J. (1981). *Concepts of leisure* (2nd ed.). Englewood Cliffs, NJ: Prentice Hall.

Murphy, P. E. (1985). *Tourism: A community approach.* New York: Routledge.

Nadler, R. S. (1999). Therapeutic process of change. In M. A. Gass (Ed.), *Adventure therapy: Therapeutic applications of adventure programming* (pp. 57–69). Dubuque, IA: Kendall/Hunt.

Nadler, R. S. & Luckner, J. L. (1992). *Processing the adventure experience: Theory and practice.* Dubuque, IA: Kendall/Hunt.

Naess, A. (1995). The deep ecology movement: Some philosophical aspects. In G. Sessions (Ed.), *Deep ecology for the 21st century: Readings on the philosophical and practical of the new environmentalism* (pp. 64–58). Boston: Shambhala.

Napier, T. L. (1981). *Outdoor recreation planning, perspectives, and research.* Dubuque, IA: Kendall/Hunt.

Nash, R. (1982). *Wilderness and the American mind* (3rd ed.). Binghamton, NY: Yale University Press.

National Association for Interpretation. (2007). Retrieved February 9, 2004, from http://www.interpnet.com/home.htm

National Council for Therapeutic Recreation Certification. (n.d.). Retrieved July 23, 2004, from http://www.nctrc.org

National Cycle Network. (2007). National cycle network. Retrieved May 9, 2007, from http://www.ctc. org.uk/DesktopDefault.aspx?TabID=3685

National Outdoor Leadership School. (2007). *NOLS history*. Retrieved April 16, 2007, from http://www.nols. edu/about/history

National Park Service. (n.d.a). Retrieved April 12, 2004, from http://www.nps.gov

National Park Service. (n.d.b). *The National Park system: Caring for the American legacy*. Retrieved May 1, 2007, from http://www.nps.gov/legacy/mission.html

National Park Service. (2006). *Yosemite National Park: Nature and history*. Retrieved May 1, 2007, from http://www.nps.gov/archive/yose/nature/nature.htm

National Park Service. (2007). *Frequently asked questions*. Retrieved May 1, 2007, from http://www.nps.gov/faqs.htm

National Parks Conservation Association. (2007). *Who We Are*. Retrieved April 3, 2007, from http:www. npca.org/who_we_are

National Parks. (2000). *George Washington birthplace national monument*. Retrieved August 9, 2004, from http://www.nps.gov/gewa/homepg.htm

National Statistics. (2007). *East of England spent the most on recreation*. Retrieved May 1, 2007, from http://www.statistics.gov.uk/CCI/nugget.asp?ID=1131&Pos= 1&ColRank=2&Rank=208

National Trails. (2007) *About the national trails*. Retrieved May 2, 2007, from http://www. nationaltrail.co.uk/text.asp?PageId=2

Natural England (2005). *England leisure visits: Report of the 2005 survey*. Retrieved May 6, 2007, from http://www.countryside.gov.uk/Images/ELVS%20Brochure%20_tcm2–31642.pdf

Natural England. (2007a) *Conservation: Designated areas*. Retrieved May 2, 2007, from http://www.naturaleng-land.org.uk/conservation/designated-areas/default.htm

Natural England. (2007b). *Recreation: Greenways and quiet lanes*. Retrieved May 1, 2007, from http://www. countryside.gov.uk/lar/recreation/greenways/index.asp

Natural Resources Canada. (2007). *Forests in Canada*. Retrieved May 14, 2007, from http://atlas. nrcan.gc.ca/site/english/maps/environment/forest/forestcanada

Nebel, B. J. & Wright, R. T. (1996). *Environmental science: The way the world works* (5th ed.). Upper Saddle River, NJ: Prentice Hall.

Neill, J. (2003). *Paul Petzoldt: Brief biography & quotes*. Retrieved August 10, 2004, from http://www.wilder-dom.com/Petzoldt.htm

Nelson, G. (2004). Towards a Grand sense of place. In G. Nelson (Ed.), *Towards a grand sense of place* (pp. 1–11). Waterloo, ON: Heritage Resources Centre.

Nelson, J. G. (1993). Beyond parks and protected areas: From public lands and private stewardship to landscape planning and management. In P. Dearden & R. Rollins (Eds.), *Parks and protected areas in Canada: Planning and management* (pp. 45–57). Toronto: Oxford University Press.

Nepal, S. K. (2000). Tourism, national parks and local communities. In R. W. Butler & S. W. Boyd (Eds.), *Tourism and national parks: Issues and implications* (pp. 73–94). New York: John Wiley & Sons.

Neulinger, J. (1981). *The psychology of leisure* (2nd ed.). Springfield, IL: C. C. Thomas.

Nicholson, J. A. (1986). Risk recreation: A context for developing client potential. *Journal of Counseling & Development, 64*, 528–530.

NSW Department of Primary Industries. (2005). *Fishing and aquaculture*. Retrieved May 1, 2007, from http://www.dpi.nsw.gov.au/fisheries

Oates, D. (1989). *Earth rising: Ecological belief in an age of science*. Corvallis, OR: Oregon State University Press.

Oelschlaeger, M. (1995). Taking the land ethic outdoors: Its implications for recreation. In R. L. Knight & K. J. Gutzwiller (Eds.), *Wildlife and recreationists: Coexistence through management and research* (pp. 335–350). Washington, DC: Island Press.

Olmstead, M. (2001). A theology of fly fishing. Retrieved July 8, 2004, from http://people.bu.edu/wwild-man/WeirdWildWeb/courses/theo1/projects/2001_olmstead/index.htm

O'Riordan, T. (1971). *Perspectives on resource management*. London: Pion.

Ostrom, E. (1990). *Governing the commons: The evolution of institutions for collective actions*. Cambridge: Cambridge University Press.

Outward Bound International. (2005). Annual Report 2005. Retrieved May 1, 2007, from http://www.out-wardbound.net/news/annual_reports/obi_annual-report_2005.pdf

Outward Bound. (2004). About us. Retrieved May 1, 2007, from http://www.outwardbound.net/about/index.html

Outward Bound. (2007). *History*. Retrieved April 16, 2007, from http://www.outwardbound.net/about/history

Outwater, A. (1996). *Water: A natural history*. New York: Basic Books.

PADI. (n.d.). *PADI website*. Retrieved May 1, 2007, from http://www.padi.com/padi/default.aspx

Page, S. J. & Dowling, R. K. (2002). *Ecotourism*. Harlow, Essex: Pearson.

Paletz, S. B. F., Peng, K., Erez, M. & Maslach, C. (2004). Ethnic composition and its differential impact on group processes in diverse teams. *Small Group Research, 35*(2), 128–168.

Palmer, J. A. & Suggate, J. (1996). Environmental cognition: Early ideas and misconceptions at the ages of 4 to 6. *Environmental Education Research, 2*(3), 301–330.

Parks Canada. (1994a). *Parks management guidelines: Pacific Rim National Park Reserve*.

Parks Canada. (2006). *National Parks of Canada ecosystem management: Inventory and monitoring*. Retrieved May 1, 2007, from http://www.pc.gc.ca/progs/np-pn/eco/eco3_E.asp

Parks Canada. (2007). *Parks Canada Agency: Parks Canada's mandate*. Retrieved May 1, 2007, from http://www.pc.gc.ca/agen/index_E.asp

Payne, R. J. & Graham, R. (1993). Visitor planning and management in parks and protected areas. In P. Dearden & R. Rollins (Eds.), *Parks and protected areas in Canada* (pp. 185–210). Toronto: Oxford University Press.

Payne, R. J. & Nilsen, P. W. (2002). Visitor planning and management. In P. Dearden & R. Rollins (Eds.), *Parks and protected areas in Canada: Planning and management* (2nd ed.). Oxford: Oxford University Press.

Peepre, J. & Dearden, P. (2002). The role of aboriginal peoples. In P. Dearden & R. Rollins (Eds.), *Parks and protected areas in Canada: Planning and management* (2nd ed.) (pp. 323–353). Don Mills, ON: Oxford University Press.

Peterson, D. (1987, June). Here's what's wrong with no-rescue wilderness. *Parks and Recreation, 39–43*, 54.

Peterson, J. A. & Hronek, B. B. (1992). Risk management for park, recreation, and leisure services. Champaign, IL: Sagamore.

Petrini, C. M. (1990). Over the river and through the woods. *Training and Development Journal, 44*(5), 25–36.

Phipps, M. & Swiderski, M. (1990). The "soft" skills of outdoor leadership. In J. C. Miles & S. Priest (Eds.), *Adventure education* (pp. 221–233). State College, PA: Venture.

Pigram, J. (1951). *Play, dreams and imitation in childhood*. London: Heinemann.

Pigram, J. J & Jenkins, J. M. (1999). *Outdoor recreation management*. New York: Routledge.

Pigram, J. J. & Jenkins, J. M. (2006). *Outdoor recreation management* (2nd ed.). London: Routledge.

Plaut, L. (2001). Degree-granting programs in adventure education: Added value? *The Journal of Experiential Education, 24*(3), 136–140.

Plummer, R. (2005). A review of sustainable development implementation through local action from an ecosystem management perspective. *Journal of Rural and Environmental Health, 4*, 33–40.

Plummer, R., Kulczycki, C., FitzGibbon, J. & Smith, A. (under review). Exploring the implications of successful fisheries management: A decade of experience with the Upper Grand River tail-water fishery. *Human Dimensions of Wildlife Management*.

Pohl, S. L., Borrie, W. T. & Patterson, M. E. (2000). Women, wilderness, and everyday life: a documentation of the connection between wilderness recreation and women's everyday lives. *Journal of Leisure Research, 32*(4), 415–434.

Polglase, K. J. (2003). Leadership is everyone's business. *Leadership, 32*(5), 24–28.

Polk, J. (1977). *Wilderness writers*. Toronto: Clarke, Irwin & Company.

Pollard, E. (Ed.). (1994). *The Oxford paperback dictionary*. Oxford: Oxford University Press.

Pomerantz, G. (1990). Understanding children's perceptions of nature through developmental theory: Implications for interpretation. *Legacy, 1*(3), 12–19.

Postma, H. & Zijlstra, J. J. (1988). Introduction. In H. Postma & J. J. Zijlstra (Eds.), *Ecosystems of the world 27: Continental shelves*. Amsterdam: Elsevier.

Price, D. (1999). Carrying capacity reconsidered. *Population and the Environment, 21*(1), 5–26.

Price, J. A. (1971). *Indians of Canada: Cultural dynamics.* Salem, WI: Sheffield.

Priest, S. (1990). The adventure experience paradigm. In J. C. Miles & S. Priest (Eds.), *Adventure education* (pp. 157–163). State College, PA: Venture.

Priest, S. (1999a). Introduction. In J. C. Miles & S. Priest (Eds.), *Adventure programming* (pp. xiii-xiv). State College, PA: Venture.

Priest, S. (1999b). The adventure experience paradigm. In J. C. Miles & S. Priest (Eds.), *Adventure programming* (pp. 159–162). State College, PA: Venture.

Priest, S. (1999c). Outdoor leadership competencies. In J. C. Miles & S. Priest (Eds.), *Adventure programming* (pp. 237–239). State College, PA: Venture.

Priest, S. & Baillie, R. (1987). Justifying the risk to others: The real razor's edge. *Journal of Experiential Education, 10*(1), 6–22.

Priest, S. & Gass, M. A. (1998). *Effective leadership in adventure programming.* Champaign, IL: Human Kinetics.

Priest, S. & Gass, M. A. (1999). Six generations of facilitation skills. In J. C. Miles & S. Priest (Eds.), *Adventure programming* (pp. 215–218). State College, PA: Venture.

Propst, D. B. & Koesler, R. A. (1998). Bandura goes outdoors: Role of self-efficacy in the outdoor leadership development process. *Leisure Sciences, 20*(4), 319–345.

Propst, D. B., Wellman, J. D., Campa III, H. & McDonough, M. H. (2000). Citizen participation trends and their educational implications for natural resource professionals. In W. C. Gartner & D. W. Lime (Eds.), *Trends in outdoor recreation, leisure and tourism* (pp. 383–392). Wallingford, UK: CABI Publishing.

Proudman, B. (1992). Experiential education as emotionally-engaged learning. *The Journal of Experiential Education, 15*(2), 19–23.

Pulaski, M. A. S. (1980). *Understanding Piaget: An introduction to children's cognitive development.* New York: Harper & Row.

Queensland Outdoor Recreation Federation (2001). *What is outdoor recreation?* Retrieved July 26, 2004, from http://www.qorf.org.au/app/index.asp?page=qorfandyou

Quick, T. L. (1988). Expectancy theory in 5 simple steps. *Training and Development Journal, 42*(7), 94–98.

Quinn, W. (1999). The essence of adventure. In J. C. Miles & S. Priest (Eds.), *Adventure programming* (pp. 149–151). State College, PA: Venture.

Rainbird, P. (2002). A message for our future? The Rapa Nui (Easter Island) ecodisaster and Pacific Island environments. *World Archaeology, 33*(4), 436–452.

Raiola, E. (199). Outdoor leadership curricula. In J. C. Miles & S. Priest (Eds.), *Adventure education* (pp. 233–237). State College, PA: Venture.

Raiola, E. & Sugerman, D. (1999). Outdoor leadership curricula. In J. C. Miles & S. Priest (Eds.), *Adventure programming* (pp. 241–245). State College, PA: Venture.

Rand, A. (1964). *The virtue of selfishness: a new concept of egoism.* New York: Signet.

Rankel, G. L. (1999). Indian land. In H. K. Cordell (Ed.), *Outdoor recreation in American life: A national assessment of demand and supply trends* (pp. 60–63). Champaign, IL: Sagamore.

Rankin, J. S. (1987). The legal system as proponent of adventure programming. In J. F. Meier., T. W. Morash & G. E. Welton (Eds.), *High-adventure outdoor pursuits: Organization and leadership* (pp. 427–431). Columbus, OH: Publishing Horizons.

Raschke, E. (2001). Is the additional greenhouse effect already evident in the current climate? *Fresenius Journal of Analytical Chemistry, 371*, 791–797.

Rasmussen, G. A. & Brunson, M. W. (1996). Strategies to manage conflicts among multiple users. *Weed Technology, 10*, 447–450.

Raven, P. H., Berg, L. R. & Johnson, G. B. (1995). *Environment.* Fort Worth: Saunders College Publishing.

Reid, D. G. (1995). *Work and leisure in the 21st century.* Toronto: Wall and Emerson.

Reimers, E., Eftestol, S. & Coleman, J. E. (2003). Behaviour responses of wild reindeer to direct provocation by a snowmobile or skier. *Journal of Wildlife Management, 67*(4), 747–754.

Reynolds, E. E. (1942). *Baden-Powell.* London: Oxford University Press.

Ricaardson, R. B. & Loomis, J. B. (2005). Climate change and recreation benefits in an Alpine National Park. *Journal of Leisure Research, 37*(3), 307–320.

373

Richer, J. R. & Christensen, N. A. (1999). Appropriate fees for wilderness day use: Pricing decisions for recreation on public land. *Journal of Leisure Research, 31*(3), 269–280.

Riddick, C. C., DeSchriver, M. & Weissinger, E. (1984). A methodological review of research in Journal of Leisure Research from 1978 to 1982. *Journal of Leisure Research, 16*(4), 311–321.

Riese, H. & Vorkinn, M. (2002). The production of meaning in outdoor recreation: A study of Norwegian practice. *Norwegian Journal of Geography, 56*(3), 199–206.

Riggins, R. D. (1986). Effective learning in adventure-based education: Setting directions for future research. *Journal of Environmental Education, 18*(1), 1–5.

Ringholz, R. (1997). *On belay!* Seattle: The Mountaineers.

Ritchie, J. R. B. (1984). Assessing the impact of hallmark events: conceptual and research issues. *Journal of Travel Research, 23*(1), 2–11.

Robert, A. (2003). *River processes: An introduction to fluvial dynamics.* London: Arnold.

Rollins, R. & Robinson, D. (2002). Social science conservation, and protected areas. In P. Dearden & R. Rollins (Eds.), *Parks and protected areas in Canada: Planning and management* (2nd ed.) (pp. 117–147). Don Mills, ON: Oxford University Press.

Roper, L. W. (1973). *A biography of Frederick Law Olmsted.* Baltimore: The Johns Hopkins University Press.

Rosgen, D. (1996). *Applied river morphology.* Pagosa Springs, CO: Wildland Hydrology

Rosol, M. (2000). Wilderness therapy for youth-at-risk. *Parks and Recreation, 35*(9), 42–50.

Runnels, C. N. (1995). Environmental degradation in ancient Greece. *Scientific American, 272*(3), 96–100.

Rusk, R. L. (1949). *The life of Ralph Waldo Emerson.* New York: Columbia University Press.

Rutledge, R. & Vold, T. (1995). Canada's wilderness. *International Journal of Wilderness, 1*(2), 8–13.

Ryan, S. (2002). Cyborgs in the woods. *Leisure Sciences, 21,* 265–284.

Sasidharan, V. (2002). Special issue introduction: Understanding recreation and the environment within the context of culture. *Leisure Sciences, 24,* 1–11.

Sasidharan, V., Yarnal, C., Yarnal, B. & Godbey, G. (2001). Climate change: What is mean for parks and recreation management? *Parks and Recreation, 36*(3), 54–61.

Savory, A. (1988). *Holistic resource management.* Washington, DC: Island Press.

Scherl, L. M. (1989). Self in wilderness: Understanding the psychological benefits of the individual-wilderness interaction through self-control. *Leisure Sciences, 11,* 123–135.

Schneider, I. E. (2000a). Revisiting and revising recreation conflict research. *Journal of Leisure Research, 32*(1), 129–132.

Schneider, I. E. (2000b). Responses to conflict in urban-proximate areas. *Journal of Park and Recreation Administration, 18*(2), 37–53.

Schumm, S. A. (1977). *The fluvial system.* New York: John Wiley & Sons.

Schummer, M. L. & Eddleman, W. R. (2003). Effects of disturbance on activity and energy budgets of migrating waterbirds in south-central Oklahoma. *Journal of Wildlife Management, 67*(4), 789–795.

Schunk, D. H. (2004). *Learning theories: An educational perspective.* Upper Saddle Row, NJ: Prentice Hall.

Schutz, W. C. (1971). *Here comes everybody.* New York: Harper and Row.

Scott, D., Bayfield, N. G., Cernusca, A. & Elston, D. A. (2002). Use of a weighing lysimeter system to assess the effects of trampling on evapotranspiration of montane plant communities. *Canadian Journal of Botany, 80*(6), 675–684.

Seabrooke, W. & Miles, C. W. N. (1993). *Recreational land management* (2nd ed.). London: E. & F. N. Spon.

Sealts Jr., M. M. & Ferguson, A. R. (Eds.). (1969). *Emerson's nature: Origin, growth, meaning.* New York: Dodd, Mead.

Searle, M. S. & Brayley, R. E. (2000). *Leisure services in Canada* (2nd ed.). State College, PA: Venture.

Sellars, R. W. (1997). *Preserving nature in the national parks.* London: Yale University Press.

Sessoms, H. D. (1984). *Leisure services* (6th ed.). Englewood Cliffs, NJ: Prentice Hall.

Seton, E. T. (1940). *Trail of an artist-naturalist.* New York: Arno Press.

Shafer, C. L. (1990). *Nature reserves: Island theory and conservation practice.* Washington, DC: Smithsonian Institution Press.

Shafer Jr., E. and Mietz, J. (1969). Aesthetic and emotional experiences rate high with northeastern wilderness hikers. *Environment and Behaviour, 1*(1), 187–197.

Shankland, R. (1970). *Steve Mather of the national parks* (3rd ed.). New York: Alfred Knopf.

Sharpe, G. W. (1982). *Interpreting the environment* (2nd ed.). New York: John Wiley & Sons.

Sharpe, L. B. & Partridge, E. D. (1973). Some historical backgrounds of camping. In D. R. Hammerman & W. M. Hammerman (Eds.), *Outdoor education: A book of readings* (pp. 57–62). Minneapolis: Burgess.

Shelby, B. & Heberlin, T. A. (1986). *Carrying capacity in recreation settings*. Corvallis, OR: Oregon State University Press.

Shelby, B. & Vaske, J. J. (1991a). Using normative data to develop evaluative standards for resource management: A comment on three recent papers. *Journal of Leisure Research, 23*(2), 173–187.

Shelby, B. & Vaske, J. (1991b). Resource and activity substitutes for recreational salmon fishing in New Zealand. *Leisure Sciences, 13*(1), 27–32.

Sheldon, N. M. & Arthur, N. (2001). Adding adventure to therapy. *Guidance and Counseling, 16*(2), 67–73.

Shuttenberg, E. M. & Poppenhagen, B. W. (1995). Current theory and research in experiential learning for adults. In K. Warren, M. Sakofs & J. S. Hunt Jr. (Eds.), *The theory of experiential education* (2nd ed.) (pp. 141–145). Boulder, CO: Association for Experiential Education.

Sibthorp, J., Paisley, K. & Gookin, J. (2007). Exploring participant development through adventure-based programming: A model from the National Outdoor Leadership School. *Leisure Sciences, 29*(1), 1–18.

Siderelis, C., Moore, R. & Lee, J. H. (2000). Incorporating users' perceptions of site quality in a recreation travel cost model. *Journal of Leisure Research, 32*(4), 406–414.

Siehl, G. H. (2000). US recreation policies since World War II. In W. C. Gartner & D. W. Lime (Eds.), *Trends in outdoor recreation, leisure and tourism* (pp. 91–102). Wallingford, UK: CABI Publishing.

Sierra Club. (2007). *Sierra Club homepage*. Retrieved April 16, 2007, from http://www.sierraclub.org

Silverberg, K. E., Backman, S. J. & Backman, K. F. (2000). Understanding parks and recreation volunteers: A functionalist perspective. *Society and Leisure, 23*(2), 453–475.

Slaymaker, O. (1999). Mountain environments. In D. E. Alexander & R. W. Fairbridge (Eds.), *Encyclopedia of environmental science*. Dordrecht: Kluwer.

Slocombe, D. S. & Dearden, P. (2002). Protected areas and ecosystem-based management. In P. Dearden & R. Rollins (Eds.), *Parks and protected areas in Canada: Planning and management* (2nd ed.) (pp. 295–320). Don Mills, ON: Oxford University Press.

Smith, A. (1997). *Economic impact analysis of sport fishing on the upper Grand River: A methodology*. Unpublished master's thesis, University of Guelph, Guelph, Ontario, Canada.

Smith, D. S. (1993). Introduction. In D. S. Smith & P. C. Hellmund (Eds.), *Ecology of greenways* (pp. xi–xvi). Minneapolis: University of Minnesota Press.

Smith, J. W. (1973a). Where we have been—what we are—what will become: the taft campus outdoor education award lecture, 1970. In D. R. Hammerman & W. M. Hammerman (Eds.), *Outdoor education: A book of readings* (pp. 487–454). Minneapolis: Burgess.

Smith, J. W. (1973b). A decade of progress in outdoor education. In D. R. Hammerman & W. M. Hammerman (Eds.), *Outdoor education: A book of readings* (pp. 107–111). Minneapolis: Burgess.

Smith, S. (1975). Toward meta-recreation research. *Journal of Leisure Research, 7*(3), 235–239.

Smith, S. (1989). Demand. In G. Wall (Ed.), *Outdoor recreation in Canada* (pp. 43–74). Toronto: John Wiley & Sons.

Snow, C. P. (1959). *The two cultures and the scientific revolution*. Cambridge: Cambridge University Press.

Snowden, J. (1984). A brief background of scouting in the United States: 1910 to today. Retrieved April 17, 2007, from http://www.troop97.net

Solomon, G. B. (2002). Sources of expectancy information among assistant coaches: The influence of performance and psychological cues. *Journal of Sport Behaviour, 25*(3), 279–288.

Soulé, M. E. (1989). Conservation biology in the twenty-first century: Summary and outlook. In D. Western & M. Pearl (Eds.), *Conservation for the twenty-first century* (pp. 297–304). New York: Oxford University Press.

Spielvogel, J. J. (1991). *Western civilization: Volume II*. St. Paul, MN: West.

Spiers, A. & Plummer, R. (2005). An exploratory study of conflict in Ontario provincial parks: Developing a framework for conflict management. *Leisure/Loisir 29*(2), 329–353.

Stankey, G. H., Cole, D. N., Lucas, R. C., Peterson, G. L. & Frissel, S. (1985). *The limits of acceptable change system for wilderness planning* (General Technical Report INT-176). Ogden, UT: USDA Forest Service.

Stankey, G. H., McCool, S. F., Clark, R. N. & Brown, P. J. (1999). Institutional and organizational challenges to managing natural resources for recreation: A social learning model. In E. L. Jackson & T. L. Burton (Eds.), *Leisure studies: Prospects for the 21st century* (pp. 435–449). State College, PA: Venture.

Stapp, W. B. (1973). Integrating conservation education into the existing curriculum of the Ann Arbour public school system (K-12). In D. R. Hammerman & W. M. Hammerman (Eds.), *Outdoor education: A book of readings* (pp. 151–156). Minneapolis: Burgess.

Stebbins, R. A. (1999). Serious leisure. *Society, 38*(4), 53–58.

Stem, C. J., Lassoie, J. P., Lee, D. R. & Deshler, D. J. (2002). How "eco" is ecotourism? A comparative case study of ecotourism in Costa Rica. *Journal of Sustainable Tourism, 11*(4), 322–347.

Stem, C. J., Lassoie, J. P., Lee, D. R., Deshler, D. J. & Schelhas, J. W. (2003). Community participation in ecotourism benefits: The link to conservation practices and perspectives. *Society and Natural Resources, 16*, 387–413.

Sterling, K. B., Harmond, R. P., Cevasco, G. A. & Hammond, L. F. (1997). *Biographical dictionary of American and Canadian naturalists and environmentalists*. Westport, CT: Greenwood Press.

Stevens, B. & Rose, A. Z. (1985). Regional input–output methods for tourism impact analysis. In D. Propst (Ed.), *Assessing the economic impacts of recreation and tourism*. Asheville, NC: USDA Forest Service, Southeastern Forest Experiment Station.

Stewart, W. P. & Cole, D. N. (2003). On the prescriptive utility of visitor survey research: A rejoinder to Manning. *Journal of Leisure Research, 35*(1), 119–127.

Stumm, W. (1986). Water an integrated ecosystem. *AMBIO, 15*(4), 201–207.

Sugerman, D. (1999). Programming adventure for older adults. In J. C. Miles & S. Priest (Eds.), *Adventure programming* (pp. 385–388). State College, PA: Venture.

Sugerman, D. (2001). Inclusive outdoor education: Facilitating groups that include people with disabilities. *The Journal of Experiential Education, 24*(3), 166–172.

Sung, H. H. (2004). Classification of adventure travelers: Behavior, decision making and target markets. *Journal of Travel Research, 42*(4), 343–356.

Swan, J. A. (1995). *In defense of hunting*. San Francisco: HarperCollins.

Swinnerton, G. S. (1999). Recreation and conservation: issues and prospects. In E. L. Jackson & T. L. Burton (Eds.), *Leisure studies prospects for the twenty-first century* (pp. 199–231). State College, PA: Venture.

Sylvester, C. (1999). The classical idea of leisure: Cultural ideal or class prejudice? *Leisure Sciences, 21*(1), 3–16.

Tasmania Parks and Wildlife Service. (2007). *Tasmania Parks and Wildlife Service*. Retrieved May 1, 2007, from http://www.parks.tas.gov.au/recreation/recreation.html

Teaching and Learning About Canada. (2007). *Rivers and lakes of Canada*. Retrieved May 14, 2007, from http://www.canadainfolink.ca/chartnine.htm

Teasley, R. J., Bergstrom, J. C., Cordell, H. K., Zarnoch, S. J. & Gentle, P. (1999). Private lands and outdoor recreation in the United States. In H. K. Cordell, B. L. McDonald, R. J. Teasley, J. C. Bergstrom, J. Martin, J. Bason & V. R. Leeworth (Eds.), *Outdoor recreation in American life: A national assessment of demand and supply trends* (pp. 183–218). Champaign, IL: Sagamore.

Thapa, B. (2001). Environmental concern: a comparative analysis between students in Recreation and Park Management and other departments. *Environmental Education Research, 7*(1), 39–54.

Thapa, B., Graefe, A. & Absher, J. (2002). Information needs and search behaviors: A comparative study of ethnic groups in the Angeles and San Bernardino National Forests, California. *Leisure Sciences, 24*(1), 87–107.

Thomson, L. A. (1992). *Leadership monograph*. Thunder Bay, ON: Lakehead University.

The British Boy Scouts. (2007). *The British Boy Scouts*. Retrieved April 16, 2007, from http://www.netpages.free-online.co.uk/bbs/bbs.htm

The Countryside Agency. (2005). *Countryside access and the new right: Helping everyone to respect, protect and enjoy the countryside*. Gloucestershire, UK: The Countryside Agency.

The Inter-governmental Panel on Climate Change. (2007). *Climate change 2007: The physical science basis* (Summary for Policymakers). Geneva: IPCC Secretariat.

The International Ecotourism Society. (2005). *Ecotourism fact sheet*. Retrieved April 24, 2007, from http://www.ecotourism.org

The Internet Encyclopedia. (2007). *Sport*. Retrieved April 15, 2007, from http://www.internet-encyclopedia.org/index.php/Sports

The Nature Conservancy. (1994). *The conservation of biodiversity in the Great Lakes ecosystem: Issues and opportunities.* Chicago: The Nature Conservancy Great Lakes Program.

Thomson, L. A. (1992). *Leadership monograph.* Thunder Bay, ON: Lakehead University.

Thoreau, H. D. (1992). Walden. In W. Rossi (Ed.), *Walden and the resistance to civil government: Authoritative texts, Thoreau's journal, reviews and essays in criticism* (2nd ed.) (pp. 1–191). New York: W. W. Norton & Company.

Tilden, F. (1977). *Interpreting our heritage* (3rd ed.). Chapel Hill, NC: The University of North Carolina Press.

Torkildsen, G. (2005). *Leisure and recreation management* (5th ed.). London: Routledge.

Toth Jr, J. F. & Brown, R. B. (1997). Racial and gender meanings of why people participate in recreational fishing. *Leisure Sciences, 19*, 129–146.

Tovell, W. M. (1979). *The Great Lakes.* Toronto: Royal Ontario Museum.

Town, H. & Silcox, D. P. (1977). *Tom Thomson: The silence and the storm.* Toronto: McClelland & Stewart.

Trent University Archives (n.d.). Retrieved November 24, 2003, from http://www.trentu.ca/library/archives

Tuan, Y. (1971). Review: Environmental attitudes. *Science Studies, 1*(2), 215–224.

Tuckman, B. W. (1965). Developmental sequence in small groups. *Psychological Bulletin, 63*, 384–399.

Turner, T. (1991). The dinosaur story. *Sierra, 76*(6), 28–30.

US Department of the Interior. (1997). *The visitor and resource protection (VERP) framework: A handbook for planners and managers.* Denver, CO: Department of the Interior, National Park Service.

Ugalde, A. F. (1989). An optimal park system. In D. Western & M. Pearl (Eds.), *Conservation for the twenty-first century* (pp. 145–150). New York: Oxford University Press.

UNESCO (n.d.). *UNESCO's Man and the Biosphere Programme (MAB).* Retrieved May 13, 2007, from http://www.unesco.org/mab/mabProg.shtml

Unger, W., Evans, I. M., Rourke, P. & Levis, D. J. (2003). The S–S construct of expectancy versus the S–R construct of fear: Which motivates the acquisition of avoidance behaviour? *Journal of General Psychology, 130*(2), 131–147.

United Nations Education, Scientific and Cultural Organization. (2007). *World heritage list.* Retrieved May 1, 2007, from http://whc.unesco.org/en/list

United Nations Framework Convention on Climate Change. (2006). *Report of the Conference of the Parties on its twelfth session, held at Nairobi from 6 to 17 November 2006* (Report No. GE.07–60260 (E)). United Nations Framework Convention on Climate Change

United Nations Framework Convention on Climate Change. (2007). *Future effects. A question of degree.* Retrieved May 1, 2007, from http://unfccc.int/essential_background/feeling_the_heat/items/2905.php

United States Fish and Wildlife Service. (n.d.). *Hunting statistics and economics.* Retrieved May 1, 2007, from http://www.fws.gov/hunting/huntstat.html

Upneja, A., Shafer, E. L., Seo, W. & Yoon, J. (2001). Economic benefits of sport fishing and angler wildlife watching in Pennsylvania. *Journal of Travel Research, 40*, 68–78.

USDA Forest Service. (n.d.). *Recreation and heritage resource integrated business systems: TRACS.* Retrieved May 1, 2007, from http://www.fs.fed.us/r3/measures/Inventory/TRACS.htm

Vaske, J. & Manning, R. E. (2008). Analysis of multiple data sets in outdoor recreation research. Introduction to the special issue. *Leisure Sciences, 30*, 93–95.

van der Smissen, B. (1998). Legal responsibility for recreational safety. In N. J. Dougherty (Ed.), *Outdoor Recreation Safety* (pp. 12–24). Champaign, IL: The School and Community Safety Society of America.

van der Smissen, B. & Gregg, C. (1999). Legal liability and risk management. In J. C. Miles & S. Priest (Eds.), *Adventure programming* (pp. 285–297). State College, PA: Venture.

Veale, B. (2004). Watershed management in the Grand River Watershed. In G. Nelson (Ed.), *Towards a Grand sense of place* (pp. 261–277). Waterloo, ON: Heritage Resources Centre.

Veblen, T. (1934). *The theory of the leisure class: An economic study of institutions.* New York: Modern Library.

Veblen, T. (1975). The theory of the leisure class [1899] (Reprinted ed.). New York: Augustus M. Kelly, Bookseller.

Venkatachalam, L. (2004). The contingent valuation method: A review. *Environmental Impact Assessment Review, 24*, 89–124.

Vickery, J. D. (1986). *Wilderness visionaries.* Merrillville, IN: ICS Books.

Victor, D. G. & Ausubel, J. H. (2000). Restoring the forests. *Foreign Affairs, 79*(6), 12–145.

Victorian Climbing Association. (2007). *Welcome to the Victorian Climbing Club!* Retrieved May 1, 2007, from http://www.vicclimb.org.au/Site/index.php

Virden, R. J. & Walker, G. J. (1999). Ethnic/racial and gender variations among meanings given to, and preferences for, the natural environment. *Leisure Sciences, 21*, 219–239.

Vogel, S. (2002). Environmental philosophy after the end of nature. *Environmental Ethics, 24*, 23–39.

von Storch, H. & Stehr, N. (2000, June). Climate change in perspective. *Nature, 405*, 615.

Walker, G. J., Deng, J. & Dieser, R. B. (2001). Ethnicity, acculturation, self-construal, and motivations for outdoor recreation. *Leisure Sciences, 23*, 263–283.

Wall, G. (Ed.). (1989). *Outdoor recreation in Canada.* Toronto: John Wiley & Sons.

Wall, G. & Wright, C. (1977). *The environmental impact of outdoor recreation.* Waterloo, ON: Dept. of Geography, Faculty of Environmental Studies, University of Waterloo.

Walton, M. (1998). Ecosystem planning within Georgian bay islands national park—a multi-jurisdictional approach. In N. W. P. Munro & J. H. M. Willison (Eds.), *Linking protected areas with working landscapes conserving biodiversity* (pp. 552–566). Wolfville, NS: Science and Management of Protected Areas Association.

Warren, K. (1999). Women's outdoor adventures. In J. C. Miles & S. Priest (Eds.), *Adventure programming* (pp. 389–393). State College, PA: Venture.

Washburne, R. (1978). Black under-participation in wildland recreation: Alternative explanations. *Leisure Sciences, 1*(2), 175–179.

WCED (1987). *Our common future.* New York: Oxford University Press.

Weaver, D. (2001). *Ecotourism.* Milton, Queensland: John Wiley & Sons.

Weaver, D. (2002). Asian ecotourism: Patterns and themes. *Tourism Geographies, 4*(2), 153–172.

Weaver, D., Faulkner, B. & Lawton, L. (1999). *Nature based tourism in Australia and beyond: A preliminary investigation.* Gold Coast: CRC for Sustainable Tourism.

Weaver, O. B. & Lawton, L. J. (2001). Resident perceptions in the urban–rural fringe. *Annals of Tourism Research, 28*(2), 439–458.

Weber, R. C. (1982). The group: A cycle from birth to death. In L. Porter & B. Mohr (Eds.), *Reading book for human relations training* (7th ed.). Alexandria, VA: NTL Institute.

Weiss, M. (1987). Self-esteem and achievement in children's sport and physical activity. In M. Weiss & D. Gould (Eds.), *Advances in pediatric sport science,* Vol. 2. Champaign, IL: Human Kinetics.

Welbourne, M. (2001). *Knowledge.* Montreal, QC: McGill-Queen's University Press.

West, M. (1997). Homer's meter. In I. Morris & B. Powell (Eds.), *A new companion to Homer* (pp. 218–238). New York: Brill.

West, P. (1983). A test of the projection accuracy of the status group dynamics approach to recreation demand. *Leisure Sciences, 6*(1), 15–45.

West, P. (1993). *The tyranny of metaphor: Interracial relations, minority recreation, and the wildland urban interface: Culture, conflict and communication.* Boulder, CO: Western Press.

Wheeler, W. & Hammerman, D. (1973). What is the education potential in the outdoor setting? In D. R. Hammerman & W. M. Hammerman (Eds.), *Outdoor education: A book of readings* (pp. 10–16). Minneapolis: Burgess.

Whisman, S. & Hollenhurst, S. (1998). A path model of whitewater boating satisfaction on the Cheat River of West Virginia. *Environmental Management, 22*, 109–117.

Whitman, D. (2000). Don't get foolish in the great outdoors; the bison do butt. *U.S. News & World Report, 129*(1), 48–51.

Wichman, T. (1991). Of wilderness and circles: Evaluating a therapeutic model of wilderness adventure programs. *Journal of Experiential Education, 14*(2), 43–48.

Wilderness.net. (n.d.). *Wilderness fast facts.* Retrieved May 1, 2007, from http://www.wilderness.net/index.cfm?fuse=NWPS&sec=fastFacts

Winzer, M. (2002). *Children with exceptionalities in Canadian classrooms* (6th ed.). Toronto: Pearson.

Witt, P. A. (1984). Research in transition: Prospects and challenges. *Parks and Recreation, 19*, 60–63.

Wolff, R. P. (1976). *About philosophy.* Englewood Cliffs, NJ: Prentice Hall.

Wood, M. E. (1998). New directions in the ecotourism industry. In J. Johnson (Ed.), *Ecotourism: A guide for planners and managers* (Vol. 2) (pp. 45–63). North Bennington, VT: The Ecotourism Society.

Woodley, S. (2002). Planning and managing for ecological integrity in Canada's national parks. In P. Dearden & R. Rollins (Eds.), *Parks and protected areas in Canada: Planning and management* (2nd ed.) (pp. 95–114). Don Mills, ON: Oxford University Press.

World Association of Girl Guides and Girl Scouts. (2007). *Our history*. Retrieved April 16, 2007, from http://www.wagggsworld.org/en/about/history

World Commission on Environment and Development. (1987). *Our Common Future*. Oxford: Oxford University Press.

World Organization of the Scout Movement. (2007). *Facts and figures*. Retrieved April 17, 2007, from http://www.scout.org/en/about_scouting/facts_figures

World Tourism Organization. (2007). *Methodological notes*. Retrieved April 15, 2007, from http://www.unwto.org/facts/eng/methodological.htm.

Worster, D. (1994). *Nature's Economy: A history of ecological ideas* (2nd ed.). New York: The Press Syndicate of the University of Cambridge.

WRI, IUCN & UNEP. (1992). *Global biodiversity strategy: Guidelines for action to save, study, and use earth's biotic wealth sustainably and equitably*. Washington, DC: World Resources Institute.

Wright, J. R. (1984). *Urban parks in Ontario*. Ottawa: University of Ottawa.

Wright, P. & Rollins, R. (2002). Managing the national parks. In P. Dearden & R. Rollins (Eds.), *Parks and protected areas in Canada: Planning and management* (2nd ed.) (pp. 207–239). Don Mills, ON: Oxford University Press.

Wright, R. (1934). *The story of gardening: From the hanging gardens of Babylon to the hanging gardens of New York*. New York: Dover.

Wright, T. (2003). Geocaching: Trees as treasure. *American Forests, 109*(2), 7–9.

Wurdinger, S. D. & Priest, S. (1999). Integrating theory and application in experiential learning. In J. C. Miles & S. Priest (Eds.), *Adventure programming* (pp. 187–192). State College, PA: Venture.

Zabinski, C. A., DeLuca, T. H., Cole, D. N. & Moynahan, O. S. (2002). Restoration of highly impacted subalpine campsites in the Eagle Cap Wilderness, Oregon. *Restoration Ecology, 10*(2), 275–282.

Zimmerman, E. W. (1933, 1951 revised). *World resources and industries*. New York: Harper and Brothers.

Zinser, C. I. (1995). *Outdoor recreation*. New York: John Wiley & Sons.

Index

Figures are indicated by bold page numbers, tables by italics.